Political
Man

Other books of interest by the same author

An Introduction to Political Analysis
    (with James D. Barber and Fred I. Greenstein)
The Regulation of Businessmen
Political Life: Why People Get Involved in Politics
The Liberties of Wit: Humanism, Criticism,
    and the Civic Mind
Political Ideology: Why the American
    Common Man Believes What He Does
Public Opinion
    (with David O. Sears)
Political Thinking and Consciousness

Political Man

Robert E. Lane

YALE UNIVERSITY

The Free Press, New York

Collier–Macmillan Limited, London

The Free Press
A Division of The Macmillan Company
866 Third Avenue, New York, New York 10022

Collier–Macmillan Canada Ltd., Toronto, Ontario

Library of Congress Catalog Card Number: 75-158930

printing number
1   2   3   4   5   6   7   8   9   10

Contents

PART III

CORE BELIEF SYSTEMS

PART IV

THE EFFECTS OF AFFLUENCE AND KNOWLEDGE ON BELIEF SYSTEMS

PART V

THE GOOD CITIZEN

Preface

"I am the doubter and the doubt." I am the observer and the observed. I am the actor and his critic. I murder to dissect, and I am the *corpus delicti* ("I am the slayer and the slain"). The proper study of mankind is man: I am the student and his studies. I am Man.

The essays and articles in this book, some five of them here published for the first time, place man and his beliefs at the center of the political stage. In this sense, they are humanist, but of course they employ the concepts and methods of the social sciences. Part I focuses on concepts of political personality and analyzes the way certain features of personality shape political decisions. Part II deals with the maturation of political ideas in the young and the ways these ideas may be changed by school and family. Part III introduces the concept of a core belief system and employs this concept in political explanation. The political effects of two major social changes, the growth of affluence and of scientific knowledge, are analyzed in Part IV. Lastly, in Part V we turn to two problems of citizenship: participation and patriotism.

ROBERT E. LANE
YALE UNIVERSITY

ACKNOWLEDGMENT

For her invaluable help in preparing the manuscript for publication, I wish to thank Betty Hanson.

R.E.L.

PART I
PERSONALITY

Introductory Note:
The Use of Personality Types
and Traits in Political Analysis

The choice for the political analyst is usually not whether he should make use of personality types and traits but rather whether he should draw attention to the ones he has settled on. Does he implicitly rely on models of rational man, natural man in a state of nature, hedonistic man? Does he choose to focus on other-directedness, aggressiveness, narcissism?

One possibility examined in this section is to employ the typologies and symptoms or traits of psychiatric medicine. Thus, following Fenichel,[1] one might build an analytic scheme on the symptoms of psychoanalysis. Here are some examples of how these diagnostic concepts have been employed:

Anxiety and anxiety hysteria (marked by inhibitions of various functions, projection, paranoid symptoms, indecisiveness, and so on). The lack of specificity of the symptoms opens up many possibilities for classification. One of these is the *politics of apathy*. Mussen and Wyszynski[2] and Morris Rosenberg[3] find that anxious people are characterized by political apathy because their energy is consumed in managing their personal problems. They have no time for the larger issues of the outside world. Because one of the medical symptoms of anxiety is inhibition, it is easy to see how this illness might lead to political and social inhibition.

A second and very different form of political expression stems from another medical symptom, the projective and paranoid traits of the anxious person. The *politics of paranoia* are reflected in the following quotation from such a person:

> This is not the first time that the Reds, Socialists, Pacifists, and their college-professor allies have attempted to prevent, and have actually prevented, murderers and other violators of the law from getting their just deserts. . . . So far as Red criminals are concerned our judicial systems are being scrapped.[4]

I

Notes to this Introduction will be found on pages 3–4

Obsession and compulsion (marked by magical thinking, fixed ideas, ritual acts designed to block out guilty feelings or denied impulses). The illustrations and manifestations of political obsessions are numerous. *Political leaders with obsessive traits* include Hitler, whose obsessions carried him through the defeat of the Munich beer hall *putsch* when more "realistic" men would have failed, and Woodrow Wilson, who was obsessed with the idea that "no man shall ever bend me to his will again."[5] *Compulsive political behavior* may include behavior towards the flag and voting under certain circumstances. Both of these are, to some extent, duty-bound acts; like other compulsive acts, they may serve to cleanse or purge oneself, or to ward off evil. *Political thinking* may be obsessive, as the following illustration from Fenichel reveals:

> Because of his obsession for neatness, a patient with geographical obsessions was troubled by the artificial boundaries between countries that are geographical units. Therefore, he referred to the entire Iberian peninsula as "Spain," ignoring the existence of Portugal.[6]

Perversions and impulse neuroses (marked by homosexual, fetichistic, sadistic, masochistic, kleptomaniac and other impulses). The relation of political behavior to psychosexual disturbances emerged as a broad field for speculation and inquiry during the Nazi domination of Germany. The sadistic behavior of storm troopers and concentration camp guards was almost sufficient evidence of such a relationship, and H. V. Dicks' study of German prisoners of war gave strong evidence of a *link between Nazi convictions and homosexual impulses.*[7] In a more speculative study, Ernest Jones outlines reasons for believing that *Quislingism has its roots in homosexuality.*[8] In a study of *American communists*, Krugman finds that some Party members use the Party to satisfy their mixed aggressive-passive impulses by giving themselves up to the Party in the service of their need for legitimate aggression against others.[9] *Nativist agitators*, according to Lowenthal and Guterman, are often in the grip of exhibitionist impulses.[10]

Depression (marked by lack of self-esteem, infantile regression, apathy, exaggerated conscience). Depression is often regarded as the consequence of self-punitive, in contrast to extra-punitive, thought and action. This line of interpretation would suggest that hostile political thought is unlikely to be found among depressives, while advocates of "selfless causes", like the champions of underdogs, might very well suffer from depression. Apparently this is the case. Ackerman and Jahoda studied forty cases of anti-Semitic persons who had been psychoanalyzed and found that none of them suffered from depression.[11] On the other hand, Adorno and associates found the equalitarians who became mentally disturbed showed signs of "neurotic depression and feelings of inadequacy."[12]

The medical diagnostic typology is useful but often does not capture particular symptoms that are most useful in political and social analysis.

For one thing, this typology deals with the problems of the ill, whereas the political world is made up of both the sick and the healthy. It was devised for individual diagnosis and therapy, not social diagnosis. Until very recently, psychoanalytic theories and interpretations were rarely subject to the kinds of tests prevalent in the behavioral sciences; hence behavioral scientists sought to employ and shape concepts more amenable to testing procedure. Hence, as noted in the second of the following pieces, a number of personality symptoms and their related types have been devised to capture facets of social behavior and thought not immediately related to illness and sometimes discovered by test rather than clinical procedures.

The three chapters in Part I deal with the employment of personality theory and typologies in political analysis. The first chapter defines political personality, briefly outlines some of the psychological theories that contribute to an understanding of personality, and then illustrates the uses of psychological interpretations of legislative, judicial, electoral, and other political behavior and thought.

The second chapter attacks the problems of interest group theory with the typologies developed by David Riesman (such as indignant-moralizer, inside-dopester, anomic, the autonomous man, the other-directed man, the inner-directed man) in order to illuminate problems of pluralism and representation under various kinds of characterological distributions, strain, and conflict. It is wholly speculative, designed to reveal the personalistic aspects of a group of traditional political problems.

The third chapter employs the concepts and measures of *The Authoritarian Personality* to analyze problems of electoral choice as reflected in the 1952 election. It serves to reveal ways in which authoritarianism and equalitarianism can guide electoral choice when one of the candidates is perceived as "strong," when there is a stalemated war in progress which especially frustrates authoritarian personalities, and when other factors permit the conservatism of the authoritarian to gravitate towards a more conservative party. Whether in the 1968 election Nixon profited from such tendencies would be an interesting question to pursue.

Notes

1. Otto Fenichel, *The Psychoanalytic Theory of Neurosis* (New York: Norton, 1945).

2. Paul H. Mussen and Anne B. Wyszynski, "Personality and Political Participation," *Human Relations*, 5 (1952), pp. 65–82.

3. Morris Rosenberg, "Self-esteem and Concern with Public Affairs," *Public Opinion Quarterly*, 26 (1962), pp. 201–211.

4. Reported in Karl Menninger, *Theory of Psychoanalytic Technique* (New York: Basic Books, 1958), p. 240.

5. Alexander L. George and Juliette L. George, *Woodrow Wilson and Colonel House* (New York: Dover, 1964).

6. *The Psychoanalytic Theory of Neurosis*, p. 301.

7. Henry V. Dicks, "Personality Traits and National Socialist Ideology," *Human Relations*, 5 (1950), pp. 111–154.

8. Ernest Jones, "On Quislingism," *International Journal of Psychoanalysis*, 22 (1941), pp. 1–6.

9. Herbert E. Krugman, "The Role of Hostility in the Appeals of Communism in the United States," *Psychiatry*, 16 (1953), pp. 253–261.

10. Leo Lowenthal and N. Guterman, *Prophets of Deceit* (New York: Harper, 1949).

11. N. W. Ackerman and M. Jahoda, *Anti-Semitism and Emotional Disorder* (New York: Harper, 1950).

12. T. W. Adorno, Else Frenkel-Brunswik, Daniel J. Levinson, and R. Nevitt Sanford, *The Authoritarian Personality* (New York: Harper, 1950).

Chapter *1*
The Study of
Political Personality

Because one cannot write about, or even think about, human affairs without some implicit concept of human nature, the idea of "political personality" is a very old one; indeed, the established classics of political philosophy from Plato through Mill almost always give it explicit attention.[1] Yet at the same time, the development of sophisticated psychology and psychiatry, especially psychoanalysis, is so recent that the modern concept of political personality is qualitatively very different and must here serve as the substance of the discussion. This article will explore the meaning of the concept, examine the ways in which the various psychological schools have left their mark on the idea of a *political* personality, and then deal more extensively with the ways in which theory and research in this area have helped in our interpretation of political outcomes.

The Concept of Political Personality

"Political personality" may be defined as *the enduring, organized, dynamic response sets habitually aroused by political stimuli*. It embraces (a) motivation, often analyzed as a combination of needs and values (the push-pull theory); (b) cognitions, perceptions, and habitual modes of learning; and (c) behavioral tendencies, that is, the acting out of needs and other aspects of manifest behavior. Each of these has obvious political implications: (a) people who are motivated by needs for power may employ political leverage to satisfy these needs rather than (or in the course of) a pursuit of

Reprinted from *International Encyclopedia of the Social Sciences* (New York: Macmillan & Free Press, 1968).

Notes to this chapter will be found on pages 17–19

some explicit policy goal; (b) cognitively, people who handle information in the defense of their partisanship, rather than as an instrument of broader learning, become dogmatic and obstruct social adaptation to new situations; (c) behaviorally, political life is vitally affected by the tendencies of leaders to act out (externalize) their psychic conflicts, projecting them onto other people and situations or, alternatively, to withdraw into inaction when threatened or, again, to make public demands to assuage their sense of worthlessness. Most simply stated, then, the habitual patterns of feeling, learning and knowing, and behaving in political situations constitute political personality.

This definition states that the elements of political personality are "enduring"; this means that they are in some sense central to the personality, not merely the response to somewhat ephemeral situations or the product of a certain occupation or, more generally, a role that a person occupies for the time being. This means that in speaking of political personality, we are dealing with patterns of thought, emotion, and acting out that may be seen in operation in many different situations over a relatively long period of time, perhaps youth, young adulthood, and maturity. Again, this implies that these patterns are laid down relatively early, though their expression and style may reveal differences over time; indeed, there may be fundamental changes in personality at a relatively mature age. Parenthetically, it may be noted that these changes are often the product of a slight change in some set of balancing internal forces (say, strong aggressive impulses held in check by fear of one's own aggression) which may produce a relatively great change in outward personality manifestations (e.g., from ingratiating to domineering behavior).

The definition of political personality includes the attribute "organized," implying some interrelationship among the constituent elements such that a change in one, say, a growing need for social approval, would modify other elements, perhaps leading to a decreased willingness to defy authority. Inquiry into this organization implies something like the following paradigm of questions: What patterns of needs, expressed through what need-coping mechanisms (repression, sublimation, ego-striving, etc.), modified by what perceptions of reality and habits of learning, screened through what ideological constellations, produce what behavioral tendencies? The organization of a political personality, then, implies a patterned relationship and interaction among these elements. And, among these elements, the manner of dealing with conflicting needs or motives is probably the most important, followed by the pattern of response to and internalization of authority.

There was a third adjective in the definition: "dynamic". Here, this overworked term refers to a capacity to produce change in something else. Operationally this means that if two ideas or emotions are brought into some kind of relationship, the more dynamic element changes the less dynamic element. For instance, the attitude toward authority is generally considered more potent than feelings toward particular leaders. Therefore, when a worshipful attitude toward authority is forced to confront a dislike of a particular political leader, more change will be effected in the attitude toward the leader than in the posture toward authority in general ("he isn't so bad, after all . . . I must have misjudged him . . . at least he looks like a president, etc."). We reserve for the term "political personality" those elements of a person's total psychic pattern which tend to shape attitudes, beliefs, and actions on new issues as they arise. Just as some authorities talk of "reference groups" and "reference persons," so we might here refer to political personality as a constellation of "reference ideas" and "reference emotions"—ideas and emotions to which new problems are referred for guidance and instruction. But, of course, this reference is usually quite unconscious.

The concept of political personality borders on other concepts from which it must be distinguished. There is, in the first place, the concept of "attitude," which has been classically defined as a kind of "mental and neural response set." We would distinguish political personality from a single attitude on the obvious ground that the latter is too narrow, and from any conceivable complex of attitudes, however broad, on the ground that such a complex lacks the organization and dynamic potential of a political personality. Personality, as has so often been remarked, is not a bundle of traits. Thus we conceive of a personality as shaping attitudes, and not vice versa.

In the second place, there is the concept of "role," usually defined as a pattern of expected behavior associated with a given position in society. In practice it is not easy to distinguish role-determined behavior from personality-determined behavior when a person is acting out his concept of appropriate role behavior or, worse, when he has accepted the values and beliefs associated with a given role and performs accordingly. Sometimes the only way to distinguish between personality and role is to observe the person in a set of different roles, say, father and bureaucrat. Conceptually, political personality has an earlier genesis, has a different organizational principle, transcends the situation or social position, is more internally motivated or autonomous of the environment, responds to different crises and conflicts, and is more idiosyncratic or individualized than is any (political) role behavior.

Finally, there is the distinction between personality and culture, a difficult one because personality must be learned somehow from available cultural elements. It is for this reason that personality is sometimes said to be the subjective side of culture. Does individual anxiety reflect an anxiety-laden culture? Does the authoritarian personality reflect an authoritarian culture? When we are dealing with individuals, the distinction is relatively easy, because no two individuals bring together an identical genetic pattern and an identical sequence of experiences; hence, each is in some way unique. When we deal with "modal personality" or "social character," that is, the features of personality which are commonly shared in a group, we have greater trouble distinguishing between these shared personality elements and the dominant themes of a culture. Obviously the carriers of the culture are people; they exemplify it, as well as conveying its themes to others through their norm-setting and norm-enforcing behavior. Perhaps the best way to distinguish between these concepts of modal political personality and political culture is through the different questions each concept poses, the different theoretical structures employed to answer these questions, and the differential focuses upon people and ideas in each instance. Questions dealing with modal political personality elicit answers employing psychological theories of individual development, learning, imitation, conflict resolution, and the like. They are designed to tell us about people, in this case individuals who happen to be in groups. Questions dealing with political culture employ theories of social change, cultural diffusion, group adaptation to ecological factors, functional requirements of a given social structure, the reinforcement of social patterns, social (rather than individual) pattern maintenance, and so forth. Both concepts contribute to an understanding of political phenomena: modal political personality, through its contribution to an understanding of group psychology; political culture, through its contribution to an understanding of the prevailing myths, beliefs, and adaptive responses of the underlying society. Yet it must be said that often these amount to the same thing.

Political Personality and Environment

It is now a truism to say that all social explanations employ some variation of what the learning theorists term a "stimulus(S)–organism(O)–response(R)" model, though sometimes it is referred to as "environment(E)–predisposition(P)–response(R)." Social and political explanations place the emphasis now on one term (S or E), now on the other (O or P). Institutional theories, such as those which claim that a separation of powers is a necessary condition for the rule of law or those which assert that the development of a middle class is necessary for the survival of representative government, emphasize the environmental part of this model. Yet while they are silent on the personalities of the actors involved, they always quietly impute to them a set of personal qualities, e.g., the universal love of power, which can be restrained only by others with power, or the reluctance of an economic elite to share power with the masses unless coerced by a balancing middle class and/or the incapacity of the masses to govern themselves. Each environmental theory, then, as mentioned in the first sentence of this article, implies a theory of personal motivation and some distribution of motives, values, and capacities in a relevant population. The study of political personality represents, in the one sense, an effort to fill in these never-empty but often unexamined cells in the great macro theories which have guided the study of nations.

On the other hand, there is a temptation to employ the new concepts of political personality in an exaggerated way, so as to imply that an individual has a set of motives or needs which are evoked in the same way in all situations or, worse, that a given public, say the German people, chose a certain leader, adopted a certain ideology, became bellicose and domineering or whatever because of some national character constellation, as though this constellation operated quite independently of the history and institutions of that particular public. One has only to glance at the early theories of political motivation to see the temptation at work: politicians choose their careers because they (all of them) love power; the Germans chose Hitler and Nazism because they were authoritarian; Americans offered economic aid to other countries because they were other-directed and wanted the world to love them—and partially turned against aid giving when they found that they could not buy love.

The lesson is clear, indeed obvious—but often neglected: it is in a combination of circumstances and attitudes, environment and political personality, that the answers to the important political questions will be found.

Theoretical Interpretations

Since, as was said at the beginning, the modern exploration of political personality is encouraged by and feeds on the developments of personality theory and research among psychologists and psychiatrists, it is not surprising that variations in these more molar fields are reflected in the interpretations of the role of personality in political life. For this reason it is useful to touch briefly upon the way in which various psychological theories affect these interpretations.

The first approach is that of Pavlov, Watson, Hull, and others in Russia and the United States.[2] Originally called learning theory, it is now more generally called behavior theory. The central doctrine of this school is that an understanding of all behavioral responses may be acquired through a grasp of the concepts of drive, cue, response, and reward and their derivatives; rewarded responses become habits through a process of conditioning, and unrewarded responses tend to be extinguished. Personality, then, is the pattern of learned responses, not all of them adaptive in long-range terms but all of them, at least once, reinforced. It has been argued that the behavior of the Soviet elite has been heavily influenced by this concept of personality, leading them, so it is said, to believe that through a fairly gross manipulation of rewards and punishments they can shape the personalities and behaviors of the populations under their control.[3] Although it is possible to translate behavior theory into the terms and constructs of other more clinically oriented theories, as Dollard and Miller[4] have shown, the product is somewhat inelegant. Because of its mechanistic emphasis and insistence upon observable (operationalized) ingredients, the theory leaves out the rich, speculative, and often fruitful concepts of internal dynamics, conflict resolution, fantasy and free-associational styles of thought, dream life, analogical thinking, and the secondary elaborations which these theories produce.

A second approach to political personality focuses upon the complex of vectors or forces which influence a person in his "life space." Kurt Lewin[5] was the originator of this theory, whose sources lie in gestalt psychology. His associates and followers have gone on into the field of group dynamics exemplified in their small group experiments.[6] The central work of this school consists of accounting for the impact of the social world, the world of inter-action and group life, upon an individual whose goals are constantly shaped and modified by these influential people—the other members of his group. This approach, reflected in the voting studies produced both by the Lazarsfeld–Berelson group[7] and the Michigan Survey Research Center group headed by Angus Campbell[8] has led to some important formulations of the way in which reference groups, interpersonal influence, cross-pressures or conflicting identifications, family, school, and work socialization, and group pressures all combine to modify electoral decisions. The findings suggest that in this area of American electoral decision making, individual differences are not so important as group differences, that is, national modal character is more important than individual personality. Another way to say this is that for any one country, more of the variance is accounted for by environmental factors than by personality factors.

The more strictly Freudian approach, now only one of several competing schools of psychoanalysis, focuses, as is well known, upon the channeling and blocking of the libido, the conflict among id and ego and superego (impulse, conscious mind, and conscience), unconscious processes, early determination of central personality characteristics, and the consequent need to return retrospectively to early experience in order to achieve fundamental personality change.[9] The view of political man which emerges from this perspective on personality and its formation is well symbolized, if not well summarized, by Lasswell's early provocative formulation:

> The most general formula which expresses the developmental facts about the fully developed political man reads thus:
>
> $$p)d)r = P,$$
>
> where p equals private motives; d equals displacement onto a public object; r equals rationalization in terms of public interest; P equals the political man; and) equals transformed into.[10]

This makes of political man the rationalized version of inadmissible private motives and reflects the early emphasis of Freudians and neo-Freudians upon those aspects of personality which could be traced to a wild and assertive id. Anna Freud, Heinz Hartmann, and many others have somewhat restored the balance by giving more weight to ego psychology.[11] But the political personality which emerges from this theoretical framework tends to under-emphasize what has been overemphasized by the rest of the world, the plain appeal and obvious influence of economic advantage.

More recently, psychoanalytic theory has been re-examined and modified by a group, sometimes called the interpersonal school of psychiatry, which has been led by three important figures: Harry Stack Sullivan, Erich Fromm, and Karen Horney. The label "interpersonal" comes from the central view of personality expressed by Sullivan in the following terms: *"Personality I now define in the particularist sense as the relatively enduring pattern of recurrent interpersonal situations which characterize a human life."*[12] His work has had less bearing on political problems than has that of his two associates, so we now turn to their formulations.

Horney, in emphasizing the reflection of the strains of society in the contemporary neurotic trends of her patients (as a sample of some larger group), reveals what social life is doing to people: making them competitive, decreasing their capacity to give of themselves and thereby reducing their capacity to love; at the same time it is increasing their "neurotic need for affection" and generally, and most importantly, making them more anxious.[13] Unfortunately, because she has no base line, Horney cannot substantiate her claim that modern man has *more* of these problems than did his predecessors —but she can make a strong case that these facets of personality damage are real and important for our time. The importance of these neurotic trends for political personality, that is, the personality faced with political decisions, is substantial, though their expression is uncertain: the anxious man may, depending upon the organization of his personality, withdraw, become assertive, cling desperately to some dogmatic belief, or yield utterly to some tendency toward "other-directedness." What is certain is that his anxiety will impair his rational functioning and prevent him from using politics to his maximum long-term advantage.

Erich Fromm, the most politically oriented figure in this group, presents three main themes with special relevance to the study of political personality. The first of these has to do with the idea of "social character," which on the one hand is the "root" of ideology and culture and on the other "is molded by the mode of existence of a given society."[14] For Fromm, "the social character internalizes external necessities and thus harnesses human energy for the task of a given economic and social system."[15] In the same sense, one might think of a modal political personality, in a world where personality and political system are in harmony, as providing the motives, values, and capacities for performing the required political acts.

Fromm's second theme has to do with the relationship of man to society and to the government thereof. It was he who in modern times first developed an accounting of the costs of "freedom," that is, autonomy won at the expense of weakened ties of family, neighborhood, community, tradition, occupation, and, in some cases, religion. In developing this accounting and in elaborating on some of the political responses which it facilitated, Fromm portrayed, or at least sketched, the atavistic political personality unable to stand alone, searching for some synthetic ties to replace the ones lost in the process of modernization. This theme assumed increased importance with the development of the theory of *The Authoritarian Personality* by Adorno, Frenkel-Brunswik, Levinson, and Sanford.[16] Another sprout from the soil of this theory, nurtured by that very original gardener David Riesman,[17] is a theory of modern man as other-directed, that is, decreasingly reliant on his own conscience and increasingly reliant on cues from other people for his ideas and actions.

A third theme in Fromm's more recent work deals with the concept of alienation; it is important because it stands for, although it did not originate, an entire school of criticism of modern society. With roots in the work of Feuerbach and Marx,[18] but now more leveled at "modernity" than at capitalism, the idea of the alienated man claims that industrialism has alienated man from his work; that commercialism and the long process of change from status to contract have created an alienated "marketing personality" where people and the self are regarded as "things"; that mass society divorces people from meaningful group life; and that mass politics creates automaton-like, meaningless political responses.[19] The alienated personality is said to be "available" for charismatic leadership and anomic destructive social movements. Unfortunately for the theory, most available evidence shows that the attitudes characteristic of alienation are more prevalent in rural societies and are especially frequent in village life relatively untouched by industrialism, commercialism, mass media, and mass politics.[20]

While the "interpersonal school" represents one variation of the original Freudian interpretation of political man, another variation is represented by Erik Erikson, whose public hallmark is the concept of *identity*. Here we have a shift in focus from instinctual libido and interpersonal relations to the concept of the self, or the self image, but it is a self image in a group context. The term is somewhat elastic: "At one time . . . it will appear to refer to a conscious *sense of individual identity*; at another, to an unconscious striving for a *continuity of personal character*; at a third, as a criterion for the silent doings of *ego synthesis*; and finally, as a maintenance of an inner *solidarity* with a group's ideals and identity."[21] It is important now because of the growing evidence that psychic breakdowns have their origins decreasingly in the repression of impulses, as was the case in the nineteenth century, and more often in "identity-diffusion," that is, the uncertainties and anxieties arising from ill-defined goals, ambiguous group identifications, conflicting self images, and vague life patterns. In its political aspects, identity-diffusion leads to low political cathexis and ideological caution.[22]

Political Personality and Political Analysis

The various concepts and interpretations of political personality are reflected in the applied work of political analysis—but often segmentally, or eclectically, by men seeking personality concepts by means of which they can grapple with the intricate workings of political institutions. The problems of such analysis are many, and the amount of research in this area is small.

Legislative behavior. Legislative behavior, the output of which is a set of laws, institutions, and appropriations, is inevitably modified by the personality constellations of the legislators. An early study by McConaughy suggests that in one American state, South Carolina, a (somewhat unsystematic) sample of legislators were, compared with the average American adult, "less neurotic . . . far less introverted, more self-sufficient and slightly more dominant."[23] McConaughy does not relate these results to legislative behavior. A more comprehensive study of Connecticut legislators by James Barber finds a large proportion of the legislators lacking in self-esteem and employing their positions in the legislature to compensate for their doubts about themselves; it is the few who are genuinely self-confident who get the legislative business of the legislature done.[24] On a closely related psychological syndrome, the sense of efficacy, evidence from a study of four American state legislatures reveals how important this sense is in affecting the manner in which a legislator sees and handles his role: those with a higher sense of efficacy (ego strength?) look beyond their immediate districts and accept responsiblity for the larger unit, in this case the state; more than others, they accept pressure groups and even welcome them as part of the play of forces necessary for developing acceptable policy; and they tend to regard their role as brokers in a cockpit of conflict with equanimity, without becoming personally upset.[25] But in these four states, as in Connecticut, it appears that more than half of the legislators have grave doubts about their efficacy or even adequacy in the legislative situation.

Another theme out of the nosology of personality syndromes is the matter of identity. It seems from Barber's Connecticut study, and from other work on the United States House of Representatives, that the more clearly a legislator perceives his role and assimilates this role concept to some vigorous and viable sense of identity, the more effective he is—i.e., persuasive, work-oriented, and hard to manipulate.

Although it does not explicitly deal with personality, Nathan Leites' work on "operational codes," first of the Politburo and then of the French parliament, embodies in different language many of the themes which are normally conceived to be the stuff of personality. Thus, Leites asserts that two themes of the operational code of the Politburo are a fear of dependency, leading to strong measures to avoid any situation where people or nations are mutually interdependent, particularly any situation where they might be "used" by others,[26] and an unusually strong insistence on "the control of feelings," leading to attacks on sentimentality and emotional responses and to an observable "hardness"—at least during the Stalinist period.[27] Speaking of the French legislator, Leites describes a series of behaviors, especially avoidance of responsibility, efforts so to arrange things that others are "to blame" for unpopular or unsuccessful decisions, inability for form permanent coalitions because of distrust of others (following from and causing this pattern of irresponsibility), and a search for a *force majeure* to get the French parlement or the nation out of its difficulties.[28] Leites would argue that these are French, as well as legislative, characteristics; hence they also fall under the category of "national character," though of course he would also argue that they are traits to some extent widely shared throughout the world. At the bottom of many of these traits, there seems to be a concept of individualism and a tendency to distrust others, a quality which Almond and Verba found central to the working of a successful civic culture.[29]

Judicial behavior. Many years ago Jerome Frank pointed to the very great variation in the treatment given to defendants in similar situations by judges of different dispositions.[30] Although at first this seemed to reflect different "philosophies," it later became evident that this was another name for the motivations, values, punitiveness, and other elements of a personality constellation. Harold Lasswell illuminated these problems in his discussion of the influence on judicial decisions of narcissistic, paranoid, latent homosexual, and other tendencies in a group of judges whose life histories were made available to him.[31] Pritchett's study of patterns of decisions made by Supreme Court justices reveals something about the influence of personal characteristics upon judicial decision making, but the personality themes here are only partially developed.[32]

Electoral behavior. As mentioned earlier, the main themes of the very substantial studies of electoral behavior in the United States, England, France, and Norway deal not with personality features but with group life, media influence, occupational and class differences, electoral laws, and the like. This is for the very good reason that, at least in the United States, and generally elsewhere, modal behavior is situationally determined to such an extent that people with many different personality syndromes tend to behave similarly. The places to look for the influence of personality are in the interstices where social pressure are conflicting or ambiguous. Lane has listed some of these as follows:

Selection of the grounds for rationalizing a political act.
Selecting topics for political discussion.
Selecting types of political behavior over and above voting.
Expression of the probable consequences of participation.
Holding particular images of other participants.
Styles of personal interaction in political groups.[33]

In general this means that, at least in the United States, there are no important personality differences between Democrats and Republicans, though radicals of the right and left have been shown to have deviant personality syndromes.[34] On the other hand, there are substantial differences between participants and nonparticipants: the nonparticipants tend to be more neurotic, more anxious, less self-confident, more autistic, less trusting of others, lower in ego strength, and more alienated from themselves and society.[35] In a cross-cultural study by Almond and Verba, in which personality and cultural differences are, as always, somewhat fused, it appears that those societies in which there is greater interpersonal trust; in which, from the beginning, people have a sense that each person is himself important and influential in the family, school, and place of work; and in which it is possible to work easily and cooperatively with others—such societies develop healthier (more effective and less destructive) patterns of participation and more conciliatory and workable patterns of partisanship.[36]

Ideology. Electoral participation inevitably leads into a discussion of ideology, but, as Campbell and his colleagues[37] make clear, the relationship between voting and ideology is often tenuous. Ideology here means not merely the attitudes and values on topical concerns (foreign aid, civil rights, welfare state) but also the fundamental views which form the ideational counterpart to a constitution: ideas on fair play and due process, rights of others, sharing of power, the proper distribution of the goods of society (equality), uses and abuses of authority, etc. It is in this sense that Adorno and his associates[38] developed their concept of an authoritarian personality and belief system, and in this sense Lane explored the ideologies of a group of working-class and lower middle-class men.[39] The problem here is to sort out the conventional beliefs which almost everyone in the society holds, not because these ideas have a special congeniality but because they are, so to speak, "given," from those ideas which are selected from among alternatives because these ideas have a special "resonance." The conventional ideas may be conceived as related to national character, though there can be a lack of congruence here, too; the "resonant" ideas, the more or less individual ones, may more properly be related to and explained by the concept of individual political personality.

In the general discussion of ideology, it appears that one central aspect is that of alienation versus allegiance, a rejection of "the system" or some substantial part thereof, compared with a fundamental loyalty to and acceptance of it. Cantril[40] found this to be a main theme among the French and Italian communists he interviewed; Almond and Verba[41] suggest that one of the main difficulties of the Italian political system lies in the high incidence of alienation and contrast this with the sense of allegiance and political pride of the Americans and British. Lane found in his Eastport, U.S.A., sample that a failure to support democratic norms and a tendency to see decisions as made by conspiratorial groups ("cabalistic thinking") were related generally to just such political alienation but that this did not extend to a more general feeling of social alienation, a rejection of the society and its values.[42] On the whole, it seems wise to think of alienation in terms of specific targets of disaffection, a series of topically specific continua, rather than in terms of a dichotomous and total classification, although the tendency of alienation in one area to infect another should be observed.

National character. The study of widespread ideologies or belief systems leads to the study of the broad distribution of political personality types or characteristics in a society. At this point we begin to study national or social character—a field which fell into disrepute because of early unsupported generalizations by Le Bon[43] and others.

Following World War II, a series of studies on the German people, sometimes based on interview data and sometimes more speculative,[44] sought to discover what led them down the path to the Nazi revolution. A few comparative studies have indeed suggested that the Germans, more than others, tend to revere both paternal and state authority and have, by a very slight margin, a higher incidence of "authoritarianism."[45] Subsequent political history has indicated that these elements of political personality are not incompatible with the functioning of certain kinds of republican institutions, and, moreover, they are not fixed in the character of a people forever.

Similar studies of the Soviet Union,[46] necessarily more limited because of the inaccessibility of most of the population to such study, have suggested the importance of certain other emotional themes: expressiveness and the felt need for external control (combined, it is true, with a strain between the controlling, overly bureaucratic elite and the mass of people still in transition from traditional to modern behavior and norms); suspicion of "outsiders," implying sharp differentiation between in-groups and out-groups, with some paranoid symptoms; and "identity crisis" posed by the long-term, but recently exacerbated, conflict between Russia and the West—and yet, withal, a lack of the "tenderness taboo" (or sadomasochism) which characterized the Nazi mentality.

We are only beginning to study the close inter-relationship of personality qualities and political life, particularly the way in which similar institutions function when manned by persons of different personality constellations. This article has not touched upon the important research done on the personality problems of the officials and publics in modernizing nations, as illuminated by Doob, Pye, and Leighton[47], among others, but this is surely an area where further work is needed. Problems of personality and bureaucracy in a world which inevitably is becoming bureaucratized deserve further attention following the seminal article by Merton.[48] Elite studies have, until now, tended to focus on the more easily accessible data, the external circumstantial forces affecting career choice and selection of the world's elites, but we need to know more about the internal dynamics and inter-personal characteristics of coopted, appointed, and elected leaders. By now, however, scholars are aware that there is no simple distribution of traits, syndromes, or personality types which is good or necessary (or at least sufficient) for the operation of an efficient and humane political system, and that hence we must direct our research toward discovering relatively subtle patterns of personality characteristics, with varying distributions, meshed into roles and institutions in complementary ways, each "way" modified by the ecology and history of a particular political system.

Notes

1. Graham Wallace, *Human Nature in Politics*, 4th ed. (Gloucester, Mass.: Smith, 1962), originally pub. 1908; and Robert E. Lane, "Political Character and Political Analysis," *Psychiatry*, 16 (1953), pp. 387–398.

2. Ivan P. Pavlov, *Conditioned Reflexes: An Investigation of the Physiological Activity of the Cerebral Cortex* (New York: Dover, 1960), first published in 1927 as *Lektsii o rabote bob'shikh polusharii golovnogo mozga*; John B. Watson, Behavior: *An Introduction to Comparative Psychology* (New York: Holt, 1914); and Clark L. Hull, *Principles of Behavior: An Introduction to Behavior Theory* (New York: Appleton, 1943).

3. Robert C. Tucker, *The Soviet Political Mind* (New York: Praeger, 1963), pp. 91–121.

4. John Dollard and Neal E. Miller, *Personality and Psychotherapy: An Analysis in Terms of Learning, Thinking, and Culture* (New York: McGraw-Hill, 1950).

5. Kurt Lewin, *Field Theory in Social Science: Selected Theoretical Papers* (1939–1947), Dorwin Cartwright (ed.) (London: Tavistock, 1963).

6. Dorwin Cartwright and Alvin Zander (eds.), *Group Dynamics: Research and Theory*, 2nd ed. (Evanston, Ill.: Row, Peterson, 1960), originally pub. 1953.

7. Bernard Berelson, Paul F. Lazarsfeld, and William N. McPhee, *Voting: A Study of Opinion Formation in a Presidential Campaign* (Chicago: University of Chicago Press, 1954); and Paul F. Lazarsfeld, Bernard Berelson, and Hazel Gaudet, *The People's Choice: How the Voter Makes Up His Mind in a Presidential Campaign*, 2nd ed. (New York: Columbia University Press, 1960), orignally pub. 1944.

8. Angus Campbell et al., *The Voter Decides* (Evanston, Ill.: Row, Peterson, 1954); and Angus Campbell et al., *The American Voter*, University of Michigan, Survey Research Center report (New York: Wiley, 1960).

9. Sigmund Freud, New Introductory Lectures on Psycho-analysis (New York: Norton, 1965), first published as *Neue Folge der Vorlesungen zur Einführung in die Psychoanalyse*, 1932.

10. Harold D. Lasswell, "Psychopathology and Politics," in *The Political Writings of Harold D. Lasswell* (Glencoe, Ill.: Free Press, 1951), pp. 1–282, orig. pub. 1930.

11. Anna Freud, *The Ego and the Mechanisms of Defense* (New York: International Universities Press, 1957), first published as *Das Ich und die Abwehrmechanismen*, 1936; and Heinz Hartmann, *Essays on Ego Psychology* (New York: International Universities Press, 1964).

12. Harry Stack Sullivan, *Conceptions of Modern Psychiatry*, with a critical appraisal of the theory by Patrick Mullahy, 2nd ed. (New York: Norton, 1953), first published in the February 1940 and May 1945 issues of *Psychiatry*.

13. Karen Horney, *The Neurotic Personality of Our Time*. (New York: Norton, 1937).

14. Erich Fromm, *Escape from Freedom* (New York: Holt, 1941, 1960), p. 296.

15. Fromm, *op. cit.*, p. 284.

16. Theodor W. Adorno et al., *The Authoritarian Personality*, American Jewish Committee, Social Studies Series, No. 3 (New York: Harper, 1950).

17. David Riesman, *The Lonely Crowd* (New Haven: Yale University Press, 1950).

18. Erich Fromm (ed.), *Marx's Concept of Man* (New York: Ungar, 1961).

19. Erich Fromm, *The Sane Society* (New York: Rinehart, 1955).

20. Edward C. Banfield and L. F. Banfield, *The Moral Basis of a Backward Society* (Glencoe, Ill.: Free Press, 1958).

21. Eric Erikson, "The Problem of Ego Identity," in Maurice R. Stein et al. (eds.), *Identity and Anxiety* (Glencoe, Ill.: Free Press, 1960), p. 38.

22. Robert E. Lane, *Political Ideology* (New York: Free Press, 1962), pp. 381–399.

23. John B. McConaughy, "Certain Personality Factors of State Legislators in South Carolina," *American Political Science Review*, 44 (1950), pp. 897–903.

24. James D. Barber, *The Lawmakers* (New Haven: Yale University Press, 1965).

25. John Wahlke et al., *The Legislative System* (New York: Wiley, 1962), esp. pp. 474–475.

26. Nathan Leites, *The Operational Code of the Politburo* (New York: McGraw-Hill, 1951), pp. 40–43.

27. Leites, *op. cit.*, pp. 20–24.

28. Nathan Leites, *On the Game of Politics in France* (Stanford: Stanford University Press, 1959).

29. Gabriel A. Almond and Sidney Verba, *The Civic Culture: Political Attitudes and Democracy in Five Nations* (Princeton: Princeton University Press, 1963).

30. Jerome Frank, *Law and the Modern Mind* (New York: Conrad, 1949), originally pub. 1930.

31. Harold D. Lasswell, *Power and Personality* (New York: Norton, 1948).

32. C. Herman Pritchett, *The Roosevelt Court, 1937–1947* (New York: Octagon Books, 1963), orig. pub. 1948.

33. Robert E. Lane, *Political Life: Why People Get Involved in Politics* (Glencoe, Ill: Free Press, 1959), p. 100.

34. Gabriel A. Almond, *The Appeals of Communism* (Princeton: Princeton University Press, 1954); and Adorno et al., *op. cit.*, 1950.

35. Lane, *Political Life*, pp. 97–181.

36. Almond and Verba, *op. cit.*

37. Campbell et al., *The American Voter.*

38. Adorno et al., *op. cit.*

39. Lane, *Political Ideology.*

40. Hadley Cantril, *The Politics of Despair* (New York: Basic Books, 1958).

41. Almond and Verba, *op. cit.*

42. Lane, *Political Ideology*, pp. 161–186.

43. Gustave Le Bon, *The Psychology of Peoples* (New York: Macmillan, 1898), first published as Lois psychologiques de l'évolution des peuples, 1894.

44. Henry V. Dicks, "Personality Traits and National Socialist Ideology," *Human Relations*, 5 (1950), pp. 111–154; David M. Levy, "Anti-Nazis: Criteria of Differentiation," *Psychiatry*, 11 (1948), pp. 125–167; and Bertram H. Schaffner, *Father Land: A Study of Authoritarianism in the German Family* (New York: Columbia University Press; Oxford University Press, 1948).

45. Donald V. McGranahan, "A Comparison of Social Attitudes Among American and German Youth," *Journal of Abnormal and Social Psychology*, 41 (1946), pp. 245–257.

46. Henry V. Dicks, "Observations on Contemporary Russian Behavior," *Human Relations*, 5 (1952), pp. 111–175; and Margaret Mead, *Soviet Attitudes Toward Authority: An Interdisciplinary Approach to Problems of Soviet Character* (New York: McGraw-Hill, 1951).

47. Leonard W. Doob, *Becoming More Civilized: A Psychological Exploration* (New Haven: Yale University Press, 1960); Lucian W. Pye, *Politics, Personality, and Nation-building: Burma's Search for Identity* (New Haven: Yale University Press, 1962); and

Alexander H. Leighton et al., *Psychiatric Disorder Among the Yoruba: A Report*, from the Cornell-Aro Mental Health Research Project in the Western Region, Nigeria (Ithaca, N.Y.: Cornell University Press, 1963).

48. Robert K. Merton, "Bureaucratic Structure and Personality," in *Social Theory and Social Structure*, rev. ed. (Glencoe, Ill.: Free Press, 1957), first published in Vol. 18 of *Social Forces*, 1940.

Chapter 2
Political Character and Political Analysis: The Case of Interest Groups

The purpose of this paper is threefold: (a) it suggests the utility of the idea of political character in political analysis; (b) it attempts to show how three specific political problems can be illuminated by the use of models, or types, of political character; and (c) it tests the particular types of political character set forth in David Riesman's *The Lonely Crowd*[1] by using them in the analysis of certain political problems.

A person's political character may be defined as his habitual responses to political situations rooted at the personality level. These responses, of course, include a wide range of attitudes and traits—such as apathy or interest, submission or assertiveness towards authority, suspicion or trust of other groups, and so on. Persons having similar responses may be grouped together as a "type"; this is sometimes done on the basis of a single significant response pattern (ethnocentricity) and sometimes on the basis of a cluster of responses which are seen to go together (authoritarian personality). It is these various typologies which are at the focus of this paper.

The Idea of Political Character in Political Analysis

Since every kind of politics implies some psychological premises, political theory has always included assumptions about the nature of man—assump-

Reprinted from *Psychiatry: Journal for the Study of Interpersonal Processes*, 16 (1953), pp. 387–898. Also reprinted in Heinz Eulau, Samuel J. Eldersveld, and Morris Janowitz (eds.), *Political Behavior* (New York: Free Press of Glencoe, 1956) and in Neil J. Smelser and William T. Smelser (eds.), *Personality and Social Systems* (New York: John Wiley, 1963), pp. 466–480.

Notes to this chapter will be found on pages 34–37

tions which were more often implicit than overtly stated. Political theorists, and economic theorists as well, have therefore created a range of characterological types to populate the systems they created. Aristotle's "good man," the Machiavellian personality, the law's "reasonable" man, the Marxian's "bourgeois" or class-bound personality, the Marshallian "economic man," Bentham's pleasure-seeking and pain-avoiding human register, and other familiar types all illustrate varieties of political character—some with sophistication but others with the implication that there is only one human nature.[2]

Contemporary insight into the nature of personality has made many of these types of political character seem archaic and quaint, thereby subverting the political theories with which they were associated. New typologies have been developed; some of them have been strictly for therapeutic reasons (such as manic depressives, schizoids, and paranoids), but there are other typologies which are more closely related to the above definition of political character. A few of these types are set forth below, with the definitions condensed from the various works cited:

automaton. A person who "escapes from freedom" by adopting culturally popular personality patterns, losing his sense of personal identity and responding to political stimuli without any individual or distinctive orientation. *Erich Fromm.*[3]

pseudo-conservative. A person who adopts the conservative's ideology at the verbal level but, because of underlying personality disorders, subconsciously seeks radical solutions—for example, the lynching of agitators in the name of law and order. *T. W. Adorno and associates.*[4]

authoritarian personality. A person who (among other things) perceives the world as made up of a small glorified in-group and despised out-groups, hierarchically arranged by power relationships, peopled by types rather than individuals. He cannot establish warm human relationships, judges people by exterior qualities, adopts a moralistic condemnatory tone toward deviant behavior, and so forth. *T. W. Adorno and associates.*[5]

political agitator. A political leader whose satisfactions are derived from arousing emotions in others and whose skills are greatest in this area of interpersonal contact. *Harold Lasswell.*[6]

political administrator. A person whose skill lies in the manipulation of things and situations whose displacement of affect upon less remote objects is associated with a better adjustment to society. *Harold Lasswell.*[7]

political theorist. A person whose skill lies in the manipulation of ideas and who has displaced his private motives and emotions upon a system of abstract concepts. *Harold Lasswell.*[8]

bureaucratic personality. A person whose interpersonal relations have been habitually formalized by the demands of his work-life and whose responses to new situations are governed by overvaluation of rules. *Robert Merton.*[9]

indifferent. A person either who has no emotional or mental relationship to politics or whose mobility or lack of orientation leads him to shun all political involvements. *David Riesman.*[10]

moralizer (indignant or enthusiast). A person whose responses to political situations are characterized by high affect and low competence. *David Riesman.*[11]

inside-dopester. A person with controlled (and low) affect and great desire to know and/or use political phenomena for his amusement and advantage. *David Riesman.*[12]

anomic. A person whose political style is inappropriate to the situations he faces and who shows other symptoms of disorientation. *David Riesman.*[13]

autonomous. A person who is neither dominated by parentally instilled conscientious views of politics nor by concern for the opinions of peer groups; a person, therefore, free to choose his own political opinions. *David Riesman.*[14]

Underlying the five political types conceived by David Riesman is another typology which has a much broader application than political phenomena. Riesman suggests a relationship between certain demographic situations and social character, and then proceeds to define three emergent types: (a) the *tradition-directed* person, who has no image of himself as in any way related to the world of government and politics; (b) the *inner-directed* person, whose orientation is given in childhood and who is not responsive to the changing moods and opinions of his associates; and (c) the *other-directed* person, whose means of dealing with each situation is determined by a sensitive screening of whatever doctrine or behavior prevails among the groups close to him at a given moment.[15]

These and other contemporary conceptions of political character have been employed to explain political phenomena in a limited but growing number of instances.[16] Their utility in political analysis is manifold, but four services seem to emerge as most important:

1. *When it appears that socioeconomic and historic factors are relatively constant in two situations but the situations develop differently, the concept of political character may serve as an auxiliary explanation of social causation.* For example, the impact of a crisis situation has often presented socialist and communist groups with similar opportunities. Is it ideology alone, or may it also be a differential selection of personality types which causes the observable difference in reactions?[17] The West invaded China and Japan with a significantly different reception in each case.[18] Cultural and geographic distinctions may seem to explain these differences—but do not the concepts of comparative culture implicitly include the concept of difference in political character? The employees in a West Virginia mill staffed by workers with rural breeding react to exploitation in a manner different from that of metropolitan-bred workers. This is more than a difference of ideology and economic alternatives; it is a difference in habitual responses to social and political stimuli—that is, a difference in social and political character.

2. *Hypotheses respecting the political character of the members of a social organization help suggest the probable development, the tropisms, and the limitations of that organization.* One might, for example, upon seeing a high percentage of pseudo-conservatives (Adorno) in an organization dedicated to

traditional values, anticipate internal friction on the appropriate means for defending these values. This would follow from the different political characters of the genuine conservatives and the pseudo-conservatives. Or it would be possible to predict that there will be recruitment difficulties in an organization that defends the interests of groups which are populated by indifferents (Riesman). Or, to cite a third instance, it was just such an analysis of defective psychological substructure which Fromm employed in his explanation of the rise of Naziism in Germany.

3. *The explicit use of types of political character in the construction of political and social models (Utopias) minimizes the use of concealed premises about the nature of man and facilitates the use of these models to clarify social goals.* In the use of such models one follows in eminent footsteps. Thus Marx constructed his model community, the eventual classless communist society, on the basis of a complaint, unaggressive, self-controlled model of human nature.[19] Another Utopia may be seen in the atomized capitalist society conceived by Marshall and Mill, a Utopia populated entirely by rational and selfish versions of economic man.[20] A third model community is seen in Lasswell's garrison state, which is inhabited by paranoids and their captives.[21] Each such hypothetical society must include assumptions regarding the natures of the inhabitants, and it is an advance to recognize that these inhabitants are not live men but are stage characters borrowed from the cast made available by contemporary views of human nature.

4. *The employment of alternate types of political character in the premises of classical political issues serves to give them a new dimension and to illuminate new aspects of these problems.* In this use, the concept of political character is employed on a hypothetical basis in such a way as to shed light where the nature of the participants has eluded attention. What one does, in effect, is to take a certain situation, make various assumptions regarding the type of political character of the participants in the situation, and then predict the results that would be likely to occur on the basis of these assumptions. For example, this might be done to shed light on the problems associated with force and revolution by comparing the typical responses of the pseudo-conservative with the genuine conservative (Adorno), the automaton with the spontaneous man (Fromm), or the indifferent with the inside-dopester (Riesman). By varying the type of political character assumed, our knowledge of a problem may be enriched and stale arguments given new meaning.

An Example of Political Character Analysis: Riesman's Typology and Interest Group Theory

The merits and defects of this last type of analysis may best be revealed by an example: the application of a political typology to the classic issues of interest group theory. "Interest group" is defined as a formally organized association exercising an influence on governmental policy; a few examples would be the American Medical Association, Americans for Democratic Action, locals of the United Steel Workers of America, and the New Haven Chamber of Commerce.

In giving such an example of the application of a political typology, the selection of the typology offers a dilemma—for the solutions to the problems presented will depend upon the style and capacities of the characters introduced. Thus electoral behavior and the democratic processes will differ in their results in societies and groups inhabited by (a) pseudo-conservatives or (b) indifferents, and in societies and groups led by (c) agitators or (d) bureaucratic personalities.

For the purposes of this paper, I have selected Riesman's troupe, not because it is the closest to reality—probably the Adorno typology deserves this honor—but because it is a more complete group, offering more variety, and is particularly serviceable in opening up hidden but real issues in the area of interest group theory.[22] In what follows, three aspects of interest group theory are discussed: (a) the pluralistic problem; (b) the interpretation of group pressures; and (c) problems of representation in the leadership of interest groups.

THE PLURALISTIC PROBLEM

The interpretation of men's actual and potential relationship to government has formed the substance of political discussion in every arena and forum of Western culture. In broad and blunt outline, the units of observation are threefold: the individual, the group and constellation of groups, and what is usually termed "the state." Today, the focus of scholarly political science attention rests upon the middle category, the group and the constellation of groups which characterize society. This mental focus is, of course, a reflection of the changing structure of society, as well as a sharpening of insight into what was, in reduced measure, always there. A society which recognizes the importance of these groups, as contrasted with a society which recognizes only the state and the individual, is termed a "pluralistic" society.

The nature and perspectives of individuals who elude affiliation with interest groups bear closer examination. In Riesman's terms, who are the isolates? Are they *anomic*—persons with no appropriate political style, lost in the maze of people and events? Or are they *inner-directed moralizers*—persons steered by a rigid conscience, who, in their isolation from others, may become a persistent and difficult force of political anomalies? Or are they *autonomous*—that is, self-possessed and in possession of a perspective which leads them to avoid close affiliations and political commitments? Of course the isolates are of all three types, but it appears from the observable evidence that they are more anomic than they are autonomous or inner-directed moralizers.[23] Analysis, prescription, and therapy must then proceed in part from this identification of isolate character. It should be understood that the problem here is one of giving guidance to disoriented people rather than one of providing opportunities for expression for oriented and politically stable citizens. And it is important to recognize that the prescription and therapy must depend upon the differential analysis of the type of isolate under consideration. Solidarity and greater group integration may be prescribed as both an individual and a social cure for the anomic; but for the autonomous person, tenuous and lightly worn group relationships may indeed be socially healthy. For the moralizer, membership in groups of fellow indignants may serve to reinforce his indignation, while membership in multipurpose groups may dull the edge of his indignation, thwart its expression, and broaden its frame of reference.

If the nature of the isolate is a fractious problem, so also is the nature of group adherence. Political theorists have been inclined to regard the problem of group adherence in terms of the undifferentiated conception of "membership" in interest groups, without reference to the variety of meanings that membership may have for different people. This is a deficiency in conceptualization which any sophisticated approach to political character should seek to repair. The approach to the problem of group membership may also proceed through the use of Riesman's typology: *anomic, moralizer, autonomous*, and also, since this problem deals with affiliated individuals, the *inside-dopester*—the person who endows his politics with little affect, treats goals and ends casually, but possesses great technical (political) competence and seeks to employ it constantly to reorient himself with respect to other people's desires and ideas.

The typology is limited in its serviceability at this point. It fails to illuminate much of the significance of group membership: for example, it is not useful for distinguishing among, say, those veterans who join the American Legion in search of solidarity or because of a "need to avoid aloneness," to use Fromm's terminology; those who join in order to recapture status formerly accorded them by military rank; and those who join because of sympathetic responsiveness to hierarchical society (Adorno). To apply Riesman's ideas on political character in an effort to develop those themes would be adventitious; it would overburden an already speculative line of argument.

But Riesman's typology does illuminate some aspects of group membership which might otherwise escape attention. I have before me the image of the New Haven League of Women Voters who recently mobilized for an all-out assault upon the weak-mayor form of government in that city in an effort to secure the adoption of a council-manager charter. For some of the members the League represented a reflection of their own strong consciences, a force for Right, and the opposition represented the incarnation of evil. These women may properly be designated "indignant moralizers" and the analysis of such a character type is fruitful and, indeed, pragmatic. For others in the

League, the association offered sources of information, a little power, opportunities for the exercise of interpersonal skills—in short, a favorable milieu for the inside-dopester. A few of the League members seemed at the same time to have both political skills and a secure conviction of the direction in which they wished to go; for such autonomous persons, compromise, minor achievements, and the higgling ways of municipal democracy were admissible without defection or despair.

The significance of this breakdown of members into types lies in the destruction of the conception of an organization as a monolith, and in its re-creation in proper molecular terms. As a result, the respective sources of weakness and strength come more quickly to attention. The possibilities of compromise, the capacity for creating and holding allies, the stock pile of emotional fuel which may give staying power to the organizational effort, the capacity to sustain defeat, to change goals, and so forth—these may all be a reflection of the political character of the interest group membership or at least of the leadership.

It is not only societies that are pluralist, however, it is also individuals. A man belongs, inevitably, to many latent interest groups, even though he may be only dimly aware of them—his ethnic group (for the native white Protestant, often a group outlined only by the presence of other groups which he does recognize), his class group (ambiguous to most Americans), his religious group, his "cause" groups if any, his sectional group, and any number, variety, and complexity of others.[24] Normally, a person will be conscious of his group affiliation with men in similar occupations—professional, union, business, farm.

It is not surprising that such a multiplicity of group affiliations creates contradictions and conflicts for the individual—particularly when they present their claims for support simultaneously.[25] It has been said, therefore, that representation by interest groups fractionalizes a person—divides him into irreconcilable component parts so that he never becomes a whole man with an orientation that overrides his subordinate interests. The conclusion follows that political-party representation, because it presents a comprehensive, if vague, orientation, is superior to the atomistic representation of unreconciled interest groups.[26] Although the conclusion may be right, it follows too swiftly at this point, for it is precisely here that it may be useful to employ the concepts of political character.

The first revelation to appear from this psychologically oriented analysis is that the question has been miscast: psychologically the choice is not between party and interest group, but between whole-hearted devotion to a few interest groups or to a narrow third party, on the one hand, and, on the other hand, a sympathetic affiliation with a broad major party and a complex of interest groups. Riesman's indignant or enthusiast will find congenial representation in a goal-oriented organization (such as the Anti-Saloon League, Prohibition Party, Committee for Constitutional Government,

People's Lobby, or Socialist Party) and will refuse to consider himself represented by other interest groups or parties. But the other-directed overpoliticized person will seek representation by many interest groups whose conflicting goals will not disturb him—since he will have a loose and tenuous interest in their goals. Such an other-directed person will also find satisfaction in representation by a broad and amorphous party whose orientation is toward power rather than toward program. Being himself a pluralist, he sees no threat in the pluralistic problem.

But the pluralistic problem has facets other than the nature of the isolate in a group-structured society, the nature of the linkage which binds men to their groups, and the nature of the role of political character in the conflict of interest groups and political parties. There is, also, the question of the relationship between social typologies and character typologies. One such social typology refers to the isolation and the group solidarity of the individuals in a given society. A society of isolated persons may be said to be atomistic; a society in which most persons have many and close group memberships may be said to be pluralistic.[27] What, then, would be the relationship of the inner-directed-other-directed character typology to such an atomistic-pluralistic social typology?

Theoretically, of course, it would be possible to have a fourfold classification (see Table 2-1); pluralistic and inner-directed; pluralistic and other-directed; atomistic and inner-directed; atomistic and other-directed.

Table 2-1. Fourfold Social Typology, Theoretically Possible

Inner-Directed and Atomistic	Inner-Directed and Pluralistic
Other-Directed and Atomistic	Other-Directed and Pluralistic

The logic of the typologies, however, is such that an atomistic other-directed society is impossible, and a pluralistic and inner-directed society is too explosive to exist in any other than transitional form. On the other hand, both an atomistic inner-directed society, such as those of earlier agrarian America, and a pluralistic other-directed society can logically exist. Perhaps with these particular variables there is no other logical choice.

The United States is a pluralistic society.[28] Furthermore, the predominant emphasis in the range of political character types seems to be other-directed: thus Mead refers to the American search for contemporary popular orientation that has resulted from distrust of tradition,[29] Jones reports on the centralist tendency in opinion formation—the fear of isolation from the median public opinion[30]—and Riesman, of course, develops the theme of American other-directedness at some length.[31] As a pluralistic other-directed society, however, the American nation—or at least the urban parts of it—may have found the best available basis for democracy, now that the earlier simpler agrarian and inner-directed basis is no longer generally available.

THE INTERPRETATION OF GROUP PRESSURES

The Constitution arranges the elements of government in such a manner that the translation of popular desires into law is difficult and often delayed; it has created a situation where political parties, the vehicles of popular majorities, are weak, and the interest groups, the vehicles of minorities, are strong. Among the interest groups, those with independent sources of strength in the economy are in a relatively stronger position than those dependent upon governmental action for protection of their interests; this results from the fact that it is easier to block governmental action under a bicameral system endowed with a separation of powers than it is to advance governmental action in such a system. The result, of course, is that not only have interest groups flourished in such institutional soil, but they have developed chiefly along the lines of thwarting governmental action. Hence the term *veto groups*, applied to them by Riesman and others, has some justice.

Institutional analysis of this variety offers a primer's answer to the question, "Why are interest groups so influential in the United States?"—a question to which I shall return. But one may as well ask, "Why, given their institutional leverage, do not interest groups achieve greater strength in the United States?" For both questions, the ideas associated with the concept of political character have relevance.

It is to this second question that Riesman addresses himself, applying his social schema to achieve an explanation of the relative restraint of interest group leaders. In summary, it appears that the inner-directed robber baron has now given way to the politically sensitive industrial statesman, frightened by the cautions of his public relations counsel, fearful lest he appear "exotic" to his fellows, anxious to avoid controversy—in short, all "radar" (other-directedness) and no "gyroscope" (inner-directedness). Furthermore, if the veto groups are acknowledged to exercise the really decisive influence in a wide range of social issues and if they restrain themselves from a blunt and overt exercise of this influence, there may be said to be a power vacuum at the top. Asking himself who is the ruling class in this situation, Riesman says there is none.[32]

But this does not dispose of the matter. In the very system that Riesman describes there are forces which sustain the power of the interest groups and impoverish the resistance which society can offer. Among the forces contributing to interest group influence is the character structure of the society Riesman describes, a society populated by men trained to yield to others' opinions, to exhibit "tolerance" towards diverse interests (within an approved framework), and to move cautiously towards acceptability by the more powerful agents of that society. Most of the remainder of the population is busily indifferent to political matters, and, of those few who are concerned, a large number possess political styles inappropriate to their times and so lack the competence to make themselves heard. Such a society offers itself helplessly to the rape of the interest group chieftain who overcomes his diffidence in this matter.

Nor can it be said that the interest group counselors are unaware of the milieu which offers them such advantages. For those interests which directly engage the public seem most often to select for emphasis themes that suggest the popularity, cultural approval, indigenous nature, and American Way of the proposed public policy. Not the merits but the orthodoxy of the proposal seems at stake, and in such manner the other-directeds, the inside-dopesters, the conformists of suburbia and pseudo-suburbia are moved to respond favorably.

Equally important is the anaesthetic appeal of the interest group which narcotizes potential indignation with "good-will" advertising and stimulates indifference and apathy toward their loosely regulated activities by elaborate devices for turning public attention toward something else.[33] Furthermore, aggregates of enormous power attempt to masquerade as "just one of the boys" (the oligopolist as a small business man) or to deny their existence completely (the union leader whose followers act "spontaneously" to quit work). Using Riesman's model to reveal a possible truth, if not a present situation, it appears that an overpoliticized society under tension to return to a happier state of indifference will respond with quiet satisfaction to the narcotizing appeal of a number of interest groups.[34]

While some interest groups engage in this variety of persuasion and discussion among the public at large, most, being small, operate in more intimate relationships with such congressmen as seem vulnerable or at least approachable. The responses of congressmen, furthermore, are guided by their political characters, which may be stylized as other-directed raised to the second power —that is, politically sensitive men selected from constituencies heavily endowed with other-directed voters and letter writers. It is not overreaching the argument to say that the tenderness of congressmen to pressures, many of which bear no conceivable relation to past or future electoral results, is partly due to this social sensitivity distilled from society and purified in the atmosphere of Washington.[35]

PROBLEMS OF REPRESENTATION: THE ELITE-CONSTITUENCY RELATIONSHIP

In addition to the pluralistic problem (the person, the group, and the state) and the interpretation of interest group strategy, there are problems emerging from the relationship of leaders to constituencies in the interest groups themselves which merit attention. Orthodox attention singles out certain aspects of this relationship: Is the leader responsible to the constituency and what are the sanctions to enforce such responsibility? Is he vested with the powers of discretion or must he act within a narrow prescription of opinions upon which he has received instructions? Does he serve only the majority faction, if any, or does he modify his actions to suit a minority view? Is he permitted to transcend the bounds of the group's apparent interest to serve the interests of a larger group, perhaps the nation, when there is conflict between the two?

If these are classic questions, how may the classic answers be illuminated by reference to a typology of political character? In the first place, the relationship between the personality characteristics of the leaders and of the constituents—the *closeness of fit*,—to use Dicks' terminology[36]—is suggestive. Since leaders and delegates respond to issues with reference both to their internal personality pressures and external political pressures, the question arises of whether leaders whose personality characteristics differ from those of their constituents will validly represent their constituents. It is for this reason that, for example, leadership responding in terms or organizational advantage, public relations considerations, and strategic concepts (inside-dopesterism) runs afoul of the fraction of membership, large or small, which is purely goal-oriented (moralizers). If there is a systematic recruitment of inside-dopesters among the elite of an interest group, it is questionable whether the indignant and enthusiastic membership may be said to be adequately represented. Thus the anything-to-win psychology which seemed to be ascendant in the leadership group of Americans for Democratic Action at the 1948 Democratic Convention—on candidates, not issues—appeared hopelessly compromising to a portion of moralizing rank and file back home. On the other hand, there are occasions when an indignant radical faction will achieve control of an organization, defy public opinion, and gladly crucify themselves and their organization on some principled issue which might, from an organizational point of view, better have been avoided. Thus recently a strong faction in a cooperative housing community, in demonstrating their breadth of view on racial matters, welcomed a mixed couple (Negro and white) into the group, heedless of the fact that the couple had not sanctified their union by marriage, and were defiant toward the probable legal action which would follow.

The psychological congruity of elite and constituency is more than a matter of the accuracy of the representation involved; it also raises a question of the significance of the various kinds of discrepancies. Thus a moralistic elite in a fraternal and other-directed community or group, will pursue the formal explicit goals of the organization at the expense of the implied and unconscious goals of solidarity and "escape from aloneness." The instrumentalist other-directed elite in a moralistic group will preserve the organization and attend to its needs for cohesion and solidarity at the expense of the formal goals. In organizations where both elite and constituency consist of inside-dopesters, the survival instrumental values of the group will tend to be accentuated at the expense of the ideological values; and in organizations made up entirely of moralizers, it is the ideological values that will tend to be accentuated. In the former case, the organization will flourish to do nothing;

in the latter, clear goals will be enthusiastically pursued by an organization of dwindling effectiveness.[37]

The case of an elite which represents a constituency of indifferent and apathetic members, neither concerned over the organization's goals nor linked to the organization by its opportunities for advancement or social stimulus, offers special problems.[38] This is, by and large, the nature of much union membership, except for bread-and-butter issues, and it is also reflected in the membership of a number of churches. It is, in fact, a special case of wide frequency. In such cases the personality responses of the leadership are given free rein and are neither confirmed nor restrained by membership responses. As a consequence of this absence of external pressures of all kinds—ideological and social—the internal pressures of the character structure of the elite are released; the personalities of the leadership find their own media and style of expression. In the case of unions, because of the pragmatic nature of the leadership, the ideological content of the union program is apt to recede, *for both elite and constituency*, into a limbo of unmentioned topics; in the case of some of the churches, the indignation of leaders with a hyper-developed social conscience may alight upon convenient issues almost indiscriminately as they erupt in the news. In neither case does representation have anything to do with the event.

In addition to being important in the study of the degree to which the wishes of the constituency are accurately reflected by the leadership and the nature of the distortion of their wishes, if any, the psychological relationship of elite to constituency is also important in the treatment of the majority-minority problem. It is in the perspective of a range of values—consensus, heterodoxy, fear of authority, concern for economic privation, and so on—that this issue is usually argued,[39] but the problem has its psychological aspects as well.

A simple diagram of four possible situations, where there is only one minority group and where only Riesman's two major political character types are employed, is set forth in Table 2-2.

Table 2-2. Fourfold Majority-Minority Typology

Inside-dopester Majority and Inside-dopester Minority	Inside-dopester Majority and Moralizer Minority
Moralizer Majority and Inside-dopester Minority	Moralizer Majority and Moralizer Minority

The resolution of these situations of course is, in fact, unpredictable; but by using them as models, it becomes possible to suggest tendencies created by the conflict of political character:

1. Inside-dopester majority and inside-dopester minority: Both groups would tend to compromise; the unity of the organization would be preserved at the expense of whatever principles were at issue. There would be consensual rule rather than majority rule, in conflict with minority rights.

2. Inside-dopester majority and moralizer minority: The majority would be inclined to yield to the resolute minority in order to save the organization from irreparable split (although the desire of the majority to be acceptable to the outside world might yet force the split). Temporarily, at least, the minority goals would be furthered and there would thus be a tendency toward minority rule.

3. Moralizer majority and inside-dopester minority: The minority would yield to the majority and the organization would pursue a strict majoritarian policy. This is the only situation conducive to strict majoritarian rule.

4. Moralizer majority and moralizer minority: Neither group would yield to the other and a split would almost inevitably follow. This would be a revolutionary situation.

There is, finally, the question of the affinity of like-minded members of an organization—those with congenial personalities—at both the leadership and constituency levels. It often appears that intraorganizational disputes which turn on questions of "principle" generate more heat than the principles involved alone would call forth. Although there are many reasons for the intensity of feeling on trivial issues—including their symbolic value, the history of factional disputes in the organization, conflict between rival leaders, and so forth—one of the sources of emotion may be the unrecognized conflicts between types of political character. Futhermore, on such occasions, the leadership itself will be drawn into an apparent affiliation with those whose responses seem most reliable—that is, whose psychological referents are most like their own. The psychological faction, therefore, should be recognized along with the economic and ideological faction of a group. The fact that these cohesions are overlaid and reinforced by what is called "friendship" tends to divert attention from their more enduring and more fundamental causes.[40]

Summary

Every politics implies a psychology. Classic political theorists relied, implicitly or overtly, on assumptions regarding the plasticity, sociability, fearfulness, ambition, conscience of mankind. Sophisticated modern political theorists, more conscious of the many dimensions of human nature, may turn to the theories of contemporary psychology and psychiatry to inform their doctrines and make their conceptions more plausible. In both cases, the combinations of traits which are thought to go together create "types"—that is, persons with similar habitual responses to political stimuli, responses which have their sources in some aspect of personality.

The conscious employment of these types of political character can serve several useful purposes in political science:

1. They can offer auxiliary causal explanations for historical events.
2. They can help in the analysis of social and political organizations.
3. They can populate social science models and clarify social goals.
4. They can be inserted as data in the arguments over classic issues and thus give them a new dimension and new definiteness for political theory.

To illustrate the possibilities of the use of types of political character in political analysis, I have selected a typology from among those available (Fromm, Adorno et al., Lasswell, Merton, Riesman) and have employed it in the analysis of interest group theory. Employing Riesman's cast of political character types, the following hypotheses emerge:

I. Regarding the pluralistic problem—that is, the interrelationships of individual, group, and state:
1. Individual isolation from interest groups takes its meaning from the political character of the individual; it may be healthy or pathological for both society and the individual depending upon the individual's degree of "autonomy."
2. The nature of the adhesives which bind people, particularly the leadership, to their interest groups will determine the capacities of the interest group to compromise, endure, broaden its membership, define its goals, and so on.
3. A person's choice of agencies of representation—among political parties and the varieties of interest groups—is partly a search for means of expression congenial to his political character.
4. The nature of a person's response to the conflicts between groups with which he identifies depends upon the nature of his connection with social groups. For goal-oriented persons, the conflict will be severely felt.
5. The relationship between the "pluralistic-atomistic" social scale and the "inner-directed-other-directed" personality scale reveals how personality types must fit the social pattern and vice versa. A pluralistic, other-directed society may give democracy its most favorable environment.
II. Regarding the power of interest groups in American culture:
1. If it is assumed that the pattern of American social relations emphasizes the sensitive, "radar screening," other-directed type of response, it seems true that the interest groups themselves are restrained by this emphasis (Riesman).
2. The interest groups are assisted in their search for influence by the open-mindedness and other directedness of the population, as well as by the large residue of indifference.
3. The interest groups take advantage of these popular traits through stressing the "general acceptance" of their positions and through narcotizing public resistance with abundant "good-will" advertising.
4. The influence of interest groups upon Congress is accentuated by the distillation of other-directed attitudes through the electoral process and the consequent supersensitivity of congressmen to the pressures of interest groups.
III. Regarding problems of representation:

1. The relationship of men with different political characters in elite and constituency positions poses special problems of representation: (a) When the political character of members of the elite differs from the political character of their constituencies, the organization may be led along lines not desired by the membership. (b) When the political character of members of the elite is in harmony with the political character of their constituencies, the policy of the organization may tend, in Riesman's typology, either towards doctrinaire indignation or disoriented drift. (c) When the political character of the constituency group is apathetic and indifferent, the elite will be guided less by external pressures and more by internal (character) pressures.

2. In the controversy over majority rule and minority rights, the respective political character types of majority and minority factions may determine the outcome: where both groups are inside-dopesters, consensus is quickly achieved without majority enforcement; where both groups are moralizers, a split is almost inevitable; where the majority is composed of inside-dopesters and the minority is composed of moralizers, there is a tendency toward minority rule; only where the majority is composed of moralizers and the minority is composed of inside-dopesters is there likely to be a clear case of majority rule.

3. The intensity of factional conflict in an organization often has its source in the types of political character of the two groups, each employing psychological referents unfamiliar and uncongenial to the other group.

Notes

1. David Riesman, *The Lonely Crowd* (New Haven: Yale University Press, 1950).

2. In a sense many classic theoretical works may best be used to illustrate model communities wherein a single psychological orientation is made the premise and the governmental forms outlined may be considered the result. Thus Hobbes' *Leviathan* (Oxford: Blackwell, 1946) may be considered as a discussion of the society and government which would follow if human beings were sadomasochistic and paranoid; Machiavelli's *The Prince* (Chicago: Packard and Co., 1941) may be considered as a discussion of government where the elite is competitive, anxious, and possessed of psychopathic personalities; and J. S. Mill's *On Liberty* and *Considerations on Representative Government* (Oxford: Blackwell, 1946) represent a Utopia where men are assumed to have democratic personalities, are thought to have their libidinous drives well under control, and are guided by reason.

3. *Escape from Freedom* (New York: Rinehart, 1941), pp. 185–206.

4. *The Authoritarian Personality* (New York: Harper, 1950), pp. 181 ff.

5. Reference note 4, *passim.*

6. *Psychopathology and Politics* (Chicago: University of Chicago Press, 1930), pp. 78–126.

7. Reference note 6, pp. 127–152.

8. Reference note 6, pp. 53–56.

9. "Bureaucratic Structure and Personality," *Social Forces*, 17 (1940), pp. 560–568.

10. Reference note 1, pp. 184–190.

11. Reference note 1, pp. 190–199.

12. Reference note 1, pp. 199–210.

13. Reference note 1, pp. 287–288.

14. Reference note 1, pp. 295–299.

15. Reference note 1, Chap. 1.

16. For a discussion of the political character of members of the Nazi elite, see G. M. Gilbert, *The Psychology of Dictatorship* (New York: Ronald Press, 1950). For a discussion of the traits of Nazi leaders among prisoners of war, see H. V. Dicks, "Personality Traits and National Socialistic Ideology," *Human Relations*, 3 (1950), pp. 111–154. For a discussion of the political character of American Fascist agitators, see Leo Lowenthal and Norbert Guterman, *Prophets of Deceit* (New York: Harper, 1949). For a discussion of the political traits of Soviet elite and followers, see H. V. Dicks, "Observations on Contemporary Russian Behavior," *Human Relations*, 5 (1952), pp. 111–176; and Margaret Mead, *Soviet Attitudes Toward Authority* (New York: McGraw-Hill, 1951). For a discussion of methodological problems, see Nathan Leites, "Psycho-cultural Hypotheses About Political Acts," *World Politics*, 1 (1948), pp. 102–119.

17. See Gabriel Almond, *The Appeals of Communism* (Princeton: Princeton University Press, 1954) on the sources of Communist party membership. See also, Howard Wriggins, "The Ideal Image of the Communist Militant," unpublished Ph.D. dissertation on file at Yale University Library, 1952; and Herbert Krugman, "The Appeal of Communism to American Middle Class Intellectuals and Trade Unionists," *Public Opinion Quarterly*, 16 (1952), pp. 331–355.

18. See: Ruth Benedict, *The Chrysanthemum and the Sword* (Boston: Houghton Mifflin, 1946). J. K. Fairbank, *The United States and China* (Cambridge: Harvard University Press, 1948). D. N. Rowe, *China Among the Powers* (New York: Harcourt, Brace, 1945).

19. Although Marxian literature does not provide a clear picture of the nature of the prophesied Utopia, a few suggestions by Marx and Engels can be found in Max Eastman (ed.), *Capital, the Communist Manifesto, and Other Writings* (New York: Modern Library, 1932), Part I, "Outlines of a Future Society." For a commentary on this and other Utopias, see Karl Mannheim, *Ideology and Utopia* (New York: Harcourt, Brace, 1944), pp. 173–236.

20. Although Jevons presents the conceptualized analysis of economic man in its purest form, both Alfred Marshall, *Principles of Economics* (London: Macmillan, 1890) and John Stuart Mill, *Principles of Political Economy* (Boston: Little, Brown, 1845) give more rounded and complete presentations of the operation of the capitalist Utopia.

21. See Harold Lasswell, "The Garrison State and Specialists on Violence," *Amer. J. Sociol.*, 46 (1941), pp. 455–468 (reprinted in Lasswell, *The Analysis of Political Behavior* (London: Routledge & Kegan Paul, 1948), pp. 146–157.

22. Riesman's focus of attention in *The Lonely Crowd* (reference note 1) and *Faces in the Crowd* (New Haven: Yale University Press, 1952) is such that many of the classic problems of interest group theory are not treated there. But with an autonomy of their own his ideas may be made to grapple with these problems.

23. Membership in formal organized groups normally increases as one goes up the social scale. Political participation and interest also increase with socioeconomic status. But at any given socioeconomic level, those with greater group connections are likely to be more clearly oriented politically, more confirmed in their political beliefs, than those with fewer group connections. See P. F. Lazarsfeld, B. Berelson, and H. Gaudet, *The People's Choice* (New York: Columbia University Press, 1948), pp. 145–147.

24. W. L. Warner and associates present a schematic version of an individual's formal group membership (*The Status System of a Modern Community*, New Haven: Yale University Press, 1942). The informal groups to which a person belongs are analyzed as voting determinants in several studies: See, for example, Angus Campbell and R. Kahn, *The People Elect a President* (Ann Arbor: Survey Research Center, 1952), pp. 20–39.

25. See W. Y. Elliott, *The Pragmatic Revolt in Politics* (New York: Macmillan, 1928), pp. 95–99, 204. See also F. W. Coker, *Recent Political Thought* (New York: Appleton-Century, 1934), Chap. 18.

26. "It is clear that my underlying assumption in this critique is that ultimate legal relationship between [group] members and the state could . . . only be one of citizenship made effective by political parties, although this citizenship is now 'filtered' by group life.

Political parties based on territorial representation must be the final means... of enforcing responsibility and registering public opinion." Elliott, reference note 25, p. 213.

27. In addition to atomistic and pluralistic societies, there are monolithic societies where the nation is *the* group and the group is solidary and demanding. This represents the kind of homogeneous consensual society implied in the works of Plato, Rousseau, and Mussolini. For a different kind of scale—irrational to rational—see Karl Mannheim, *Man and Society in an Age of Reconstruction* (New York: Harcourt, Brace, 1948).

28. See David Truman, *The Governmental Process* (New York: Knopf, 1951) and Earl Lathan, *The Group Basis of Politics* (Ithaca: Cornell University Press, 1952).

29. Margaret Mead, *And Keep Your Powder Dry* (New York: Morrow, 1943), pp. 27–53. Almond seems to agree with Mead in her estimate of the "faddistic" nature of American orientation, but his stress upon the privatization of interests in the United States appears to qualify his conception of the other-directed American character. See Gabriel Almond, *The American People and Foreign Policy* (New York: Harcourt, Brace, 1950).

30. See A. W. Jones, *Life, Liberty and Property* (Philadelphia: Lippincott, 1941), pp. 318–354.

31. "Bearing [certain] qualifications in mind, it seems appropriate to treat contemporary metropolitan America as our illustration of a society—so far, perhaps, the only illustration —in which other-direction is the dominant mode of insuring conformity." Reference note 1, pp. 20–21, see also Chaps. 10 and 12.

32. Reference note 1, Chap. 11, "Images of Power." In support of this position, it may be said that in all probability those interest groups with a stake in governmental decisions fail to treat lobbying costs as they would some other more explicit and formalized cost factor (such as wages or capital or advertising) and consequently underspend in this area. In further support, it appears that the failure of business to accept what may be called "Brady's solution"—the establishment of a hierarchical organization of business groups to absorb political power in their own interest, on a scale comparable to the German pattern of the 1920–1932 period—suggests indeed a marked restraint of these dominant veto groups. See Robert Brady, *Business as a System of Power* (New York: Columbia University Press, 1943).

33. Thus Thurman Arnold suggests that the chief utility of the Sherman Anti-Trust Act has been to lull the public into a sense of security and permit the normal activities of trusts, cartels, and oligopolies to proceed without serious public concern or governmental interference. See Thurman Arnold, *The Folklore of Capitalism* (New Haven: Yale University Press, 1937), pp. 207–229.

34. Kris and Leites found the German people generally seeking to escape the politicization of their lives during the Nazi era, and they suggest that this phenomenon is present in less degree in all Western countries. (E. Kris and N. Leites, "Trends in Twentieth Century Propaganda," pp. 393–409; in *Psychoanalysis and the Social Sciences*, edited by Geza Roheim (New York: International Universities Press, 1947).) Reisman argues that the mass media constantly present political stimuli to people who are constantly trying to escape it. (Reference note 1, pp. 244, ff.) Thus if interest groups can offer reassurance that attention is not needed, this theme will chime with an already present and poignant desire.

35. The responsiveness of United States congressmen to pressure groups is often described, but any effort to appraise motivation or the role of personality and character requires more information than has hitherto been available. See L. E. Gleeck, "98 Congressmen Make Up Their Minds," *Public Opinion Quarterly*, 4 (1940), pp. 3–24; or Jerry Voorhis, *Confessions of a Congressman* (New York: Doubleday, 1947), *passim*.

36. See H. V. Dicks, "Observations on Contemporary Russian Behavior," reference note 16, pp. 168–174. Much of Dicks' discussion centers on the problem of the divergent personality characteristics of the new Bolshevik elite and the mass of the Russian people.

37. It is well to keep in mind throughout that this essay represents a stylized account of possible factors to take into consideration; it is not a descriptive account. Furthermore,

there is an implied *ceteris paribus* at every stage of the reasoning. Here, for example, it appears that the Anti-Saloon League, surely an indignant organization if there ever was one, was eminently successful in attracting adherents (see Peter Odegard, *Pressure Politics: The Study of the Anti-Saloon League* (New York: Columbia University Press, 1928). Furthermore it is at least possible that one reason Hitler achieved success was his obsessive, indignant nature (see Gilbert, reference note 16, p. 295). These two exceptions suggest a modification of the principles stated above: Where there is a constituency available with strong indignant feelings in certain areas, an indignant elite may be both uncompromising with respect to these areas and successful in attracting adherents.

38. This is, of course, Michels' problem, although he deals with it in terms of divergent and conscious interests rather than in terms of divergent psychological referents. Much of Michels' argument rests upon the capacity of the elite to change from their revolutionary (and representative) position to their position of leaders with vested interests and conservative orientation. If this change is the product of material and status considerations, it may be easy and rapid. If, however, the change requires characterological changes as well, it will necessarily be a slower and more difficult process. See Robert Michels, *Political Parties* (Glencoe, Ill.: Free Press, 1949) (first published in 1915), pp. 205–234.

39. See, for example: H. S. Commager, *Majority Rule and Minority Rights* (New York: Oxford, 1943). Edward Mims, *The Majority of the People* (New York: Modern Age, 1941). Willmoore Kendall, *John Locke and the Doctrine of Majority Rule* (Urbana: University of Illinois Press, 1941).

40. Friendship itself is a combination of many things, among them "frequency of interaction" as the result of purely external pressures (Homans), common group memberships and identifications, common foci of attention (sports, shopping, and so on), and congenial response patterns to political and social stimuli (political and social character). See George C. Homans, *The Human Group* (New York: Harcourt, Brace, 1950).

Note: This article was stimulated by David Riesman's guest appearance with my graduate class in political parties and public opinion. I wish at the same time to express my debt to Professor Riesman and to repeat his warning that no typology is good for every purpose. Where one fails, another designed for a different purpose may succeed. At this point I would like also to express thanks to Charles Blitzer for his help in clarifying several points made in this paper.

Chapter *3*
Political Personality and Electoral Choice

The most widely-held and well-supported theories of electoral choice today relate such choice to group membership, socializing, so to speak, the vote decision. In this process the personality of the individual voter has tended to be overlooked or its influence minimized. In focussing in this discussion upon the relationship of authoritarianism to electoral choice, therefore, we hope not only to contribute to our knowledge of a particular personality pattern in a political context but also, more generally, to restore the individual, as contrasted to the group, to an important place in a theory of the electoral process.

In an electoral situation, as in any other situation, personality factors play a double role: (a) they affect the perceptions of the individual, screening out some stimuli, distorting others, and admitting others intact; and (b) they shape the responses of a person, selecting among the various possible responses those which are most serviceable to basic personality needs. Every personality develops certain attitudes to assist in this process of selecting among the possible responses. For example, interest in the election,[1] sense of duty,[2] sense of political efficacy,[3] or sense of social integration with the community[4] might form the nucleus of the attitudes bearing on the decision whether or not to vote. Identification with a political party,[5] position on current political issues,[6] candidate preference,[7] anticipation of economic or political advantage,[8] prestige considerations,[9] or identification with a partisan social group[10] might affect the vote itself.

Reprinted from *American Political Science Review*, 49 (1955), pp. 173–190. Also reprinted in Nelson W. Polsby, Robert A. Dentler, and Paul A. Smith (eds.), *Politics and Social Life* (Boston: Houghton Mifflin, 1963).

38

Notes to this chapter will be found on pages 54–56

Circumstances Limiting the Influence of Personality

We have said that dimensions of personality can help to explain certain attitudes which in turn help to explain participation decisions and partisanship decisions. But the influence of personality in making these contributions to the ultimate political decisions is not constant, due to variation in the strength of the personality factors which may be present. In addition, the situations themselves provide either a broad or a narrow scope for the influence of personality. Undoubtedly many elements of the situation tend to affect the degree of influence that personality may have on any single electoral decision, but among the important elements of the situation the following four are surely significant.

1. *The degree to which the national or local culture has established an approved norm.* Where the individual perceives a latitude of decision, elements of his personality can guide his decision in a way which is not possible where the culture provides sanctions against all those who deviate from a specified position.

2. *The degree to which the choice is guided by personal experience and illuminated by personal information.* It is a commonplace that a structured situation gives rise to fewer rumors and less projectivity than a vague situation where knowledge is little and guideposts few. But where there is personal information, the projective possibilities are limited and internal referents are displaced by clearer perceptions of the outside world.

3. *The degree to which the choice is guided by perceived economic, social, or political self-interest.* A person who believes that some clear gain to himself or to his group will result from a victory of one or another candidate generally narrows the scope of "expressive" responses. In other words, when dealing with tax and subsidy matters, the expression of aggression, passivity, projectivity, and authoritarian-submission will be inhibited when they entail the prospect of economic loss, although they may be pressed into the service of the economic interest in the manner or style of argument employed.

4. *The degree to which a person's group memberships create cross pressures.* When a person belongs to groups whose political attitudes are homogeneous, the scope of personality factors is somewhat limited by his narrowed perception of alternatives. When he belongs to several groups whose political views are different, he must choose among them, compromise, or withdraw from the field.

Even if the above four factors are kept constant and the strength of personality forces in the individual himself is fixed, there is another way in which the influence of personality on electoral choice may be varied. Not all elections evoke the same kinds of personality responses. For example, Paul Lazarsfeld suggested (in a recent talk at the Survey Research Center) that the 1896 campaign between Bryan and McKinley might have brought forth a difference between the inner-directed and the other-directed persons of Riesman's typology in a way never again reproduced, whereas the 1928 campaign in which Prohibition was a campaign issue might have been more discriminating on certain elements of the authoritarian syndrome. Each election, then, varies not only in the degree to which it evokes decisions determined by personality, but also with respect to the nature of the personality syndromes which are relevant.

In spite of these various opportunities for personality-shaped determinations, it must be repeated that under many circumstances the social forces, the group memberships, and the stimuli of the media, which have been at the focus of traditional attention, exercise their influence without regard to personality factors. So to speak, they slip unscathed through the screening influences of the personality. It is for this reason, among others, that analyses of political decisions employing solely demographic data and data of exposure to the media have been able to achieve considerable success. Yet always behind the demographic relationships there lurk the unexplored problems of motivation, both for the portion of the vote that is "explained" in this fashion and even more for that portion which is considered deviant.

Method

Although the literature contains many suggestions of personality factors which might provide the basis for fruitful exploration, the authoritarian "syndrome" isolated by the pathbreaking study on *The Authoritarian Personality*[11] has been selected for the following case study. Recent criticism[12] has tended to highlight the methodological weaknesses of this work, but further research with the instruments devised by its authors has amplified our knowledge of the several personality factors involved in the "authoritarian personality" and has corroborated a significant proportion of the original findings.[13] The set of attitudes which make up the authoritarian syndrome may be briefly described as follows: desire to submit to strong leaders; desire to dominate persons and groups seen as weaker than oneself; tendency to seek destructive and aggressive solutions to problems as contrasted to an attitude of tolerance and compromise; tendency to accept superstitious or supernatural explanations and to avoid scientific explanations; tendency to see individuals as members of favorable or unfavorable types rather than as unique human beings; cynicism regarding other people's motives (and regarding the integrity of the political process); tendency to project one's own motivations upon other people—to see them responding in the same way the individual himself responds; tendency to value conventional attitudes and behavior and to reject deviants—tendency to conformity; tendency to avoid introspection and to "externalize" explanations for the events in one's life (anti-intraception); tendency to see situations in terms of power and to see one's own part in such situations as a function of one's own power and toughness; tendency for sex drives to be inadequately integrated with the rest of the personality, and therefore a fear of sexual impulses.[14]

But to move from a promising and indeed demonstrably fruitful concept to a test of the concept in some relevant situation is difficult. The authoritarian personality was originally measured by a battery of thirty items, called the F (for Fascist) Scale. Ten of these thirty items were included in a battery of questions asked of a portion of the national sample, interviewed by the Survey Research Center in their November, 1952, post-election survey, thus opening up an opportunity for significant research on the relation of personality to electoral behavior.

The use of these data, however, posed a number of methodological questions, a few of which must be mentioned. First, there emerged the question of the *representativeness* of the sample. Only a portion (585) of those interviewed in the post-election national survey were asked the authoritarian-equalitarian (AE) questions. Since the 585 were randomly selected from a random stratified sample, there was assurance that they were about as close to a representative national sample as could be secured with this size group. Second was the question of the *nature of the scale* to be used. It would have been possible to construct a simple Likert-type scale on the basis of all ten of the questions, but this type of scale is open to the criticism of multi-dimensionality; the scale may be measuring more than one dimension of personality. For this reason, after some experimentation a Guttman-type four-item scale (hereafter referred to as "the AE scale") was constructed which met the minimum requirements for this type of scale—a Coefficient of Reproducibility of 90.4.[15] This type of scale has the virtue of more nearly measuring a single dimension. The items in this scale, with their distributions, are as follows:

1. What young people need most of all is strict discipline by their parents. (agree: 76%; disagree: 23%; NA: 1%)

2. Most people who don't get ahead just don't have enough will power. (agree: 64%; disagree: 35%; NA: 1%)

3. A few strong leaders could make this country better than all the laws and talk. (agree: 51%; disagree: 48%; NA: 1%)

4. People sometimes say that an insult to your honor should not be forgotten. Do you agree or disagree with that? (agree: 25%; disagree: 73%; NA: 2%)

In some ways this four-item scale purports to measure, by a less complex method, an aspect of personality already explored by the authors of *The Authoritarian Personality*. Although there are areas of difference, the series of attitudinal and behavioral relationships obtained with this shorter AE scale do suggest that the scale measures some of the main dimensions of the 30-item F Scale. By and large, the evidence presented below reveals that those who show high authoritarianism on the four-item AE scale are less tolerant of ambiguity, more ethnocentric, more projective (at the lower educational levels), more moralistic, and more tough in their attitude on foreign affairs (at the lower educational levels) than are the equalitarian types.

The demographic characteristics of the authoritarian and equalitarian personalities are of interest, but space permits discussion of only the educational factor. As might be expected, the more education a person has the more likely he is to be equalitarian, but the relationship between education and authoritarianism is not a very close one. Suffice it to say that those with only a grade school education are the most authoritarian group by a moderate margin.

Political Participation

Political participation can be conveniently classified in terms of three modes of behavior: (a) non-voting; (b) voting without further political activity; and (c) voting plus such further political activity as going to meetings, ringing doorbells, and contributing funds. How does authoritarianism relate to these levels of participation?

Theoretically, the expectation is unclear. Voting implies faith in a democracy (equalitarian), but it is also a conventional act (authoritarian). Political activity implies social responsibility (equalitarian), but it also suggests power-oriented activity (authoritarian). Other studies have indicated that authoritarians tend to vote less than equalitarians;[16] but since authoritarianism and non-voting are both class-linked and the data are not broken down by classes, one cannot be sure of the validity of this conclusion. Similarly, Fillmore Sanford concludes that "equalitarians are more politically participant,"[17] but his data suffer from the same lack of class breakdown and, therefore, the same possible invalidity.

When our data are not broken down into two class groups, it also appears that there is a significant personality difference ($p < 5\%$) between authoritarian and equalitarian patterns of participation, but when the class breakdown is made, this significance disappears. On this basis of the class-controlled (education) data there appears to be almost no difference in non-voting between the two personality groups and only slight differences ($p < 17\%$) in political activity of the meeting-going, money-giving type.

Yet such evidence in no way proves that the authoritarian syndrome does not play a part in decisions on political participation. It is possible for people to arrive at the same decision for different reasons, to vote for different reasons, and to go to meetings for different reasons. Although with the data at hand we cannot probe deeply into motivation, we can make a rough test of the way two important influences on participation bear on authoritarians and equalitarians in our sample.

The first of these influences is a set of attitudes relating to a person's belief in the effectiveness of voting in a democracy. In a battery of five questions, the Survey Research Center probed people's beliefs on whether public officials "care what people like me think," the effectiveness of the vote in influencing policy, and the sense of bewilderment at the complexity of public problems, summarizing the responses in a score on "sense of political efficacy." Theory would suggest that the authoritarian, with his cynicism and his belief that weak people do not have to be consulted, would score low in such a test. The data for non-high school graduates are given in Table 3-1. There was no significant relationship for the better-educated group.

Table 3-1. Authoritarianism and Sense of Political Efficacy for Non-High School Graduates

Sense of Political Efficacy	AUTHORITARIANISM	
	Equalitarian N=53	Authoritarian N=147
Low	38%	55%
High	62	45
Total	100%	100%

$\chi^2 = 5.04$ $p < 5\%$.

But if a sense of the importance of his vote helps lead the equalitarian into political participation, why does the authoritarian participate? Is it from a sense of duty? The members of the sample were asked about their concept of a person's duty to vote under various circumstances and were scored on their responses. On the whole, it appears that authoritarians and equalitarians do not perceive the duty to vote in different ways—it is too heavily laden with cultural approval for such personality dimensions to show through.

Why, then, does the authoritarian vote and become active in approximately the same degree as the equalitarian? It is at least possible that he is responding less to inner feelings of responsibility and self-confidence and more to external pressures. The nature of such pressures is such that they tend to increase with the number of social contacts a person has in a community, or the number of groups to which he belongs. Therefore, greater number of group memberships of authoritarians revealed in Table 3-2 is significant in appraising the context of "civic" influences on the two personality groups.

Table 3-2. Authoritarianism and Number of Formal Group Memberships

	AUTHORITARIANISM	
	Equalitarian	Authoritarian
Non-High School Graduates	(N=60)	(N=172)
0–2 group memberships	72%	62%
3 or more group memberships	28	38
Total	100%	100%
High School or College Graduates	(N=68)	(N=97)
0–2 group memberships	68%	51%
3 or more group memberships	32	49
Total	100%	100%

$\chi^2 = 6.58$ $p < 5\%$.

Yet the data probably have another meaning as well. The very thing which makes the authoritarian a joiner of groups (although, according to Sanford,[18] not a leader) may also make him politically active: that is, it is the perception of some personal or material advantage which makes him both join groups and work for a political party. Sanford has shown that the authoritarian, more than the equalitarian, is reluctant to join the less prestigeful groups but eager to "head up" some community committee work.[19] Similar considerations probably enter into the authoritarian's calculations regarding political activity.

From the evidence, therefore, it appears that although there is little difference in voting and political activity between the two personality groups, there may be differences in the personal meanings of these forms of participation to the two groups. The equalitarian, in part at least, seems motivated by a feeling that his voice in a democracy is significant; the authoritarian may be responding more to the group (conventional) pressures around him, and to the hope of some increment in prestige and power associated with his political activity.

Orientation

While this portrayal of personality forces operating covertly in a series of political acts helps to illuminate the level of participation, it does nothing to reveal the direction. Other studies have suggested that there is a relationship between ideology and authoritarianism,[20] between Communist Party identification and authoritarianism,[21] and between candidate orientation at the rightist margin and authoritarianism.[22] This last study, however, also shows that in the spring of 1952 there were only minimum differences between Eisenhower and Stevenson supporters at the upper-income level, and the Adorno study shows the small difference in authoritarianism between "Willkie Republicans" and "New Deal Democrats" in 1946 and 1947. Theoretically, therefore, there was no clear reason for assuming that the vote in the 1952 election would reflect important differences in authoritarian personality orientation. The data are given in Table 3-3.

The interrelationship of personality, education, and the 1952 vote shows a pattern of some interest. It is clear that at every educational level authoritarianism tends to be associated with the Republican party. Furthermore, it is pertinent to note that those at the middle level of education, the high school graduates who did not go to college, are most influenced by the personality dimension. It is at this level, roughly upper working and lower middle class, where social group memberships exert cross pressures, and, as noted above, cross pressures open up the way for personality influences which are blocked out by solidly partisan group identifications.

If it is legitimate to make a rough equivalence between education and socio-

Table 3-3. Authoritarianism and the 1952 Vote Preference

1952 Vote and Vote-Preference of Non-voters	AUTHORITARIANISM	
	Equalitarian	Authoritarian
Grade School	(N=30)	(N=124)
Democratic	60%	49%
Republican	40	51
Total	100%	100%
High School	(N=70)	(N=98)
Democratic	51%	34%
Republican	49	66
Total	100%	100%
College	(N=26)	(N=41)
Democratic	38%	24%
Republican	62	76
Total	100%	100%

$x^2 = 8.60$ $p < 5\%$.

economic status, certain of the cell groups are especially significant. The authoritarian grade-school Republicans and equalitarian college Democrats suggest the influence of personality operating not merely to structure an ambivalent situation but in opposition to socio-economic pressures. These may be the groups for whom personality influences are the greatest of all. The equalitarian grade-school Republicans and authoritarian college Democrats represent groups for whom both socio-economic and personality forces are thwarted by some other more significant force, such as regional party loyalty, religious identification, or a particular stand on the issues of the day.

The relation of education to personality (authoritarianism) differences between the parties tells us something about the way in which equalitarians and authoritarians at every educational level behave politically. Their voting history is also informative in this respect. If one were to ask, for example, whether it was something distinctive about the 1952 election that attracted the authoritarians to the Republican standard, a clue would be given by the 1948 vote of each group. Examination of the data in Table 3-4 shows that, on

Table 3-4. Authoritarianism and the 1948 and 1952 Vote

Voting Decision	EQUALITARIAN		AUTHORITARIAN	
	1948	1952	1948	1952
	(N=126)	(N=127)	(N=247)	(N=241)
Democratic	37%	41%	36%	30%
Republican	21	38	28	43
Non Voters	42	21	36	27
Total	100%	100%	100%	100%

$x^2 = 20.87$ $p < 1\%$.

balance, the 1952 election had, in a small degree, opposite effects on the Democratic vote in the two personality groups, and that these effects were largely the result of the effects upon the non-voters. Put differently, 1948 equalitarian non-voters divided between Democrats and Republicans, while 1948 authoritarian non-voters probably went solidly for Eisenhower. In addition, some 1948 authoritarian Democrats switched to Eisenhower.

But, as with the problem of participation, once the fact of difference has been established, the explanatory hypotheses crowd the stage. Why, in 1952, were authoritarians drawn to vote for the Republican candidate, General Eisenhower? The line of attack on this question will use three elements in the vote decision: party identification; position on current and relevant issues; and attitudes towards the candidates.

Party identification. Party identification, that is, a sense of personal attachment to a political party, is a significant feature of a man's group orientation; it helps him to decide not only which candidate to support but also which issues to endorse and to oppose. It is related to many things which define a man's living space, such as his family and friends, his religion, and his socio-economic status. In view of this significance, how do authoritarians and equalitarians tend to relate themselves to political parties? The data are presented in Table 3-5.

Table 3-5. Authoritarianism and Party Identification

Party Identification	AUTHORITARIANISM	
	Equalitarian	Authoritarian
	(N=117)	(N=241)
Democratic	48%	47%
Independent	35	23
Republican	17	30
Total	100%	100%

$x^2 = 9.71$ $p < 1\%$.

Among other things, it is clear that there are many more Democratic party identifiers than Republican party identifiers or independents. One consequence of this fact is that, for both equalitarian and authoritarian groups, there are more Democratic partisans than Republic partisans. The significant feature is the difference in proportion of partisans in each personality group. Among the partisans, the equalitarians are about nine to three Democratic, while the authoritarians are only about five to three Democratic, a relationship due partly to socio-economic factors. It is also clear that the equalitarian is more likely to be independent (tolerant of ambiguity)[23] than the authoritarian. Put another way, one might say that personality (authoritarianism) does not make so much difference in terms of identification with the Democratic party, but does make a lot of difference as to whether one

says he is an independent or a Republican. For those who do not identify
with the Democratic party (because of demographic considerations, group
pressures, or ideological conviction), authoritarian motivations will move
them towards Republican partisanship, while equalitarian considerations
will move them toward an independent position.

Although it would be fruitless to attempt here to catalog the many kinds of
attitudes which impel a man to identify with one party rather than another
as a regular feature of his orientation, surely one of the elements in this choice
lies in his perception of the kind of group with which he is aligning himself. It
was clear enough in the Survey Research Center study of the 1952 election, for
example, that most members of the electorate perceived the Democratic party
as being more closely associated than the Republican party with labor union
members, and the Republican party as being more closely linked than the
Democratic party with big business. For those people who regard unions as a
negative reference group, and who wish to disassociate themselves from union
and possibly the working class in general, identifying with the Republican
party offers a means of so doing; and in reverse the same thing is true of
"big business." Equally, it is true that for those who wish to vote Democratic
for other (family, regional, economic) reasons, a means of escape from this
conflict is offered by changing the perception of the disliked labor union group
so that one "doesn't know" how union members will vote, or so that they are
seen as voting Republican. Projection of this kind offers a kind of index to the
social distance a person wishes to place between himself and a specified group.

Specifically, we would hypothesize that authoritarians would tend to
disidentify from whatever party they perceived as the party of Negroes,
immigrants, and "social inferiors." If this were true, authoritarians would
tend to see these groups voting for the other party rather more than did the
equalitarians; that is, their effort to identify with the more respectable party
would be measured by their projective perceptions of the way the less pres-
tigious groups voted. This hypothesis can be tested with perceptions of the
Negro vote in 1952. The data for the better-educated group (high school or
college graduates) who stated a perception on this point are given in Table 3-6.

Table 3-6. Authoritarianism and White Perception of the Negro Vote among High School or College Graduates

Perception of the Negro Vote	Equalitarian	Authoritarian
Negroes will vote "like me," i.e., Democrats think Negroes will vote Democratic, Republicans think Negroes will vote Republican.	(N=44) 59%	(N=74) 41%
Negroes will not vote "like me," i.e., Democrats think Negroes will vote Republican, Republicans think Negroes will vote Democratic.	41	59
Total	100%	100%

$\chi^2 = 3.99$ $p < 5\%$.

Why this relationship attains significance only among the better-educated portion of the population is not clear, although the presence of "split" and "don't know" categories left the less well-educated groups means of "escape," which they used relatively more frequently. What the data suggest, however, is that political parties are reference groups with positive and negative images in the minds of the electorate and that further research into the properties of these reference groups might be rewarding.

Political issues. The part which political issues play in national elections has never been adequately appraised and certainly not measured. The lore of political science is filled with historical judgments: the Democrats lost the 1920 election on the question of the League of Nations and the issue of "normalcy"; the Republicans lost New York in 1884 because of a "rum, Romanism, and rebellion" statement left uncorrected by James G. Blaine; Woodrow Wilson won the 1916 election on the basis of an implied pledge to keep the United States out of war, and so forth. More recently Campbell, Gurin, and Miller have minimized the role of issues in the 1948 election, while Julius Turner elevates them into a much more significant position in that election.[24] The relative importance of issues, candidates, and traditional party loyalties assumes varying proportions in each campaign and there remains much to be done in discovering how each of these factors, and particularly issues, relate to other campaign phenomena.

Whatever their particular influence in each election, issues are significant features of the electoral process and the stand a person takes on the important issues of the day will contribute to his electoral decision.[25] The extent of the awareness of the issues of the day taken all together will, of course, vary greatly in the population, just as the significance of any one issue will be differently appraised by different people. Here, again, personality will affect this determination. An illustration of this is provided by the "coders' " estimates of the main reason why each respondent in the 1952 study who had arrived at a vote decision prior to election day would cast his ballot as he planned. (The coders were neutral staff persons in the Survey Research Center who were required to go through every interview and indicate how the interview was to be coded on the IBM cards.) Although in a number of areas there were no differences, it appeared that equalitarians were more likely to be concerned with domestic issues and authoritarians with foreign policy (projective?) issues. Of more significance, perhaps, is the finding that of the 35 cases of persons whose main reason for voting for Eisenhower was the corruption issue, the distribution was as follows: equalitarians, 17 per cent; medium, 26 per cent; authoritarians, 57 per cent. Although the number is small, the evidence suggests that the authoritarian is, in politics as elsewhere, more concerned with conventional moral values than is the equalitarian; if he is a reformer, he is a moralistic reformer and not a social reformer.

The Survey Research Center study makes the statement that the voters favored Eisenhower "because a central aspect of his appeal was his presumed ability to do something personally about Korea and the cold war."[26] How does personality relate to voters' attitudes on Korea? If it could be shown that personality factors such as authoritariansim were related to popular attitudes on Korea, it would follow that personality probably made some contribution to vote decision in 1952.

Curiously enough, in the attitudes on foreign policy authoritarianism plays a role only among those who have at least some high school education. Although this was not expected, in retrospect one might argue that those with less education either answer "don't know" or, if they have views on foreign policy, take their cues from their party alignment in a way not true of the better-educated groups. Earlier we made the inference that lower-class individuals are less influenced than others by personality considerations in their party choice because of the preponderance of group and demographic forces. It now appears that this holds true for issues as well as for party identification.

Specifically, on the Korean question we would hypothesize that the authoritarian would be less likely to tolerate continued peaceful negotiation in Korea at a time when progress there seemed minimal (intolerance of ambiguity) and would prefer a policy of pulling out or of bombing the Chinese and committing other aggressive acts (authoritarian aggression and destructiveness, orientation toward power and toughness). The data for the better-educated groups controlled for the 1952 vote decision, are given in Table 3-7.

Table 3-7. Authoritarianism and Attitudes on United States Korean Policy among High School or College Graduates

Policy	Authoritarianism and the 1952 Vote			
	DEMOCRATS		REPUBLICANS	
	Equalitarian	Authoritarian	Equalitarian	Authoritarian
	(N=42)	(N=39)	(N=58)	(N=98)
Pull out of Korea entirely	5%	15%	5%	14%
Keep on trying to get a peaceful settlement	67	49	38	29
Take a stronger stand and bomb Manchuria and China	26	36	48	52
Other	2	0	9	5
Total	100%	100%	100%	100%

$x^2 = 8.26$ $p < 10\%$.

The evidence tends to support the hypotheses, although the relationship is least strong (where we would expect it to be strongest) in the "bomb China" responses. In certain areas of foreign policy, then, we may say that the personality dimension of authoritarianism tended to contribute to or to reinforce a decision to vote for the Republican party in 1952.

The most salient question among the various domestic policies was the overall attitude towards what may be referred to as "welfare-statism," the notion that the state should serve the interests of the less privileged through housing, health and social security measures. It is not normally associated with governmental aids to the business community or subsidies to manufacturers. For the lower-income groups, then, it has a quality of self-interest which obscures and overrides the relationship of personality (authoritarianism) to attitudes toward the welfare state, but there is no such clear self-interest (except indirectly, the tax interest) for the upper income and education groups. For these latter groups, in accordance with our theory of the circumstances which facilitate the influence of personality, some relationship might be expected.

On the question of services to lower-income groups, one would hypothesize that among the better educated, the equalitarians would be more likely to favor welfare services than would the authoritarians. The responses of those who wanted more governmental services and those who wanted less are compared in Table 3-8 "About right" responses were ambiguous (conventional or "liberal"?) and hence not included in the analysis.

Table 3-8. Authoritarianism and Attitudes toward the "Welfare State," among High School or College Graduates

Authoritarianism and the 1952 Vote

	DEMOCRATS		REPUBLICANS	
	Equalitarian	*Authoritarian*	*Equalitarian*	*Authoritarian*
	(N=22)	(N=18)	(N=28)	(N=46)
Not enough	86%	78%	61%	26%
Too much	14	22	39	74
Total	100%	100%	100%	100%

$x^2 = 9.38$ $p < 1\%$.

Note: Responses were determined by the question: "Some people think the national government should do more in trying to deal with such problems as unemployment, education, housing, and so on. Others think that the government is already doing too much. On the whole, would you say that what the government has been doing is about right, too much, or not enough?"

The hypothesis is confirmed, although the relationship is much more significant among the Republicans and the numbers involved are small. On the whole, it would seem that for the equalitarian Republicans who believed in more governmental services (17 in number), a force had been set in motion which, given the right circumstances, would make them more likely than most Republicans to switch to the Democratic party.

It is important, however, to issue a *caveat* at this point, and to raise the possibility that issue-orientation may be the result of a vote decision, as well as a contributing cause. Belknap and Campbell have demonstrated the manner in which certain policy attitudes flow from party identification,[27] and Lazarsfeld and associates have shown how a person resolves his cross pressures in a voting situation by adjusting his attitudes so that they are in conformity with his vote preferences.[28] Using only the partisan attitudes employed in this paper, the sequence of events, then, could take any one of three forms:

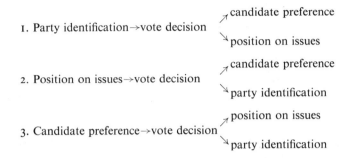

1. Party identification→vote decision
   ↗ candidate preference
   ↘ position on issues

2. Position on issues→vote decision
   ↗ candidate preference
   ↘ party identification

3. Candidate preference→vote decision
   ↗ position on issues
   ↘ party identification

Party identification in the second and third forms, of course, would not be likely to develop out of a single election.

Candidate orientation. The literature of political science has dealt extensively with the problem of candidate appeal to the electorate. Much of this discussion has been in terms of the demographic or experimental characteristics of the candidates, such as the advantage of a humble origin, the advantage or disadvantage of military titles, the handicap of being a non-Protestant and the importance of coming from a pivotal state. To some extent the personality of the candidate has entered into discussion, as in references to Wilson's coldness, Roosevelt's charm, and Dewey's apparent conceit. Furthermore, to an increasing degree the personality of the electorate or constituency has come under examination, as in Sanford's Philadelphia study,[29] James Davies' study of charisma in the 1952 election,[30] Hyman and Sheatsley's analysis of Eisenhower's appeal,[31] and studies of the followers of American demagogues.[32]

On the surface it appears that the 1952 election offers a unique opportunity for studying the part which personality plays in drawing people toward one or another political candidate. It was hypothesized, for example, that the authoritarian, more than the equalitarian, would be drawn toward Eisenhower, partly because he was endowed with the attributes of a victorious general, partly because he was presented as a "strong" leader, a role which he himself attempted to enhance by his selection of the term *crusade* to describe his campaign, and partly because his opponent could well have been seen as a weak and indecisive intellectual. With this hypothesis in mind, an effort was made to test the relation of personality to the perception of the candidates.

A precondition of this test was the elimination of those who supported a candidate because he was their party's candidate or because his position on issues was more congenial to them. The first step, therefore, was to select all of those who responded to open-ended questions on the candidates in personal terms ("I like him," or "He is a marvelous man"). With data available on these responses, several hypotheses seemed plausible and were tested. The first of these was to the effect that authoritarians would respond more to candidates in this way than would equalitarians, a hypothesis in line with the theory expressed in *The Authoritarian Personality* that authoritarians tended to personalize politics.[33] The data showed that there was no such relation, at least as measured by the number of voluntary responses of this character.

A second hypothesis was to the effect that the group limiting its comments to pro-Eisenhower and anti-Stevenson statements would be more authoritarian, an hypothesis not borne out by the data. One of the interesting findings, incidentally, was that one of the most authoritarian patterns of response was given by those who made only favorable references to Stevenson with no other personal references of any kind. Inspection of the data, however, showed that most of the equalitarian patterns included some critical remarks about Eisenhower, whereas most of the authoritarian patterns did not. The data were then arranged as shown in Table 3-9.

The similarity of responses of equalitarians and authoritarians suggests that the authoritarian syndrome is unrelated to attitudes towards Stevenson and Eisenhower. Yet since this facet of personality is related to attitudes on political issues, to party identification, and to some elements of participation, it seems likely that it is also related to the selection of the candidate. As in the case of political participation, it seems probable that authoritarians and equalitarians arrived by different routes at similar decisions on the candidates. To some, "Ike" may have appeared as a *warm, friendly, democratic man*; to others he may have been a *strong, military leader* who would shoulder the

Table 3-9. Authoritarianism and Criticism and Support of Eisenhower and Stevenson

Expression of Criticism and Endorsement	Equalitarian (N=121)	Authoritarian (N=251)
Expressed criticism of Eisenhower in personal terms	60%	48%
Did not express criticism of Eisenhower in personal terms	40	52
Total	100%	100%
Expressed endorsement of Eisenhower in personal terms	72%	68%
Did not express endorsement of Eisenhower in personal terms	28	32
Total	100%	100%
Expressed criticism of Stevenson in personal terms	37%	43%
Did not express criticism of Stevenson in personal terms	63	57
Total	100%	100%
Expressed endorsement of Stevenson in personal terms	58%	56%
Did not express endorsement of Stevenson in personal terms	42	44
Total	100%	100%

nation's burdens; to still others, he may have been specially trained in international affairs and hence a *competent man* who might solve the problems posed by the Korean war; in short, his special strength may have been the ambiguity of his public personality.

That there is a difference in the basis of support for the two candidates is suggested, although not proved, by the figure in Table 3-9. Equalitarians tend to support Eisenhower as much as do the authoritarians, but they are also markedly ($p < 11\%$) more critical. What is the meaning of this?

One interpretation might be that equalitarians liked Eisenhower as much as did the authoritarians, but voted Democratic either because they liked Stevenson better or because of the greater influence of party identification and issue orientation.

Another possible interpretation is that while the equalitarian is capable of neutral and detached attitudes toward political leaders, the authoritarian tends to see competing leaders in black and white terms, endorsing one and criticizing the other.

A third interpretation, based upon the theory of the origin of authoritarianism, is that each group sees the political leader as a father image modeled after his own father, the authoritarian recalling a father whom it was unsafe to criticize publicly, and the equalitarian remembering a less frightening father, a person about whom one could be objective.

Whatever the correct interpretation, it appears that the factors that led the authoritarians to be uncritical of Eisenhower may have been important in their vote decision. On the other hand, the factors that led the equalitarians to be generous in their praise for Eisenhower were apparently less important in theirs. Expressed in another way regardless of personality, criticism may be a better index of candidate preference than is support of a candidate.

Summary

We have suggested a theory to explain the part which personality features play in electoral choice, showing the manner in which they affect a man's perception of his economic interests, group memberships, and the stimuli of the media, and the manner in which they shape political responses through certain politically relevant attitudes. Taking the authoritarian syndrome for illustrative purposes, we have shown its influence upon political participation (voluntary "persuasive" activities and voting) in terms of a sense of political efficacy and the effect of multiple group memberships. It was suggested that these two influences had differential effects on equalitarians and authoritarians, often balancing out and leading them to participate politically in approximately equal degree.

In terms of political orientation, it appeared that authoritarians were relatively more Republican in 1952 and that this Republican orientation had increased since 1948 in two ways: a defection from authoritarian (1948) Democrats and an increase of Republican voters from the ranks of authoritarian (1948) non-voters. The Republicanism of the authoritarians was due partly to a greater traditional identification with the Republican party, which in turn could be traced partly to disidentification with the underdog groups seen as allied to the Democratic party. The better-educated authoritarians' position on Korea is in accord with what would be expected of people with this personality characteristic and is in accord with the position of the Republican party; and the same is true of their position on the welfare state. With respect to their candidate orientation, authoritarianism seems to inhibit criticism of General Eisenhower but not to be associated with praise of the General in personal terms. The relationships revealed by the data suggest that the ambiguity of the electoral image of Eisenhower may have led both authoritarians and equalitarians to perceive in him traits congenial to their own respective personality structures.

Notes

1. See, for example, Elmo Roper's interpretation of "concern" in "New York Elects O'Dwyer," *Public Opinion Quarterly*, 10 (Spring, 1946), pp. 53–57. Charles E. Merriam and Harold F. Gosnell treat this attitude under the head of general apathy in *Non-voting* (University of Chicago Press, 1924); Paul Lazarsfeld, Bernard Berelson, and Hazel Gaudet consider the significance of "interest" in *The People's Choice* (Columbia University Press, New York, 1944), pp. 40–41.

2. Angus Campbell, Gerald Gurin, and Warren Miller, *The Voter Decides* (Evanston, Ill., 1954), pp. 194–199; Harrison Gough et al., "A Personality Scale for Social Responsibility," *Journal of Abnormal and Social Psychology*, 47 (Jan., 1952), pp. 73–80.

3. See The *Voter Decides*, pp. 187–194.

4. See Alice Kitt and David B. Gleicher, "Determinants of Voting Behavior," *Public Opinion Quarterly*, 14 (Fall, 1951), pp. 393–412; the idea forms an important part of the analysis of Bernard Berelson, Paul Lazarsfeld, and William M. McPhee, *Voting* (University of Chicago Press, 1954), and is further developed in *The Voter Decides*, pp. 199–206.

5. The idea of traditional loyalty to political parties has been discussed by such writers as MacCauley, Bryce, and Holcombe, and has been analyzed by V. O. Key in his *Southern Politics in State and Nation* (Alfred Knopf, New York, 1949). See also *Voting* and *The Voter Decides*, pp. 88–111.

6. For the relationship of issues to electoral choice see Stuart Rice, *Quantitative Methods in Politics* (Russell, New York, 1928, reprint 1969); Julius Turner, *Party Constituency* (Johns Hopkins Press, Baltimore, 1951); George Belknap and Angus Campbell, "Political Party Identification and Attitudes toward Foreign Policy," *Public Opinion Quarterly*, 15 (Winter, 1951–52), pp. 601–623; *The Voter Decides*, pp. 112–135; Angus Campbell and Robert L. Kahn, *The People Elect a President* (Ann Arbor, 1952), pp. 54–60.

7. See Fillmore Sanford, "Public Orientation to Roosevelt," *Public Opinion Quarterly*, 15 (Summer, 1951), pp. 189–216; Jerome Bruner and Sheldon Korchin, "The Boss and the Vote," *Public Opinion Quarterly*, 10 (Spring, 1946), pp. 1–23; *The Voter Decides*, pp. 136–143; James C. Davies, "Charisma in the 1952 Campaign," *American Political Science Review*, 48 (Dec., 1954), pp. 1083–1102.

8. Although the assumption that man behaves economically in political situations has

been prevalent in the literature, the nature of this type of motivation has rarely been analyzed. Much of the discussion has dealt with group economic interests, confusing the appeals of group solidarity and economic gain. Other discussion, that of Bean, Lundberg, Holcombe, Lubell, and others, shows the economic basis for the vote, without reference to the psychology of economic self-interest. On this latter point, see Stephen Sarasohn and Vera H. Sarasohn, *Political Party Patterns in Michigan* (Detroit, 1957).

9. Samuel Lubell, *The Future of American Politics* (Harper, New York, 1951), pp. 75–80.

10. Howard Freeman and Morris Showell, "Differential Political Influence of Voluntary Associations," *Public Opinion Quarterly*, 15 (Winter, 1952), pp. 703–714; *The People's Choice*, pp. 137–158; Berelson et al., *Voting*; and Morris Janowitz and Warren Miller, "The Index of Political Predispositions in the 1948 Elections," *Journal of Politics*, 14 (Nov., 1950), pp. 710–725.

11. T. W. Adorno, Else Frenkel-Brunswik, Daniel S. Levinson, and R. Nevitt Sanford, *The Authoritarian Personality* (Harper-Row, New York, 1950).

12. Richard Christie and Marie Jahoda, "The Authoritarian Personality," in *Continuities in Social Research* (The Free Press, Glencoe, Ill., 1954), pp. 50–122.

13. *Ibid.*, pp. 123–196.

14. *The Authoritarian Personality*, pp. 222–279.

15. The coefficients of error for each question were: 1-7.6; 2-12.7; 3-12.0; and 4-7.4. On computation and use of the Guttman Scale, see L. Guttman, "The Basis for Scalogram Analysis," in Samuel Stouffer et al., *Measurement and Prediction: Studies in Social Psychology in World War II* (Princeton University Press, Princeton, 1950).

16. Morris Janowitz and Dwaine Marvick, "Authoritarianism and Political Behavior," *Public Opinion Quarterly*, 17 (Summer, 1953), pp. 185–201.

17. Fillmore H. Sanford, *Authoritarianism and Leadership* (Philadelphia, 1950), p. 159.

18. *Authoritarianism and Leadership*, p. 181.

19. *Ibid.*, pp. 159–169.

20. *The Authoritarian Personality*, pp. 151–207.

21. See Edward A. Shils, "Authoritarianism: 'Right' and 'Left'," in *Continuities in Social Research* (cited in note 12), pp. 24–49.

22. See Ohmer Milton, "Presidential Choice and Performance on a Scale of Authoritarianism," *The American Psychologist*, 7 (Oct., 1952), pp. 597–598.

23. *The Authoritarian Personality*, pp. 461 ff., 480 ff.

24. See Julius Turner, "Responsible Parties: A Dissent from the Floor," *American Political Science Review*, 45 (1951), pp. 143–152.

25. See *The Voter Decides*, pp. 112–135.

26. *Ibid.*, p. 67.

27. "Political Party Identification and Attitudes towards Foreign Policy" (cited in note 6), pp. 621–622.

28. *The People's Choice*, pp. 56–64.

29. *Authoritarianism and Leadership* (cited in note 17). See also Dorothea E. Johannsen, "Reactions to the Death of Roosevelt," *Journal of Abnormal and Social Psychology*, 41 (April, 1946), pp. 218–222.

30. James C. Davies, "Charisma in the 1952 Campaign" (cited in note 7).

31. Herbert Hyman and Paul Sheatsley, "The Political Appeal of President Eisenhower," *Public Opinion Quarterly*, 17 (Winter, 1953–54), pp. 443–460.

32. Bruno Bettelheim and Morris Janowitz, "Reactions to Fascist Propaganda—A Pilot Study," *Public Opinion Quarterly*, 14 (Spring, 1950), pp. 52–60.

33. *The Authoritarian Personality*, pp. 664–671.

Note: This analysis is based on data from a national sample survey conducted by the Survey Research Center, University of Michigan, under the sponsorship of the Political Behavior Committee of the Social Science Research Council. While the author is grateful to the Center and the Committee for access to the data, neither the Center nor the Committee bears any responsibility for this analysis. The author also wishes to acknowledge his debt to Angus Campbell for clarification of the relationship of personality and perception in a political context, and to Warren Miller for help in learning the intricacies of survey analysis.

PART II

POLITICAL

SOCIALIZATION

Introductory Note: Political Socialization and the
Democratic Order

The five essays and research reports that follow address themselves to the question: How do people learn political attitudes and behavior? Let us add to this the normative question: What ought people to know and feel to prepare them for participatory democracy? At the outset we must state that it is a positive advantage to have a diversity of beliefs and attitudes in a pluralistic system. Here we speak of modes and commonalities, human properties that should be widely distributed for the system to work well.

Belief in shared as well as contested power. The findings and opinions in the material below argue that those persons who had shared family power as children (compared to those who had not) are as adults less likely to be alienated or anomic and more likely to be active in politics in both the United States and Germany. Similarly, from a comparison of those who had damaged relations with their fathers with those who had good relations, I have inferred that an experience of "pawnship" in the family causes a man to lose interest in things over his immediate horizon and to focus on the personal, the immediate, the "practical." Furthermore, it seems that the process of modernization is a process of including more and more groups in decision-making processes, beginning with the emancipation of women and then proceeding to the democratization of the family so that children, too, have a sphere of appropriate influence. In this way they are prepared for their roles as participatory citizens. The schools can reinforce either the idea that only elites exercise political power or the idea that members of all groups, however humble, may appropriately employ political power. From the evidence it seems that teachers in the United States employing standard materials communicate to lower-class children that theirs is to be a passive role in politics, their contribution to be chiefly obedience; while these same teachers teach the appropriateness of more active roles to middle-class children. Finally, let us distinguish between shared power and contested power. The rebel and the authoritarian may wish to displace the authorities after a contest of some kind. It is something else to attempt to change policy through petitioning, pressuring, committee work, and persuasion. The electoral process implies a belief in both contested power and shared power; the latter is a necessary feature of a democratic belief system, for it encourages a government to work with its opposition and not merely to frustrate it.

Ego-syntonic tolerance. As we shall see in Chapter 4, an "official" tolerance of others can emerge from a quarrel with an intolerant father; it is a way of scoring on the old man—or, indeed, on any hated person or group who happens to be ethnocentric. An "ego-syntonic" tolerance, however, is the product of a democratic and tolerant home and a democratic and tolerant classroom. The case study in Chapter 7 suggests that ethnocentrism arises when a person hates the weak and oppressed because he hates his own weaknesses and underdog qualities. As with a belief in shared power, the process of modernization makes a difference in this case by introducing universalistic criteria that imply that all men with similar experience and skills should be treated equally. In a modern society the important differences are not familistic or tribal or ethnic; they are work-related, meritocratic differences with legal standing, and the law is blind to particularistic distinctions among persons. Education reduces ethnocentricity (Chapter 6); perhaps literature provides a number of models of life, a variety of characters who are accorded dignity as human beings whatever their racial or religious backgrounds. The study of humane literature is a rehearsal in experiencing diversity (Chapter 8). Finally I will argue in Chapter 7 that self-awareness is a protection against unconscious acts and thoughts that violate one's basic values; in the American community these values include the tolerance of others. More than that, the analysis of the roots of prejudice in the self brings to light their sources in unacceptable thoughts and impulses. Once brought to light, they begin to lose their power, which is often the power of darkness or ignorance. (But one should beware of identifying hostile feelings towards another group with "prejudice"; they may be realistic and based on experience, knowledge, and acknowledged self-interest.)

Openness to change. One suspects that one of the little-appreciated values of the going-away-to-college pattern is the opportunity it provides for weakening the students' family traditions. In many ways, enlisting in the armed services (or running away to sea) fulfills the same function for other youth in other social classes and cultures. The value of this device in attenuating the son's quarrels with his father—thus relaxing the polarization of views and providing him with some true options to be made at leisure—is evident in the cases presented in Chapter 6. College is also important in providing a break with tradition for other reasons; whereas high schools tend to teach the traditional culture, college often offers criticisms. Nevertheless, any situation that offers an alternative group to the family in which men may anchor new ideas—a peer group, marriage (another family), a work group— tends to break up the family traditions. Perhaps, too, the finding in the discussion of "Fathers and Sons" to the effect that those with damaged relations with their fathers do not believe in the possibility of successful social change tells us something about the conditions of "openness to change." This is in line with the finding (Chapter 5) that the German youthful rebel becomes more orthodox than his parents when he grows up. In this analysis I argue that the guilt over the rebellion creates an orthodoxy and resistance to alternative views that impedes political flexibility in later life. If, as has been said,* the capacity to imagine situations contrary to fact is a feature of modern society, of mobile man, then it is very likely the case that stretching the imagination through literature is a training for modernization (Chapter 8). One inference from these findings is that early and frequent exposures to alternative ways of life and alternative philosophies offers more encouragement to heterodoxy than early and intense rebellion against parental hegemony in the home.

Civic obligation. If the Protestant ethic and Victorian morality were to lose their grasp on modern men, as they seem to be doing, what would happen to concepts of civic obligation? Taking civic obligation to mean a sense of responsibility for social justice, for alleviating the problems arising from corrupt or inefficient government and misguided foreign policy, it is apparent that it is rooted neither in the Protestant ethic (which relates to work and thrift and not to the obligation to others, which is the Christian ethic) nor in Victorian morality, which has to do with social mores, especially sexual standards. It is rooted in a view of the world larger than the self and family, which seems to be produced by undamaged father-son relations, by having experienced influence (and responsibility) as a child, by the belief that the world can be changed for the better, by viewing authority as effective to challenge Fate, and by sufficient analytical skills to penetrate the obscurity of current events and what is said about them in the media. That is one route. Another is to use public affairs as material in working out unresolved conflicts generated in the family, to "kill the father" with a view he despises, to kill the "bad self" by rejecting one's own hated symptoms when they appear in others, to satisfy dependency needs by loyal allegiance to a strong leader, and so to assume one's civic obligation in the service of old quarrels and current weaknesses. Which of these routes is to be pursued depends, of course, on psychic health and maturity—hence the plea in Chapter 7 to employ ideological self-analysis to hasten such maturity.

Of course other influences are at work. One could argue that the study of great literature enlarges one's vision of the world and gives a sense of purpose

* See my "The Decline of Politics and Ideology in a Knowledgeable Society," *American Sociological Review*, 31 (1966), pp. 649–662, reprinted in Chapter 15.

to life. It suggests the enduring features of "the western traditions" that are worth the effort. Concern for the opinions of others, "other-directedness" works through the mechanisms of shame to bolster the flagging civic mind. And if alienation leads away from civic responsibility, then education, which seems to reduce alienative feelings, leads the young man towards his guardianship of society (Chapter 6).

Capacity to criticize the social order. The men with damaged relations with their fathers could speak no evil of political leaders; they had once been terrified by authority and taught that rebellion was futile. This argues that the capacity to criticize society is developed by nurturant parents (Chapter 4). College helps men to differ with their parents and to be different from them; in this sense the college men are standing outside of their personal traditions and able to appraise and to criticize what they once believed (Chapter 6). To criticize is to have an idea of how things might be different; it is to imagine, once again, a situation contrary to fact and it implies (unless one is wholly negative) a view of a different order, such as one learns about in college, perhaps through literature, perhaps through the study of other societies (Chapter 8). Intelligent criticism emerges from a clear idea of long-term self-interest, a self-interest that embraces whatever one cares about (whatever one cathects as part of the self). Such a long-term view of the self and its interests is a product of self-knowledge, perhaps aided by ideological self-analysis (Chapter 7). The guilty former rebel is not a good critic of society; he has too much at stake in psychologically undoing what he once did (Chapter 6).

"Mental clarity" and analytical skills. In order to take positions of leadership in society, a person should, of course, think clearly about social problems, and in order to do that he should have an adequate model of social thought. The humanistic disciplines tend to confuse people in these respects, for their model of analysis remains untouched by the current thought about thinking that has clarified so much else. The discussion in Chapter 8 shows both the values and the dangers in the study of literature; in a capsule, humanistic study contributes more to moral and emotional clarity than to mental clarity. Beyond this, however, there are the risks of analogical and projective thinking to which the immature and unexamined self is prone. To think clearly one must be able to distinguish between what is "out there" (the test being what other people think is "out there") and what is in the self, whether one sees the "communist menace" in terms of numbers and influence of known communists or in terms of nameless fears, paranoid impulses, fantasies of vermin, or whatever (Chapter 7). Finally, let us note the risks to mental clarity in "the magic of language," that is, some implicit and unconscious belief that by naming things one controls them or explains something about them and by manipulating words one manipulates their referents.

Self-knowledge and self-confidence. Self-confidence in the child is related to the high sense of political efficacy in the American culture. Persons who have not shared family power as children and who believe that children should not have any influence in family decisions tend to be politically submissive and never to develop a belief that they can change things. The idea that the self is important is a crucial support for the assumption of civic responsibility, although the idea that the self is worthless may lead a man to throw it away in a rebellious moment or a lost (or victorious) cause. As for self-knowledge, there is no evidence that this is necessary for morality or psychic health (although self-acceptance surely is), but there is evidence that self-knowledge helps a person to organize his emotions and his life in such a way as to serve his enduring purposes. Combined with self-confidence these purposes then tend to extend beyond the self to embrace some aspects of society.

Chapter *4*
Fathers and Sons:
Foundations of Political Belief

Loosely speaking, there are three ways in which a father lays the foundations for his son's political beliefs. He may do this, first, through indoctrination, both overt and covert as a model for imitation, so that the son picks up the loyalties, beliefs, and values of the old man. Second, he places the child in a social context, giving him an ethnicity, class position, and community or regional·environment. And, he helps to shape political beliefs by his personal relations with his son and by the way he molds the personality which must sustain and develop a social orientation. The combination of these three processes produces the "Mendelian law" of politics: the inheritance of political loyalties and beliefs. But while imitation and common social stakes tend to enforce this law, the socialization process may work to repeal it. It is the socialization process, the way in which fathers and sons get along with each other, that we examine in this paper.

Some perspective is gained by noting a number of possible models of the way fathers through their rearing practices may affect their sons' social outlook. The German model of the stern father who emphasizes masculine "hardness" and "fitness" in the son, and who monopolizes the opportunity for conversation at the dinner table, is one that has been explored at length.[1] The Japanese father, partially deified like his ancestors, strictly attentive to protocol and detail in the home, is another.[2] The Russian father image—the gruff, indulgent, somewhat undisciplined but spontaneous and warm individual—is a third.[3] And the American father is said to be more of a brother

Reprinted from the *American Sociological Review*, 24 (1959), pp. 502–511. Also reprinted in Roberta S. Sigel, *Learning About Politics: A Reader in Political Socialization* (New York: Random, 1970), pp. 119–131 and William J. Crotty, Donald Freeman, and Douglas Gatlin, *Political Parties and Political Behavior* (Boston: Allyn and Bacon, 1966).

Notes to this chapter will be found on pages 75–76

than a father, joined with his son under the same female yoke, uninspired but certainly not frightening.[4] Here is an image to compare with others and, as with the other models, its caricaturistic exaggeration nevertheless represents an identifiable likeness.

The father-son relationship may be explored with the help of data on the lives and politics of fifteen men interviewed recently at considerable length. These men represent a random sample drawn from the voting list of 220 citizens living in a moderate-income housing development in an Eastern industrial city. Out of fifteen asked, fifteen (prompted by a modest stipend) agreed to be interviewed, even though these interviews ranged from ten to fifteen hours, administered in from four to seven installments. The characteristics of the sample are as follows:

> They were all white, married, fathers, urban, and Eastern.
>
> Their incomes ranged from 2,400 to 6,300 dollars (with one exception: his income was about 10,000 dollars in 1957).
>
> Ten had working class occupations such as painter, plumber, policeman, railroad fireman, and machine operator. Five had white collar occupations such as salesman, bookkeeper, and supply clerk.
>
> Their ages ranged from 25 to 54 years—most of them were in their thirties.
>
> Twelve were Catholic, two Protestant, and one was Jewish.
>
> All are native-born; their nationality backgrounds include: six Italian, five Irish, one Polish, one Swedish, one Russian (Jewish), and one Yankee.
>
> All were employed at the time of the interviews.
>
> Three concluded their schooling after grammar school and eight after some high school; two finished high school, one had some college training, and one went to graduate school.

The interviews were taped, with the permission of the interviewees, and transcribed for analysis. There was an agenda of topics and questions but the interviews were not closely structured, being conducted with probes and follow-up questions in a conversational style. The topics included: (a) current social questions, such as foreign policy, unions, taxes, and desegregation; (b) political parties; (c) political leaders and leadership; (d) social groups and group memberships; (e) ideological orientation toward "democracy," "freedom," "equality," and "government;" (f) personal values and philosophies of life; (g) personality dimensions—partially explored through standard tests; (h) life histories, including attitudes towards parents, brothers and sisters, school, and so forth.

In addition to the interviews, a group of tests were administered on anxiety, authoritarianism, anomie, information, and certain social attitudes.

The characteristics of the sample, as in any study, affect the relationships discovered. It should be stressed that this is a sample of men who, by and large, are well adjusted to society: they are married and have children, hold steady jobs, they are voters. This probably implies that any warping of personality which may have taken place in childhood was marginal. We are, then, dealing with the relationships of childhood experiences and political expression in a moderately "normal" group. We are not involved with the extremes of personality damage, or the bottom rung of the social ladder, or a highly socially alienated group. Unlike the studies of American Communists[5] or of nativist agitators,[6] this paper is concerned with middle and normal America, with more or less adjusted people. This is an important point because our findings differ in certain respects from those of other studies, but they do not necessarily conflict with them.

The Unfought War of Independence

The influence of the son's rebellious attitudes towards his father has often been said to be important in explaining radical movements, particularly "youth movements." The son's basic position is one of growing from complete dependence to independence. During the later stages of this growth he and his father each must make a rather drastic adjustment to the changing relationship called forth by the son's maturation. Under certain circumstances the son may rebel against the family and particularly against the father. Is this the typical American pattern—as Erikson denies? Unlike German youth, he argues, American youngsters do not rebel, although willing and able to do so, because the paternal discipline is not something to rebel against.[7]

We explored the question of rebellion, particularly in its political aspects, with our fifteen men and found that there was indeed very little evidence of the kind of relationship that Erikson describes in the German situation. Apparently, only rarely did a family-shattering clash of wills occur when the son thought himself old enough to behave as a man. The father-son opposition took relatively minor forms: the question of what hour to come in at night, the use of the family car, the son's conduct in school. Concerning the political expression of such rebellious feelings, there were strong indications that this subject remained on the periphery of the men's world of experience.

Although the major evidence comes from the biographical material, answers to a question on youthful rebellion or radicalism are revealing. Rapuano, an auto parts supply man with a rather undisciplined tendency to vent his aggression on social targets (communists and doctors), responds in bewilderment and finally denies any such tendency. O'Hara, an oiler in a large factory and one of the more class-conscious interviewees, is confused and takes the question to mean rebellion against his brothers and sisters. Woodside, a policeman who rejected his father with venom, responds to an inquiry about his own youthful rebellion or radicalism:

I do remember through the depression that my folks mentioned that it seems as though more could have been done—that the parties should have made more means of work so that the poverty wouldn't be existing so much around you— and, not only around you—but with you yourself.

He turns the question of his own rebellion and radicalism into a family matter: the family was more or less disgruntled. Only one man, better educated than others, speaks of his own moderate radicalism in a way which could be interpreted as a search for independence from or opposition to his parents.

There are several reasons why political expression of youthful defiance failed to come off. One is the low salience of politics for the parents. Few of the men could remember many political discussions in the home and some were uncertain whether their parents were Democrats or Republicans. If the old man cared so little about politics, there was little reason to challenge him in this area. Another reason is that when there is a need to assert independence there are ways of doing it which come closer to the paternal (and generally American) value scheme. One of these is to quit school. Four or five men sought independence and the economic foundations for a life no longer dependent on paternal pleasure by leaving school shortly before they were ready to graduate—thus striking directly at the interests of parents determined to see their children "get ahead in the world." Of course this act had compensations for parents in need of money, but there seems to have been more of a genuine conflict of wills in this area than in any other. Quitting school, in some ways, is the American youth's equivalent of his European opposite of conservative parentage joining a socialist or fascist party.

Two reasons then for the apolitical quality of youthful revolt are the low salience of politics in the American home and the opportunity for rebellion in other ways. A third reason may be—to use hyperbole—the relatively low salience of the father in the American scheme. We asked our men, "Who made the important decisions in your parents' household?" One replied that they were jointly made, two that their fathers made the important decisions, and twelve testified that mother was boss. The statement of Ruggiero, a maintenance engineer and supply man from a remarkably happy home, typifies the most frequent point of view:

> Which of your parents would you say was the boss in your family?—I'd say my mother. My father was easy-going in the house. . . . We found that mother ran the house exactly the way she wanted to. She took care of the money, too. Paid all the bills. She still does.

Now it may be that from a child's perspective that Mother is usually boss. But the near unanimity on this point is convincing, all the more so because the accompanying comments generally show no overlord in the background. Even in this immigrant and second-generation population Mom had taken over.[8] Why, then, rebel against Father?

There is a fourth reason for the generally low rate of political rebellion.

In the American home a child is given considerable latitude. "Permissiveness" is the term used currently to express this idea and although the term and idea are in bad odor among some critics, it is clear that the prevailing standards of child care even twenty years ago allowed a degree of freedom in school, neighborhood, and home not generally prevalent in Europe or Asia.[9] To a large extent, the boy is on his own. This is Erikson's point, but we can illustrate it in detail. Thus Farrel, a man from a working class background whose schooling included graduate study, reports on his tendency to political radicalism in his youth: "I think there must also be the adolescent revolt aspect, which was never acute with me. . . . There was, as far as I was concerned, no necessity for it to be acute. I didn't feel hemmed in by my parents." Rapuano talks of his "reckless" youth in which he ran free with other boys, and some of the men speak of their parents' preoccupations that gave them opportunity to live a "free life." Many of the boys had earned money for their own as well as their families' use by selling papers, working in grocery stores, or cleaning up the school. Nor was this freedom attributable to parental indifference. When Rapuano was struck by a school teacher, his mother (*not* his father) visited the school to beat the teacher with a stick. A free child assured of supportive parental assistance when in need does not need to rebel.

A minority of four or five of these children, however, had suffered under controls which seem strict by most American standards.

Four Men Whose Fathers Failed Them

Although it is true that the symptoms of *rebellion* are rather slight and that its political expression in miniscule, it does not follow that the American son, particularly the son of immigrants, identifies with his father—introjects the paternal ideal, as the psychoanalysts might say—and accepts the male role as it has been played on the home stage. At least four of our fifteen men probably had experienced seriously damaged relations with their fathers and even in the roseate glow of remembered childhood do not like the old man. Interpretation of this situation must be circumspect, since people are supposed to love their parents and are even commanded to honor them. During the interviews, however, interstitial comments, reportorial selection of incidents, and graphic silences, as well as the explicit expressions of like and dislike, present a clear picture of father-son relations.

There are, of course, many varieties of both bad and good father-son relations. In these four cases of damaged relations we note two patterns. One is *identification without affection*, represented by only one case. The other, the *rejection pattern*, is illustrated by three cases. This section briefly pictures the father-son relationships of these four men. In the following sections their political expression is explored.

Identification without affection. The American youth, as we have noted, typically does not invest much emotional energy in a father rebellion on the European scale. But of course the latter does occur. And sometimes the process resembles the German pattern where the youth identifies with his father, struggles for his approval, gradually asserts himself against him as though assaulting a fortress, departs, and returns to be like him—another paternal fortress against his own son.

Sullivan, a railroad fireman and former semi-professional boxer follows this tradition. Now, at the age of 25, he stresses his respect for his father, but his report shows little affection. Of discipline he says:

> He was pretty strict—very strict. He'd been brought up strict, and in an old Irish family there, and of course, all the way through school it was very strict [the father went to a Catholic seminary]. So he was pretty strict with me, more so than with the two girls.

When asked about his father's good points he responds in the same terms as though everything else were blotted out: "Well . . . (long pause) . . . his good points were that he knew when to be strict and when to be lenient." Except on the question of sports (where the father gave instruction, but nothing is said of a good time), there is little joy in this relationship.

Yet there is identification. The son has adopted his father's strict manner. Sullivan had left his family because his wife would not follow his orders about the management of the home; he now sees that the children should, properly, give instant obedience. His rebellion—and he did rebel—is over:

> Oh, I knew everything when I was 19. Nobody could tell me nothing. Boy oh boy I found out, though. That's one thing my father would always try and . . . teach me things, and offer advice and so on. But no, I wouldn't listen. He told me especially about discipline and orders and so on. I never used to like to take orders. I don't think I was in the service a month when I wrote and told him, "Boy, you were right. You said some day I'm going to say that—and boy, you are." The service was a good thing for me.

Sullivan is a "hard" man to deal with, not mean, but there is a steely quality about him which reflects his experience in an exaltation of the Marine Corps, as well as his father's values.

Rejection of the father. Unlike Sullivan, three others, Woodside, Dempsey, and DeAngelo, reject their fathers outright. There is no effort to cover over their feelings, to take back the criticism, undo the damage, unsay the words. Something within them is quite clear and solid on this matter and they are not shaken by fear or guilt at the thought of such rejection.

DeAngelo is a factory machine operative, whose father and mother separated when he was an infant; he subsequently acquired a step-father. Of his father, who lives in the same town, laconically he says: "I don't bother with him." Of his step-father:

He was a good guy when he was sober, but he was bad when he was drunk. I never had too much respect for him. . . . When he was drunk he wanted to argue, you know. But my mother was bigger than him—didn't have too much trouble taking care of him. After a while my mother left him, you know, and we were on our own.

DeAngelo narrowly missed reform school when in high school—from which the principal ordered him to leave, possibly through a misunderstanding. But some maternally inspired internal gyroscope kept him on an even keel through a series of such adversities. Today he is the father of six boys, a steady breadwinner, and union shop steward in the plant.

Woodside, a policeman with a conscience, remembers his childhood with horror because of the irresponsible drunken behavior of his father and particularly his father's "outside interests," women. He says, quite simply: "At one time I felt I'd hate my father—that if anything ever happened to him it would be a wonderful thing." But today he plays checkers with the pathetic old man and helps him when he's in trouble. He hated his father in the past for the beatings he gave his mother, the humiliation he brought on the household, and the physical suffering to the children: "It's a pretty gruesome thing to tell anybody that a father could neglect his kids so much. Believe me, a good many days I've seen where I had just water, and I was lucky to have water—for a meal for the whole day."

Dempsey is an older man who married a widow when he himself was 40, having previously lived with his mother and, until they were married, with his brothers. In comparison with DeAngelo and Woodside, his reactions to his father are more veiled and he identifies somewhat more with him. He thinks of him as "a hard working man, the same as I am now, and couldn't get much further than I probably will . . . although my hopes are probably a little bit higher." But through the veil we see more granite than flesh and blood:

Did your father have a sense of humor?—Well, that I couldn't say. As I say, we were never too chummy with him. He never was a fellow to be chummy with us children. . . . He was one of them guys—it had to be it, or there was no way out of it.

There apparently were few family outings, little fun, and strict curfews. What things did Dempsey admire about his father? "Only that he was a hard worker, and gave us a chance to do—to choose what we wanted to—at the time [reference to choice of religion in which they chose the mother's religion.] Outside of that he was a very hard man." And a few minutes later he repeats, "he was a hard—a very hard and stern man."

The Politics of Filial Alienation

Having examined a modal American pattern of father-son relationships and isolated four deviant cases, we turn to an inquiry into the politics of these latter four men.

Low information and social interest. The question of political information is considered first, partly because it indicates the degree of interest in the social world outside oneself. Our measure of political information is made up of questions on local, national, and international institutions and events. The local events, in particular, are not usually learned in school, since they include such items as "Who is the local boss of New Haven?" and "How would you go about getting a traffic light put on your corner?" It is therefore especially significant that these four men, concerning political information, rank as the four lowest of the fifteen cases.

There are several reasons for this. The loss or lack of a secure parental model encouraged each of these four to frame his own life style and to engage in the lifelong business of self-discovery. Each man is his own Pygmalion. More importantly, the development of a personal sense of security, of being a loved and wanted and respected person, which is a bulwark against psychic conflict, is lacking. This lack seems to be borne out by the evidence of severe anxiety in all four cases. Dempsey and DeAngelo rank among the four highest scorers on the "neurotic anxiety" scale. Sullivan ranks third on a social anxiety scale and shows evidence of severe sex-tension, as indicated by his top score in this area (and his marriage is breaking up). DeAngelo ranks fourth on this sex-tension scale. Woodside, while less troubled by sexual problems and not "neurotically" anxious, ties for first place on the scale of social anxiety; he is, by his own account and other evidence, a worrier, a searcher for all-around "security" and has somatic difficulties.

Anxiety can lead into politics as well as away from politics. People can defend themselves against anxiety by knowing more than others—or people may succumb to the demands of anxiety by knowing less. Generally in the American apolitical culture the anxious man does not employ politics as a defense against his conflicts. One of the little appreciated benefits of such a culture is the low premium on politics for the anxious and neurotic.

Authoritarianism. Three of the four men score strongly on authoritarianism: DeAngelo has the highest score in the group, and Sullivan and Woodside tie for fourth; only Dempsey's ranking is moderate. The genesis of authoritarianism and its close connection with father-son relations are well known. Here it is sufficient to note that in order to believe that people can live and work as cooperative equals or at least as trusting partners, a person must have experienced such a relationship. In their relations with their fathers, these men had no such experience.

Speak no evil of the political leader. There is a third area of political outlook which seems to be shared by these four men with damaged father relations, a quality which in some measure sets them apart from the others. Although political lore would have it otherwise, people generally prefer to speak well of political leaders than to speak ill of them.[10] But the average citizen can criticize such leaders, designate those he dislikes, and weigh the good and bad points of each on occasion. Our four deviant cases found such criticism or even objectivity more difficult than the others.

Sullivan admires Monroe, Lincoln, Truman, and Eisenhower. He defends Truman against those who believe that his attack on the music critic was out of order. He defends Ike for the vacations he takes. When asked about political leaders he dislikes: "Well, from what I learned in history, Grant seemed to be pretty useless ... [pause]. He didn't seem to do too much [mentions that he was a drunkard]. And [pause] I mean I don't dislike him, either, but—I don't dislike any of them." Question: "How about living leaders, or recent leaders, which of these would you say you had the least respect for?" Answer, after a pause: "Well [long pause], none that I could think of."

Dempsey likes Washington and Lincoln, and, when probed, Wilson and Truman, for whom he voted. Asked about "any particular feelings about Dewey" he says, "No I wouldn't say that." Roosevelt was "a very good man." Eisenhower is also a "very good man, doing everything he possibly can." He can think of no mistakes he has made.

DeAngelo says he doesn't particularly admire any political leaders. But: "I like them. I mean I didn't think anything bad about them, y'know." Questioned about an earlier reference to Robert Taft, he replies:

> Well, I mean, I thought for being President, I thought he'd be a little better in know-how and savvy than Eisenhower, y'know. I ain't got nothing against Eisenhower—he's good, he seems to be honest enough, but I don't ... I don't ... I don't think he should have run again because I think his health is—his health was good enough.

DeAngelo has trouble expressing his reservations about Eisenhower even on the question of health. When asked specifically about people he dislikes, distrusts, or thinks to be weak or wrong for the job: "Well, I don't know, not offhand."

Woodside's views are a little different. He likes Eisenhower but is more willing to discuss his weaknesses (particularly his signing of an order to execute a deserter). He likes MacArthur as a "big man" and mentions Lincoln favorably. Asked about his dislikes and those he thinks did a poor job, he mentions others' criticisms of Roosevelt but then rushes to his defense, except to say that he thinks Eisenhower is "a little bit more mannish" than Roosevelt. The only political leader he mentions unfavorably is Adlai Stevenson, who strikes him as a man who could say "yes" when he means "no."

With the possible exception of this last comment, these remarks convey three themes: (a) Conventional leaders like Washington, Lincoln, and Monroe are admired. (b) The independent leader who doesn't let outsiders tell him what to do is admired—Truman would stand for no nonsense (Sullivan), Stevenson is too much influenced by his advisors (Woodside). (c) Authority figures are not to be criticized—an especially important point.

These four men are not notably deficient in their general ability to criticize or to express hostility. Why, then, do these four, whose relations with their fathers are strained, find it so hard to criticize political leaders in a whole-hearted way?

In answering this question, Sullivan's case should be distinguished from the others. Sullivan feels guilty about his negative feelings toward the original political authority in the family. He cannot bring himself to express his hostility without quickly withdrawing his remarks and saying something of a positive nature. The expression of hostility to authority figures is painful and Sullivan simply avoids this pain.

The other three men express outright hostility toward or unrelieved criticism of their fathers. Why not also of political authority? In the first place, there is a carryover of fear from the childhood situation which has not been obliterated by the adult emancipation. Men do not easily forget those childhood moments of terror when the old man comes home drunk, abuses the mother, or gets out the strap to deal with the child in anger unalloyed with love. Secondly a combined worship and envy of strength exists, which father-hatred fosters in a child, for it is the father's strength in the family that penetrates the childish consciousness. Finally, there is the persistent belief in the futility and danger of countering and rebelling against authority. Although DeAngelo was a rebel in high school and was expelled and Woodside stood up to his father threatening him with a log behind the wood shed, both are successful now partly because they have curtailed these anti-authority impulses that threatened to bring disaster once before. Their consciences are composed of anti-rebellion controls; this is why, in part, they can be good citizens.[11]

Utopia and conservatism. The basis for a hopeful view of the world lies in the self; the world is ambiguous on this point. In the self, the notion that we can move toward a more perfect society is supported by the belief that people are kindly by nature and considerate of one another. Moreover, when the idea of a better social order is developed even a little, the mind quickly turns to the nature of authority in such a society. Is there a kind of authority which is strong and directive, yet at the same time solicitous and supportive of the weak in their infirmities—in short, paternal?

We asked our subjects about the nature of their vision of a more perfect society (with results which must await detailed analysis). At the end of the discussion we inquired whether or not there is evidence that we are moving closer to such a society. Although the men were not asked if the world was possibly moving in the opposite direction, some volunteered this answer. Our fifteen men answered the questions on an ideal society as follows:

	Damaged Father-Son Relations	Others
We are moving closer to ideal society	0	8
We are not moving closer to ideal society	3	2
(volunteered) We are moving away from ideal society	1	1

The pattern is clear. Woodside first touches on the drift from a peacetime to a wartime society. Then speaking of only the peacetime society, "like we're in peace now, the society is about the same as it has been back along. . . . I would say that throughout history it has been about the same." Asked if people are happier now than they were a hundred years ago, he is reminded ironically of the phrase, "There's nothing like the good old days," and he digresses to say that people adjust so quickly to mechanical progress that their degree of satisfaction and dissatisfaction remains about constant.

Dempsey, as always, is more laconic. Asked the same question about possible progress toward a better society, he says: "No. I don't think so. I think we're going to stay on the same lines we are on right now."

And Sullivan: "Never. We'll never get any place close to it, I think." He first modifies his answer by noting that "prejudice" may decline but is skeptical because "you can't change human nature."

DeAngelo takes the dimmest view of all: "I don't think we'll ever get any closer [to a more perfect society]. We're getting farther and farther way from it, I guess. All indications are we're moving away from it. There's not enough people trying to make the world perfect." Asked why we are retrogressing, he cites what he regards as the drift away from religion and the rise of communism. These are perhaps the two most convenient pegs today on which to hang a deeply rooted pessimism regarding the social order.

Contrast these views with those of five cases selected because of their close identification and warm relations with their fathers. One says flatly that "I don't think we're far from it." Another points out that the population increase will bring about troubles but he is hopeful because of the parallel increase of the proportion of good people. A third declares that every mistake we make teaches us something, ¯hence the world is getting better. A fourth believes that a socialist society is developing, which he thinks is probably a "good thing" although socialism is not an "ideal" society. Only one of these five holds that such progress is unlikely, attributing this to the increase of governmental controls; but he adds, characteristically, "Maybe concurrently with such controls you're getting more of the things that most people seem to want made available to them."

Fathers and Sons—and History

The state is "man writ large;" the family is a microcosm of society. The history of a nation may, in considerable measure, reflect the changes in the ways children and parents, sons and fathers, struggle to get along with one another. Some of the characteristics of a nation's politics may rest on the resolution of these struggles.[12] With this point in mind, we turn to certain aspects of American and foreign politics.

To recapitulate, in American society: (a) "good" father-son relations are the norm; (b) of those youth with rebellious feelings against their fathers there are few for whom the rebellion takes political form; and (c) there is a tendency for moderately damaged father-son relations to be associated with relatively low levels of hope, interest, and capacity to criticize political leaders. These tendencies are revealed in what may be called the American political "style" in the following ways:

1. American politics is often said to embody a kind of consensualism in which both sides tend to come together, rather than a bipolarization or radicalism. At the same time, campaigns become quite heated with highly critical comments passed between the partisans of one candidate and those of another. This situation parallels the qualities we find associated with sons of strong but nurturant fathers: lack of alienation but a capactiy for outspoken criticism.

2. Compared with the citizens of other nations, the American citizen is reported to be relatively well informed about current events and civic matters. On the other hand, his intensity of concern is relatively low. He can exchange blows during campaigns and then accept the victory of the opposition without much trouble. This pattern (a considerable cultural achievement) is difficult, as we have seen, for the poorly socialized and again suggests an important family component in American democracy.

3. It is often noted that a strain of idealism exists in American international politics which distinguishes it from the hard-boiled realism of the Continent. Wilson's Fourteen Points, Roosevelt's Four Freedoms, and Truman's Point Four illustrate the character of this idealism, an idealism nourished by the hope that we can do away with war and establish a peaceful world order. Behind these beliefs and supporting them in their many expressions lies that quality of hope and trust which are forged in boyhood, when the son is apprenticed to a protective and loving father.

Summary: Some Hypotheses

With a humility based on an appreciation of the great variety of experience that goes into the making of political man, we suggest the following hypotheses.

1. Compared with other Western cultures, American culture discourages youthful rebellion against the father. It further discourages political expression of whatever rebellious impulses are generated. This is because: (a) There is less need to rebel in a permissive culture. (b) Rebellious impulses are less likely to be expressed against the father because of his relatively less dominant position in the family. (c) The low salience of politics for the father means that rebellion against him is less likely to be channeled into politics or political ideology. (d) The high salience of the father's ambition for the son (and the resulting independence) means that rebellion against the father is more likely to be expressed by quitting school and going to work, or by delinquent conduct.

2. Damaged father-son relations tend to produce low political information and political cathexis. This is because, *inter alia:* (a) Without an adult model the youth must give relatively greater attention to the process of self-discovery and expend greater energy in managing his own life problems. (b) Failure of father-son relationships creates anxiety which is often (not always) so preoccupying that more distant social problems become excluded from attention.

3. Damaged father-son relations tend to develop an authoritarian orientation.

4. Damaged father-son relations tend to inhibit critical attitudes toward political leaders because: (a) The damaged relations encourage an enduring fear of expressing hostility toward authority figures. (b) They stimulate a reverence for power over other values. (c) In children they provoke the belief that it may be useless to rebel or petition authority.

5. Damaged father-son relations discourage a hopeful view of the future of the social order because: (a) The damaged relations often give rise to a less favorable view of human nature. (b) They help to create skepticism about the possibility of kindly and supportive political authority. (c) They encourage a cynical view of the political process: it is seen in terms of corrupt men seeking their own ends.

6. The history, political style, and future development of a political community reflect the quality of the relationship between fathers and sons. The permissive yet supportive character of modal father-son relationships in the United States contributes to the following features of the American political style: (a) a relatively high consensualism combined with a capacity for direct an uninhibited criticism; (b) a relatively large amount of interest and political information combined with relatively low emotional commitment; and (c) a relatively strong idealism in foreign affairs (and in general social outlook).

Notes

1. See Bertram H. Shaffner, *Father Land, A Study of Authoritarianism in the German Family* (New York: Columbia University Press, 1948); David M. Levy, "Anti-Nazis:

Criteria of Differentiation," in Alfred H. Stanton and Stuart E. Perry (eds.), *Personality and Political Crisis* (Glencoe, Ill.: Free Press, 1951).

2. See Ruth Benedict, *The Chrysanthemum and the Sword* (Boston: Houghton Mifflin, 1946).

3. See Henry V. Dicks, "Observations on Contemporary Russian Behavior," *Human Relations*, 5 (May, 1952), pp. 111–176.

4. See Erik Erikson, *Childhood and Society* (New York: Norton, 1950).

5. Gabriel Almond, *The Appeals of Communism* (Princeton: Princeton University Press, 1954); Morris L. Ernst and David Loth, *Report on the American Communist* (New York: Holt, 1952).

6. Leo Lowenthal and N. Guterman, *Prophets of Deceit* (New York: Harper, 1949). For an interesting case analysis of father-son relationships and virulent fascism, see Robert Lindner, "Destiny's Tot," in his *The Fifty Minute Hour* (New York: Rinehart, 1955).

7. Erikson, *op. cit.*, pp. 280–283.

8. Compare Margaret Mead, *And Keep Your Powder Dry* (New York: Morrow, 1942).

9. On this point, see Robert R. Sears, Eleanor E. Maccoby, and Harry Levin, *Patterns of Child Rearing* (Evanston, Ill.: Row, Peterson, 1957); and Robert J. Havighurst and Allison Davis, "A Comparison of the Chicago and Harvard Studies of Social Class Differences in Child Rearing," *American Sociological Review*, 20 (August, 1955), pp. 438–442.

10. In 1948 between a quarter and a third of a national sample could find nothing unfavorable to say about Truman or Dewey, but almost everyone could mention something favorable about both candidates. See Angus Campbell and Robert Kahn, *The People Elect a President* (Ann Arbor, Mich.: Survey Research Center, 1952); and Angus Campbell, Gerald Gurin, and Warren Miller, *The Voter Decides* (Evanston, Ill.: Row Peterson, 1954).

11. The view that men with damaged father-son relationships do not like to criticize authority figures may seem to fly in the face of a popular interpretation of radicalism. This contradiction is more apparent than real. The effect of failure of socialization on normal populations is more likely to be apathy than radicalism (see, e.g., P. H. Mussen and A. B. Wyszinski, "Personality and Political Participation," *Human Relations*, 5 [February, 1952], pp. 65–82). There are exceptions, of course, as relationships are always expressed as probabilities. In radical groups, moreover, the tendency to criticize authority figures is focused on those who are seen as illegitimate, usurpers, or leaders who are considered to be weak. This was Woodside's approach to Stevenson, and it was precisely the latter's "weakness," his lack of decisiveness, that Woodside criticized. Our findings are complementary, not contradictory, to other similar studies in these respects.

12. Melancholy experience suggests that it is prudent to note that I am not denying the importance of a nation's history or of its geography and economics, or of its current leadership, in shaping its destiny. I do not imply, for example, that German Nazism arose because of an authoritarian family pattern rather than the Versailles treaty, or Article 48 of the Weimar Constitution, or the weakness of von Hindenberg, or what not. Within Germany, however, those whose fathers forbade them from speaking at the dinner table were more likely to be Nazis than those whose fathers were more indulgent (see Levy, *op. cit.*). German fathers were more likely to be repressive in this and other ways than fathers in certain other nations. The *combination* of defeat in World War I, the nature of German family life, and other factors, no doubt, helped to create a public responsive to Hitler's appeals.

Note: I wish to acknowledge financial assistance in the form of a Faculty Research Fellowship from the Social Science Research Council, a Fellowship at the Center for Advanced Study in the Behavioral Sciences, and a modest but indispensable grant from the former Behavioral Sciences Division of the Ford Foundation. This article is a revised version of a paper presented at the annual meeting of the American Political Science Association, September, 1958.

Chapter *5*
Political Maturation in the United States and Germany

The problem to which this paper is addressed is this: How does a sense of appropriate influence in adolescence, or its lack, affect a person's political life in the United States and Germany?

It would be pretentious to say that there is a developed theory to guide research along these lines; what is available is an arsenal of ideas, some of them very close to common sense (as this has itself been shaped by recent psychology), that have a bearing on character formation and political expression. But these ideas lead in different directions, with respect to both participation and partisanship. Let us consider the probable political expression of three types of people, those who were influential as adolescents, those who were not and resented it, and those who were not and accepted this as appropriate to their youthful status.

With respect to his participation in political life the adolescent who grows up feeling that he is appropriately influential in his family will:

(a) adopt the political norms of his social groups, that is, he will participate in the same ways and to the same extent as the members of these groups do (this is the meaning of "adjustment"); or

(b) have the inner strength and self-confidence to seek leadership positions and be more than ordinarily active in the service of his political interests and ideals.

This is the original text of a paper published in translation as "La Maturation politique de l'adolescent aux Etats Unis et en Allemagne" in *Revue Francaise de Sociologie*, 7 (1966), pp. 598–618. The published paper is a revised version of a paper presented at the Sixth World Congress of the International Political Science Association, Geneva, 1964. The English text has also been reprinted in Mattei Dogan and Richard Rose (eds.), *European Politics* (Boston: Little, Brown, 1970).

77

Notes to this chapter will be found on page 96

With respect to partisanship (left or right orientation), he will:

(c) adopt group-modal positions, shun extremism and deviance, and work within the political tradition of his group membership; or

(d) transcend the limits of his group tradition in either direction (left or right), thus pursuing his own convictions, rather than the group convictions.

If the central differentiating ingredient is self-esteem in the character of the adult who, more than others, believes he indeed did have influence as an adolescent, one would be hard put to it on theoretical grounds to say in which fashion this self-esteem would be expressed in political life.

Or take the rebel: how will the person who felt he had little influence in adolescence and resented this, express his rebelliousness in political life?

Theoretically we might expect any one of the following patterns, or perhaps a vacillation among them.

The adolescent who grows up feeling that he had little authority in his youth, and resents this, will follow one of the following participation patterns:

(a) become hyperactive in politics to assuage his feelings of worthlessness and to demonstrate that he is after all an important and powerful person; or

(b) become politically inactive because he has never had the experience of influence, has not learned the necessary skills, has no sense that he can control events; or

(c) become modal and compulsively conformist in all things, following the cues of his social group, and participate exactly according to the social norms as he reads them.

And he will adopt one of the following partisanship (directional) patterns:

(d) choose political positions deviant from those of his parental traditions, moving left, if they are rightist, or moving right, if they are leftist; or

(e) choose political positions which are nationally deviant, selecting national authorities as his targets rather than immediate group leaders and group conventions; this implies a more extremist and perhaps destructive style; or

(f) seek to restore his sense of worth and importance, damaged in adolescence, by adopting a modal, conformist pattern of partisanship within which he seeks recognition, power, and affection as outlined in pattern (a) above.

Finally, take the submissive person, one who feels he had little influence in adolescence and that this lack of influence was an appropriate state of affairs. Overtly at least he does not resent this situation. What of his political life?

The adolescent who grows up feeling that he had little authority in his youth and approves of this situation on the grounds that adolescents should not be influential will, first, adopt one of the following patterns of participation:

(a) become conformist and participate modally, doing what is expected of him, no more and no less; or

(b) continue his pattern of submissiveness, let others take over the burden of voting, talking politics, following distant events, and so forth.

And one of the following patterns of partisanship:

And one of the following patterns of partisanship:

(a) become a conformist partisan of the political tradition of the parental social group; or

(b) if his own adult social group differs from his parental group, adopt the political coloration of his group, or some compromise between them; or

(c) because some resentment of his inhibited youthful autonomy, although overtly denied, may yet fester and seek expression, become cynical, hostile, politically alienated.[1]

There are more or less substantial reasons for believing any one of these (hence, any finding will be liable to the attack that it is only what common sense would have told us in the first place), and indeed, the most sensible view might well be to assume that the stated positions of the three types of adolescent influence responses mentioned are too blunt for useful analysis. Each type may be only a necessary condition for the indicated behavior; for prediction one needs to know more. Of course it would be better to know more, and for more refined analysis it is essential; nevertheless there may be summary trends, rather weakened by cross-currents, which each of these adolescent states might reflect. Many people have thought so, and the subject is worth examining further.

Methods and Cautions

We are talking about how a situation at one stage of a person's life affects his later behavior; in this case the later behavior ranges from only a few years later to some fifty-five years later. There are two ways to proceed: The best way is to capture and record youthful experiences at the time they occur and to observe how the subjects thus studied behave five, ten, or more years later—the longitudinal study. We cannot do this now. The other way is to take people at various stages in their lives and ask them about their youthful experiences. As is well known, there are grave deficiencies in this method: People's memories are faulty, often systematically distorted by some irrelevant bias; a bad report on childhood may stem from frustrating later experiences; parents may be unjustly blamed or may benefit from a conventional compulsion to say only good things about parents and family, and so forth. Nevertheless, as the questions are important and other methods not immediately available, the retrospective report is often used. This retrospective method was used to acquire data for the following study.

In 1959 and 1960 Gabriel Almond and Sydney Verba arranged to have responsible survey organizations in each of five countries interview a sample of about 1,000 in each country on a range of issues dealing with patterns of citizenship. Included in these surveys were questions on political participation (voting, following public affairs in the media, talking politics, membership and leadership of various voluntary associations); on attitudes toward various governmental acts; on preferred methods of influence, if any; on various more general opinions of human nature; on patterns of partisanship; and, what is crucial for our purposes, memories of influence and family life during adolescence (age 16). These authors have interpreted their data in *The Civic Culture*,[2] and they have generously made their basic data available on cards distributed through the Inter-University Consortium for Political Research. It is these data that I employ for the following analysis of United States and German patterns.

The Typology and Its Validation

How shall we isolate those who were, or retrospectively feel that they were, appropriately influential as adolescents, those who were not and resented it, and those who were not and accepted this lack of influence as appropriate? There are two questions in these cross-cultural surveys which will guide us:

As you were growing up, let's say when you were around 16, how much influence do you remember having in family decisions affecting yourself? Did you have much influence, some, or none at all?

Table 5-1. Basic Typology of Adolescent Influence and Per Cent of National Samples in Each Type

"In general how much voice do you think children of 16 should have in family decisions?"		Much or Some *Influentials*	None *Rebels*
	Great Deal or Some	U.S.=65% (577) Ger.=42% (349)	U.S.=15% (137) Ger.=14% (120)
		Privileged	*Submissives*
	Little, None	U.S.=12% (111) Ger.=18% (153)	U.S.= 8% (67) Ger.=26% (214)

"As you were growing up, let's say when you were around 16, how much influence do you remember having in family decisions affecting yourself? Did you have much influence, some, or none at all?"

In general, how much voice do you think children of 16 should have in family decisions? (Great deal, some, little, none.)

By cross-analyzing the answers to these questions we arrive at the four types shown in Table 5-1.

It is worth spending a moment to consider the meaning of this cross-analysis. The two questions deal respectively with perceived own influence at age 16 and whether or not 16-year-olds in general should have influence. We assume that if a person feels that in general 16-year-olds should be influential, he will extend this to his own case: if he had influence, he will think this appropriate, and we call him an "Influential." On the other hand, if a person believes that 16-year-olds generally should be influential and perceives his own situation as having lacked influence, he will be resentful, and we call him a "Rebel." Yet there are many who think 16-year-olds should have little or no influence in the family; in fact, 20% of the American sample and 44% of the German sample think so. We would assume that those who believed this and perceived their own situation as having lacked influence would be much less resentful, indeed, would feel it was appropriate for them to submit to this proper situation, hence the term "Submissive." The fourth logical category, those who feel that 16-year-olds generally should not be influential, but perceive their own situation as having been influential, we term "Privileged," but the logic of this situation is somewhat obscure and the predictions as to how such people might behave uncertain, hence I will limit my analysis to the other three types.

One other observation is in order. Many people are reluctant to criticize their parents or express dissatisfaction with their behavior even though they feel this rather intensely. Our typology avoids an open criticism, such as that implied in the question, "Were you satisfied or dissatisfied with the amount of influence you had in family decisions when you were 16?" Thus, although 18% of the American sample were willing to say that they were "dissatisfied,"

Table 5-2. Validation of Adolescent Influence Typology: Per Cent of each Type with Certain Attitudes on Their Own Influence in their Families and on Parental Understanding

	Dissatisfied with amount of influence in family		Better not to complain about disliked decisions		Complaints affected parents' decisions		Never did complain		Parents understood respondents' needs	
	%	(N)	%	(N)	%	(N)	%	(N)	%	(N)
United States										
Influential	14	(79)	18	(104)	73	(422)	18	(104)	85	(489)
Rebel	46	(63)	64	(88)	18	(25)	43	(59)	55	(76)
Submissive	16	(11)	70	(47)	13	(9)	64	(43)	78	(52)
Germany										
Influential	3	(12)	11	(38)	84	(295)	25	(89)	85	(299)
Rebel	23	(28)	52	(62)	31	(37)	57	(69)	50	(60)
Submissive	8	(17)	53	(114)	23	(49)	54	(116)	68	(147)

Note: Chi squares for all subtables (by question in each country) are significant beyond the 1% level; differences between Influentials and Rebels are all significant beyond 1% level; differences between Influentials and Submissives are significant at the 1% level in seven of the ten cases; differences between Rebels and Submissives are significant at the 1% level in six out of ten cases.

only 7% of the German sample responded accordingly. We would expect our measure of "rebellion" to correlate with these answers but also to capture some people with resentments who could not say so. And we would expect, unfortunately, to lose some natural Rebels for whom the logic of their answers was obscure, or for some other reason. The question, of course, is whether this measure is, in fact, capturing the sets of attitudes and beliefs one might properly think associated with the terms Influential, Rebel, and Submissive we have given them and described. To find out, we can examine the answers the three types give to other questions about their influence situations in their youth (Table 5-2).

As a validation of the typology, and ignoring for the moment the cross-cultural differences, this pattern holds up pretty well in both the United States and Germany. It will be observed that the Influentials in both countries have the least dissatisfaction with their family influence, the least sense that the best policy was never to complain, the greatest confidence that their complaints would make a difference, did, in fact, complain most frequently, and as a correlate or cause of these attitudes believed that they were best understood at home.

On the other hand, the Rebels were most dissatisfied with their influence in their families and, although they were surprisingly sanguine about being understood, nevertheless had less confidence than the others in this respect.

Finally, the Submissives had the least confidence that any complaint would affect family decisions and, perhaps for that reason, felt it was better not to complain. Moreover, in the United States they did actually complain the least. On the other hand, because they were more likely than the Rebels to believe they were fairly well understood by their parents, they may have felt not only that it was useless, but also that it was unnecessary. Their state of dissatisfaction with their influence was, in any event, very like that of the Influentials and very unlike that of the Rebels.

The Sense of Influence: Causes and Effects in Two Cultures

As we examine the causes and political consequences of these adolescent experiences in the United States and Germany, two general observations are in order. In the first place, because of some of the observations just made about the method employed (retrospection) and the ambiguity of the theory, we would not expect large differences to occur; we are grateful for patterns that indicate the direction of the forces at work. Second, in comparing the effects in two cultures we are much more struck by similarities than by differences, although one significant difference in the political meaning of adolescent rebelliousness will be presented at the end of the paper.

As may be seen in Table 5-1, there are more Influentials in the United

States sample and more Submissives in the German sample, whereas there is about the same proportion of Rebels in both. The difference in sense of influence in adolescence in the two countries is in the direction the literature would suggest and the Almond–Verba report led us to believe, but the similarity in rebellion is somewhat surprising. On the one hand Germans are, by many reports, more accepting of authority, but on the other hand, it has been suggested by Erikson that the German boy, at least, tends to rebel against his father in adolescence and to return to the fold later.[3] As indicated above, we sought to avoid relying on an explicit expression of dissatisfaction for our measure (the rebels, it will be recalled, are those who felt 16-year-olds *should* have some influence but felt *they had had none*) in order to tap *latent* rebellion. Many more Americans express dissatisfaction with their adolescent influence situation than do Germans, but at this latent level of strain, there seems to be about the same proportion in each country. Now let us turn, in order, to some of the causes and consequences of each of these three adolescent influence situations.

The Genesis of the Three Types

What is it that produces these three postures toward adolescent influence? In neither country does the rural-urban difference or size of town have any consistent effect, even when it refers to the place one was brought up. We do not have available data on the subjects' family income during adolescence, but if their current income is taken as a reflection of family income we find only a very moderate indication that the better-off were more likely to experience a sense of appropriate influence—and this only in the United States.

Table 5-3. Relation of Education to Adolescent Influence Typology; Per Cent of Demographic Group in each Type, by Education Levels

UNITED STATES

	Primary	Secondary	Some Higher
Influentials	56%	80%	88%
Rebels	25	16	9
Submissives	19	4	3
(Number of Cases)	(251)	(369)	(161)

GERMANY

	Primary	At least Some Secondary
Influentials	45%	77%
Rebels	19	11
Submissives	36	12
(Number of Cases)	(563)	(120)

Note: Chi squares for the United States are significant beyond the 1% level for the entire table and for each paired comparison of types separately. For the German data the entire table and the paired comparisons between the Influentials and each of the other types show chi squares significant at the 1% level.

There is no clear pattern among occupational groups; at least status of current occupation seems almost irrelevant, when controlled for education. Curiously, there is no consistent difference between men and women in Germany. In the United States there is only a slight difference; the women feel more satisfied with their adolescent influence *and* feel that others should have more influence too (data not shown).

The things that do make a difference are education, age, and, to some extent, religion, with education the strongest and most persistent influence in both countries (Table 5-3). The more education, the more likely a person is to recall having influence in the family as an adolescent and to wish this for others, too. Submissives tend to have the least education, with Rebels somewhere in between. This means that, at least as reported in retrospect, those who were going to school at age 16 were more influential in their families than those who were working, but more importantly, those who came from homes where the parents sent their children on to higher education probably were, in fact, better treated. There is, too, the possibility that adolescents who continued their education were more responsible and reasonable—their complaints were worthy of attention. (As occupation is so tenuously related to our typology, it seems unlikely that higher adult status leads to a selectively more favorable memory of adolescence; we may accept the patterned relationship to education as reflecting true adolescent situations, at least to some extent.)

A person's age tells us two things of relevance here; it tells us something about him *now*, and it tells us something about the historical period of his youth. In general, one would expect that the process of aging would have had

Table 5-4. Relation of Age to Adolescent Influence Typology; Per Cent of Demographic Group in Each Type, by Education Levels

United States

	PRIMARY			SECONDARY			SOME HIGHER		
	18–35	36–60	61+	18–35	36–60	61+	18–35	36–60	61+
Influentials	55%	63%	47%	88%	78%	62%	94%	84%	86%
Rebels	32	19	30	11	19	25	6	12	9
Submissives	13	18	23	1	3	13	0	4	5
(Total N)	(22)	(123)	(106)	(160)	(157)	(52)	(66)	(73)	(21)

Germany

	PRIMARY			AT LEAST SOME SECONDARY		
	18–35	36–60	61+	18–35	36–60	61+
Influentials	60%	45%	27%	90%	72%	54%
Rebels	16	20	20	8	12	15
Submissives	24	35	53	2	6	31
(Total N)	(164)	(280)	(119)	(49)	(58)	(13)

Note: Chi squares for United States data are significant at the 1% level for the secondary education group where each paired comparison of types is also significant at the 1% level; other groups not significant and pairs not generally significant. The German data are significant at the 1% level for the primary education group, and almost at the 2% level for the secondary education group; paired comparisons of Influentials and Submissives are significant at the 1% level, others somewhat lower.

roughly similar effects in the United States and in Germany; therefore the fact (Table 5-4) that there is no relationship shown between age and feelings about adolescent influence in the United States for two of the three educational levels suggest that the very real influence shown for Germany has something to do with historical change and changing family patterns. In Germany, the older a person is the more likely he is to be a Submissive or a Rebel and the less likely to be an Influential. In effect, whether or not he approves of adolescent influence in general, the older he is, the more likely he is to feel he did not have much himself. And this progression has occurred over the pre-Nazi, Nazi, and post-Nazi periods. The fact that people born in an earlier historical period now recall their youth as one characterized by less family influence may be a product of selective memory. But if it accurately reflects the course of social history, it leads one to wonder whether "modernization," that is, increased urbanization, industrialization, and wealth, does not somehow increase adolescent influence in society.

On all educational levels in both countries religion makes a difference (Table 5-5); Protestantism, as contrasted with Catholicism, is associated with a sense of appropriate adolescent influence. The corollary is also true in both countries at every educational level, except for higher education in the United States, that Catholics are more likely to be Submissives, or Rebels— in this limited adolescent sense. In some manner not easily explained, the Reformation and its modern tradition seems to have given greater freedom

Table 5-5. Relation of Religion to Adolescent Influence Typology; Per Cent of Demographic Group in Each Type, by Education Levels

United States

	PRIMARY		SECONDARY		SOME HIGHER	
	Protestant	Catholic	Protestant	Catholic	Protestant	Catholic
Influentials	60%	44%	83%	71%	92%	87%
Rebels	23	27	14	24	5	10
Submissives	17	29	3	5	3	3
(Total N)	(179)	(52)	(264)	(75)	(102)	(32)

Germany

	PRIMARY		AT LEAST SOME SECONDARY	
	Protestant	Catholic	Protestant	Catholic
Influentials	51%	39%	84%	64%
Rebels	18	20	8	18
Submissives	31	41	8	18
(Total N)	(283)	(252)	(73)	(39)

Note: Chi squares for the United States data are significant at the 10% level for the primary and secondary education groups but are not significant for the higher education group; in the primary group, the paired comparison between Influentials and Submissives is significant at the 5% level; in the secondary group the comparison between the Influentials and the Rebels is significant at the 5% level; in the German sample, the data for the primary and secondary educational groups are significant at the 5% and 10% levels respectively. The paired comparisons between the Influentials and the Submissives are significant at the 1% and the 10% levels; the comparison between the Influentials and the Rebels is significant at the 5% level for the higher educated sample.

and authority to its youth. It would be interesting to have this measure over time,[4] for the evidence on a related quality, the need to achieve, suggests that what was once a substantial difference between Catholics and Protestants in Germany has now become much less important.[5] Perhaps it is true that in some respects the Catholic Church has been "protestantized," but the difference between Catholic and Protestant adolescent family influence persists.

The Center of Family Authority

But, after all, it is in the intimate relations between parents and children that the sense of appropriate influence is generated, and this, of course, is the area where it is hardest to get good information. Is it the father-dominated home (at least where he is seen to make the important decisions) or the mother-dominated home, or the home where both are seen to be coordinate in authority where rebellious or submissive feelings are born? The pattern turns out to be rather complex, and, indeed, in Germany it is very difficult to discern any pattern to the answers at all. But in the United States, one thing is clear: homes in which the parents shared authority were more likely to produce Influentials and least likely to produce Rebels than any other pattern of parental authority. And this is true regardless of the sex of the respondent or of the dominant parent. While the tendency is apparent in the less educated group, it achieves statistical significance only in the two thirds of the sample with more than primary education (Table 5-6). Perhaps it is the case that, in the United States, parents who share power between themselves also share it with their children, thus giving them a sense of influence at an early age.

Table 5-6. Center of Parental Power in the United States by Adolescent Typology (At Least Some Secondary Education)

"By and large, how were decisions made in your family?"

	MEN		WOMEN	
	One Dominant Parent, Either Father or Mother	Parents Acted Together	One Dominant Parent, Either Father or Mother	Parents Acted Together
Influentials	77%	94%	67%	90%
Rebels	20	5	27	7
Submissives	3	1	6	3
(Total N)	(101)	(95)	(94)	(158)

Note: Chi squares for male sample and for female sample are each significant at the 1% level; in each case it is the paired comparison between the Influentials and the Rebels which makes the difference; for both men and women these differences are significant at the 1% level.

We have presented evidence (Table 5-2) showing that adolescents in the United States are more willing to express dissatisfaction with their status at home and are more likely to complain to their parents if something bothers them. Perhaps it is also the case that American wives and mothers are more likely to exercise independent influence in the home; after all, Germany is, by repute, a nation marked by father-domination[6] (and the United States by mother-domination). Yet the evidence runs against this hypothesis (Table 5-7). There are only the most tenuous differences between perceptions of father-domination or of mother-domination in the two countries. Although it may be true that "shared power" is exercised differently in the two countries (perhaps in Germany this represents a coalition to minimize adolescent influence), we see no reason that Germans should misperceive who makes the important decisions in their households more than Americans. Hence we accept this indication of similar patterns of parental dominance, tentatively, as a valuable modification of current socialization beliefs about both countries.

Table 5-7. Per Cent of United States and German National Samples Reporting Family Decisions Made by Father, Mother, or Both Together

	United States	Germany
Father made the decisions	28%	32%
Mother made the decisions	17	14
Both together made the decisions	55	54
Total N	(751)	(796)

Mediating Attitudes

The experience of influence in adolescence, and one's reaction to it, should, if it is to affect later life decisions, modify one's outlook on the social world. And to some extent it does so. Thus the Influentials in both countries, backed by their own experiences of such matters, are more likely to disagree with the statement. "No one is going to care much what happens to you, when you get right down to it" (Table 5-8A). In the United States they are more likely to believe that "people can be trusted," and there is in both countries a very slight tendency to be more sanguine about human nature. Yet we should not expect the Submissives to be distrustful; after all, their experience of submission was, apparently, not unpleasant. Thus they do not think people will take advantage of them. It is the relatively sanguine nature of the Rebels that is surprising (data not given).

Having experienced and appreciated influence, the Influentials at every educational level in both countries are more likely to disagree with the view that "A few strong leaders would do more for this country than all the laws and talk," while the others see more advantages in the strong leader idea (Table 5-8B). But it is important to observe how much less the contribution of personality is in Germany where there has been recent experience with "a few strong leaders."

Table 5-8. Adolescent Influence Typology and Certain Attitudes toward Human Nature, Political Leaders, and Political Influence. Per Cent of Each Type with Indicated Attitudes

| | United States | | | | | | Germany | | | |
| | PRIMARY | | SECONDARY | | HIGHER | | PRIMARY | | SOME SECONDARY | |
	%	(N)	%	(N)	%	(N)	%	(N)	%	(N)
A. "No one is going to care much what happens to you, when you get right down to it." Per cent disagree										
Influentials	44	(62)	70	(208)	82	(117)	22	(57)	32	(30)
Rebels	42	(26)	62	(37)	67	(10)	15	(16)	8	(1)
Submissives	22	(11)	36	(5)	75	(3)	13	(27)	29	(4)
B. "A few strong leaders would do more for this country than all the laws and talk." Per cent disagree										
Influentials	46	(65)	61	(180)	68	(97)	37	(94)	44	(41)
Rebels	34	(21)	53	(32)	66	(10)	33	(35)	38	(5)
Submissives	35	(17)	14	(2)	25	(1)	29	(59)	42	(6)
C. "People like me don't have any say about what the government does." Per cent agree										
Influentials	45	(63)	29	(87)	9	(13)	68	(174)	48	(45)
Rebels	61	(38)	45	(27)	27	(4)	73	(78)	69	(9)
Submissives	73	(36)	57	(8)	25	(1)	75	(150)	64	(9)

Note: The chi square for each United States table, taken as a whole, is significant at the 1% level. On the first question, A, the differences between the paired Rebels and Submissives especially are significant, and those between Influentials and Submissives are significant at the 1% level for two of the three educational groups. On the second question, B, the more significant differences occur in the paired comparisons between Influentials and Submissives, and are generally higher in the secondary education groups; on the third question, C, the significant differences (1% and 2% and 10%) are between the Influentials and the Rebels and between the Influentials and Submissives (1%, 1%, N.S.). The chi squares for the German data are lower: For the three questions, taking each table as a whole, the significant levels are, in order, 10%, N.S., and 1%. On the first question, A, the important differences lie between the Influentials and Submissives, especially in the primary group. On the third question, C, the Influential-Submissive comparison again contributes most of the important differences.

Finally, it is clear that the Influentials have the greatest sense of under-standing, and hence control over, political affairs, and the Submissives the least with the Rebels usually some place in between. This belief is found, with various patterns of local and national issues, in both countries (data not given). It follows logically, and also empirically in our data, that the Influentials are the most likely to disagree with the view that "people like me" have no "say" about what the government does (Table 5-8C).

In summary, then, it appears that the sense of appropriate influence in adolescence tends, though somewhat tenuously, to increase the feeling that people care about you, gives one a sense of understanding complex affairs and having influence over them and leads away from a search for a strong leader to take over the country's burdens.

Participation in Civic Affairs

Of the three types of persons, we would expect those with no influence experience who also believed that adolescents generally should *not* have such experience, the Submissives, to participate least in civic affairs. This is the case. In both cultures the Submissive is most likely to be a non-voter, least likely to talk politics, least likely to follow accounts of political and govern-mental affairs, and in the United States least likely to be a leader of the groups he does join (Table 5-9).

But the interesting question is the pattern of participation one might expect from the Influentials and the Rebels. After all, each has a psycho-logical base for participation; the Influential because he has had the ex-perience and hence the self-confidence to do it, the Rebel because, although he lacks the experience, he feels he should have had it. As a corollary of the above findings on the Submissive, of course, both would be expected to, and do, vote, talk and "follow" more than these Submissives.

As it turns out the tendencies in the two countries are similar, but the differences between Influential participation and Rebel participation are stronger in the United States. Considering the similarities first, in both countries there is a modest tendency for Influentials to follow public affairs more than the Rebels, and there is also in both countries a tendency for Influentials to assume greater leadership in their organizations compared to Rebels. As for talking politics, it is clear in both countries that Influentials tend to talk politics more often than Rebels at every educational level and, furthermore, that Influentials have a substantially larger range of people with whom they feel free to talk politics (data not shown). Aside from non-voting, then, it appears that across a fairly wide range of activities, the Influential is more likely to participate than the Rebel. Resentment of having been inadequately influential as a youth does not usually lead into politics—except, perhaps, under the influence of special charismatic leadership and

Table 5-9. Adolescent Influence and Patterns of Political Participation, by Education: Per Cent of Type Not Voting, Never Following Political News, Never Talking Politics, and Ever Serving as an Officer of a Voluntary Organization

A. United States

| | Non-Voters | | | | | | Never Follow Political News | | | | | |
	PRIMARY		SECON-DARY		HIGHER		PRIMARY		SECON-DARY		HIGHER	
	%	(N)	%	(N)	%	(N)	%	(N)	%	(N)	%	(N)
Influentials	30	(46)	14	(41)	11	(16)	21	(30)	15	(43)	2	(3)
Rebels	35	(22)	8	(5)	29	(4)	34	(21)	12	(7)	7	(1)
Submissives	41	(20)	29	(4)	—	(0)	49	(24)	29	(4)	—	(1)

| | Never Talk Politics | | | | | | Officer of a Voluntary Organization | | | | | |
	PRIMARY		SECON-DARY		HIGHER		PRIMARY		SECON-DARY		HIGHER	
	%	(N)	%	(N)	%	(N)	%	(N)	%	(N)	%	(N)
Influentials	35	(50)	17	(49)	5	(7)	24	(33)	26	(77)	56	(79)
Rebels	50	(31)	17	(10)	20	(3)	8	(5)	20	(12)	47	(7)
Submissives	55	(27)	36	(5)	—	(0)	8	(4)	7	(1)	—	(2)

B. Germany

| | Non-Voters | | | | Never Follow Political News | | | |
	PRIMARY		AT LEAST SOME SECONDARY		PRIMARY		AT LEAST SOME SECONDARY	
	%	(N)	%	(N)	%	(N)	%	(N)
Influentials	4	(9)	6	(5)	20	(52)	6	(6)
Rebels	4	(4)	0	(0)	26	(28)	18	(1)
Submissives	7	(11)	10	(1)	36	(72)	14	(2)

| | Never Talk Politics | | | | Officer of Some Voluntary Organization | | | |
	PRIMARY		AT LEAST SOME SECONDARY		PRIMARY		AT LEAST SOME SECONDARY	
	%	(N)	%	(N)	%	(N)	%	(N)
Influentials	34	(87)	15	(14)	9	(22)	16	(15)
Rebels	37	(40)	23	(3)	6	(6)	8	(1)
Submissives	53	(107)	14	(2)	3	(7)	7	(1)

Note: For the United States, taking the tables for each type of participation as a whole, the chi squares for non-voting, not following the news, and not talking politics are significant at the 1% level, while the table for serving as officer of an organization is significant at the 10% level. The important comparisons between the Influentials and the Rebels are, unfortunately at the margin of significance. In two cases (non-voting and not following news) they are just short of the 10% level; the other two are above the 5% level. For not following the news, the Influential-Submissive comparison is significant at the 1% level and the same is true for not talking politics. The data on serving as officer of a voluntary organization show the Submissive-Rebel comparison significant at the 1% level. For Germany, taking the tables for each kind of participation as a whole, neither the non-voting nor the officer of an organization tables are statistically significant; the other two tables are significant at the 5% and 1% levels. In the paired comparisons, the comparisons between Influentials and Rebels in no case is significant, while, except for the non-voting table, the differences between the Influentials and the Submissives are significant (1%, 1%, 10%). The differences between Rebels and Submissives are significant (5% and 10%) in two cases.

more destructive appeals than have been usual in post-war Germany and the United States. On this point, it should be noted that in neither country is there much difference between the two groups in their choice of "organizing a protest demonstration" as a method of influencing government (data not shown).

But why should the effect of personality differences on political behavior be less in Germany than in the United States—so much less that these differences tend not to achieve statistical significance in Germany? One can only guess, of course, but it is usual for these kinds of differences in the effect of personal disposition to reveal themselves where the culture is more ambiguous and the environment less controlling. It seems likely that in Germany political behavior and attitudes are more usually controlled by community pressure and expectation, whereas, at least in the political area, the American environment is more permissive. This seems certainly true of voting, and therefore, by extension, may be believed to be the case in the other areas of participation we are examining.

Direction and Partisanship

As we observed earlier, there are reasons for believing that Influentials might closely conform to their group tradition, lower-class left, upper-class right, and the like, or might transcend it. There are reasons to think that Rebels might deviate from their group parental norms, or move toward some national radical norm, or become embittered and alienated apathetics (though the participation findings deny this). There are, also, reasons for thinking of submissives as, more than others, content to remain in their group political traditions or, on the other hand, more likely to find support in the national conservative tradition, that is, with a preference for parties upholding the status quo. And, of course, to match conflicting theories, conflicting tendencies are revealed in the data.

The data, themselves, require a parenthetical comment. Because of the nature of the material available to me I must use somewhat different indicators of political orientation in the the two countries: for the United States, the measure is the vote in the 1956 election, an unfortunate one because that particular election tended to blur religious and income differences and hence to weaken whatever relationships might be revealed by breakdowns along these lines. For Germany, the measure is "usual vote" in local elections, a better measure because it avoids the distorting effect of a single election and, especially, of the attractiveness of a particular candidate. The analysis relies primarily on income and religion. (As background information, it should be pointed out that the influence of religion works in different directions in the two countries: in the United States the Catholic tradition is Democratic (more liberal), while in Germany it is Christian Democrat (more conservative).) How, then, do Influentials, Rebels and Submissives differ in their political orientations?

Submissives. As the Influentials are the largest group, the most active politically, and the group with the fewest pathological symptoms, we will use them as a standard against which to compare the others. In the United States the Submissive group is so small that their main usefulness is a kind of suggestive counterpoise to the German submissive pattern. Yet one negative finding is in order. It might have been thought that the submissive personality would swing more readily to support the candidate with the "strongest" or most charismatic appeal, General Eisenhower. This was certainly not the case; indeed, if anything, the Submissives tended to be more Democratic than others (data not given).

Table 5-10. Adolescent Influence and Group (Religion and Economic Class)
Unorthodoxy in Voting Patterns, by Nation:
Per Cent of Type with Unorthodox Vote Preference

	United States				Germany		
	LOWER-INCOME CATHOLICS VOTING REPUBLICAN IN 1956		HIGHER-INCOME PROTESTANTS VOTING DEMOCRATIC IN 1956		LOWER-INCOME PROTESTANTS VOTING CDU IN LOCAL ELECTIONS		HIGHER-INCOME CATHOLICS VOTING SPD IN LOCAL ELECTIONS
	%	(N)	%	(N)	%	(N)	%	(N)
Influentials	80	(20)	27	(40)	43	(23)	38	(12)
Rebels	61	(8)	36	(10)	18	(5)	10	(1)
Submissives	—	(4)	—	(2)	34	(10)	18	(3)

Note: Chi squares for the United States tables and paired comparisons by types are not significant. For Germany: chi squares for lower-income Protestants are significant at 10% level; for paired comparison between Influentials and Rebels the significance levels are 5% and 10%; if combined (3 d.f.) they are at about the 7% level.

But the German pattern is more interesting. The Submissives, a larger group in that country, were more responsive to group tradition than the Influentials; further, one should comment that the very conservative nature of the Catholic Submissive group, a tendency manifested on all income levels (data not shown). I doubt if the answer lies in Catholic doctrine, but rather in the acceptance of a Catholic political tradition of Christian Democratic voting, reinforced by formidable institutional organized support.

Rebels. The Rebels, it will be recalled, are those who had little experience of influence as a youth and resent it. One might expect them to become radicals, but would they express this radicalism as a protest against their parental group tradition, lower income moving right and higher income moving left (unorthodox) or against the national status quo "establishment" tradition, possibly towards some radical extreme? Perhaps there are national differences in this respect, although our United States findings are largely heuristic here for they do not achieve statistical significance. The data suggest that, if anything, the American Rebel is more likely to be Democratic than his matched group member who is an Influential (data only partly shown in Table 10). But this is important, if at all, only as a possible contrast to the rather interesting German pattern. Compared to the Influentials, the German Rebels are *not* generally more leftist. A finer economic breakdown (data not shown) reveals that a middle-income Rebel group is exactly modal in its partisanship and an upper income group is very slightly more rightist. But perhaps the Rebel is more likely to be unorthodox, in the sense that whatever his group tradition may be, he tends, more than others, to violate it or transcend it. Eliminating the cross-pressured groups (lower-income Catholics and upper-income Protestants) in order to isolate groups where the influence of religion and social status reinforce each other, we can compare the Rebel pattern with the pattern of the Influentials in the two countries, as in Table 10. The result is a surprise; instead of being less orthodox, we find the Rebels *more* orthodox, according to these data. Among the Rebels, higher-income Catholics are more likely to support the Christian Democratic party than the Influentials, and lower-income Protestants are more likely to support the Socialists.

Obviously, as this finding was partially unexpected (but see item "f" in the introductory comments), the reversal of one relevant theory and a marked difference between the two national patterns requires the search for new theoretical considerations. What could account for this pattern? One very good possibility is that it is an artifact of the measures, but their fine performance according to (some of) our predictions in the validation tests above makes that a little less likely. The possibility that the pattern could happen by chance is greater then one would like, but still it is only one chance in about fourteen that sampling variation is the correct interpretation. Perhaps there is a clue in Erikson's statement mentioned above to the effect that the German male adolescent tends to be more rebellious (more than Americans) against his parents, but then, returns to the fold and shapes himself in the parental mold, becomes a father like his own father. That is, guilt over the rebellion may be great enough to create a counter-force to restore the Rebel to the parental tradition.

There are indications in our data that this may, in fact, be the case. Not only are expectations and standards different, but also, Germans probably find *overt expression* of criticism of their status in the home more difficult than do Americans. This hypothesis is supported by the fact that the measure of latent dissatisfaction and rebellious feelings uncovered as many covert Rebels among the German population as in the American population. Latent rebellious feelings come more easily to the surface in the United States: 46 per cent of the American Rebels expressed open dissatisfaction with their adolescent influence while only 23 per cent of the German Rebels did so (Table 5-2). These are indications of suppression of critical feelings which might reasonably be interpreted as reflecting guilt. This guilt, then, could be the force which, during the course of maturation, brings a person back into the parental fold, political and otherwise, with some of the force of a compulsion. Hence the Rebels are more orthodox than the Influentials, and they over-conform.

Summary and Implications

In the foregoing discussion, I have developed a typology of adolescent influence experience and certain adult responses thereto designed to measure (a) an appropriate sense of influence in adolescence, the Influential, (b) a sense of appropriate lack of influence, the Submissive, and (c) a sense of inappropriate and resented lack of influence, the Rebel. By and large, these measures seem to capture for each type an attitude syndrome that supports an intuitive view of what they should be like. Three basic sets of questions have been explored: (a) What kinds of causes produce these types? (b) How do they affect political participation? (c) How do they affect political partisanship?

Causes. The strong relationship between adolescent influence and education at first suggested that more education simply creates in the educated person a sense of generalized influence in society, a sense that is projected back into adolescence: The later educational experience affects memories of the earlier adolescent experience. Probably this is true, but since occupational status (which should create a similar sense of influence) is not related to these memories, other factors must be important as well, among them two important ones. I would hazard the guess that the family that values education also values children and children's opinions. These are correlated values. Second, the child who drops out of school early is a different kind of child from the one who persists in his education. The "complaints" of the one who goes on may be more worth listening to.

Why is it that there is a strong relationship between age and adolescent influence typology in Germany but much less in the United States? Could it be that the United States, without the residue of a feudal order to be broken and overcome through difficult historical trauma, passed through the last fifty years with far less change in social relationships than is true of Europe and especially Germany? McClelland has found that modernizing societies are more "other-directed" than static societies, their members more sensitive to each other's opinions.[7] Almond and Verba have found that the American is far more trusting of others than the German, Italian, or Mexican.[8] Part of the modernizing process, then, is an increased acceptance of the opinions, influence, and trustworthiness of others. And this includes adolescent sons, and daughters. The age differences in Germany may reflect this aspect of modernization, a movement, if I may put it this way, toward the American position established some years ago.

I have discussed the idea that the strong relationship in both cultures between Protestantism and adolescent influence is part of the general Protestant movement to set men free from institutional (including family) restraints. If a man can directly influence God, without intercession of another (Church) authority, he may properly influence lesser authorities, such as parents. But does this also work the other way? Is the Protestant reformation in part a product of the growing sense that youth can modify paternal authority? Kardiner says that religion is in large part a projection of social relations.[9] If this is so, what shall we say of the religious changes that the modern revolution in social relations may bring about?

These changes are the indirect influences of society on adolescent freedom and authority; they work through parental behavior. In the United States, where the parents share authority with each other, they also share it with their children. But in Germany this connection is not so clearly the case. Does this mean that joint parental decision-making in Germany is more like a joint adult management of affairs in which children do not participate? In Germany fathers and mothers are seen as jointly deciding how to vote more often than in the United States, where they are seen more often as making this decision individually (though, of course, they usually do agree).[10] The particular nature of the family solidarity in Germany may include a set of constraints which the German child, imbued with a familistic loyalty and even ideology, views as appropriate. Thus the "togetherness" of German family decisions implies something different from what is implied by the joint decisions of the American family. Perhaps there is more freedom for the German child when the parents do *not* decide matters jointly. "Divide and rule" is a maxim that children as well as emperors can learn.

Participation. A sense of appropriate influence in adolescence and the experience which it gives form a better basis for participation than resentment over lack of influence. At least in democratic politics, as we have observed elsewhere, damaged father-son relations tend to inhibit participation,[11] particularly when the father is not interested in politics. Now it seems more generally true in other cultures, as well, that damaged parent-child relations are more likely to lead away from politics than back into the fray; except of course, for the radical fringe.[12] In the simplest terms this can be expressed as follows: one learns to use democratic influence by an early exercise of democratic influence; one believes what one has experienced.

Orientation. As for the political orientation of the Rebels (in our limited sense), again a cross-national difference is apparent. In every social group, the American rebel is more likely to be Democratic (leftist?) than his matched Influential group; at least, it seems he was not "available" to the personality appeal of what was generally regarded as a strong candidate. Moreover, he acts out his feelings without too much guilt; all along he has been able and willing to express, more than the German, his feelings of resentment.

But the German Rebel tends, more than his peers among the Influentials, to return to the parental tradition in an exaggerated way. If he is a lower-income Protestant, he is more likely than other lower-income Protestants to vote Socialist. If he is a higher-income Catholic, he is more likely than others with these characteristics to vote Christian Democrat, FDP, or DRP. The mature former Rebel violates his own earlier rebellious idealism. Erikson writes, "this regular split between precocious individualistic rebellion and disillusioned, obedient citizenship was a strong factor in the political immaturity of the German: this adolescent rebellion was an abortion of individualism and of revolutionary spirit. . . ." For once a patriarchal superego is finally established in early childhood, you can give youth rope: they cannot let themselves go far.[13] And more of them come "home" politically, than if they had never rebelled in the first place.

Notes

1. See Russell Middleton and Snell Putney, "Political Expression of Adolescent Rebellion," *American Journal of Sociology*, 68 (1963), pp. 527–535; Eleanor E. Maccoby, Richard E. Matthews, and Anton S. Morton, "Youth and Political Change," *Public Opinion Quarterly*, 18 (1954), pp. 23–29.

2. Princeton, N.J., Princeton University Press, 1963.

3. Erik Erikson, *Childhood and Society* (New York: Norton, 1950), pp. 289–294.

4. See, for example, *ibid.*, p. 247.

5. David C. McClelland, *The Achieving Society* (New York: Van Nostrand, 1961), pp. 360–362.

6. See Bertram H. Shaffner, *Father Land, A Study of Authoritarianism in the German Family* (New York: Columbia University Press, 1948).

7. D. C. McClelland, *op. cit.*, pp. 192–197.

8. G. A. Almond and S. Verba, *op. cit.*, p. 267.

9. Abram Kardiner, *The Psychological Frontiers of Society* (New York: Columbia University Press, 1945), pp. 38–46.

10. Unpublished data from the Almond and Verba study.

11. Robert E. Lane, "Fathers and Sons: Foundations of Political Belief," Chapter 4; see also preceding discussion in this chapter.

12. See Gabriel A. Almond, *The Appeals of Communism* (Princeton, N.J.: Princeton University Press, 1954), pp. 258–294.

13. E. Erikson, *op. cit.*, p. 293.

Note: I wish to acknowledge the help given me by Gerry Ruth Sack and Elizabeth Warren in making the statistical calculations presented below. Miss Warren programmed the data for computer calculation of chi squares. I am also grateful to John Helliwell, of Nuffield College, for consultation on various statistical matters, but hold him free of blame for any errors I may have committed in interpreting his advice.

Chapter 6
Political Education in
the Midst of Life's Struggles

College does change young people's political outlook, or at least people come out of college rather different from the way they were when they went in, and people who go to college are markedly different from those who do not. Unfortunately, the studies of these matters are not always clear on what actually happened; they tend to confuse two pairs of things. One common error is to confuse maturation with education. Because they often fail to compare changes within the group of 18- to 22-year-olds who went to college with changes in similar young people who did not, one is not sure what contribution college made to the evident differences. Many studies also fail to separate the influence of students' backgrounds from the effects of education; children whose parents send them to college may be different to start with from those whose parents do not.

Nevertheless, the weight of the evidence suggests that college has the following effects:

POLITICAL INFORMATION

It is clear from masses of evidence that the better-educated are better-informed on most political matters and, moreover, it seems from recent evidence that the difference between college and high-school graduates is greater than the difference between high-school and grade-school graduates.[1] But the caution just mentioned seems to apply with force, even on this simplest aspect of politicization. McClintock and Turner compared the political information of freshmen and seniors at seven California colleges and universities and found that if they controlled for sex and grade-point average,

Reprinted from *Harvard Educational Review*, 38 (1968), pp. 468–494.

Notes to this chapter will be found on pages 119–120

there was no important difference in information between the two class levels. Most groups of seniors were no better informed than the freshmen, except that seniors with low grade-point averages were somewhat better informed than freshmen with low averages. Yet even here the inference is obscure: is this because college has a greater effect upon those who have least to start with or is it because a number of the worst freshmen had flunked out, leaving a different and "better" set of low-average students in the senior year?[2]

There is one other point on this matter of information. Most questions about politics ask about "school-type" national information such as the number of years a Senator serves, the protections in the Bill of Rights, or the functions of the United Nations. There is some slight evidence in the interview material reported in my *Political Ideology*, that in local practical matters such as "Who is your alderman?" or "How would you go about getting a light put on your street corner?" the less-well-educated may "know the ropes" fully as well as the better-educated.[3]

LIBERALISM–CONSERVATISM

The terminology is obscure, but if we sort out from the class of attitudes sometimes called "liberal" only those supporting government intervention in national economic life with welfare state implications (leaving aside the civil libertarian, internationalistic, and ethnocentric dimensions of liberalism), we will have a rough set of common referents. Liberalism in this sense does seem to increase with greater exposure to college, for reasons which are still obscure. The phenomena seem to be relatively stable over time and in different places, with some important exceptions to be noted.

The studies in the 'thirties and early 'forties of politico-economic liberalism all suggest that this kind of liberalism increases with formal school right up through the college years.[4] Later the matter becomes more complex. The most extensive study of political and other values, conducted by a Cornell group but not limited to Cornell, during the period 1950-62, suggests several things. At Cornell, a panel study suggests that the general movement is from liberalism to conservatism, on a philosophy-of-government scale composed of the following items:

Democracy depends fundamentally on the existence of free business enterprise.
The welfare state tends to destroy individual initiative.
Government planning almost inevitably results in the loss of essential liberties and freedom.
The best government is the one which governs least.[5]

But the amount of movement was not great at Cornell, and comparable studies with the same items elsewhere reveal a somewhat different pattern. At

Harvard there is a change toward conservatism between freshman and sopho-more years, followed by an unpatterned movement; at Yale and elsewhere there is a great variety of changes in many directions.[6]

A more recent study suggests that the general movement is again toward a more liberal philosophy (at least on the item "Should the government provide medical and dental care for citizens who cannot afford such services?"), although the sample is an elite scholarship group, and the engineering students *move* in the opposite direction.[7] (The effect of field of study will be examined in a moment.)

PARTY AFFILIATION

One's political philosophy, as indicated by one's attitudes toward laissez faire, for example, and one's political party have a rather loose affinity; they are separable, learned from different sources and at different times. The party affiliation is learned earlier and is more closely linked to family preference.[8] But these party affiliations are then subject to erosion over time as other experiences and groups modify the original family choice, though the majority of people remain in the party of their fathers. This erosion through exposure to contrary group and community influences takes place in high school: Republicans in predominantly Democratic high-school populations tend to change from their parents' affiliation more than do Democrats, and the reverse is true of Democrats in predominantly Republican high-school populations.[9] At Cornell, where there were about three times as many Republican identifiers as Democratic partisans (in the early 'fifties), only one out of about 25 sons of Republicans became Democrats, while about one out of every 14 sons of Democrats became Republicans.[10] Obviously at Cornell the rate of defection from Democratic homes is greater than the rate from Republican homes. These defections are much more likely in individuals whose father's political preference does not follow the usual partisanship of his socio-economic group (as defined by religion and income). But a *later* study of the *brighter* students in *many places* concentrating in the *humanities* revealed a net shift from Republican to Democratic for the men and Republican to Independent for the women.[11]

Maccoby and associates compared the rates of change for a group of Cambridge, Massachusetts, young adults and found that college experience had increased the rates of partisan change in both directions, Republican to Democratic and vice versa. These authors believed that college experience, with its exposure to a variety of points of view, facilitated partisan flexibility.[12]

POLITICAL PARTICIPATION

Like all educational experiences, college tends to increase political partici-pation of all kinds. This is partly because it changes certain attitudes which directly support participation, such as a sense of citizen duty (the obligation to vote under various circumstances), and a sense of political efficacy and competence (the feeling that one's voice counts and that one can effect desired changes). But the process is more subtle than one would have supposed. A study at Ohio Wesleyan in the early 'fifties found declining intention and desire to participate in political affairs combined with an increase in somewhat "cynical" attitudes about politics.[13] This was also true at metropolitan New York University, and variations in the curriculum seem to have had little effect on these intentions.[14]

A more recent study summarizes student attitudes as being "dutifully responsive toward government" but without any inclination to extend oneself in this area, or much of a desire to engage in public affairs.[15] Any evaluation of these relatively "cool" responses and political detachment should take into consideration Burgemeister's earlier finding that students who tended to avoid social participation were likely to be those with considerable intellectual interests; this finding should be viewed as a caution only, since the temper of the times (1940) and the character of the students who comprised the sample (Barnard girls) probably affected the outcome of the study.[16]

AUTHORITARIANISM

Although it was not entirely clear from Adorno's original study of authoritarianism that this trait was greatly reduced by education, subsequent studies have established this beyond a doubt.[17] On the other hand education seems to make the authoritarian "ideology" an operative force in affecting attitudes on topical issues, while this is less true of the uneducated.[18] In some later research Sanford shows that while there is a general tendency for authoritarian attitudes to decline over the college years, some high scorers do not change—a matter which he suggests deserves further investigation.[19] Further work by Brown and Bystryn shows the differential effect of different kinds of institutions: education in a Catholic liberal arts college for women and a nondenominational liberal arts college for women produced declines in authoritarianism, but this was not the case in a large Eastern coeducational university.[20]

ETHNOCENTRISM

Ethnocentrism declines with education. The early *Study of Values* by Allport, as well as the more recent study by Jacob, shows this to be a persistent phenomenon.[21] Perhaps the most convincing demonstration is that of Plant, whose study employed the California "E" (for ethnocentrism) scale and compared students who withdrew from San Jose State College with a group matched for ethnocentrism and intelligence who remained in college. Two years later those who remained in college had become significantly less ethnocentric, while the dropouts had not.[22]

CONFORMISM AND TOLERANCE OF HETERODOXY

Stouffer has established that college graduates are consistently more tolerant of religious and political heterodoxy than those who have not been to college.[23] Jacob found a little later that college students "typically" have considerable "tolerance of diversity," but he also finds that students become more conformist in their tolerance, a finding that suggests a paradoxical turn of mind.[24] Webster found that college produces a greater diversity of interests and greater heterogeneity of values, something which the alarmists over college conformity might consider.[25]

ALIENATION

Keniston has described the general nature of alienation in college and delineated with artistic skill the portrait of an alienated young man at Harvard. Referring to the measuring of this young man's alienation, he includes such items as "distrust, pessimism, resentment, anxiety, egocentricity, the sense of being an outsider, the rejection of conventional values, rejection of happiness as a goal, and a feeling of distance from others . . . self-contempt, interpersonal alienation, dislike of conventional social groups, rejection of the culture, and the view of the universe as an unstructured and meaningless chaos."[26] Keniston's longitudinal data on changes are not yet published, but elsewhere he argues that many of the elements of modern intellectualism tend to encourage these alienated feelings.[27]

There is a little information, however, on how some of these symptoms change among women during the college years, especially "the sense of being an outsider . . . a feeling of distance from others . . . interpersonal alienation," for it appears that a measure of social integration developed at Vassar captures part of these attitudes. "Social integration" is defined this way: "High-scorers are likely to be quite conventional and free of symptoms of social alienation; low scorers usually feel that they are unhappy social isolates,"[28] A comparison of Vassar freshmen and seniors shows almost no difference, while a comparison of Bennington freshmen, sophomores, juniors and seniors reveals a steady increase in social integration (decrease in social alienation) over their college years. Thus, as far as these measures go, they indicate that at the very least college does not increase this kind of alienation, and may very well reduce it.[29]

EXTREMISM AND CAUTION

Although it seems well-established that college increases what is called "impulse expression," it also seems to be the case that this does not lead to ideological extremism or political impulsiveness. The concepts are slippery, but an early study by Hunter found that while students had become more liberal over their college years, seniors were more careful about endorsing extreme statements.[30] Similarly, Newcomb found in his Bennington study that seniors were more likely than freshmen to show a pattern of greater caution in agreeing with liberal statements combined with greater willingness to disagree with conservative statements—a more critical response set.[31]

CRITICAL SOCIAL THINKING

A report by Dressel and Mayhew summarizing a major American Council on Education study of social science teaching in the colleges has the following to say:

> In general it was found that students gained in ability to think critically in social science over a period of a year, although the size of these gains varied widely, depending on the institutions that students attended. Attempts to teach critical thinking in social science by making minor changes in particular courses did not appear to result in greater growth than was found in courses not making overt attempts to teach this skill.[32]

Since the study developed and employed a special test for measuring critical thinking, this is a useful and independent confirmation of the tendency reported above: increased avoidance of extreme statements and greater caution in responding to ambiguous questionnaire items after a few years of college education.

What Causes these Changes

Of course, these dimensions of change have different causes, and these various causes interact in a variety of very complex ways. We may summarize a few of the findings, particularly as they relate to politico-economic liberalism, but with a glance at the other dimensions.

1. Higher scholarship, "bookishness," and perhaps "seriousness," are related to greater economic and social liberalism and lower ethnocentrism in college.[33]

2. Economic status or wealth in college seems not to make much difference among college students on broad economic philosophy questions, but is more likely to be associated with greater conservatism on specific economic questions.[34]

3. The field of study makes a difference. Summarizing the older studies, Kerr says, "Evidence on the liberalizing effect of various courses of study is conflicting, but there is a tendency for students in the social sciences to be more liberal than students in almost any other curriculum." A later study of National

Merit Scholars shows that in contrast to others in mathematics and humanities, engineers become *more* conservative during their college years.[35]

4. Specific changes in curricula to increase intention to participate in political life are not effective, as revealed in studies in a small college and a large metropolitan university. The same lack of effect is true of attempts to teach "critical social thinking," as reported above.[36]

The focus quickly comes to rest upon the college environment, the larger student culture exemplified by attitudes toward dating, sports, "campusmanship," deviance, "grinds," "meat-balls" or "wienies" (why meats?), "odd balls," scholarship, and so forth. On this point Freedman states that such a student culture "is the prime educational force at work, for . . . assimilation into the student society is the foremost concern of most new students," and "academic aims and processes of the College are in large measure transmitted to incoming students or mediated for them by the predominant student culture."[37] This view is reinforced by Jervis and Congdon's study of New Hampshire students which showed that between the freshman and senior years, student vocational and educational values come little closer to those of the faculty.[38] The marked decline in evaluation of high academic achievement during the freshman year further corroborates this point.[39]

Politically, these student values seem to vary substantially from campus to campus, as Tables 6-1 and 6-2 show.

But, of course, as Newcomb has shown in his Bennington study, a student may or may not choose to accept the values of his college culture, even in a small and intensely political college such as Bennington in the 'thirties. The major inhibiting force is a continued *reference* to a different family culture, but the degree of *awareness* of the prevailing campus values is also an important consideration. A person may be insulated somehow against this perception. Lipset's finding that attitudes toward the faculty oath at the University of California were more pro-faculty for those who lived on the campus than for those who lived at home probably represents a mixture of both awareness and reference-group effects.[40]

A closer inspection of the impact of smaller social subsystems on a large campus reveals some important processes at work. It will be recalled that the authors of the Cornell study found that the students on that campus tended to become more conservative over the course of their college years. This was because those who were uncertain at the beginning of college tended to crystallize in a conservative direction; among the few switchers, the liberals lost more than they gained, and those who were conservative at the beginning tended to be more constant. Looking at the reasons for this, these authors found that certain social subsystems, particularly the fraternities, reinforced the conservatism of the larger college community; students who were *not* embraced by these social groups, the independents, were much less likely to crystallize in a conservative direction, or, if liberal initially, less likely to

Table 6-1. Proportion of Positive Responses at Universities to the Question: "Do you ever get as worked up about something that happens in politics or public affairs as you do about something that happens in your personal life?" (1950)

University	Percentage Saying "Yes"	Total Number Asked
Wayne State	46%	519
Yale	44	297
Wesleyan	44	277
Cornell (men; 1952)	42	655
Harvard	41	453
Dartmouth	39	365
Texas	39	516
U.C.L.A.	38	467
Michigan	38	488
Fisk	37	134
North Carolina	34	414

Source: Rose K. Goldsen et al., *What College Students Think* (New York: Van Nostrand, 1960), p. 218

Table 6-2. Votes Cast in College Polls and Mock Elections, Fall, 1964

	PERCENTAGE				PERCENTAGE		
College	Johnson	Goldwater	Un-decided	College	Johnson	Goldwater	Un-decided
Radcliffe	93%	7%	—	Iowa	66%	34%	—
Amherst	90	10	—	Princeton	66	27	7
Harvard	87	13	—	Illinois	63	37	—
Ricker (Me.)	78	22	—	Pennsylvania	62	38	—
Pembroke	77	18	5	Rider (N.J.)	62	38	—
Moravian (Pa.)	74	20	6	Brown	61	29	10
Penn. State	70	30	—	Ohio State	61	39	—
Michigan State	70	30	—	Lehigh	57	43	—
Yale	70	20	10	Tulane	57	43	—
Western (O.)	70	30	—	Minnesota	55	45	—
Dartmouth	69	25	6	Northwestern	52	48	—
Lafayette	68	32	—				

Source: American Institute of Public Opinion release, November 15, 1964.

defect from this position. In any event, to achieve the same constancy ratio as the conservatives, the liberals had to feel more intensely about the rightness of their philosophy of government than the conservatives.[41]

The influence of the curricula and the faculty, of the larger college community, of special social subsystems, and of various on-campus and off-campus reference groups is received by individuals who are working through enormously complicated adjustments to parents, peers, and self, the specific nature of which is bound to affect their political and other orientations. They are surprisingly fluid in many respects. Among freshmen at a small coeducational college, Walter Wallace reports a high rate of turnover in the freshman year on such values as "importance of being accepted and liked by other students," "importance of falling in love and getting married," "importance of pleasing parents," and "importance of getting high grades," although there was a marked decline in the importance attached to the last of these until the freshman average approximated the low evaluation of upperclassmen on this point.[42] Less satisfactory cross-sectional data suggest, but greatly understate, the fluidity of political attitudes at Yale (see Table 6-3). We shall examine this in greater detail in a moment.

Table 6-3. Philosophy of Government among Students at Yale University

PERCENTAGE HOLDING EACH ATTITUDE BY YEAR IN COLLEGE

Attitude	Freshman	Sophomore	Junior	Senior
Support laissez faire	45%	24%	33%	46%
Intermediate	15	23	22	20
Do not support laissez faire	39	52	45	35

Source: Rose K. Goldsen et al., *What College Students Think* (New York: Van Nostrand, 1960), p. 220

This fluidity is suggested also by the curious pattern of support for Johnson and Goldwater among the four classes in 1964 (see Table 6-4).

Table 6-4. Political Choices of Yale Students, October, 1964

PERCENTAGE FOR EACH CANDIDATE BY YEAR IN COLLEGE

Candidate	Freshman	Sophomore	Junior	Senior	All years
Johnson	73%	64%	57%	75%	69%
Goldwater	19	24	30	15	20
Undecided	8	12	13	10	11

* *Source:* Yale Political Science Research Library and *Yale Daily News* Survey.

Obviously a great deal is going on that these measure hardly capture. It is to this point that we now turn.

Parties to the Central Struggles: Parents, Peers, Self

One must take a closer view. To this end I will make use of material from some candid and courageous political autobiographies of Yale men who sought to answer the questions: "Of what use to me is my 'liberalism' or 'conservatism'?" and "How did I become a 'liberal' or 'conservative'?" Over the years I have collected some thirty-five of these self-analyses; here I wish to report on eight, not substantially different in tenor from the others, though richer in detail than most.

These eight young men are obviously better-off than the average, and some of them are very wealthy indeed. One of them comes from a distinguished old family, but most are the sons of upper-middle-class professional and business people; only one is from a relatively lower-middle-class home. It is hard to report what their political orientation *is*; it is easier to say in what direction it is *changing*. Caught between the stability of earlier unthinking parental identification and the stability reinforced by established status in adult life, six of the eight were moving, though often within the framework of their father's political party. Five of these were becoming more liberal, one more conservative. All of them talk about their political lives with reference to their father's views (and sometimes their mother's), and most refer to the views of their friends and enemies at college, but only two talk about what takes place in their classes or the views of the faculty.

Case material here, as elsewhere, has the defects of its virtues; it illuminates detail, intricacy, the flavor of emotion, but obscures general patterns, general relationships, the grounds for general findings. Hence, the following points:

1. Newcomb's Bennington study (and the Cornell study, too) stresses the importance of positive reference groups; students who accepted the college community as their social ground were compared with those who accepted and retained their parental group for this purpose. These eight cases, and many more, indicate the importance of negative reference groups: the push as well as the pull. Those who are most influenced by their father as a reference person, at least at a conscious level as revealed in these reports, are fleeing from him, fighting him, differentiating themselves from him. Is the Newcomb analysis as it applies to political orientation *primarily relevant for girls*? In the same way, at Yale where fraternities are less important, those who report their responses to the Yale environment speak more of fighting the elites, the "preppies," even the larger student culture, than of accepting it and striving within its framework. But of course, kicking and screaming (*sotto voce*, perhaps, and privately to me), they do accept a good part of it. Still, without being "odd-balls," they do fight it, and its elite spokesmen.

2. So much that is said about political orientation and its development seems totally irrelevant to what is happening outside the campus in the world that it is as though these young men were living private and group lives, but lives in a historyless age, an age without headlines, political crises, loved and hated leaders. Perhaps it is an artifact of the method; but given the freest possible choice, they chose to focus on themselves and their highly personal environments.

3. In the classroom, but more especially in the corridors and dining halls, these young men give an extraordinary impression of self-assurance and a talent for good fellowship. But here, in their private revelations, almost all of them talk about their "feelings of insecurity," "fear of seeming weak," "fear of loss of friends," "fear of standing out in some odd way." Their politics comes from an attack upon these problems, and is used in the war against these unhappy feelings and fears. They forge their political (and other) identities out of their weaknesses and so try to make themselves strong.

4. At the same time, their views of their parents and themselves are, for many, amazingly accessible to their conscious thought. It is a source of strength, for it makes their political views more susceptible to conscious change. Insight alone will not effect such changes, of course, but it is the first step.

5. There is evident a phasing process in political development in the college years; one must first solve the "father problem" or one cannot solve the "peer problem." And one must solve both of these before one can solve the "self problem." This is to suggest that the formation of a satisfactory identity is, in

Sullivanian manner, the product of felicitous interpersonal relations. More of this later.

The Father Problem

Around the world the story is much the same: father is the source of political orientation, especially for sons.[43] For this reason, politics, even more than most other issues, gets caught up in the son's struggle to discover a mode of accommodation with father, a style of continuity and independence which does not deny what he has admired and may still, but which reflects his own autonomy. Three of our cases will reflect three different resolutions of this struggle and, to some extent, the role that college played by giving them a four-year "furlough from father."

TRUMBULL, TOWARD AUTONOMOUS MISANTHROPY

Trumbull's father was a member of a distinguished family, a fact the older gentleman seems not to have accepted lightly. He never settled into a useful career (as his son reports it) and, with leisure at his command, devoted much time to his family. After discussing his own part in early family history, our young Trumbull says:

I distinctly remember my father as a person whose entire life was oriented around being unfair and punishing in every trivial instance which could be manufactured. Unfortunately, I lacked the maturity at that time to realize that all punishment and arguments were merely reflections of his unfailing desire to weld my character into a more nearly perfect mold. That his methods were ill-designed to the end he wished to realize was indeed unfortunate, for they have left marks which have been extremely difficult, if not impossible, to erase. It is indeed ironic that at the time when I most needed love and affection, he had little to offer, yet now that I am more nearly a finished product, he has little else to give.

Trumbull went to an excellent preparatory school, where he says he was miserable and had few friends, and then came to Yale. He reports that as he looks inward upon himself, he finds that "behind the mask that I, like others have devised to shield myself from the barbarity of society, lies an individual who is scared and insecure about his relations to society in general, and who covers his lack with a veneer of self-sufficiency and independence." He attributes this insecurity to his upbringing and states that as a consequence he protects himself with snobbish airs and ethnocentrism.

I feel that for one reason or another I am better than many of my countrymen and that many of them are obnoxious and undesirable. I feel that I am one of the more intelligent people in this country; I feel that I am one of the wealthier people in the nation; I feel that Catholics as a group are objectionable, but I refer only to their religion, not their persons; I feel that Jews are obnoxious.

He accounts for this partly on the grounds of his need to belong to a group and so tends to categorize others as either in his group or outside. He is, as one might imagine, a conservative Republican, who believes that government should be run by a select elite composed of people like himself. Yet he says he finds it hard to make up a credo of policy matters in which he has any confidence.

Yale enters into this situation in a curious way. For one thing, he reports that his years at Yale have been "the happiest and most fruitful of my life. I can now honestly feel that with work and luck my future looks promising indeed." Thus independence and the sense that his father no longer controls his destiny have given him an enormous release from the heavy burden of criticism which he had endured up to then. Also, he finds that he can identify with the wealthy and elite without necessarily identifying with his father; he has an alternative base for his snobbishness, one that is supportive and in some sense "his own." He has been able to achieve some perspective on his father, and reports with some sympathy his father's unhappy childhood and miserable experiences. Thus, in some sense, he has a social and psychological preparation for the extremely candid view of himself and others which he offers in his biography, and can find the strength to question his beliefs, even though he continues to hold them. He has, in short, solved the problem of alienation from a misanthropic father by adopting his own misanthropy, but tempering it with doubt, and converting some of his elitist thinking to a class and wealth basis, than a family base. His furlough from father gave him surcease from paternal correction and criticism; he could not *transcend* the paternal tradition, but he could *master* it.

SVENSON, A CLASSIC REBEL

I am not at all sure that Svenson loves his fellow more than Trumbull, and he certainly has no greater affection, in this stage of his life, for his father. Nevertheless, he is a "liberal" where Trumbull is a conservative, each rather more intense about their politics and rather more unsure underneath it all than those who came by their views following a different route. Of his father, Svenson says:

I have numerous memories of physical punishment administered by my father in an effort to maintain discipline. I reacted to this usually by a temporary retirement into phantasy, imagining various ways of getting revenge. My father is generally undemonstrative of emotion, and I received little affection from him. I can recall at the tender age of about five a feeling of repugnance when asked to "kiss Daddy." In fact, my family is particularly loveless.

His mother is well-educated; his father never finished high school. As a consequence, he says, "my mother constantly berated my father for making 'inane and stupid remarks.' " His father's politics is based on a view that the world is made up of "chiselers and phonies," and, says Svenson, "He is probably ripe for anti-democratic, fascist propaganda."

Svenson hardly mentions Yale or his friends here; he is absorbed with himself and his family. His views are what might be called reactively liberal. His father is isolationist; he is internationalist. His father is suspicious of the civil rights movements; Svenson is all for the integration of the schools. He says, "My father's 'stupidity' also contributes to my dislike of anti-intellectualism," but it is characteristic that he puts it negatively in this fashion; he does not seem, on the basis of other evidence available to me, to be on the way to becoming an intellectual himself.

Under these circumstances, it is not surprising that Svenson's views are thus marked by intensity *and* uncertainty. He complains of his own gullibility, a quality which he attributes to his mother's protective influence. He finds that he has trouble stating his views with conviction: he cannot decide exactly where he stands; in conversation he leaves his sentences unfinished. He hates arguments and believes that they settle nothing. In short, his self-confidence and capacity for assertion have been damaged or stunted and he is finding this process at Yale of self-discovery and the achievement of an independent view of the world a difficult one to carry through. Even the matter of party identification is difficult: "I do not identify specifically with any political party. The reasons for this lie in an attitude of indifference and a certain unsureness about what my beliefs really are. . . . I prefer to judge on the basis of ideas expounded by individuals or groups within the parties, but I do not make positive decisions and identifications, and remain essentially indecisive and uncommitted."

One can only hazard a guess why, under these circumstances, Trumbull stayed on the right and Svenson went radically but insecurely left. The greater division in Svenson's home gives one clue: perhaps he has an ally, his mother, in the war against Father. Perhaps she secretly welcomes the father-son quarrel in her own war against her husband.

Under these circumstances the furlough from father which four years at Yale offers to Svenson does not serve him so well as a similar leave does for Trumbull. The war goes on; he cannot find within him the materials for a cease-fire. His politics is still father-dominated, or rather, anti-father dominated. He can use the liberal materials available for him in college, he can find the arguments and doctrines that he needs for his verbal war, but they are not really "his." And, perhaps (the caution is needed) he is being secretly encouraged and coached by his "educated" ally, his mother.

MCGREGOR, THE APOSTATE'S RETURN TO CONSERVATISM

The alienation of a son from his father has many meanings. While Trumbull and Svenson seem cruelly scarred by their hostility to their fathers (Svenson more than Trumbull), others of our group escape through this period of antagonism relatively whole. For McGregor, whom we consider here, the estrangement does not carry with it the same freight of conscious or unconscious bitterness and hatred. In this case a variety of adjustive strategies have facilitated a return from apostasy and McGregor is now already "home" again.

McGregor certainly went through a crisis of bad relations with his father. At one point he says, "I can remember how relaxed and relieved I felt whenever my Dad went away on a business trip. I used to be so afraid and fearful of him that I would spill milk all over the table at dinner because I would be watching him instead of what I was doing." The situation got progressively worse, until his mother intervened to have him sent away to boarding school. In his terms this developed as follows:

> Although my Father is a rational man, if one did not conform to the pattern he set down, he would use any means possible to return one to this pattern. I was afraid of not knowing exactly what this pattern consisted of. He demanded perfection, and I could not live up to it. . . . In each instance Dad would claim that I was trying to flout his authority on purpose. This continued to the point where, at the age of fourteen, I began to do the very thing he accused me of. This just reinforced his feelings that I had been doing it all along. What had originally been his projected aggression as an interpretation of my actions, had become a reality. He accused me long enough until my every energy was involved in trying to make him mad at me. I kind of revelled in the punishments he gave me and this reinforced my belief that he was a wicked individual.

When he went away to boarding school, McGregor became a flaming liberal, militantly anti-business because his father was a businessman. But as he kept out of his father's way, the tension subsided; he started working for some businessmen in the summer and found them decent men, and he himself began to wonder how he was going to become a success in the world if he were so anti-business. Then, his father was promoted to vice-president in his company and as McGregor said, "This bothered me because it questioned and shook the foundation of my values." How could it be that such a man could be successful?

From the perspective of Yale (when he was a freshman) McGregor could see that in fact his father was a fair and decent man in his working relations with his business associates. But the son only goes part way; he says of his father: "His family is a different matter from his business. In this realm he 'owns us,' and thus can treat us as he pleases. The rules of the game are different in these two spheres. This discovery has helped to clear up many problems." With this settled, and his hostility diminished and his antipathy toward the father-associated business world weakened, McGregor says:

> I swung more and more away from the liberal idealistic political philosophy that I so hurriedly and blindly rushed into. I have come to slowly and carefully examine my beliefs. *The fact that I was able to identify with conservative values and still not with my Father marked an important turning point.* My family relations now seem to be strange ones. As I came out of my liberalistic shell, no longer did it have to be "me versus my Dad." I was able to recognize and accept him for what he is. This took quite a while and was a bitter pill to swallow. I think he, too, saw that he could no longer get me tied up in an argument. . . . Now if I will pay lip service to him for the sake of expediency, things go wonderfully well. (My italics. R. E. L.)

While McGregor feels guilty about this deceit he is well on the way to an integrated conservative position which reflects his values and accommodates himself to his family and associates.

The Peer Problem

A student's associates, much more than the faculty, are with him early and late, eating, drinking, and sleeping, in sports, dating, studying. They are the audience for most of his remarks and the commentators who daily grade and judge and evaluate his performance. Unlike the tutorial system, the classroom and seminar system requires collective learning; there is, therefore, a shared response and a search for the appropriate mode of response (not unlike the search for a common standard in reporting the illusion of movement of a point of light in a darkened room). As we observed above, colleges foster a mixture of conformism and heterogeneity; they create the conditions where social pressures are very strong. As we have seen, a sense of social isolation does not usually develop in college; if anything, quite the reverse, and while we may regard this with favor, it represents a symptom of the collectivizing quality of everything collegiate. But in detail, how does this work?

As noted above, judging from the entire group of cases the peer-group orientation is a function of the abatement of the father-orientation. I am sure that the possible patterns are multiple, but the starting point is a recognition of the fact that one cannot attend to, or hear, or see the men around you if you are preoccupied with father-dominated responses. One can of course "use" peers in the war against the father and give an appearance of peer-group orientation; but it is their usefulness as allies, all unknown to them, and not as friends or even as whole people, which marks this relationship. This point comes out in the following two cases, each of which reflects a variety of other themes.

KING, THE FEAR OF EXTREMISM

Unlike the three cases reported above, King seems to have been able relatively early to develop an adjustive strategy towards his parents and to have settled down to the problem of achieving the esteem of his friends and associates. Of his parents he says:

> Any rebelling that I ever did was more in the form of pouting than in hostility to the thing being done or achieved. As a result of this, I was able to benefit from their [parents'] pushing. In scouting I became an Eagle Scout and a member of an honorary organization at the camp I attended. In school I made good marks. I was able to win some money in the speech contests. . . . I have more of a feeling of guilt when I do not conform, than a tendency to rebel.

King's father, a self-made man, took an interest in his son and joined him in his scouting activities and watched and encouraged his progress at school; indeed, King feels that he was "oversteered" by his father. Yet, on the whole, he identifies with his "strong" father more than his oversolicitous mother, something he attributes to his fear of weakness stemming from early illness and isolation.

At high school, King grew out of early fears of "standing out" and, finding himself excluded from the popular ruling clique, he organized a "people's party," became a politician and ran for school office, being careful not to attack the ruling clique because "that would have made me stick out and classed with the 'odd-balls'." He lost the election but through some maneuvering became the editor-in-chief of the school paper, and went on to become Student Council President, a success he attributes to his habit of saying "hi" to everybody and identifying with the "plain folks."

His parents are Democrats; "on a liberal-conservative scale I believe," he says, "that I should rank well *within the extremes*, but definitely on the liberal end of the scale." (My italics, R.E.L.) It is therefore a surprise to find that he has joined the Conservative party in the Yale mock assembly known as the Political Union. He explains it this way:

> It is true that the prevailing undergraduate opinion at Yale is anti-Democrat, anti-New Deal, and really anti-Truman. . . . Since I have been at Yale I have done some things which might be considered in line with conformity to this new and different environment. In the Political Union, I am a member of the Conservative Party, for instance. It goes without saying that most of the other members of the party are not New Dealers. I feel, however, that *my decision to join this party was less an attempt to conform than an attempt to avoid the extremism* which I felt might be prevalent in the Liberal party. . . . I have a fear of extremism.

From his further remarks it seems clear that it is not his fear of extremism or his putting up a Conservative front that bothers him, but rather his failure to change parties in line with the prevailing norms both of Yale and his home community (though not, as observed above, of his family). He explains this apologetically on the grounds that it is not necessary to be popular or have power at Yale because it is only a transient residence, and he affirms that later he will pick up these threads again.

COLEMAN, THE POLITICIAN AS LIBERAL

Coleman's father was away a great deal when he was a child, but he has pleasant memories of him and speaks of him as a gentle man. Yet he feels that his father somehow failed to support him in the major battles of his young life, his quarrels with his mother. He is ambivalent about her, but feels that from his relationship with her he both learned the techniques of dominance and developed a need to dominate and achieve. At an early age he learned, moreover, that he was, as he says "a natural leader," and he exploited his talents to the full in high school. Furthermore, at the same time that he is a student at Yale, he is running for precinct leader in his native Arkansas, thus he is political to the hilt, with some sense of unknown mission and destiny alive inside him.

He refuses to accept either of the terms "liberal" or "conservative," but says that his friends managing his campaign back home speak of him as a "moderate liberal." He is for desegregation of the races, partly, he says, because he realizes if he is to become a national political figure he must have this record. On welfare-state issues, his father is a mixed liberal-conservative and Coleman is, too, having had his conservatism modified by his freshman adviser at Yale. On labor he tends to be conservative: "I never had reason to identify with the working class and therefore could never see their struggle for power in terms of my own."

These conflicting tendencies, combined with very strong political interests and ambitions, present Coleman with a problem at Yale.

> At high school I had the position and recognition that I needed. But at Yale most people are in higher economic levels than I. I cannot easily be at the top of my class and my athletic prowess did not meet the competition. I have been reasonably successful in what little campus politics there are here . . . but these are insufficient to give me any real sense of position. I have thus tended to seek strength in "rebelling against the system." I am a liberal in a hotbed of conservatism. I paint a picture of myself as the "angry young man." The more conservative the people around me are, the more liberal I become. I have no doubt that much of my liberalism is due to the fact that I cannot realize the ideals of "shoeism" [i.e., the right thing in the right set] as I see them and thus to have stature must deny these goals.

And, of course, with his talents, he can manage this without losing status or becoming that most dread thing, "an odd-ball."

The Self Problem

We now move on to the third party in this triangle, the self. Much has been made these days of the crisis of identity; and it is thought somehow to center in adolescence, the time when youth is marginal both to its own childhood and to its own adulthood. The themes running throughout these biographies suggest the nature of part of the problem: How to give the appearance of strength when one knows oneself to be weak? How to select a platform for life's drama where one can "show them" (whoever they may be) that one merits that attention and respect too long withheld? How to find an inner voice that is convincing to the self, confident, resolute, able to be heard without shouting?

Our data reveal one thing: the exaggerated uncertainties of an uncertain age are found among those who have not resolved by acceptance or rebellion their warfare with their parents, especially their fathers. It is as though parental polarization of any kind gives structure and continuity and direction to political choice, and probably other choices as well, regardless of whether it is the negative or the positive pole that the young man has selected. Similarly, it is true that the overt problems of identity are greatest when the problem of association with peers is still unsettled and remains as cause and symptom and result of an unresolved identity. But unlike the situation with the parents, there must be some group with whom the lad is at home, to which he responds positively. He must have friends. Thus, in the following three cases we find the unresolved material of the earlier situations. These men are either uncertain in their politics, or certain *and* changeable.

MARTIN, THE SELF AS UNIVERSE

> Right now I actually think I feel no love for my father and that I would oppose nearly everything associated with him. To me his only virtues are his ability to work for his goals and his ability to fool everyone into thinking he is a good fellow.

This frame of mind reflects a history of multilateral acrimony in the home. Martin's parents were divorced after a long period of fighting, about which he is bitter. He resents the insecurities of his childhood, worries intensely about himself, and feels that the major problems of his life are bound up in finding some balance between being an independent individual and finding some secure niche in society. Neither parent seems attractive to him, but as indicated in the above quotations he particularly dislikes his father, with whom he is currently embroiled over college bills.

Martin's politics are most confused. His father is a Democrat and so is he, a matter which gives him no satisfaction. He cannot easily become a Republican because of certain attitudes he has toward the elites of this world, hence he moves farther to the left, speaks of himself as "radical" and adopts an uncompromising posture of equalitarianism, based, as he says, on his deep and abiding insecurities and "consequent" (?) sympathy with the insecure everywhere.

Yale does something for him, but only when he is away from her grey stone walls, for then he finds his self-esteem enhanced in his home circles by being known as a "Yale man." Within the walls it is different. His Eastern roommates make him feel insecure. "They looked upon my friends as clods and hicks," he said (did he mean himself?), "and I retaliated by regarding them as playboys and preppies. Even the bull sessions we had degenerated into an antagonistic comparison of beliefs." He felt that he was being grilled and that his opponents won their points by deceptive means. "This experience," he said, "acted quite decisively to discourage any feelings of conformity that I possessed." Being unable to identify with any group, even his circle of "clods" and "hicks," he returns to his studies and seeks distinction in that realm, but he is too preoccupied with himself to succeed there either. He concludes his account as follows:

> I must realize that . . . I must constantly be re-evaluating my own opinions. I must also continually recognize that my values are different in periods of feeling depression and insecurity than they are in periods of elation and security. I can now recognize these influences momentarily but my compensation must be made a continuous affair if my opinions are to be as valid as possible. Also, I must continue to evaluate my personality and the influences acting upon it to determine when additional compensation must be made.

One casts a figurative arm around this rounded shoulder and wishes him somewhere a little peace.

COHEN, BETWEEN TWO WORLDS

Here is an attractive, sensitive, responsible young man, who starts out his account with the question "What right has a Jew to be a Republican?" His father worked his way up from illiterate beginnings to some wealth in a family business. His mother comes from a somewhat better-educated family and as Cohen says, "She likes neither the way her husband dresses nor the way he talks and eats and she does not hesitate to criticize him. My sister and I regard our father as a slob." Cohen had a lonely childhood. "I recall with some bitterness," he says, "that my father preferred to sleep or eat rather than accompany me to a movie, go to school on parents' night, or even tell me some of the facts of life." He identifies with an uncle, the head of the family firm, who, as he idealizes him, has more culture, charm, warmth, poise—in fact, everything. His uncle is a Republican.

Unlike some others, Cohen brings the question of his Judaism to the surface immediately. He says he becomes very nervous when he is introduced to non-Jews since "his name is 'so Jewish'." He worries intensely about his "disgust and resentment" over the Eastern European nonassimilated Jews he has seen in New York. He likes to associate with non-Jews, but is terribly concerned lest it be true, as he is taught at home: "Scratch a Gentile and you'll find an anti-Semite." With this background and torn by this religious problem, he reports that at Yale:

> I feel very insecure; it does not seem to me that I belong anywhere or that I am in any particular group of friends. I feel alone. I find myself criticizing my friends and myself for small and insignificant things.

He has, he says, "a great obsession to be successful in whatever I do, but I am somewhat pessimistic about the future." Like Martin, then, he is absorbed with a search for identity and, especially, an identity which can give him the illusion of belonging to the right crowd, being successful, overcoming these doubts about himself. But he has a conscience about repudiating the others, too, and seeks some middle road. Thus he is not a Zionist (for fear of being called "traitor"), but rather a pro-Zionist. For Cohen, coming as he does from a relatively small town, this being among the successful means being a Republican, just as at Yale it means the same thing. But at Yale there is; for Cohen, although apparently not for many others, a competing attraction on the other side of the political fence: the faculty. He says "Most of my instructors at Yale seem to be Democrats. These are successful, distinguished, and important men and I find myself identifying with some of them." And later in his summary, after noting the reasons why he is a Republican, he says "I could change my party affiliation without too much difficulty; the more I come in contact with older men and women whom I respect and admire and who are Democrats, the greater the chance that I will also become a Democrat." For Cohen, the search for identity, with its political implications, is just beginning, and just as his uncle was a father-substitute, perhaps some member of the faculty at Yale will be an uncle-substitute or provide an alternative model.

DEMMING, A SWITCH IN TIME

Our last case, Demming, comes from a lower-middle-class family with strong Republican conservative views and an emphasis upon education and rising in the world. Today, however, Demming says he has a distrust of business, feels that labor has not achieved the influence it deserves, and feels that "capitalism is not a good system unless the government exerts a good deal of control and coordination." He is now the only Democrat in his family.

Some groundwork was laid in a former factory job where he found the working conditions deplorable and the respect accorded the workers almost nil. But this is ideologically useful to him only later. At Yale, he says, he became "more aware of the existence of social and economic in-groups and out-groups," something encouraged by the fact that he was a scholarship student and by this, he says, cut off from much of the normal social life of the university. He came into conflict with the "in-group" over the system of apprenticeship and trial at the Yale broadcasting station, a high-prestige campus organization. The trial period was so time-consuming that students with scholarship jobs couldn't afford to compete. Although most students agreed with him (he says), the radio station so commanded the means of influence that he was not able to make any headway. At a meeting with certain elite members of the *News* and radio station he received a number of psychic wounds and "a great change occurred":

> I became hostile to everything "shoe" ["in" or "U" or "O.K."] and quite ex-
> pressive about my sentiments. This naturally provoked reactions which merely
> made me all the more adamant in my feeling. I began to think more about con-
> formity at Yale . . . and I began to conform to nonconformity.

He attempted to become "unshoe" in everything, including dress, very independent of Yale, hostile to the authorities, and a leader of somewhat-alienated groups. All of this, moreover, was fed by personal feelings of insecurity, a sense that he was not and could not be a success in conventional terms, and an abiding loneliness.

> In addition to this feeling of loneliness, I was always very fat and this contributed
> more than anything else to my feelings of inferiority. In order to be accepted
> one may laugh at derisive remarks by the in-group but attempt to punish such
> remarks from a weaker group. In addition, I might associate with smaller or
> less-popular boys in order to vent my desires to dominate and be a tough leader.

He brought these feelings of inferiority to bear on political matters for the first time at Yale. He says:

> In childhood I did not associate economic standing with any feelings of in-
> feriority, but at Yale this added to a certain feeling of hostility towards society
> because of my failure to identify successfully. The Democratic party always
> represented to me the party of change and of the poorer classes. . . . The Re-
> publican party seemed to embody the group in which I wanted to be accepted
> and couldn't, and so I accepted the Democrats as the opposite.

Moreover, he discovered that his new-found liberalism,

> so opposed to the extreme conservatism of my parents, acted as a good medium
> both to express hostility and to show that I have a mind of my own. This may

explain why my ideology is often based on the New Deal and Franklin Roosevelt, because it is in these fields that my parents show their greatest disgust for the Democrats.

Finally, there is, for almost the only time in the biographical material, a reference to the content of the courses.

At Yale I found that the education placed more emphasis on methods of discovering the truth and methods of investigation of problems, rather than on one's final opinion. In this way the education at Yale was more liberal [sic]. . . . Yale provided an intellectual pattern which could justify my ideas. Without exposure to this other way of thinking, the other factors could not have, by themselves, caused the changes in my political thought.

Thus the undergraduate life at Yale made a liberal-Democrat out of Demming, while his professors gave him material he could use in this new political role. But the plot is not nearly so much a story of political choice as a story of social friction and the search for an ideology that would satisfy his war against all those others.

Political Change in a Maelstrom

Briefly let us now glance back at the earlier reports on the effects of college education on various dimensions of political life.

1. On balance it was not clear exactly what kinds of political information were learned in college; in some cases it seemed none. But consider what needs our eight men have and how political information can be serviceable to them. They need information in their arguments with their peers and fathers; they need it to fill in and flesh out their shifting ideologies. No doubt that they are learning what they can use, though for many this is limited, and for all of them it has little to do with civic knowledge. It will be polemical and for special purposes.

2. Their increases in liberalism and their decreases in ethnocentrism are in part (how large I do not know) products not of any increased love of their fellow men but of their hostilities toward certain fellow men, especially their fathers, who are conservative and prejudiced. Unlike Newcomb's sample, these liberals are very likely to be recidivists in later life, for their reactions to father-domination and peer elites seem a poor base for a life-long philosophy. College people *are* more liberal than others matched for income, but their liberalism and their tolerance for heterodoxy wanes as they age. Perhaps in part this basis in interpersonal hostility is the reason; it didn't have much to do with the issues anyway.

3. The problem of conformism and extremism, dealing respectively with modality in a group and modality in a range of issues, is so complex it defies easy conceptualization. Several studies show that nonconformity to parents' views is encouraged if the parents are nonconformists to *their own* social traditions. Thus the nonconformist to parental modes becomes in his social group a conformist.

These eight boys certainly worry about it, for it is a feature of the very real problem: "Am I strong enough to stand alone?" versus "Am I, in some sense, odd, extreme, or as one put it, 'unlovable'?" In any event, looking over these cases, one gets almost no sense that these young men were exploring issues and taking stands on which their reading convinced them on a point where others, who had read different things, disagreed. On the contrary, they were exploring social relationships in which they could employ political issues to achieve the payoffs associated with being different, hostile, or agreeable. The choice in such cases seems hardly to fall under the rubric of "conformity" or "independence" from any point of view.

Political choice "in the midst of life's struggles" is inevitably affected by the nature of these struggles. Taking them into account seems essential to understanding how youth blends the public and the private and draws on insitutions and individuals in developing a political orientation.

Notes

1. See Hazel Gaudet Erskine, "The Polls: The Informed Public," *Public Opinion Quarterly*, XXVI (1962), pp. 668–677.

2. C. G. McClintock and H. A. Turner, "The Impact of College upon Political Knowledge, Participation, and Values," *Human Relations*, XV (1962), pp. 163–176; see also comment in Robert E. Lane and David O. Sears, *Public Opinion* (New York: Prentice-Hall, 1964).

3. Robert E. Lane, *Political Ideology: Why the American Common Man Believes What He Does* (New York: Free Press, 1962), pp. 321–345.

4. See Gordon W. Allport, "The Composition of Political Attitudes," *American Journal of Sociology*, XXXV (1929–30), pp. 220–238; W. A. Kerr, "Correlates of Politico-Economic Liberalism-Conservatism," *Journal of Social Psychology*, XX (1944), pp. 61–77; Gardner Murphy and Rensis Likert, *Public Opinion and the Individual* (New York: Harper, 1938).

5. Rose K. Goldsen, Morris Rosenberg, Robin M. Williams, Jr., and Edward Suchman, *What College Students Think* (New York: Van Nostrand, 1960), p. 111.

6. *Ibid.*, pp. 123, 220.

7. Harold Webster, Mervin Freedman, and Paul Heist, "Personality Changes in College Students," in Nevitt Sanford (ed.), *The American College* (New York: Wiley, 1962), p. 827. I wish to express my gratitude to these authors for their excellent guide to the relevant literature.

8. Herbert Hyman, *Political Socialization* (New York: Free Press, 1959), p. 46.

9. Matilda White Riley, John W. Riley, Jr., and Mary E. Moore, "Adolescent Values and the Riesman Typology: An Empirical Analysis," in Seymour Martin Lipset and Leo Lowenthal (eds.), *Culture and Social Character* (New York: Free Press, 1961), pp. 370–386.

10. Rose Goldsen et al., p. 100.

11. Reported in H. Webster et al., p. 827.

12. Eleanor E. Maccoby, Richard E. Matthews, and Anton S. Morton, "Youth and Political Change," *Public Opinion Quarterly*, XVIII (1954), pp. 23–39.

13. *The Development of Attitude Scales in Practical Politics* (Delaware, Ohio: The Evaluation Service, Ohio Wesleyan University, 1955), pp. 21–26 (mimeographed).

14. Albert Somit, Joseph Tanenhaus, Walter H. Wilke, and Rita W. Cooley, "The Effect of the Introductory Political Science Course on Student Attitudes Toward Personal Political Participation," *American Political Science Review*, LII (1958), pp. 1129–1132.

15. Philip E. Jacob, *Changing Values in College* (New York: Harper, 1957), pp. 1–3.

16. Bessie R. Burgemeister "The Permanence of Interests of College Women Students," *Arch. Psychology*, XXXVI (1940), pp. 1–59, as reported in Webster et al., p. 823.

17. T. W. Adorno *et al.*, *The Authoritarian Personality* (New York: Harper, 1950), pp. 220–279.

18. Angus Campbell, Philip E. Converse, Warren E. Miller, and Donald E. Stokes, *The American Voter* (New York: Wiley, 1960), pp. 514–515.

19. Nevitt Sanford, "The Approach of the Authoritarian Personality," in J. L. McCary (ed.), *Psychology of Personality* (New York: Grove, 1956), pp. 282–315.

20. D. R. Brown and Denise Brystryn, "College Environment, Personality, and Social Ideology of Three Ethnic Groups," *Journal of Social Psychology*, XLIV (1956), pp. 279–288.

21. Gordon Allport, P. E. Vernon, and Gardner Lindsey, *Study of Values*, rev. ed. (Boston: Houghton-Mifflin, 1951); P. E. Jacob, *op. cit.*

22. W. T. Plant, "Changes in Ethnocentrism Associated with a Two-year College Experience," *Journal of Genetic Psychology*, XCII (1958), pp. 189–197.

23. Samuel A. Stouffer, *Communism, Conformity, and Civil Liberties* (Garden City: Doubleday, 1955).

24. P. E. Jacob, *Changing Values in College.*

25. Harold Webster, "Changing Attitudes During College," *Journal of Educational Psychology*, XLIX (1958), pp. 109–117.

26. Kenneth Keniston, "Inburn, An American Ishmael," in Robert W. White (ed.), *The Study of Lives* (New York: Atherton, 1963), p. 43.

27. Kenneth Keniston, "Alienation and the Decline of Utopia," *American Scholar*, XXIX (1960), pp. 1–40.

28. Webster, et al., p. 830.

29. *Ibid., loc. cit.*

30. E. C. Hunter, "Changes in General Attitudes of Woman Students During Four Years in College," *Journal of Social Psychology*, XVI (1942), pp. 243–257.

31. Theodore Newcomb, *Personality and Social Change* (New York: Dryden, 1943).

32. Reported in Webster, et al., p. 818.

33. See footnote 4 above for references to W. A. Kerr, G. W. Allport, and Murphy and Likert.

34. Here the Goldsen et al. study reinforces and refines the earlier findings of Kerr and Murphy and Likert.

35. W. A. Kerr, pp. 76–77; on the engineers see Webster et al., p. 827.

36. Reported in Webster et al., p. 818.

37. Mervin Freedman, "The Passing Through College," *Journal of Social Issues*, XII (1956), p. 14.

38. F. M. Jervis and R. G. Congdon, "Student and Faculty Perceptions of Educational Values," *American Psychologist*, XIII (1958), pp. 464–466; cited in Webster, et al., p. 836.

39. Walter L. Wallace, "Institutional and Life-Cycle Socialization of College Freshmen," *American Journal of Sociology*, LXX (1964), pp. 303–318.

40. Seymour Martin Lipset, "Opinion Formation in a Crisis Situation," *Public Opinion Quarterly*, XVII (1953), pp. 20–46.

41. Rose K. Goldsen, et al., pp. 119–124.

42. Walter L. Wallace, *loc. cit.*

43. Where mothers and fathers disagree on party affiliation, children are likely to agree with the mother. This implies that women strong enough to differ with their husbands (an unusual event) are strong enough or care enough about politics to determine their children's politics. See M. Kent Jennings and Kenneth P. Langton, "Mothers versus Fathers; The Formation of Political Orientations Among Young Americans," *Journal of Politics*, XXXI (1969), pp. 329–358.

Chapter *7*
Ideological Self-Analysis as Political Education

Political learning is heavily influenced by the way a student perceives ideas and events to be useful in his quarrels with his family and friends, his attempts to impress others with his sound views (or his independent views, or his moral views), and his ongoing search for ideas congenial to the evolving personality he is coming to know.[1] Under these circumstances, I believe, one might well improve political learning, and socialization more generally, by addressing oneself directly to this aspect of the problem. One might ask students (and oneself) to answer the questions: "Of what use to me are my political ideas?" and, given this focus, "How did I come to take on these particular ideas?" This is what I have done for fifteen years in political science classes. That experience forms the basis of this discussion.[2]

In almost all teaching and learning situations the role of the "knower," in contrast to the subject matter to be known, is left out of account. It is frequently observed that learning situations involve both the text or speech which serves as stimulus and the mind of the learner with its own special capacities for selectivity, inattention, distortion, and imaginative reconstruction. As this focus on subject matter alone is characteristic of all subjects and classrooms, it takes a special effort to direct attention back to the student's own mind in teaching (and learning) about the formation of a political ideology. The "oddness" of this kind of learning serves as a barrier to its introduction into the educational process.

Then, too, there is the student's own resistance to self-knowledge. This resistance is not so much the product of any particular sense of what is appropriate to political learning or based on the misleading epistemologies of the other academic disciplines as it is the product of two other things: ignorance of the self and fear of the self. Elsewhere I have noted that Americans without

Notes to this chapter will be found on page 139

much education tend to treat themselves in their life histories in the third person. They objectify themselves, and it is as though their feelings and emotions about their own lives were irrelevant.[3] This is true to a much lesser degree among the very able college and graduate students with whom I have dealt, but there is a very considerable "self-ignorance" to be overcome and remedied. Equally important, although again the extent should not be over-emphasized, is the resistance to self-exploration that comes from fear or suspicion of what one might find. Everyone has repressed material, secrets from himself; some are afraid to explore themselves lest these be uncovered. But, as we shall see, this reluctance is rare; the proportion of students who welcome an opportunity for ideological self-analysis and rejoice in it after-wards, is very large.

There is another impediment to political learning which the focus on self-knowledge may not overcome but rather, indeed, enlarge. Once you feed a student a little psychology, a few categories about human personality, he starts his pigeonholing: "This is a that," "I am a this." The naming of symptoms, types, illnesses, scale positions often satisfies students that they somehow understand processes and causes, just as it did the psychiatric profession before Freud. One has to get them out of this rut somehow. The only way I know is to encourage them to let the unconscious do its work and to test the "truth" by the feel of truth. While this approach is retrograde in the philosophy of science, it is consistent with its real meaning, namely, that the nature of the investigation determines the appropriate instrumentation. Here the nature of the investigation is such that the instrument is the psyche and the object is the self; the two must be both detached and related in a delicate process of self-observation and evaluation.

The Process of Self-Analysis

I have experimented with three different kinds of ideological self-analysis. The first is the autobiographical essay answering the questions mentioned above: "Of what use to me is my liberalism (conservatism)?" and "How did I come to be a liberal (conservative)?" The second form of self-analysis answers the same questions but involves oral, "therapy-type" interviews, so that there is more probing and probably more revelation of the self. I have found that this works best after students have written autobiographies and that these in turn are better if they are mulled over and thought about for a period of some weeks or even months before they are committed to paper. The third method follows the "group therapy" model. Two to five students who trust each other write the essays as before, exchange them (if they want to), and come together for the exploration of common themes that disturb the group members. The following themes and "problems" recur in the group sessions: attitudes toward and meaning of "underdogs," authority, conformity, commitment, and involvement. Problems of alienation (acceptance or rejection of common cultural norms), the uses of hostility and conflict, and postures towards "bourgeois morality" are also resonant with current ideological dilemmas.

In all of these analyses, attitudes towards parents, peers, and self will form a substantial part of the analytical material. Here we will focus on the written essay that comprises a crucial element in all three variants of ideological self-analysis.

The method is instructive in several ways. In the first place, the ordinary process of setting forth one's own belief system, without reference to its functions or sources, helps to clarify the mind on a difficult and important area of thought. What one took for granted has to be examined, what was only partly conscious has to be made conscious, what was self-contradictory has to be made consistent; assumptions must be questioned and inferences reviewed. None of this is easy and people do not do it unless an occasion for this self-examination is created for them. Second, the attempt to answer a functional question such as "Of what use to me are my ideas?" probes the way ideas serve the purposes a man seeks to achieve in his life and reveals important truths about the self-analyst. Furthermore, such a question inquires into a man's tendencies to conform or to provoke or to rebel, his dependency on others, his desire to put a moral face on things, his avoidance of competition, his apathy and withdrawal, the paralysis of his decision-making capacities. From this phase of the analysis, third, the self-analyst learns something about his own personality and life strategies, things which interest him quite apart from his political life. One should not claim too much for this general self-revelation. After all the subject is not guided through therapy; the instructor is not competent to heal and must avoid giving this impression. Nevertheless, the evidence we shall present does suggest that self-knowledge and the beginnings of "an examined life" may commence here; a process and habit of mind, however small, may be given impetus. And fourth, in learning about the self the self-analyst learns about others and about general processes of opinion formation. This tendency to generalize must be limited and guided; other people are different. But if one finds that ideas are not just "true" but also functional, that personality and belief are really linked, that lifetime quarrels are served by political ideas as are lifetime purposes and goals, then the path is cleared to a sensitive inquiry into what motivates others to believe what they do. A way of thinking and a new branch of meta-knowledge is opened up.

As ideological self-analysis has a certain resemblance to other forms of self-analysis, even to psychotherapy, one should point out some important distinctions. In psychotherapy, the patient is driven to self-revelation because of the pain of his illness. If it works, the pain involved in searching for the sources of a person's difficulties is invited because of the greater pain of the illness, the depression, the phobias and fears, the inability to achieve life goals or to get along with others. In ideological self-analysis these motives are present in a much attenuated form, for the student may not be at all unhappy with his political belief system—at least not until he examines it. He is not ill; he may not even come to the task of his own volition (although I have always allowed students the option of doing something else—a courtesy that the classroom situation requires). The motives for self-analysis lie elsewhere. They are curiosity (a strong force), narcissism (which makes the self an endlessly interesting topic), perhaps some exhibitionism, and for some a malaise or uneasiness regarding special problems they would like to clarify and solve if possible. Among these problems, which are connected with their social beliefs, are their unwanted hostilities towards others, their own apathy and tendencies towards withdrawal, their tensions when confronted by authority, and their conformist tendencies. Only in this last set of motives do we tap the main motives for therapy connected with illness.

Another problem concerns not the motive for analysis but the subject matter. It is an almost universal experience, even among the best educated, for persons starting to state their own beliefs to find the cupboard almost bare. What they had supposed was a well-stocked mind, perhaps even full of Locke, Kant, Marx, Mill, turns out to be an unsystematic collection of fairly conventional statements and beliefs, apothegms, clichés familiar to a certain group, undigested borrowings from family axioms and sayings, a note from yesterday's columnist, a roomate's phobic reactions, some beloved "quirk" that the individual takes to be his own contribution, a defensive reaction for not living up to the normative standards of one's time and place, an attack on threatening ideas or people, and so forth. The "system" is provided by the underlying themes of the personality, not the interlocking logic of the ideas. The individual is disappointed with himself. He cries, "But I have no ideology." His course in the history of political thought taught him something of the thoughts of others and gave him the materials out of which he might frame a superior political philosophy of his own, but he did not take that last step.

The Problem of Authenticity

One cannot expect students to make the best use of the opportunity to analyze their own belief systems without preparation. It is usually foreign to whatever else they may have done in school. But the preparation presents a major problem; students may be cued by their materials to respond in ways aimed to please the instructor. If one assigns psychological interpretation of politics (for example, M. B. Smith, J. Bruner, and R. White, *Opinions and Personality*; H. D. Lasswell, *Psychopathology and Politics*; T. W. Adorno and associates, *The Authoritarian Personality*) one may be giving them explicit cues as to what they should find. Similarly, if one were to assign material on the influence of great books in helping to form ideas, one would find students writing accounts of how great books influenced their own beliefs. Consequently, is it not the case that if one presents them with material on the influence of their own personalities and private motives on their beliefs one may expect them to discover, sure enough, that they are conservative because of their "other-directed nature" in a conservative milieu, they are radical because their father is conservative and they need to rebel against him, their ethnocentrism is a product of their insecurities?

I have puzzled a great deal about this criticism, which is always raised when I speak about ideological self-analysis, and there is no easy answer. Such answer as there is may be developed as follows. In the first place, all of the forces of academia have combined to teach the individual that what he believes and knows is simply a product of what he has read and been told. He does not want for instruction along these lines. This is reinforced by the emphasis on rationality, on what is in books rather than in the self, on cognitive processes in education.

In the second place, the accounts ring true. (On only one occasion did I "smell a rat." I queried the student further and realized he had made it up. One should watch for this, but in my experience it is exceedingly uncommon.) What makes the accounts persuasive is the unhackneyed detail of experience, the variety of interpretations among the student papers (yet all had done the same reading), the relative scarcity of pat psychological answers. The evidence from personal probing is often persuasive. This is especially true where the bookish inference, if challenged, would be exposed if there were not supporting experiences and incidents that come to mind under examination. The accounts of how a student went about observing himself and keeping notes over some period of time, revising his thoughts about himself under the impetus of new observations, carries conviction. But there is nothing so convincing as to read (or listen to) the accounts themselves and what they say about the experience.

This self-reported value of the experience, as a third indication of the authenticity of the student reports and hence of the method, is persuasive to those who are already open to persuasion, but probably stops there. I will quote, for example, the statement of one of the undergraduate analysts. DeVita, as he comes upon a "finding" about himself that surprises and pleases him. A lower middle class boy on scholarship at elite Adams College, DeVita felt that he was a young man without a "home," an identity, or identifiable social class, and hence very much "on his own." He says:

I had always imagined myself to be a very independent type and had therefore believed that I could always turn to myself for reassurance in time of stress. However, while tracing through moments during which I had been forced to turn to myself, I found that always these were times which were accompanied by frustration and depression. They were usually times which followed an occurrence in which I was rebuffed by someone upon whom I had depended. My moments alone were usually soul-searching sessions where I tried to figure out what I had done to bring about disagreement. I turned on myself the aggression which I had refrained from turning on the other person, for I felt that an open show of hostility on my part would mean the withdrawal of affection on the part of the other.

Later, DeVita draws a more general lesson from this insight, a lesson he applies to his understanding of some of the roots of his anti-ethnocentric tolerance, which he now believes is a bid to propitiate others. Here he continues with his discovery of his dependency needs:

I know now that my self-image of independence was only a defense used to cover up a thwarted drive for dependence upon others. Once this striving for affection was uncovered, a very neat history of events verified the finding. I always had a feeling, which up to now I couldn't understand, that I am never really doing things for myself. I am always working to please someone else.

And he believes government should also strive to please, at least in foreign policy, tracing out these beliefs in some detail. Then at the end he summarizes his attitude towards the ideological self-analysis.

In conclusion I wish to apologize for the more or less disjointed form of this paper. [Of course, I regard "disjointedness" as further evidence of authenticity; the neat explanations are unlikely to follow the disjointed character of life and thought. R. E. L.] Not only did I fight with contradictory ideas while I planned the work, but even during the writing I was never quite sure where an idea would lead me. Needless to say the work has been extremely rewarding. I am indeed glad that I grasped the opportunity to do a work of this type.[4]

Hammer, a very different kind of young man, handed in a first installment of about forty typewritten pages, then a week later submitted a postscript of twenty-five handwritten pages trying to straighten out some of the dangling problems that disturb him. Hammer is about six feet four inches tall, with a build to match. Formerly a football player in another college, he transferred to Adams because he wanted a better education, but he seems uncertain about what to do with it, where to go with it, how to employ his skills and life. Silent in class, he surprises me with the quality of his reflection, the literary power, and the depth of analysis revealed in his autobiography. He writes one of the most beautiful and vulgar of all the self-analyses. If the reader will bear with a rather long quotation and tolerate the unvarnished vulgarity, he may find the frame of mind of this analyst informative. Hammer starts this way:

I very much want to steer away from the sham of intellectualizing that is the Adams [college] trademark. If this is going to be of any value, I think it has got to be honest. I am going to try to imagine that I'm bullshitting with one of my excellent and incomparable friends from [Southwest college], like we used to do to such profit and delight over a couple of six-packs of beer, and let it seem that someone took down my monologue from behind a curtain without my knowing it. Indulge me in the use of language and expression that I would in fact use in baring my soul to old Bill and Tim. If it seems unbearably crude, that's just the way I am, I suppose. . . . That is the way I would talk so that we could *really* get down to the core of whole business.

Then Hammer faces the problem of what he believes and what good it is to him. He starts with a theme common to many analyses: the cupboard is surprisingly empty—or so it appears at first.

Trying to write this paper has proven to be a real bitch. I found that I don't really have any definite opinions, any logically constructed philosophy of life, not one of the way that society should be constructed or administered. Moreover, in searching out these ambiguities of mind, I've had to mull over some things in the past that are embalmed in my memory in bitterness and humiliation. It is pretty painful sometimes to think about what a colossal botch I've made of things.

In the paragraph that follows, and throughout the work, Hammer explores his humiliation and self-deprecation. One clue to the basis of this low self-evaluation occurs in the last sentence:

But at the same time, I was very excited by the proposition of writing this paper. . . . I have had a lot of bitter, angry and disappointed feelings that I have wanted to pour out for as long as I have been screwing around with this college business. . . . It seems to me that it would be good to dump the whole putrid business out, mull over it and see if there is any clue for me as to where to go from here. Nowhere but up, that seems certain. My whole achievement in twenty-two and a half years seems to have been to become a well-rounded, but nevertheless undeniable, bum. It's such a shame that all of this was wasted on such a turd as I sometimes think I am. My father could have done so much with the same opportunities, if fate had just seen fit to bestow them on him rather than me.

Here the reader must pause to consider whether he believes that Hammer's reference to his father is the product of having *read* that one's relationship to his father is important in developing personality and ideology or whether, given the tone and content of these few paragraphs, he does not believe Hammer refers to his own untutored feelings about a very real man, a father who is a skilled but officially uneducated telephone lineman.

A week after handing this in, Hammer returns with his postscript:

I can't seem to leave this thing alone. The damned thing is always gnawing away at the back of my mind. . . . I've pointed out some of the wholly negative things that run through my cloddish mind. Let me say some things about what I think in those moments when I tense up and start to shudder in frustration and bitterness, and then get hopeful and begin to think about where I might want to try to start again.

My dearest "political" romantic notion is that of the West. . . .

Then Hammer develops a kind of Utopian idyll of a life lived close to nature, isolated, away from the troublesome metropolitan problems and life styles, clean, fresh, beautiful. He was uncomfortable talking to me about his analysis; he wanted not to see me after he had handed it in. But he came for advice: Should he join the Marine Corps or the Peace Corps? He chose the latter, where he performed supremely well.

Hammer was least influenced by the reading, but his essay shows that he understood it. Others have been more influenced by it, but none, I think, allowed their analyses to be determined by it. The problem is less that these men have been given clues as to what to look for than that they have been inadequately prepared by too small a range of reading, too brief an exposure to the rich variety of interpretation of the human mind and personality.

Now I wish to turn to the analysis of a single abbreviated case. The purpose of this analysis is first to give body and example to the preceding discussion and second to illustrate how the case may be analysed so as to extract meaning for the student of ideology and give help to the self-analyst himself.

Novak: One Road to Reaction

The following case can illustrate only a few features of the method, for the cases are highly individualized, very different from each other in style and content. I will present an abbreviated version of the case (unchanged except for omission), commenting on certain features in the form of running footnotes at the bottom of the page. These footnotes are, of course, only suggestive; the subject could very likely set me straight on a number of points. As in a therapy situation the subject's response to an interpretation is an important clue to its validity.

Personal Background: Novak is a small, nervous young man from the Middle West, the son of a former professor of law in a state university. He was born in the early thirties. As an only child he was comparatively isolated from his own age group. The greatest influences on his early development seem to have been his anxious submission to his father and his sense of inferiority.

Political Position: Novak calls himself a "pseudo-conservative." In 1952 he was a supporter of Robert Taft for the Presidency, but he later came to have a great respect for President Eisenhower as a strong figure. He respected Joseph McCarthy for his strength and sincerity rather than for his virtue. He advocates immediate confrontation with Russia, and he believes that capitalism is the only proper form of contemporary economy, for it allows freedom for "conspicuous consumption" according to individual ability without subordination to a hierarchical system (communism).

What follows in slightly abridged form is Novak's ideological self-analysis in his own words. (I have numbered the paragraphs in Novak's text for easier reference to the notes.)

BACKGROUND

1. My father has always seemed a distant force in my life.[1] He early represented strength, authority, and its concomitant punishment. His punishments were severe and unpredictable. His affection always has been balanced by a sharp temper. In early and later stages his strength and authoritarian characteristics have not been counterbalanced by provision for the successful solution of problems created for me in my own age group.

2. His college yearbooks made clear to me that my father had been very successful in his extracurricular activities while in college. He is a vaguely religious and highly moral person. He has dominated the family and made its decisions. He is very attentive to his children, broken by periods when he is suffering headaches. He has been very consistent in his work.

3. My father always had abhorred intensity, whether it be in the intellectual or business world.[2] A high-strung person himself, he enjoys a casual atmosphere where he may relax. This contrasts to the intensity which unconsciously surrounds him when he is working. He always had admired scholastic distinction and urged such for me. He considered himself a scholar but never published a book. I equated publication with an important scholar.

4. My father is a liberal Republican. He says he believes in "controlled capitalism." However, he likes such proposals as socialized medicine. He insists on my mother's and his own complete lack of prejudice. However, both of them frequently criticize Jewish acquaintances on the basis of their

[1] Although the main themes in paragraphs 1–4 are critical of the father, a comparison with other biographies suggests the important point is the inclusion of some supportive views, as in the references to "affection," paternal success, work consistency. Novak is revealing an ambivalence he will later comment upon, an ambivalence that suggests that much of his striving is partially oriented towards impressing and even pleasing his father. It also comes close to paralyzing his decision-making capacity and, as he notes himself, reduces his capacity for assertive action. As further evidence of this ambivalence, the last line of this paragraph seems to be a complaint that the father did not guide young Novak enough, while other sentences complain of discipline and over-guidance.

[2] As one reads these comments on the hypocrisy of the father, one must reserve judgment on two counts: (a) Novak wants to see paternal weaknesses, for he is in bitter competition with his father's college record and would find his task easier if the record were tarnished, and (b) he may be projecting his own ambivalent attitudes on his father, framing these to make a picture of an ambivalent and hypocritical man. Neither of these factors imply that the judgment is not substantially correct.

"Jewism." They pity Negroes but wish my sister did not have to attend a school where they are a strong minority.[3]

5. My mother also is a nervous person, quite prone to crying when a disturbing situation arises in the family.[4] She always has been submissive to my father on the surface. At times this is broken through by periods of moodiness and "tiredness" when she explains that she is unable to take part in what my father wants to do.

6. Her affection towards me has seemed shallow in that she would submit to my father in punishing me or allow him to punish me without handling the situation herself. Whenever she discovered my having indulged in genital play with the children in the neighborhood she reported it to my father. He punished me severely. However, whenever my age group attacked me or made me feel unhappy in some way, my mother showered attention on me.

7. I lived in a small western New York town until I was ten. There were five children in my age group in the area in which I lived. However, one of the five was three years older than I, two were two years older and two were one year older. There were none my age or younger. I was the only child in the family.[5]

8. Because of my music lessons, I had to leave school promptly at the end of each day, precluding a possible means of synthesis into the larger group from other parts of town. The second smallest in my class, I backed out of a fight when chance afforded it. When having to fight I cried during it and for some time afterward. This continued into secondary school.[6]

[3] Young Novak also is anti-Semitic and punishing towards the weak or the members of out-groups. He avoids hypocrisy by not pretending to be otherwise. Unlike other biographers, he fails to take advantage of this situation to reveal his greater humanism or morality by adopting a more tolerant stance, thus scoring on his father. I interpret this to mean that his needs do not include a need to put a moral face on things; rather he desperately wants to be thought of as strong, an image which means to him wealthy, powerful and successful.

[4] The lack of a nurturant mother, of course, contributed to Novak's uncertainty about himself and his innate worth. Further, as the following comments suggest, especially when taken together with the comments in paragraph 15, Novak's mother at the same time "babified" him and gave forth ambivalent cues as to the masculinity expected of him. No doubt her own worries about sex were thus communicated to him.

[5] The reference to "only child" is illuminating. Later (paragraph 21) Novak speaks of having been a "first child." Nowhere is there any discussion of brothers and sisters; Novak simply reads them out of the picture, wishing them away. It seems that his complaints about having been isolated and alone have a wish component; at the same time that he wanted to have other children his own age to play with, he resents the younger child who appeared in the family some time later. His demands for attention "without working for it" (his phrase) are probably related to his resentment of his younger brother or sister. Further, his combined fear of minority out-groups and his belief that it is appropriate to aggress against them because of their weakness (as he wished to do against his baby sibling) may have roots in this submerged sibling rivalry.

[6] This fear of fighting combined with a desire for victory and dominance creates a life-long difficulty for Novak. The syndrome helps to explain his association with a strong

9. I was very talkative and always wanted to lead, to "take the ball" in touch football, to "pitch" in baseball. I relished the chance to have a part in two school plays.

10. My friends had houses larger than mine. I recall once at the age of ten I invited a "girl friend" to the house to visit me. She left soon after arriving. I blamed it on the house. When my father bought an electric vacuum cleaner it was smaller than those I had seen in my friend's houses.

11. An older boy in my neighborhood was very mechanically minded. He built model airplanes and constructed a scale village on a platform where he ran his electric train. I tried to do the same and would lose interest. Such "failures" repeated themselves.[7]

12. When I lived in Albany, New York, Fresno, California, and Richmond, Virginia, during the war, I felt the same desire for attention from a group, but met with successive failures despite early popularity. I "talked too much" was the usual criticism. I could entertain myself only at the piano, which I rarely enjoyed apart from a few public recitals in which I played. Despite my relative lack of popularity, I preferred being with the group to being alone.

13. At the age of 13 I entered Elite Academy and attended it for two years. I found studying very difficult. I frequently stopped studying early in the evening, reading various "light" magazines. I began reading biographies of men such as Theodore Roosevelt, Abraham Lincoln, Woodrow Wilson, and other political leaders.[8]

14. I had one close friend—he ranked second in the class scholastically. I tried to copy his study habits. He kept his Latin vocabulary on sets of cards. I tried this but did not keep it up. During this period at Elite, I changed my handwriting four times: in copy of my senior counselor who was a very

leader and eagerness to do battle under the leader's aegis and protection. Further, it helps to explain his combativeness in support of the conventional, established, strong forces in society, the conservative business interests.

[7] Paragraphs 9, 10, and 11 reveal three themes that run throughout the analysis. Novak wants constantly to *draw attention to himself* and to be at the center of the stage (literally, in the high school plays, but also in sports, where he is not a good performer). He is filled with *envy* of others, whether they have larger houses or are more successful academically (paragraph 16), and is always making comparative rankings. He is *imitative*; he copies his father's and his friends' handwriting, he imitates their interests, their styles of speech, their studying habits. These themes are reflected in his political beliefs: he adopts a flamboyant ideology that singles him out on the campus as reactionary—he relishes the term. He adopts a political line that, he believes, will help in the race to success and wealth. These are the very grounds for his support of capitalism. And he accepts the political teachings of a strong campus leader without, as he says, really understanding the philosophy behind it.

[8] The interest in politics and political figures reflects several of Novak's needs and interests: the need to be with others, the interest in words (orality?) and the usefulness of talking skills, the need to express aggressive feelings in a protected environment, the need for immediate rewards. Novak's weak ego cannot easily accept delayed gratification; hence studying is difficult for him and twice he must drop out of school. As with acceptance of anti-Semitism, Novak imitates his father's behavior in reading "light magazines" in the evening.

popular fellow and a high-ranking student; in copy of my friend who was second in the class; in copy of my father; and finally, in copy of my "mechanically minded" friend with whom I had grown up and who was a class ahead of me. Each change meant a period of vacillation. I consulted my counselor and my roommate on it. They thought it funny but I thought it might change my grade average. With each attempt I felt somehow inferior to the person whose script I was copying—because I could not copy it exactly. It was not so neat. Whenever I returned to my style of writing I would compare mine to others', feeling somehow this style caused my scholastic deficiency. During a change of handwriting I felt like a new person. This continues today. I am at present copying the style of my former room-mate at college.[9]

15. At the end of two years I lost my scholarship because of my low grades. I was called "Lord Fauntleroy" by some of the boys. At this time a rather effeminate boy from an upper class family became a good friend of mine. I was not cognizant of this fact until my mother mentioned it. I stopped spending my time with him.[10]

16. I entered Adams College in September 1950. I quickly grew envious of my roommate who did very well scholastically. I attempted to copy his study habits. I copied his manner of talk at intervals. I frequently tried to obtain from him the reasons why he was so successful scholastically and socially. I would try to be very neat and orderly in my study habits and in organizing my belongings. When the pattern collapsed I became quite despondent. However, I never seriously attempted to make it a consistent pattern.[11]

[9] The lack of any sense of true identity is apparent in these changes of handwriting. One might also observe the unrealistic, almost magical thinking here which makes him believe that by changing certain external and superficial characteristics he can change fundamental ones—without the hard work necessary to achieve these latter changes. In the same way, he adopts views on politics that offer easy solutions: threats to Russia, "capitalism" (unexplained) to solve social problems. Later (paragraph 17) he acknowledges his acceptance of ideas without an effort to understand them. His love of words may come in part from his belief in their magical properties.

[10] The repudiation of persons and groups who are neither "strong" nor conventionally acceptable is reflected in both personal and political behavior and thought. Marginal man is very often the most aggressive defender of the dominant group and exponent of the dominant values because of both the internal pressure to keep down the latent out-group affinity and the external pressure to conform. This is true of sexual identifications, ethnic identities, and political partisanship.

[11] The repeated pattern of weak attempts to succeed followed by failure (as with the imitation of the mechanically minded friend, the loss of scholarship at Elite, the academic failure at Adams [paragraph 18], and the imitation of the roommate here) suggest an ambivalence about success and a covert desire to fail. No doubt both the wish to punish the parents, who want Novak to succeed, and to punish himself because he does not like himself contribute to this series of failures. For one who wants political power, the adoption of an extremist political philosophy is another means of ensuring failure—but Novak wants attention more than power and the success in getting attention is more important than the political failure at first.

17. At this time I met George Zeal, a former chairman of the Student Council. When I learned who he was I began talking to him after Math. class. I discovered he was leading a group attacking the (college) President for his liberalism. I began attacking the President on this same basis among my friends. I wrote an article for *The Defender*, an undergraduate magazine, in which I "reinterpreted" academic freedom. I joined a conservative society, and later became an officer. I know relatively little about conservative philosophy.[12]

18. I became a member of the Broadcasting station, the varsity debating team and a fraternity. I had little time for dating. Among my close friends I included three former chairmen of the Student Council. At the end of two years I was asked to resign from college because of my poor scholastic record.[13]

19. After a year at the University of Chicago, I returned to Adams. At Chicago I did quite well scholastically but was unhappy—I felt that if I weren't able to return to Adams I would lose social position. I made few friends at Chicago. Those with whom I did associate were strong leaders on the campus—including the president of the Student senate and the editor of the paper. I spoke of my close friendship with Zeal and I described myself as a "Zealist conservative," not quite certain what that meant. However, I argued liberally at times. Upon my return to Adams I improved myself scholastically, receiving an average of 88. I was interested in "living down" my previous reputation for scholastic weakness. I hoped to become a "grand old man" to whom younger students would turn for advice. I became extremely conservative in political attitudes. Some labeled me a "reactionary", which I rather enjoyed. I associated "reactionary" with "capitalism," I always wanted wealth, but my family never had very much money. It was due to a loss of scholarship that I had to leave Elite. I entered Adams with a scholarship. I felt that the pressure of having a scholarship and the necessity of working brought on my scholastic difficulty. I always had felt quite inferior to those with a great deal of money.[14]

[12] Observe the usefulness for Novak of a situation where he can attack an authoritative figure while yet remaining in the protection of another strong personality, George Zeal. His ambivalence towards his own father and his uncertainty about himself can thus be neatly expressed and protected. See my comments on the acceptance of ideas for their symbolic and magical properties without attempting to understand them (footnote 9).

[13] See footnote 11.

[14] In spite of the many symbolic and projective themes in the above analysis (bragging about his relationship to George Zeal, associating only with the strong and successful, seeking the limelight through the "reactionary" label), there is evidence of growing maturity and realistic thinking here. Apparently, having tested the limits of tolerance by academic authorities and having found them when he was asked to resign, Novak now begins to see certain connections and act upon his insight. He sees that to get good grades he must work for them and that to make his way in the world he will have to earn money (scholarship awards) and not just wish for it. Punishing his parents and himself has short-run "rewards" but long-run disadvantages, and he begins to think of the long run and to defer

20. I had few dates with girls until this past summer. They seemed superficial, and involvement meant a boy had to spend a great deal of time which I felt was wasted. During this past summer I secretly dated a girl with whom I had my first sexual relationship. She was a secretary in my father's office. I disliked her as a person. My father never learned of my dating her.[15] At the end of the summer I "fell in love" with another girl. She is four years younger than I, is a freshman in college, and is very submissive to me. She visits Adams whenever I invite her. Although I have no evidence I am very suspicious of her background. I worry about this suspicion. I worry more, however, about her having dates with others when I am not with her. I am not as concerned with her loving me as I am with her remaining true to her pledge of not dating others. At times I hope to discover some blemish in her past which would mean our immediate breakup. At other times I feel that I cannot do without her. She does not offer any real strength. To the contrary, I feel she detracts from my strength. I spend a great deal of time with her which I often regret having spent so. I would like to marry a girl with strength, a great deal of "life," very high moral standards, high intelligence, and a word I can trust. This is an "ideal" girl whom I may never find.[16]

UNDERLYING PSYCHOLOGICAL MANIFESTATIONS

21. My early isolation from children my own age conjoined with parental devotion to a first child cut deeply a desire for attention. Such attention was obtained without "working" for it. Such a passive means of attention created conflict when I was thrust suddenly into a play group in which I was foreign and in which all were older than I. I was unprepared to adapt myself to "adaptive" aggression to obtain the attention I craved.

22. Such a trait may have come from fear of aggression itself created by my father's unpredictable and severe punishments. I became very submissive

---

interpersonal and narcissistic gratifications. His conservatism has found increased support in economic self-interest, something that may change as his self-confidence grows and his interests change (see paragraph 37).

[15] The meaning of seducing one of his father's secretaries (whom he didn't like) is probably complex, but it suggests two ways of "becoming a man": getting even with his father as well as consummating heterosexual intercourse.

[16] As with earlier school and family relations and politics, sexual relations are treated as competitive, somewhat loveless, and suffused with dominant-subordinate properties. He is possessive—indeed he has selected a girl whom he can almost "own"—jealous, and eager for an easy escape from the situation. Like other biographers, his accounts of his sexual relations tend to serve as revealing and heightened glimpses of general interpersonal relations, and as such they tell us about preferred political style. Novak's lack of clear identity, desire and fear of dominating, over-the-shoulder glances at competitors, desire to possess or own a girl as he wishes to possess property, idealized version of conventional (conservative) thought, and self-defeating behavior come to the surface in both sexual and political relationships.

and could not translate any aggressive tendencies into my own age group.[17]

23. I was not accepted by the in-group—I was myself at an early age the out-group. I became very introspective and self-blaming at an early age. Feelings of guilt assailed me. I "talked too much" in order to gain attention. When this lost me friends I blamed myself severely. I came to idolize the "leader" of every in-group. He seemed to have powers which were beyond my grasp.[18]

24. *Dependence.* My dependence upon my mother and the desire for her affection may have been a basis in my taking piano lessons for so long without any real desire for music myself. However, real mother affection might be upset at any time by my father's severity which my mother submitted to. My direct submission to my father followed. I could never lie to him—not because of conscience but for fear of being discovered. In later years I did lie to him when I myself could handle the secret.[19]

25. My dependence was accentuated not only by the natural need for mother-love but also by the fear of being rejected by my father. My mother did not offer a protection against this potentiality. The capacity for conscious or strong rebellion may have been eliminated. I not only submitted to my father but came to depend on his authoritarian manner. I adopted many of his mannerisms. I not only idolized him but began to respect his severity in

[17] The nature and content of a person's self-blame or guilt has important consequences for political thought. On the basis of comparative analysis of a variety of ideological biographies, it seems to me that liberal and conservative-reactionary belief systems are the products of two different aggression-control mechanisms. While both groups may be quite aggressive—indeed I see no differences on that score—the liberal is inhibited in his aggression by his concern for the victims of his aggressive acts, while the conservative-reactionary is inhibited by his concern for the consequences to himself. Novak, it seems to me, is self-blaming not because of his attitudes towards the weak or the out-group, but because he has not been able to express his aggressive feelings adequately. He is ashamed of his "fear of aggression." His conscience is self-regarding without concern for his victims. (See *Political Thinking and Consciousness,* Chapter 9.)

[18] One must ask why Novak does not accept out-group status and become a rebel, a leader of the "outs." This would satisfy some need for revenge, need to attract attention to himself, give him a different definition of "success" and a chance to achieve it. The answer, of course, lies in the possibility afforded him to attack "liberal authority" in the person of the college President and to associate himself with wealth and status at the same time—a better solution for one so reverential and envious of the wealthy, the possessors (phallicly strong)—and to disassociate himself from the weak or marginal men whose underdog status frightens him and even disgusts him. The disgust, of course, given his own definition of himself as historically "an out-group," is self-disgust. Perhaps in the end it is this self-rejection—rejecting the weak, economically deprived, sexually insecure features of himself—that makes a liberal, pro-out-group, pro-underdog stance impossible.

[19] If the capacity to "lie," that is, to give accounts of the world contrary to experience becomes identified with assertiveness against minatory authoritarian pressures, there develops a positive pressure to falsify experience and to develop fanciful ideas of politics, e.g., of Senator Joseph McCarthy, Communism, and foreign policy. The usual method of rooting honesty in the internalized parental directives here has found its obverse: rooting dishonesty in a "satisfactory" relationship with the father.

dealing with me. In actuality I do not believe I turned to his "love" naturally. I was dependent against my wishes. Yet the incapacity to assimilate with a group, and the void which mother-symbols seemed unable to fill probably enhanced my father's impress on my personality structure.[20]

26. *Ambivalance.* The artificiality of this relationship with my father may have produced its effect at Elite Academy. I base this in two factors. First, as stated before, my father's authoritarian impression of himself and his values did not bring solution to the problems raised for me in my age group. Second, his actions belied many of his expressed beliefs, thus setting an insecurity in my own pattern of thinking.

27. The dichotomy between what my father expected me to do and what the group demanded created unconscious rebellion without confidence in myself to exploit the questionable advantages of rebellion—i.e., the creation of an independent aggression even though artificial. A cautious meandering within the conventional framework, as delineated by my father, thus has been spotted by "weak-kneed" rebellion. This always has been followed by a period of depression and ultimate acquiescence to his will.

28. The second factor which, I believe, marked the essential artificiality of this dependence was created by the dichotomy between my father's unconsciously "being" and consciously "seeming." One example has been given: a nervous father, impatient with others' intensity and nervously created enthusiasm, when he himself fell into the same pattern. His claims to nonprejudice and scholarship are other examples.

29. The product of these two factors was not only an insecurity as to my own concept of reality, but an acquiescence to and adoption of those thoughts, beliefs and values of one who represented authority—my father—without associated power to discriminate among these thoughts, beliefs and values and to assimilate them with reality.[21]

30. The ready acceptance of the viewpoint of Zeal now may be partially explained. My adherence to his beliefs cannot have been determined ration-

[20] In these passages it becomes apparent that part of the tie with his father lies in what has been called "identification with the aggressor," and forms part of the syndrome of the worship of the strong, the identification of goodness with strength, the idea that rebellion (but not deception) is both wrong and futile, and that the self, being sinful and weak (which is sinful), is unworthy and appropriately punished. Novak seems to have learned this submission in part from his mother. He has never seen two mature independent persons relating to each other in a community of shared power.

[21] The ambiguous cues issuing from his father were important for Novak, because neither a clear call to rebellion nor a clear model for imitation was presented. Hence the insecurity and the pathetic search for other models. Nevertheless, the reader should note that Novak has the strength to present this penetrating and courageous self-analysis, belying in some ways his denigration of himself and revealing a mind that, sooner or later, may provide him with the independence and identity he claims he does not have. Here, as when Novak returned to Adams with determination to do what was necessary to prove himself academically, one senses maturity and growth sufficient to indicate that many of the problems presented may, in time, find adaptive solutions.

ally. Furthermore, they ran contrary to the beliefs of my father. Finally, I have not maintained a consistent conservative attitude.[22] Such a pattern may lie behind my attachments to "successful" figures at college.

31. *Orderliness and disorder.* The discrepancies between orderliness and disorder have been described. At times, sleep and apathy destroy any attempt at adhering to an organized pattern. These are counterbalanced by periods of extreme neatness, and an insistence on personal cleanliness and orderliness. With such return to orderliness I have a feeling of control over myself and superiority towards others.

32. During a period of extreme orderliness I frequently have quarrels with the family because of an attitude of superiority. I have broken off ties with girl friends and have hurt the feelings of good friends at such times. At the end I generally return to a disorganized state, sleep a great deal, and if I have a chance for a date, I grab it.[23]

33. A summary of the psychological bases to an authoritarian susceptibility produces a picture of conflicting personality organization: dependence upon and dissatisfaction with the father image, a strong desire for leadership and conscious rejection from the in-group, a search for a mother-symbol and despairing submission to the force from which it could not protect me, and an oral and anal dichotomy. Perhaps description of such relationships begins to describe a pattern. However, it denies a clear solution and, in case of such a paper as this, a clear-cut "solution."

MY PERSONALITY AND MY POLITICS

34. My wide participation in extracurricular activities points partly to the striving to raise myself in the hierarchy of my social environment. One important element in a society allowing such mobility is flexibility in income and purchasing power. Capitalism represents possibilities and opportunities for rising in that society. My relationships at Elite and Adams with members of

[22] Novak does not see that one of the reasons why Zeal's philosophy was attractive to him was *because* it differed from his father's views. Nor does he know that the inconsistencies in his views represent both confusion as to values, a handicap to further thinking, *and* an experimentation with different points of view, a useful learning and trying-on process.

[23] Although there were a few hints on the problem of "orderliness" in the preceding material, this is the introduction of a new theme. Although Novak (in some omitted material) identifies this with "anal" characteristics, I doubt if the concept of anality will prove helpful here. Rather it seems to me that orderliness and its concomitant quarrelsomeness represent feelings of mastery, of "ordering" things and people to obey, of the beginnings of a sense that life, things, and others are under control. Perhaps the references to "breaking ties with girl friends" during these orderly periods and having dates when he becomes *dis*orderly imply that cleanliness and sex are considered incompatible states, probably a reflection of his mother's concerns. The identification of "orderliness," "order," and "ordering people" is congenial to the authoritarian view of the world, as is the view that sex and disorder are somehow linked.

the upper economic strata have enhanced the earlier concept of "bigger houses" and "bigger vacuum cleaners" with which money provides. The "having" of such objects represents a symbol of assimilation into and acceptance by the in-group.[24]

35. The early impossibility of opposition to my father created an equation between strength and goodness. I do not attack groups at Adams which are strong, institutionalized, and widely accepted. I attack the unaccepted and the out-group representatives. My association of good with power comes in the case of Senator Joseph McCarthy, whom I "feel sorry for" because I believe he is sincere. My readings of Theodore Roosevelt represented an outcome of such a relationship. His authoritarian character as reflected in his writings seemed to give me a moral strength and temporary self-justification in acting in the manner in which I felt he had acted.[25]

36. Actual out-group intolerance has been strong. I reject members of the out-group in striving to enter the in-group. I wished to return to Elite and Adams partially because of a feeling of being separated from in-groups. I have few Jewish friends and am suspicious of the motivation of those. I associate with a prestige-powerful element at Adams and have attempted to be an "inside dopester" in friendship formed with former chairmen of the Student Council. The greater the fear of being associated with an out-group, periodically occurring in my background, the greater have been my leanings toward authoritarian figures and strong leaders among the in-group from whom I need to draw strength.[26]

---

[24] One must ponder why it is that a young man who seems to have a low opinion of himself and to have sought failure at various stages in life believes that he can make a success of it in a competitive society. Why does he not seek the security of a protected welfare state, or the security of academia, or of a government job? The answers rest on the following facts, I believe: (a) He seeks competitive advantage more than he seeks security, and he needs invidious distinctions in his favor to compensate him for his self-doubts. (b) His attention-seeking personality would shrivel in a bureaucracy, and his need for immediate rewards would not be satisfied by the long latency period of academic training and research. (c) His rejection of the weak and subordinate (a rejection of this portion of himself) would deprive him of self-love if he were to join the bureaucrats or the relatively impotent (in his eyes) teachers of this world. (d) His father went from academia to a quasi-business position; Novak earns more credits in his own and, he must imagine, in his father's eyes by besting him at the game he chose for his "success." (e) Worshipping strength, wealth, and power he moves to where these are centrally located, the business world. Finally (f), he *is* able and may have a realistic sense that for all his sinfulness (perhaps because of it) and worthlessness, he can make his way. He can meet the challenge.

[25] This is the first hint of a need to justify or license Novak's authoritarian and ethnically prejudiced behavior. I think it indicates more of a liberal conscience than he was prepared to admit. Whereas most men repress their hostilities, Novak tends to repress his pacific and humane impulses. When he achieves more self-confidence, these may emerge and temper his authoritarianism.

[26] Here again, the contrast between the explicit authoritarian, ethnocentric, and ego-centric ideology on the one hand and the insightful, self-revelatory exposition poses a problem. One wonders whether one of the gains in this account is the "shock" delivered

37. Politically, the conventionalism represented in acceptance of the *status quo* provides security in itself. Through its own consistency in contrast to changing liberal doctrines it provides a ready-made rigidity which imposes itself on the ego to prevent the eruption of certain unconscious forces. This situation is dual faced: it represents not only susceptibility to emotional forces but to authoritative commands from without. At present the conservative philosophy represents such a command. However, because of no real rational synthesis with the basic tenets of conservatism, an environmental change could create a superficial change in ideology but not real change in my relation to authority on which I am dependent and towards which I am respectful.[27]

Notes

1. See "Political Education in the Midst of Life's Struggles," Chapter 6.
2. To preserve anonymity, the identifying characteristics of the students have been changed.
3. *Political Ideology* (New York: Free Press, 1962), pp. 383–384.
4. This case is presented in more detail in my *Political Thinking and Consciousness* (Chicago: Markham, 1969), Chapter 1.

---

to Novak's liberal reader, myself. At the same time he may enjoy shocking himself by stating "the worst" about himself. The need to dramatize the self is expressed elsewhere in his biography; hence we would be surprised if he did not engage in self-dramatization at this point. I suspect that all of these elements were present in Novak's unconscious as he wrote the analysis. For this reason, and because he tends to repress his humane instincts (for fear of appearing weak), it will be well to suspend belief in the stark version of authoritarianism and selfishness as it is presented, although to a considerable degree in this complex and many-sided person the main features of the personality given in the account are probably accurately described.

[27] I don't know where Novak got these ideas about the usefulness of a *status quo* philosophy for him, but I think it is accurate and most insightful, perhaps even a contribution to the theory of personality and politics. On the question of the flexibility of his conservatism and the fixed nature of his authoritarianism, one can only guess. However, judging from observation of other biographers over some period of time, I suspect that the tendencies marked by both these features of his social outlook will remain evident, while their particularly vivid and pronounced features will be modified as Novak finds what he is searching for, and may someday be pleased to call, himself.

Chapter 8
The Study of Literature as Political Education

Literature and Citizenship

It has been a long time since anyone took seriously the question of whether the study of poetry, or at least certain kinds of poetry, is detrimental to the development of civic virtue. To the modern ear this proposition seems to be foolish, although the spirit behind it has certainly been heard in recent investigations on the effects of comic books and television on the young. But it is not a foolish question, nor was Plato's answer foolish, however wrong it may seem to us now. He argued, as is well known, that poetry that did not uphold his views of justice, or that implied that the unjust might be happier than the just or that they could avoid the consequences of their injustice by appealing to the Gods, or that portrayed the Gods as indulging in violence or other evil practices should be banned. He opposed dialogue in poetry because it required impersonation, which led to evil consequences. Poetry that enphasized "the image of the good" and that developed the heroic qualities and courage of men was to remain and to serve important purposes in the training of guardians of the society, He said:

> Let our artists rather be those who are gifted to discern the true nature of the beautiful and graceful; then will our youth dwell in a land of health, amid fair sights and sounds, and receive the good in everything; and beauty, the effluence of fair works, shall flow into the eye and ear, like a health-giving breeze from a purer region, and insensibly draw the soul from earliest years into likeness and sympathy with the beauty of reason.[1]

Reprinted from *The Liberties of Wit* (New Haven: Yale University Press, 1961, and Hamden, Conn.: Archon Books, 1969), pp. 1–2, 4–6, 106–122, 127–136.

Notes to this chapter will be found on pages 156–157

How do we "draw the soul from the earliest years into likeness and sympathy with the beauty of reason"? This is our problem. Like Plato, I am concerned with the citizen and, in a sense, with the "guardian," for most of what I have to say refers to college education of those who will be guardians in one way or another. My concern is with the way the humanities and the social sciences together prepare men for an adult life in which they must bear some responsibility for themselves and for others as well. Like Plato, too, I am concerned with how education shapes the mind so that it may "discern the true nature" of things. . . .

What do we want of the citizen? Aristotle and Bryce think of the answer in terms of the citizen's political functions, Bryce as a member of the democratic public, Aristotle as a man eligible for governmental and jury duty.[2] Both are concerned with his skills and his moral qualities. Most nations have codes of behavior and attitudes that are essential for decent citizenship. C. E. Merriam, in a study of nine of them, finds that these codes usually include obedience to law, loyalty to and respect for the regime and its ideology, a certain amount of self-control, a willingness to sacrifice for the community, and sometimes a sense of the mission or destiny of a people.[3] But one might also focus upon how a citizen solves the conflicts between his private needs and his public duties. Thus, as H. M. Roelofs suggests, a citizen must at the same time be loyal and yet independently critical; he must support the authorities but be ready to defy them; he must sacrifice for the common good but protect himself against exploitation.[4]

We want all these things and more. We want citizens to have democratic values and the personality structure to sustain them effectively. We want them to have the skills to take part in civic or social life. We want them to understand their heritage. We want them to have mental clarity, the mental habits and equipment to cope adequately with the public questions they confront. Here is our second focus: the mental clarity of the citizen, the "sound mind" that comes to terms with life, seeks to understand it, and, understanding, deals with it.

Mental clarity could mean anything from a platform on which to say "I disagree with you" to a concept of complete order and rationality—as in the Mind of God. I mean the following things: First, I mean an understanding of the philosophical foundation on which an inquiry is premised and an awareness of the consequences of this foundation for the type of question asked. Second, I mean an awareness and analysis of the theoretical propositions that underlie statements of fact, historical accounts of events, evaluations of poetry or politics, and casual comments on the events of the day. (For example, knowing that the statement, "President Kennedy is doing a good job," involves an implicit theory of the Presidency and of current domestic and international affairs.) Third, I mean by mental clarity a sophistication about the way concepts are formed and the uses of the classificatory systems we inevitably use in every statement. Very close to this, in the fourth place, I mean a knowledge of the relations between language and the real world. I mean, fifth, an idea of how propositions about reality may be tested, a firm grasp on the more reliable methods of verification either actually available or useful as a way of thinking about "truth." Sixth, mental clarity, as I use it, means a knowledge of the processes of evaluation and judging and employment of these processes when evaluation is required. Seventh, I mean a capacity to differentiate between fantasizing and directed thinking—an awareness and control over thought processes. Finally, I mean the organization of experience to give a general clarity to life, which might embrace the emotional, the moral, and the purposive, as well as the purely instrumental clarity we have been considering. I cannot imagine any field of learning, particularly not my own, *establishing* clarity of this kind. In what sense does the example set by the study of literature contribute to it?

[*The Liberties of Wit*, from which these extracts are taken, then proceeds to argue that literary criticism, as an example of humanistic thinking, reveals much confusion on the first seven of the elements of mental clarity set forth above. There is much opaque thinking on the nature and uses of "ideas," substitution of implicit theory for explicit theoretical statements, unsystematic use of typologies and classificatory schemes, ignorance and ignoring of verification procedures for general theoretical statements, subjectivistic evaluation without revealed criteria, and confusion between imaginative and logical thought. Nevertheless, on the eighth criterion, the "organization of experience," the study of literature and literary criticism (which is different) makes a contribution for which there is no substitute. The following discussion explores this contribution and argues for the unity of the humanities and the social sciences.]

Some Human Values in the Study of Literature

The study of literature—and more generally, the humanities—yields to the reader a beneficence of untold, much discussed, and little understood values. Richards speaks of this as the organization of experience, the sorting out of impulses and development of discrimination; Auden speaks of the organization of emotions; John Dewey speaks of "reconstructive doing," of the creative element of aesthetic experience.[5] Of course, every important psychic event organizes experience—as those familiar with the way Orson Welles' broadcast of *The War of the Worlds* organized the experience of those who fled in terror into the streets will recall.[6] A beneficial organization is implied.

In the broadest sense, we are talking about what literate people get from their literacy. In Richard Hoggart's study of *The Uses of Literacy*, he describes the situation of the least educated in the following terms.

Their education is unlikely to have left them with any historical panorama or with any idea of a continuing tradition. . . . A great many people, though they may possess a considerable amount of disconnected information, have little idea of an historical or ideological pattern or process. . . . With little intellectual or cultural furniture, with little training in the testing of opposing views against reason and existing judgments, judgments are usually made according to the promptings of those group-apothegms which come first to mind. . . . Similarly, there can be little real sense of the future. . . . Such a mind is, I think, particularly accessible to the temptation to live in a constant present.[7]

Among other things, then, the study of literature gives a sense of tradition, provides an ideological framework which, in turn, gives a certain consistency to thought and confers on individual opinions a larger "meaning"; it provides an exercise in making judgments and a time perspective to life.

Hoggart's study suggests that education tends to *civilize* people. If we may draw this distinction, it also tends to *humanize* them. Stouffer found that "in *all* age groups the better educated tend to be more tolerant than the less educated."[8] They also are less likely to categorize people in terms of their weakness and their strength and are more likely to encourage a tolerant and permissive upbringing for children. They are more optimistic about the future, too, a factor which probably "permits" them to be more relaxed and generous with older people.[9] Authoritarianism studies, which bear some relation to Stouffer's questions, also show that education is likely to reduce authoritarian tendencies.[10]

If we take a somewhat closer look, not at education or literacy, but at what is called "bookishness," a preference for reading rather than mere exposure to it, we find in Murphy and Likert's study of a quarter of a century ago that this factor is one of the main ingredients of liberalism—at least as they conceived of liberalism.[11] Their concept of liberalism as a unidimensional and relatively undated set of attitude does not survive, and the relation of liberalism to "information" and to "intelligence" which seemed so certain in the thirties has pretty well been worn away, but a central ingredient of their scale is a kind of concern for the underdog, an equalitarianism, and this, I think, continues to be a function of education and, probably, of bookishness.[12]

It is apparent that these inquiries barely touch the surface of the problem. We must ask in more intimate detail how the experience of reading Dante, Shakespeare, Dostoevsky, restructures a man's emotions, perceptions, personality. Three distinctions must be kept in mind. First, these experiences, like almost every other kind of experience, will have different effects on different people. Studies of the effects of television on children show that while the isolated and withdrawn child and the normal child may both watch the same gruesome programs, they use their material differently: the withdrawn child evolves an autistic and somewhat morbid fantasy life out of what he has seen; the normal child selects material to be used in his active and social play life. Or, again, when comparable audiences are presented with arguments for a course of action, one audience exposed to one side only, the other to two or more sides, the persuasiveness of the two techniques is seen to vary substantially with intelligence. The more intelligent are more likely to be persuaded by the argument which deals with opposing considerations, the less intelligent by the one-sided appeal.[13] One thing that vitiates most philosophical and critical discussion of value, then, is this failure to consider the wide range of values affected by the personality, intelligence, and experience of the various readers.[14]

A second preliminary matter is the time period considered. The effect of reading a poem is almost certain to be different at the time of reading it, and later when its effect, if any, has been assimilated into the main body of the ongoing experience of life. In the persuasion studies the so-called sleeper effect has demonstrated how very deceiving about long-run influence a measurement immediately after an experience may be.[15] For the sake of precision, then, we would need to divide what is called "the aesthetic experience" into a short-term "aesthetic effect" and a longer term and more enduring "aesthetic organization."

A third distinction, too obvious to mention except for the tendency to speak of "the aesthetic experience" as a homogeneous concept, is the difference between reading Dickens and T. S. Eliot, Homer and Faulkner. The nature of the work makes a difference.

An outline for analysis of the values of the study of literature, then, allowing implicitly for these distinctions, would go something like this. In the first place I would suggest a kind of *placing* function, that is, the placing of the individual in a broader and more complicated world, with a greater variety of cultures, people, experiences than he might otherwise dream of. This, in turn, would be composed of two parts: (a) orientation, which might be understood to mean a picture of the variety of life, and (b) perspective, that is, an understanding of where a person fitted into this situation, combining, thus both cultural perspective and individual perspective. I take this to be the heart of W. H. Auden's comments on how the critic can help the reader. He says:

> First, he must show the individual that though he is unique he has also much in common with all other individuals, that each life is, to use a chemical metaphor, an isomorph of a general human life . . . for example, the coal miner in Pennsylvania can learn to see himself in terms of the world of Ronald Firbank, and an Anglican bishop find in *The Grapes of Wrath* a parable of his diocesan problems. And secondly the critic must attempt to spread a knowledge of past cultures so that his audience may be as aware of them as the artist himself.[16]

Such a perspective on oneself leads through a process of self-discovery to an understanding of one's own *identity*. There is considerable discussion these days of the problem of identity; it is an important emphasis for our time. Identity means a knowledge of "who" you are; such knowledge gives a sure sense of self, awareness of what is ego-syntonic to one's nature, an avoidance of "phoniness," false fronts, poses, expression of unexperienced emotion, capacity to judge one's own skills and talents—in short, a reality sense and consciousness about oneself. One learns about oneself partly through comparison with other people.[17] I would argue that the "other people" of literature serve this function, and that the constant vicarious living of the literary experience gives one a basis for a rich and meaningful comparison. The more complex, deep, and true the portrayal of characters in drama and fiction, the more one learns through identification and contrast about oneself.

Two facets of this aspect of the literary process have special significance for our time. One, a reservation on the point I have just made, is the phenomenon of pseudo-thinking, psuedo-feeling, and pseudo-willing, which Fromm discussed in *The Escape from Freedom*. In essence this involves grounding one's thought and emotion in the values and experience of others, rather than in one's own values and experience. There is a risk that instead of teaching a person how to be himself, reading fiction and drama may teach him how to be somebody else. Clearly what the person brings to the reading is important. Moreover, if the critic instructs his audience in *what* to see in a work, he is contributing to this pseudo-thinking; if he instructs them in *how* to evaluate a work, he is helping them to achieve their own identity.

The second timely part of this sketch of literature and the search for identity has to do with the difference between good and enduring literary works and the ephemeral mass culture products of today. In the range and variety of characters who, in their literary lives, get along all right with life styles one never imagined possible, there is an implicit lesson in differentiation. The reader, observing this process, might ask "why not be different?" and find in the answer a license to be a variant of the human species. The observer of television or other products for a mass audience has only a permit to be, like the models he sees, even more like everybody else. And this, I think, holds for values as well as life styles. One would need to test this proposition carefully; after all, the large (and probably unreliable) *Reader's Digest* literature on the "most unforgettable character I ever met" deals with village grocers, country doctors, favorite if illiterate aunts, and so forth. Scientists often turn out to be idiosyncratic, too. But still, the proposition is worth examination.

It is possible that the study of literature affects the conscience, the morality, the sensitivity to some code of "right" and "wrong". I do not know that this is true; both Flügel and Ranyard West deal with the development and nature of conscience, as do such theologians as Niebuhr and Buber.[18] It forms the core of many, perhaps most, problems of psychotherapy. I am not aware of great attention by any of these authors or by the psychotherapeutic profession to the role of literary study in the development of conscience—most of their attention is to a pre-literate period of life, or, for the theologians of course, to the influence of religion.

Still, it would be surprising if what one reads did not contribute to one's ideas of right and wrong; certainly the awakened alarm over the comic books and the continuous concern over prurient literature indicate some peripheral aspects of this influence. Probably the most important thing to focus on is not the development of conscience, which may well be almost beyond the reach of literature, but the contents of conscience, the code which is imparted to the developed or immature conscience available. This is in large part a code of behavior and a glossary of values; what is it that people do and should do and how one should regard it. In a small way this is illustrated by the nineteenth-century novelist who argued for the powerful influence of literature as a teacher of society and who illustrated this with the way a girl learned to meet her lover, how to behave, how to think about this new experience, how to exercise restraint.[19]

Literature may be said to give people a sense of purpose, dedication, mission, significance. This, no doubt, is part of what Gilbert Seldes implies when he says of the arts, "They give form and meaning to life which might otherwise seem shapeless and without sense."[20] Men seem almost universally to want a sense of function, that is, a feeling that their existence makes a difference to someone, living or unborn, close and immediate or generalized.[21] Feeling useless seems generally to be an unpleasant sensation. A need so deeply planted, asking for direction, so to speak, is likely to be gratified by the vivid examples and heroic proportions of literature. The terms "renewal" and "refreshed," which often come up in aesthetic discussion, seem partly to derive their import from the "renewal" of purpose and a "refreshed" sense of significance a person may receive from poetry, drama, and fiction. The notion of "inspiration" is somehow cognate to this feeling. How literature does this, or for whom, is certainly not clear, but the content, form, and language of the "message," as well as the source, would all play differential parts in giving and molding a sense of purpose.

One of the most salient features of literary value has been deemed to be its influence upon and organization of emotion. Let us differentiate a few of these ideas. The Aristotelian notion of catharsis, the purging of emotion, is a persistent and viable one. The idea here is one *discharge* but this must stand in opposition to a second view. Plato's notion of the *arousal* of emotion. A third idea is that artistic literature serves to *reduce emotional conflicts*, giving a sense of serenity and calm to individuals. This is given some expression in Beardsley's notion of harmony and the resolution of indecision.[22] A fourth view is the transformation of emotion, as in Housman's fine phrase on the arts: they "transform and beautify our inner nature."[23] It is possible that the idea of *enrichment* of emotion is a fifth idea. F. S. C. Northrop, in his discussion of the "Functions and Future of Poetry," suggests this:

One of the things which makes our lives drab and empty and which leaves us, at the end of the day, fatigued and deflated spiritually is the pressure of the taxing, practical, utilitarian concern of common-sense objects. If art is to release us from these postulated things [things we must think symbolically about] and bring us back to the ineffable beauty and richness of the aesthetic component of reality in its immediacy, it must sever its connection with these common sense entities.[24]

I take the central meaning here to be the contrast between the drab empty quality of life without literature and a life enriched by it. Richards' view of the aesthetic experience might constitute a sixth variety: for him it constitutes, in part, the *organization of impulses*.[25]

A sketch of the emotional value of the study of literature would have to take account of all of these. But there is one in particular which, it seems to me, deserves special attention. In the wide range of experiences common to our earth-bound race none is more difficult to manage, more troublesome, and more enduring in its effects than the control of love and hate. The study of literature contributes to this control in a curious way. William Wimsatt and Cleanth Brooks, it seems to me, have a penetrating insight into the way in which this control is effected:

For if we say poetry is to talk of beauty and love (and yet not aim at exciting erotic emotion or even an emotion of Platonic esteem) and if it is to talk of anger and murder (and yet not aim at arousing anger and indignation)—then it may be that the poetic way of dealing with these emotions will not be any kind of intensification, compounding, or magnification, or any direct assault upon the affections at all. Something indirect, mixed, reconciling, tensional might well be the stratagem, the devious technique by which a poet indulged in all kinds of talk about love and anger and even in something like "expressions" of these emotions, without aiming at their incitement or even uttering anything that essentially involves their incitement.[26]

The rehearsal through literature of emotional life under controlled conditions may be a most valuable human experience. Here I do not mean catharsis, the discharge of emotion. I mean something more like Freud's concept of the utility of "play" to a small child: he plays "house" or "doctor" or "fireman" as a way of mastering slightly frightening experiences, reliving them imaginatively until they are under control.

There is a second feature of the influences of literature, good literature, on emotional life which may have some special value for our time. In B. M. Spinley's portrayal of the underprivileged and undereducated youth of London, a salient finding was the inability to postpone gratification, a need to satisfy impulses immediately without the pleasure of anticipation or of savoring the experience.[27] Perhaps it is only an analogy, but one of the most obvious differences between cheap fiction and fiction of an enduring quality is the development of a theme or story with leisure and anticipation. Anyone who has watched children develop a taste for literature will understand what I mean. It is at least possible that the capacity to postpone gratification is developed as well as expressed in a continuous and guided exposure to great literature.

In any inquiry into the way in which great literature affects the emotions, particularly with respect to the sense of harmony, or relief of tension, or sense of "a transformed inner nature" which may occur, a most careful exploration of the particular feature of the experience which produces the effect would be required. In the calm which follows the reading of a poem, for example, is the effect produced by the enforced quiet, by the musical quality of words and rhythm, by the sentiments or sense of the poem, by the associations with earlier readings, if it is familiar, by the boost to the self-esteem for the semi-literate, by the diversion of attention, by the sense of security in a legitimized withdrawal, by a kind license for some variety of fantasy life regarded as forbidden, or by half-conscious ideas about the magical power of words? These are, if the research is done with subtlety and skill, researchable topics, but the research is missing.

One of the most frequent views of the value of literature is the education of sensibility that it is thought to provide. Sensibility is a vague word, covering an area of meaning rather than any precise talent, quality, or skill. Among other things it means perception, discrimination, sensitivity to subtle differences. Both the extent to which this is true and the limits of the field of perceptual skill involved should be acknowledged. Its truth is illustrated by the skill, sensitivity, and general expertise of the English professor with whom one attends the theatre. The limits are suggested by an imaginary experiment: contrast the perceptual skill of English professors with that of their colleagues in discriminating among motor cars, political candidates, or female beauty. Along these lines, the particular point that sensitivity in literature leads to sensitivity in human relations would require more proof than I have seen. In a symposium and general exploration of the field of *Person Perception and Interpersonal Behavior* the discussion does not touch upon this aspect of the subject, with one possible exception; Solomon Asch shows the transcultural stability of metaphors based on sensation (hot, sweet, bitter, etc.) dealing with personal qualities of human beings and events.[28] But to go from here to the belief that those more sensitive to metaphor and language will also be more sensitive to personal differences is too great an inferential leap.

I would say, too, that the study of literature tends to give a person what I shall call *depth*. I use this term to mean three things: a search for the human significance of an event or state of affairs, a tendency to look at wholes rather than parts, and a tendency to respond to these events and wholes with feeling. It is the obverse of triviality, shallowness, emotional anaesthesia. I think these attributes cluster, but I have no evidence. In fact, I can only say this seems to me to follow from a wide, continuous, and properly guided exposure to literary art. Like so much else in this discussion, it is researchable, but so far as I know has not been researched.

Finally, we turn to a value which will have markedly different valences for different people: the maintenance of myth and illusion. "Without his myths," says Richards, "man is only a cruel animal without a soul."[29] O'Neill said as much about dreams and illusions in *The Iceman Cometh.* The matter is closely tied in with religion and the view one takes of the Bible, the Koran, the Talmud, and other writings of this nature.[30] It is, in my own case, reflected in a sense of loss that the cliffs, coves, and fields of the New Haven area (with a few exceptions) do not have stories told about them, are legend-free, do not have Gods and heroes, or even ghosts and pirates, associated with their names and features. But the moment I came to Hannibal, Missouri, I felt it; and I felt it playing on the Brandywine as a boy. A study of literature can do this; it can make history sing, and find books in the running brooks, and, if not good, at least a kind of human meaning in everything.

There are certain things claimed for literary study which seem to me un-likely: I doubt that it produces kindness or empathy. Work on an empathy scale seems to have run into trouble,[31] but even if it were a valid instrument, I doubt that it would show much relation between empathy and the study of literature. (The emotionality of "depth" need not be empathy or kindness.) I doubt, too, whether the study of poetry, or fiction, or drama makes people more democratic, or *per se*, induces any particular political or personal ideology. The "bookishness" that I said earlier was associated with liberalism included history, religion, sociology, travel—everything. A particular social outlook is probably a function of a particular range of reading.

And there is probably a negative side. One of these is the one I have stressed—a tendency to misunderstand the role and proper function of figurative and emotive language, imaginative discourse, the collapse of logical categories, the nature and uses of verification. All of this, and more, I have included in my concept of mental clarity. A second risk is the danger of withdrawal from real life into a substitute, vicarious, or even fantasy life. Rudolph Arnheim suggests that this is the case with the "daytime serial";[32] Paul F. Lazarsfeld and Robert K. Merton have argued that the mass media represent a substitute for social and political participation.[33] I am dubious of the extent to which this is true but it may be more applicable to the study of literature. A third risk lies in the confusion of the nature of authoritative statement: one comes to respect and love the authors of the literature one loves and then to extend their sphere of competence to politics, public opinion, social maladjustment, an interpretation of "the times." This "halo effect" is a problem with all authoritative figures, but the nature of the attachment to well-loved authors (and their tendency to express themselves boldly) serves to intensify the problem in their case.

In all of this the critic serves as guide and counselor. But he must guide and counsel and interpret and evaluate in the language of the analyst, if he is not, while guiding through this wonderland, to teach habits of thought, speech, and mystery which take away from the value of his services and lead men and boys astray. This is not an impossible task. We will in the concluding chapter, consider in the broadest terms, the conditions of an effective union among the various disciplines: the conditions of a good education.

A Humane Education in the Modern Age

There is something radically wrong at the heart of things. How is it that universities can so order their affairs as to slight the very essence of their function: imparting an understanding of how to understand, explaining the nature of explanation, showing how to weigh, test, verify the knowledge that we think we know? Surely the better part of wisdom is in knowing how to be wise.

The crux of the problem, I think, lies in the doctrine that there are "two worlds of truth" and "two methods of investigation" and that a chasm exists between the sciences and the humanities. Hence the crux of the solution lies in the knowledge that this is not so; that there is not, in particular, any formal difference between the humanities and the sciences in the appropriate method of theory formation, conceptualization, classification, verification, and evaluation—although the substantive differences will modify research strategies and the availability of proof will vary considerably. However one looks at it, there are not, in any event, *two* sets of methods. Perhaps it could be said there is a wide variety of analytical methods and schemes, but there is only one logic (with different notations) that gives to each of these schemes its rationale. . . . If these observations are correct, it follows that our educational system, partly because it is the guardian of knowledge and the repository of civilization, and partly because it is the tutor to the young, must set about correcting the situation as rapidly as possible. There must be an understanding of the problem and then remedial action.

First, no discipline can afford to exempt itself from the constant effort to formulate and systematize the theoretical presuppositions on which its classifications, typologies, "approaches," "interpretations," even hunches and intuitions, rest. No discipline can afford, either, to permit these endeavors to become excessively private, individual, atomized, and heavily larded with references and terms understood only by the theorist who developed them. I have argued and would defend, too, the idea that in order to serve one of the most important functions of theory, theoretical statements must be stated in such a way that their propositions can be used, by subsumption, to explain or partially explain particular cases. This means that it must not be merely classificatory; it must have causal components.

In the second place every discipline must work toward a univocal language; if this involves the invention of terms, the hyphenation of terms, the appropriation of general terms for specific well-understood special meanings, let us mourn privately about this. It is a casualty of a larger good—the communication of knowledge. But, I think, this does not mean that one must write badly all the time.

There is nothing in our scheme which demotes the analysis of values, the development of moral clarity, the search for the ends and purposes and meanings of life. Hence, third, these must be preserved. But, in the fourth place, every discipline must clarify its procedures so that the comparison, analysis, and postulation of values is divorced from the evaluation of specific instances, must employ some form of "due process" in these evaluation procedures, and must keep these, in turn, separate from the functional analysis of the various relationships with which the discipline deals. The behavioral sciences, like the humanities, are not value-free; but they are, or try to be, value-clear. And, in the true spirit of humanism, all disciplines should be value-fair; that is, they should proceed judicially in making judgements.

Fifth, every discipline must look at parts and wholes; if analysis is reductionist in some sense, there must be a holistic and reconstitutive portion that redresses the balance. There is an enormous nonsense about the reductionism of the behavioral sciences; but while I reject much of it, I know what is meant. Robert Redfield expresses it in the following terms:

> It is the fact that it is the nature of humanity . . . to cease to be itself in so far as it is decomposed into parts or element. . . . The effort of the scientific mind to reduce the reality to elements amenable to analysis, comparison, and even mensuration early results in a distortion or in the disappearance of the subject matter as common sense knows it.[34]

I have asked behavioral scientists about men and they have told me about variables. That is not what I asked. But, still, Redfield and I understand behavior better because someone has "decomposed" the whole and analyzed the variables. If those who fear the reductionism of analysis imply that one should not penetrate vague concepts with precise instruments, one should not look at the morally sanctified portions of culture with a secular and skeptical mind, one should avoid taking apart some whole, perhaps a myth, a mood, a poem, or a man, to see how he or it is put together, then the work of scholarship stops dead and curiosity becomes an anachronism.

When the Royal Society was in its first decade, some of the subjects which came under the scrutiny of the members of the society elicited great scorn among the learned of the time. Robert Hooke, for example, Boyle's assistant and the author of *Micrographia*, devoted great pains to the analysis of insects and engaged Sir Christopher Wren, also a member of the Society, to make detailed drawings of "a louse, a flea, and a nit."[35] This, of course, was trivial beyond measure, reductionist, and, moreover, probably against the will of God. On the occasion of the dedication of the Sheldonian auditorium at Oxford, Dr. South, the University Orator, declared of these early scientists "They can admire nothing except fleas, lice, and themselves," and he went on to damn what was called "comprehension and the new philosophy."[36] At another time, the ridiculous obsession with instruments and measurement caused King Charles to be greatly amused. As Pepys reported on February 1, 1663/4, the King "mightily laughed at Gresham College for spending time only in weighing of ayre and nothing else."[37]

One of the casualties of the bifurcation of knowledge is the understanding of man. Of course everyone claims him; in a sense he is all we have. Allen Tate remarks that it is the man of letters who must "recreate for his age the image of man, and he must propagate standards by which other men may test that image, and distinguish the false from the true."[38] Douglas Bush, the Gurney Professor of English Literature at Harvard, conceives it to be the mission of the humanities to save mankind on the grounds that by studying them "one is never allowed to forget the individual person, to lose sight of one's self and others in a large blur of social and economic forces and formulas."[39] It comes to me as something of a shock and a matter of great regret that, to the extent that there is a "plain sense" meaning in these phrases, precisely the reverse is true—at least this is the case with the critical literature. For the fact of the case is that, except when dealing with biography, critical literature treats large aggregations of undifferentiated human collectives, usually under the categories of "the reader," "the poet," "the artist," or the greatest collectivity of all, "man." One searches almost in vain for something closer to the individual that is not quite biography: certain kinds of poets doing certain kinds of things under certain kinds of conditions; certain kinds of readers enjoying certain effects produced by certain qualities of a poem.

The conclusion, unfortunately, must be that in their concern for words and "a close reading of the poem" some humanists have forgotten about human nature and its wide and interesting variety. Those who are studying man, individually and in his various postures of behavior, are, of course, the behavioral scientists. But do they make their studies lovingly? Do they treat man tenderly? Are they interested in "purposes" as well as "functions"? Do they face squarely the question: "Why are we here?" Lovingly? Perhaps—it is a fact that social scientists are generally more concerned with and about the real sufferings of the underprivileged than humanists.[40] Tenderly? Perhaps not; they must dissect and this is considered untender by some. Purposes? Individually, yes. They deal with men's intentions as well as their actions. But for all mankind, as in the question on the purpose of life, no they do not. Hence they do not seek answers to the question "Why are we here?" But they know how real people all over the world answer this question, and that is something. This is simply saying that the behavioral scientist knows about human beings, although he does not know the Divine Will. But it is human behavior, not Divine Behavior which is his speciality.

The opening up of communication between the humanities and the social sciences, and the development of common languages and methods, wherever appropriate, will not, then, face one "image of man" with another. But it will do something else. Mythology has lent its names to psychoanalysis (Oedipus, Narcissus, Eros, Thanatos) for a very good reason. Characters in fiction, like Micawber and Oblomov, focus attention upon styles of behavior and attitudinal types. I have seen courses in public administration starting with Trollope *The Three Clerks*, and have heard it argued that the best way to approach the study of Soviet politics is through nineteenth- and twentieth-century Russian novels. There is some congruence between national character and national literature; the study of culture as a social product leads to the study of literature and art. In short, the humanities stimulate the behavioral sciences, give "inspired" subjectively screened portraits of men and societies in motion, and give life and drama to the behavioral scientists' categories and findings. Max Eastman says they help us to understand what, through the sciences, in another sense, we already know.[41] "Understand" means round out, fill in the details, give motion to static concepts, engage empathic sentiments, enlist, in short, *verstehen*. But for this purpose, the behavioral scientist must meet the literary critic half way; he must join in the analytic critical process.

What I have been saying may lead some to the conclusion that a proper method will give proper answers. That is wrong. The proper questions, plus the proper method, will be more likely to give proper answers. Any method may be abused, as Aristotle noted in his *Rhetoric* when he cautioned that the Sophists might abuse certain verbal tricks and methods. Any method can give sterile answers if the questions asked are not fruitful, and the substance of literature, as well as its theory, can help to pose fruitful questions.

An alternative and equally wrong conclusion that might be drawn from these remarks would be to the effect that some separate course of instruction —a course in logic, say, or in scientific methods isolated from the substantive matter to be taught—could solve the problem. There might be voices raised in behalf of this suggestion, for it would permit men to go on thinking and teaching in their accustomed ways, happy to have their consciences cleared with so little effort on their part. Such courses should, of course, be central to the curriculum—they are as important to the liberal arts as mathematics is to the sciences. Yet, although it is true that one of the foundation stones of my entire argument is that the ways of thinking encouraged in one area of learning tend to be applied in another, I must nevertheless maintain that the teaching of logic and the scientific method isolated from the subject matter of learning, empty of poetry and politics alike, promises only a little improvement. Unless it is wedded to the materials for which it is a guide, unless it is *used* over and over again, unless the teachers of the subject themselves employ a clarity of mind such as we have spoken for, the learning in methods will be the Sunday morality of the weekday sinner. One of the most forceful teachings of psychoanalysis is that insight is not enough; one must "work through" the new learning to make it useful.

The lowly scope and methods courses of the behavioral sciences, humble and abused as they are, offer some slender thread of hope. The thread is slender because we have had enough experience with the methods courses of the teachers colleges to have earned a massive skepticism about this vehicle of learning. To the extent that they focus upon how to use a library, how to collect a bibliography, how to interview, how to build a maze for rats, how to scan a poem, and so forth, they belong to the janitorial services of learning—indispensable, but janitorial. But for those moments when they deal with the problem of how to think about the structure of knowledge in their discipline, how to infer from evidence, how to construct a theory, and how to test it, how and when to generalize and how to limit generalization—all in close connection with a substantive body of material, and all dirtied by data—those moments, I believe, are fruitful for a discipline and pregnant with possibilities for the advancement of understanding.

But they are only moments, and, as Dewey remarks, experience is continuous. There is no other solution than the continuous re-examination of the objective foundations of our concepts, theories, and beliefs in a hard-headed and scientific way by all concerned with learning. Imagination and feeling are tender growths; do not damage them. But all the same and all the time for all of us there must be that grinding molecular process milling out the answers to the questions how do we know? how good is the evidence? how far can we generalize? what are the theoretical premises? what is the definition? how is this information structured, classified, organized? The human values of the humanities speak to our emotions; that is where love is located. But civilization rests also upon the mind, the hard cruel mind, the desiccating, withering analytical mind. And this is not memory—that is what a library is for—but analysis.

What I am talking about here is a kind of self-conscious attention to the organization of thought and evidence, values and experience within the context of a subject matter. No trivial part of the usefulness of such organization is sorting out of the various kinds of mental functioning discussed above; the autistic and the directed thought processes, the immediate and mediated perception, the referential and nonreferential expression, the employment of analyzed and unanalyzed concepts. These distinctions are crucial to the entire thinking operation. Richards says of the distinction between making a referential statement and the incitement of an attitude:

There is hardly a problem outside mathematics which is not complicated by its neglect, and hardly any emotional response which is not crippled by its irrelevant intrusions. No revolution in human affairs would be greater than that which a widespread observance of this distinction would bring about.[42]

And this is true of all of them. Suddenly—or rather gradually—we would find that we were communicating with each other, often for the first time.

The emphasis upon the organization of thought and the verification of knowledge is often unwanted because it seems to challenge two specialists: the man of sensibility and the man of information. The man of sensibility who can himself discriminate and make refined judgments, who claims and often has something that is loosely called intuition, but who cannot systematize his skill or state the principles according to which he operates, inevitably feels threatened, even degraded by the efforts of others to analyze the very processes of sensibility. To the extent that he opposes the effort, he is indeed challenged—and he will be overwhelmed by the glacial advances of science. To the extent that he continues to do what *he* can do best, better than anybody else, he maintains standards of performance for the systematizers to emulate, and to explain.

The man of information feels threatened because his strength lies in his memory drum, which, like a computer, can recall an infinite assortment of relevant data when asked the right question. But information alone does not lead to understanding. The confusion of information and thought is a central problem for historians whose discipline tends to stress information, because, in a sense, history is social memory, but it also arises in the discussions of the arts and the social sciences. The critic who is best informed on the allusions of a work of art is not, by that reason alone, best able to explain how it achieves its effects or to interpret its powers to communicate. In order to do this, he must raise to the conscious level the theoretical premises he employs, clarify his concepts and classification schemes, have a sense of what is verifiable and verified, and draw logical deductions about any present instance.

But the strengths of the man of information are no less important to the processes we have in mind; this is not a counsel of ignorance. So many dialogues come to mind of the following nature: the theorist says "Modern civilization tends to make men live longer." The man of information answers "Methuselah." The theorist re-examines his theory and it appears that the life expectancy of those over eighty years old has remained constant for 3,000 years; a modification of his theory, and an interesting point to pursue further, and incidentally, probably true.

By now it must be clear that the diversity of scholarly needs, combined with the wide range of skills and interests, makes a happy situation where the division of labor is a felicitous principle. The systematizer—and there must be one and he must know his business—the model builder, the middle-gauge theorist, the intuitive interpreter, the historical scholar, the experimentalist, the methodologist, the inter-disciplinary explorer or emigré, are all required.

A discipline that neglects any of them does so at its peril, impoverishes itself, invites anemia, and begs for invasion. But the lush variety of specialisms and generalisms suggested must be endogenous, or partly so. The stranger is seen as an invader and men gather together and forget their own differences to resist invasion. Yet I must believe that this stranger in the present case has a stake in all learning processes, for he is a citizen, not of a far country, but of the same nation, and a peripatetic neighbor in the same sacred grove.

Notes

1. *The Republic*, Jowett translation (London, 1927 ed.), Book III, p. 401.

2. James Bryce, *Promoting Good Citizenship* (Boston, Houghton Mifflin, 1913); Aristotle, *Politics*, Ellis translation (London, 1912), especially Chaps. V–XIII.

3. *The Making of Citizens* (Chicago: Chicago University Press, 1931).

4. *The Tension of Citizenship, Private Man and Public Duty* (New York: Rinehart, 1957).

5. Dewey, *Art as Experience* (New York: Putnam, Capricorn Books, 1958), pp. 53–54.

6. Hadley Cantril, Hazel Gaudet, and Herta Herzog, *The Invasion from Mars* (Princeton: Princeton University Press, 1940).

7. Richard Hoggart, *The Uses of Literacy* (Boston: Beacon, 1961), pp. 158–159.

8. Samuel Stouffer, *Communism, Conformity, and Civil Liberties* (Garden City, N.Y.: Doubleday, 1955), p. 91.

9. Stouffer, pp. 91–104.

10. See, for example, Robert E. Lane, "Political Personality and Electoral Choice," *American Political Science Review*, 49 (1955), pp. 173–190. Reprinted in Chapter 4.

11. Gardner Murphy and Rensis Likert, *Public Opinion and the Individual* (New York: Harper, 1938).

12. A reservation on this point might be registered here. Recently as chairman of a panel for the political sociology section of the American Sociological Association meetings, a study passed through my hands showing not only that social science faculty members were more liberal than other faculty members when they selected their fields and started their careers but that they were also likely to become even more liberal than others during the course of their careers.

13. Carl Hovland and others, *Experiments on Mass Communications* (Princeton: Princeton University Press, 1949), pp. 201–227.

14. A fine piece of analysis on "Literary Experience and Personality" by Robert Wilson may be found in *Journal of Aesthetics and Art Criticism*, 15 (1956), pp. 47–57. See also Paul Goodman, *The Structure of Literature* (Chicago: University of Chicago Press, 1954).

15. Hovland, *Experiments on Mass Communication*, pp. 182–200.

16. "Criticism in a Mass Society," in D. A. Stauffer (ed.), *The Intent of the Critic* (Princeton: Princeton University Press, 1941), p. 132.

17. See George Herbert Mead, "The Problem of Society—How We Become Selves," in Anselm Strauss (ed.), *The Social Psychology of George Herbert Mead* (Chicago: University of Chicago Press, Phoenix Books, 1956), pp. 17–42.

18. John C. Flügel, *Man, Morals and Society, A Psychoanalytic Study* (New York: International Universities Press, 1945); Ranyard West, *Conscience in Society* (London: Methuen, 1942); Martin Buber, "Guilt and Guilt Feelings," *Psychiatry*, 20 (1957).

19. Quoted in I. A. Richards, *Principles of Literary Criticism* (London: Kegan Paul, Trench, Trubner, 1925).

20. "The People and the Arts," in Bernard Rosenberg and David M. White (eds.), *Mass Culture* (Glencoe, Ill.: The Free Press, 1957), p. 75.

21. William E. Hocking says this sense of purpose is conveyed to an entire nation through its art: "And whatever a nation accepts as giving valid and effective expression to its feeling—its song, dance, poetry, graphic art, architecture—in that, it avows something beyond its ideology but wholly pertinent thereto, namely, the quality of its purpose, its dream-of-worth, pointing beyond what it is toward what it aspires to be." *Strength of Men and Nations, A Message to the USA and the USSR* (New York: Harper, 1959), p. 26.

22. *Aesthetics, Problems in the Philosophy of Criticism* (New York: Harcourt, Brace, 1958), p. 574.

23. Quoted by Edmund Wilson in his essay on "A. E. Housman" in his *Eight Essays* (Garden City, N.Y.: Doubleday Anchor Books, 1954), p. 115.

24. *The Logic of the Sciences and the Humanities* (New York: Meridian Books, 1959), p. 179.

25. *Principles of Literary Criticism*, pp. 44–57.

26. *Literary Criticism, A Short History* (New York: Knopf, 1957), p. 741.

27. *The Deprived and the Privileged* (London: Routledge & Kegan Paul, 1953), p. 84.

28. "The Metaphor: A Psychological Inquiry," in Renato Taguiuri and Luigi Petrullo (eds.), *Person Perception and Interpersonal Behavior* (Stanford: Stanford University Press, 1958), pp. 86–94.

29. *The Philosophy of Rhetoric* (New York: Oxford University Press, 1936), p. 172.

30. "If the New Testament . . . had been written by a modern social scientist in the jargon of his profession, it would have died at birth, and Mithraism, or Manichaeanism, or Mohammedanism would have taken possession of the European mind." Henry A. Murray, "A Mythology for Grownups," *Saturday Review* (January 23, 1960), p. 12.

31. A. H. Hastorf, I. E. Bender, and D. J. Weintraub, "The Influence of Response Patterns on the 'Refined Empathy Score,'" *Journal of Abnormal and Social Psychology*, 51 (1955), pp. 341–343.

32. "The World of the Daytime Serial," in Paul F. Lazarsfeld and Frank Stanton (eds.), *Radio Research*, 1942–43 (New York: Duell, Sloane, and Pearce, 1944), pp. 507–548.

33. "Mass Communication, Popular Taste and Organized Social Action," in Lyman Bryson (ed.), *The Communication of Ideas* (New York: Harper, 1948), pp. 95–118.

34. "Relations of Anthropology to the Social Sciences and to the Humanities," in A. L. Kroeber, *Anthropology Today* (Chicago: University of Chicago Press, 1953), p. 732.

35. Dorothy Stimson, *Scientists and Amateurs, A History of the Royal Society* (New York: Abelard-Schumann, 1948), pp. 76–77.

36. Quoted in Stimson, p. 77.

37. Quoted in Stimson, p. 80.

38. Allen Tate, *The Man of Letters in the Modern World* (New York: Meridian Books, 1955), p. 11.

39. "The Real Maladjustment," in the Harvard Foundation for Advanced Study and Research *Newsletter*, September 30, 1959.

40. See note 12.

41. *The Literary Mind: Its Place in an Age of Science* (New York: Scribner, 1935).

42. *Principles of Literary Criticism*, p. 274.

PART III

CORE BELIEF
SYSTEMS

Introductory Note

We make political ideas out of other ideas, not from the raw material of personality. In the subtle and painful processes of growing up we learn concepts of self, human nature, social causation—meta-ideas, ideas that serve as the anvil under the hammer of experience, forging political beliefs. Thus it is reasonable to follow a discussion of personality and socialization with a discussion of these meta-ideas, the core belief system that a person uses to interpret experience.

None of the three chapters in this section has previously been published.

Chapter 9
Belief Systems
and Political Explanation

The thesis of this chapter is that an adequate explanation of public policy is achieved only through an understanding of the political belief systems prevalent in a society. Later we shall expand on the idea of a political belief system: for the moment, perhaps, it will suffice to say that a political belief system is a set of values, beliefs, and attitudes regarding one's place in a human scheme of things marked by politics and government action. It embodies the most primitive, unexamined ideas, those which an individual and a society take for granted partly because they are never challenged, as well as the more articulated views of government. The political belief system gets its importance from the functions it performs.

In the first place, it contributes to each individual's sense of identity and helps inform him who he is and what he is worth. In so doing, it tells him what demands he may make upon government and society.

Second, it provides cues for the members of the society concerning the goals worth striving for: status, power, honor, "face," wealth. By doing so, it gives to men, both in and out of government, content for their concepts of success, criteria for self-management and estimation of others.

Third, it informs men about the elements of human nature. Generally it implies rather than states whether or not men are trustworthy, whether they are plastic and educable, or it may designate some who are either or both and some who are not. At its core there is a concept of the nature of man.

Fourth, it provides guides for interpersonal behavior so that there is among men that comity which comes with realistic expectations of how others will behave and how they ought to behave. First and last, government is an interpersonal process, marked, when it is functioning smoothly, by reciprocal understanding of interpersonal behavior codes.

Notes to this chapter will be found on page 169

Fifth, a political belief system provides men with the means for interpreting the roles they and others occupy. How shall the sheriff employ his powers? How shall the judge, the legislator, the President? Just as they interpret their own roles by reference to a belief system, so also do they interpret the roles of others.

Sixth, in a variety of ways the political belief system borrows from a more general belief system certain explanatory or causal concepts. What makes things happen in politics? Does it emphasize Divine interpretation? If it does, a separation of church and state is a grave mistake. Let the Caliph employ the secular *and* religious powers. Great men or impersonal forces—in what proportions will these inform men's explanations of political events?

Seventh, a belief system provides a setting in time and place for relevant political events; and, in turn, things are made relevant by their time and place setting. Is the time focus upon some distant third generation when the new utopia, perhaps a communist one, will come to power, or are the living members of society more important? Is it parochial in its scope, or national, or are the horizons marking the real and important world broader in scope?

Eighth, closely linked to the idea of explanatory concepts is the epistemological basis of belief offered by a general belief system, borrowed and used for political purposes. This gives clues to the appropriate ways of knowing, learning, and understanding. This is not just myth versus science or science versus magic and religion but rather a posture towards inquiry, towards "experts" and men of knowledge, even towards intellectuals; a way of dealing with rumor, with tendencies towards dogmatism and opinionation; an openness to experience. Perhaps it may be said to center in questions of the relationship of theory and evidence, of systematic investigation.

Ninth, a political belief system assigns to some men the imprimatur of legitimate authority and to others the stigma of usurpation. Authority, we now know, is both specific and general. It is specific in that some have one sphere and others another in which their authority runs; it is general in that one sphere of authority can often be converted to another or that authority in one sphere can be interpreted as legitimate and binding in another.

Tenth, a political belief system, borrowing from the broader culture, provides an ethical code and what may be called an ethical style. On the basis of this belief system a legislator must answer Socrates' question, "What is justice?" He will make decisions based upon his concepts of fair play; he will sort out good from bad, good behavior from bad behavior. Here will be found the attenuated idea of sin, the uses of blame, the sources of guilt.

Thus an *individual* must have a belief system to guide him in his daily tasks, to orient him towards others, to provide purposes and to give them sanction, to place himself in the ongoing stream of events. *Groups* must have belief systems to permit their members to work together and to provide their members with legitimate common goals. A political party, a union, or an ethnic association needs a rationale for its existence, a rationale that helps to define membership, moralize organizational claims on society, justify the sacrifices required of members, articulate some division of labor and role-structures, and explain a mission to others. And a *nation* must have one to indicate why its people and purposes are different from, and perhaps better than, others. Nations, in any event, develop belief systems to explain and justify their origins and destinies. Nationalism is sometimes useful in nation-building and always useful in war, and it must be based on special myths and beliefs. These not only justify and rationalize the national policy and culture, but also help to organize and institutionalize social drives.[1]

Embodying much of the above, the belief system will embrace, channel, and limit the uses of social change, for no matter what is demanded of them, "Human groups cannot effectively carry out acts for which they have no underlying systems of belief."[2] In making this point Leighton is, perhaps unknowingly, echoing a theme with distinguished ancestry. It is the idea epitomized in Rousseau's concept of "the fourth" class of law regulating social action.

First, he says, there are the fundamental laws of a commonwealth, that is, the organic laws, the constitution. These are followed by the civil laws and criminal laws. And then:

> Along with these three kinds of law goes a fourth, most important of all, which is not graven on tablets of marble or brass, but on the hearts of the citizens. This forms the real constitution of the States, takes on every day new powers, when other laws decay or die out, restores them or takes their place, keeps a people in the ways in which it was meant to go, and insensibly replaces authority by the force of habit. I am speaking of morality, of custom, above all of public opinion; a power unknown to political thinkers, on which none the less success in everything else depends.[3]

And this is so because "what makes the constitution of a State really solid and lasting is the due observance of what is proper, so that the natural relations are always in agreement with the laws on every point, and law only serves, so to speak, to assure, accompany and rectify them."[4]

Burke elaborates on this scheme. Arguing against the conception of a constitution as a devised instrument stemming from men's fallible powers of reason, he pleads for constitutional change following "the method of nature," by which he means accepting the inherited rights and duties accorded to men in a given time, modifying them only in so far as minimally necessary to meet the demands of changing circumstances. "All you sophisters," he says with reference to the French revolutionary theorists, "can not produce anything better adapted to preserve a rational and manly freedom than the course that we have pursued, who have chosen our nature rather than our speculations, our breasts, rather than our inventions, for the great con-servatories and magazines of our rights and privileges."[5] The engraved breast, like the engraved heart, provides the best legislative tablet. Had Burke lived into the nineteenth century he could have seen just how persuasive this lesson could be to the observers of post-revolutionary France, for the Great Engraver had, up to that point, written an authoritarian inscription into much of his human material.

The policy-making process, then, is properly understood by reference to a set of fundamental beliefs held by significant portions of the population. Nevertheless, in political discourse there are several approaches that minimize or ignore the belief systems of a people and employ what seem to be alternative ways to account for public policy. In what follows I will sketch some of the ways philosophical, legal, and historical approaches to political explanations need to be supplemented by more explicit attention to the kinds of belief systems we have been discussing.

One of these explanatory schemes relies upon the dominant political philosophies, the products of the great political minds, of the time. I contrast these to the fundamental belief systems, the political cultures of the political actors, for they differ in several respects. The philosophies are elite products of the "political speculators" that Burke referred to; they are articulate, rationalized, designed to persuade, conscious, more or less systematic, literate in expression, and designed for the literate and sophisticated reader. Core belief systems are only partly conscious, often assumed rather then expressed; they are held by the literate and the illiterate alike (though the belief systems of the literate differ from those of the illiterate in many fundamental respects) and are the premises of thought and action. There is a strong case for explaining great events by reference to the dominant philosophies. I am arguing that this is inadequate and that reference to both philosophy and common culture is crucial; the two are related in a special way.

Political philosophy as the study of the influence of a great man's thought upon political history or upon policy decisions seems to explain much. The study of the framing of the American constitution is a study, to some extent, of the influence of John Locke, the Baron de Montesquieu, and perhaps James Harrington upon the decisions at Philadelphia. The study of the French Revolution is a study, to some extent, of the influence of the *philosophes* and Rousseau on social thought. And the study of socialism in our time seems to hinge upon the influence of Karl Marx and his interpreters. It appears on the face of things that the influence of the great political philosophers upon history, and especially upon the political belief systems of a people, is the most powerful feature of historical explanation.

But before arriving finally at this conclusion, let us consider the alternative interpretation. It is made up of two parts. First, perhaps, it is the case that the great theories are really in very substantial degree rationalizations and codification of an already prevailing set of beliefs and practices. This would be William Graham Sumner's argument, when he says that changes in life conditions produce changes in the folkways and "then new philosophies and ethical rules are invented to justify the new ways. . . ." "Of course," he adds, "the view which has been stated is antagonistic to the view that philosophy and ethics furnish creative and determining forces in society and history."[6] But Sumner is in many ways somewhat fragile support for this idea.

Exponents of the sociology of knowledge argue that case more forcefully. In somewhat prejudicial language, Karl Mannheim says: "If . . . we are to rise to the demands put upon us by the need for analyzing modern thoughts, we must see to it that a sociological history of ideas concerns itself with the actual thought of society, and not merely with self-perpetuating and supposedly self-contained systems of ideas elaborated within a rigid academic (philosophical) tradition."[7] But the history of ideas is a history of the ways social circumstances have shaped ideas, for "morality and ethics themselves are conditioned by certain definite situations, and . . . such fundamental concepts as duty, transgression, and sin have not always existed but have made their appearance as correlatives of distant social situations."[8] Elaborating on this argument Mannheim seems to show how the political philosophies of each age are themselves responsive to the social and economic requirements of the men of the age. Thus a political philosophy, like any other kind, emerges from the needs, beliefs, experiences of the men of the age in which it comes to light.

Karl Marx, writing against Hegel and what he calls "The German Ideology," makes another case against the rule of ideas as an independent force in history. He says that concept is based on a failure to understand that the philosophers accepted in a given time are the spokesmen of a ruling class and that, therefore, their ideas are inevitably the products of a given arrangement of the means of production. The illusion that ideas have this life and force independent of the social circumstances and, hence, independent of the needs and beliefs of the ruling segment of society follows from taking at face value the arguments of the philosophers themselves and their interpreters and historians. He says:

> The individuals composing the ruling class possess among other things consciousness, and therefore think. In so far, therefore, as they rule as a class and determine the extent and compass of an epoch, it is self-evident that they do this in their whole range, hence among other things rule also as thinkers, as producers of ideas, and regulate the production and distribution of the ideas of their age: thus their ideas are the ruling ideas of the epoch.[9]

There is in this interpretation at least a suggestion that the political theory of a given period is a rationalization of the needs and, to some extent, the beliefs of the ruling class. If it is accepted that Hobbes' *Leviathan* was an elaboration of an earlier argument to justify the absolute sovereignty of the Crown *vis-a-vis* Parliament, and that Locke's *Second Treatise on Government* is a justification of the Glorious Revolution, it seems to follow that Karl Marx has some substance on his side.

As will be observed, Sumner, Mannheim, and Marx are at variance on a number of points, but they all agree that political philosophy is a rationalization of experience and an interpretation of current beliefs arrived at by other means. But what of Marxism itself; this seems to give the lie to the arguments of all three. Yet does it? If we look at the transformation of Marxism around the globe, there is considerable evidence to suggest that in considerable part it has served as a convenient theory or set of ideas to moralize, historicize, and rationalize the already-established beliefs of important elements of various national cultures. In Russia it adopted certain communal features of Russian culture, embraced the absolutist ideology of Old Russia, assumed the paranoid symptoms of a nation with a history of invasion going back beyond the Time of Troubles, and, in short, became thoroughly Russian.[10] In Germany Marxism assumed in the writings of Bernstein and Kautsky a more accomodationist tone and has today, in the platform of the Democratic Socialist Party, a moderate reformist program. In its most influential aspects British Marxism became Fabian Socialism and to some extent Guild Socialism and then merely the Welfare State doctrines of the Labor Party. In the United States Marxism was interpreted in the American vein by de Leon, Debs, and the alternate versions of the American Communist Party and the several Socialist groups. But in the main it has been rejected because it was incongruent with the prevailing belief systems in the United States.[11]

The lesson to be learned from this sketchy excursis is not that political philosophies are powerless to affect policy, but rather that in order to be effective they must correctly interpret the experience of a stratum of the population. And in order to do this they must be congruent with important elements of the cultural premises, the values, norms, mores—in short, the belief system of a society. It is the interaction of the two which gives a clue to the importance of each. If one modifies Fromm's views so that the less psychological implications of the term *belief system* are accepted for his term *social character*, we would agree that "ideas can become powerful forces, but only to the extent to which they give answers to specific human needs prominent in a given social character."[12] To give these answers they must speak the language of the prevailing core belief system.

We are examining some alternative explanations for public policy which minimize or ignore the importance of popular systems of belief, and we have briefly glanced at one of these, the approach through political philosophy. There is a second familiar approach to the explanation of public policy, that of legal analysis. The analysis of the legal structure of government tells us, by and large, the nature of the constitution, that is, the arrangement of offices and their powers and duties. It deals with such matters as the admission to the franchise, the number and terms of legislators, the war powers of the President, the requirements of "due process," the degree to which legislative power may be delegated, and so forth. By interpreting the influence of this legal framework and the powers of office, legal analysis can go some distance towards explaining why policy develops as it does, for it contributes to the understanding of how certain men, selected in certain ways, operating within a certain jurisdiction, make these decisions. This certainly is important.

Yet the limits of this mode of analysis are very great. Consider, for example, an interpretation of the policy differences among the states of Alabama, California, Wisconsin, and Rhode Island on such matters as welfare, civil liberties, and education. The constitutions of these states, as with almost all American states, are very similar; reference to these constitutions would contribute relatively little to an explanation of these differences. Or on a wider stage one might compare the public policies of countries with a parliamentary system to those with a presidential system. By and large one would find that the presidential system was characteristic of the United States and many Latin American nations, while the parliamentary system was characteristic of Great Britain and the Commonwealth, most of the European nations, and many of the African and Asian nations recently emerging from colonial status. Matching countries for relative wealth or relative "modernity," we would not expect to find that the differences between presidential and parliamentary constitutions had much to do with the nature of the public policies the governments had established.

The reason for this limited influence of the legal structure upon policy is that the belief systems of these various states and countries so shape the values and goals and behavior of men that the formal structure has in the end only a residual effect. The belief system does this through the ten kinds of functions mentioned above, but one of them, role interpretation, is most immediately relevant to legal study. The constitution establishes certain roles, such as President, Supreme Court Justice, and Senator, and the laws establish many others. To these roles are assigned certain legal (expected) kinds of behavior. But the belief systems of the various incumbents provide many of the cues to proper behavior in these roles. These cues may be codified into operational codes, but for the moment it is enough to understand how role analysis brings together an important part of the belief system and the legal structure.

If legal analysis is most useful when wedded to a complementary interpretation of the belief system, a third approach, the study of government through *history* may be said to find fruition in the same way. Perhaps this is made most clearly evident through an example. In *Southern Politics* V. O. Key, Jr., undertakes to explain the pattern of voting in the South and relies with good effect upon historical events. In one striking set of maps, the similarity of voting patterns in the 1940's and in 1860 strongly suggests a historical explanation for political preferences. Referring to these maps he says:

Tennessee's Democratic-Republican cleavage stands as a monument to the animosities of Civil War and Reconstruction. Even before The War a sense of separatism set off East Tennesseans from their fellow citizens to the west, although partisan divisions did not follow closely geographical lines. The dispute over slavery and secession, however, forges Tennessee partisan alignments into a form which has persisted to this day. . . . The areas that voted against secession became centers of Republican strength; the secessionist counties became steadfast in their Democracy.[13]

We take this to be an excellent explanation because we supply certain missing ingredients. Clearly the distribution of slave ownership in 1860 and the vote on secession affects *current* voting decisions only through a series of events affecting the attitudes of living people that are relevant for voting decisions. One can infer what these are: loyalties to a different tradition, family party attachments, more accommodationist attitudes towards Negroes, different political heroes—all the kinds of attitudes on which a survey would give us information. And it is these attitudes and beliefs which are operative in framing the vote decisions Key is talking about. Obviously they form part of the belief system of the people of Tennessee, nor are they isolated elements thereof. According to the principles of congruence[14] they are fitted into a larger framework of ideas, values, and beliefs so that, at least to some extent, there is a kind of harmony, a reduction of dissonance.

From this illustration it will be seen that history (a chronological sequence of events) affects current political policy in two ways: it changes the character of institutions through which policy is decided, and it changes people's belief systems and hence their ideas about an appropriate policy to pursue. It changes the environment of decision making, and it changes the predispositions of the decision-makers. It changes society, and it changes men. It is this latter aspect, of course, which interests us here, and perhaps a word or two about the nature of this change is in order. Again, the Civil War: one of the changes in the belief system had to do with the change in identity, that is, for some being a "Southerner" became more important than being a citizen of the United States. When this happened, a shift of attitudes towards things Southern came about. The new identity required a reinforcement of what was conceived to be the Southern way of life. A reevaluation of history provided in Southern heroes new models for behavior and new sources for those maxims by which people justify their acts. To support these views men developed a defensive, hence dogmatic, apology for the South's "peculiar institution." And for others in Tennessee, there developed a "reverse" set of identities and identifications, opening the way for an enduring embrace of things Union, Republican, and, for the South, different.

If the historian tends to rely on antecedent events for causal explanations, the sociologist prefers to reduce causes to the workings of social categories: social class, sex, age, religion, neighborhood. Yet, social categories of these kinds influence policy through their capacities to affect *both* environmental stimuli (selective exposure to the media, intensified group interaction, role assignment) *and* the shaping of beliefs about self and society. The identification of relationships between social categories and policy outcomes does not provide a satisfactory explanation.

Perhaps the point has been hammered with a sledge when a lighter touch would drive it home. Let us turn in the following chapter to the characteristics of a core belief system, the basic beliefs out of which political beliefs are made.

Notes

1. See the discussion of the "telos" and the social functions of ideologies in the next chapter.

2. Alexander Leighton, *The Governing of Men* (Princeton: Princeton University Press, 1945), p. 292.

3. Jean Jacques Rousseau, *The Social Contract*, trans. G. D. H. Cole (New York: Dutton, Everyman's Library, 1913), p. 48.

4. *Ibid.*, p. 47.

5. Edmund Burke, *Reflections on the Revolution in France* (New York: Doubleday, Dolphin Books, 1961), p. 47.

6. William Graham Sumner, *Folkways* (Boston: Ginn & Co., 1940 ed.), pp. 36, 38.

7. Karl Mannheim, *Ideology and Utopia*, trans. Louis Wirth and Edward Shils (London: Routledge & Kegan Paul, 1949), p. 65.

8. *Ibid.*, p. 72.

9. Karl Marx, "The German Ideology" in Erich Fromm (ed.), *Marx's Concept of Man* (New York: Ungar, 1961), p. 212.

10. See Dinko Tomasic, *The Impact of Russian Culture on Soviet Communism* (New York: Free Press, 1953).

11. See the discussion of this point in my *Political Ideology* (New York: Free Press, 1962), pp. 425–432.

12. Erich Fromm, *Escape from Freedom* (New York: Rinehart, 1941), p. 281.

13. V. O, Key, Jr., *Southern Politics in State and Nation* (New York: Knopf, 1949), pp. 75–76.

14. See note 11 above.

Chapter 10
The Core Belief System

The area of inquiry vaguely designated as political ideology or political belief systems (and the two can be distinguished) has many referents, many modes of analysis, each relevant to the interests of a particular set of scholars. Let us start, then, with a brief review of some of the ways in which the general field is conceptualized by leading scholars. I present this in almost digest form to give as comprehensive a picture as possible in a short space.

Some Attributes of Ideology[1]

Relation to action. Daniel Bell writes, "Ideology is the conversion of ideas into social levers. . . . For the Ideologue, truth arises in action." David Apter says of ideology, "It is the link between action and fundamental belief." But most authors would be content to confine this function to a smaller sphere: ideology "may serve as a guide to action" (Sutton), but it also serves many internal, adjustive functions as well.

Empirical reference versus mythology. It is common to stress the non-empirical, non-veridical features of ideology, although some authors, like Lowenstein, speak only of the source of ideology in religion and mythology. Parsons divides belief systems into empirical and non-empirical categories: among the empirical he places science and ideology, while the non-empirical are religion and philosophy. He refers here, not to their "truth," of course, but to their real-world reference. One difference between static and dynamic societies, according to Billy, is the way in which their ideologies relate to religious or supernatural matters; if they have a close relation, they imprison their host societies in the past and present.

Notes to this chapter will be found on pages 189–190

Evaluative and moral components. All observers hold that ideologies are evaluative, although often it is largely through their efforts to "justify" the going order. Parsons refers to the way in which ideologies serve "the evaluative integration of the collectivity."

Opposition versus status quo. Mannheim and Lasswell employ the term *ideology* only for conservative thought designed to support the going order; they use the term *Utopia* for reformist and revolutionary ideas. For most scholars, however, ideology can be either conservative or radical, although there is a tendency to think of the latter as *counter-ideologies.* The important point here is the way in which a counter-ideology must somehow use features of the prevailing and accepted thought pattern to persuade members of a society to become critical—a requirement that often induces strain in the radicals themselves.

Conscious or unconscious. Although some authors contrast conscious *doctrine* to unconscious *ideology* (Kim), most scholars are content to believe that an ideology is properly thought to straddle this line, being partly conscious and partly unconscious. The frequent use of the term *rationalization* implies a partly unconscious process of thought, and Kardiner's idea of ideologies as "compounds of projective systems, in the interest of which empirical evidence is mobilized" is a good one.

Telos, or goal reference. Lasswell says that ideologies "clarify the goal values" of society, Parsons speaks of their reference to "the future course of events," and Friedrich and Brzezinski think of ideology as referring to some "perfect final state of mankind . . . a chiliastic claim." Surely this latter point is overstated.

Mode of thought or expression. Lowenstein says: "Effectiveness and ideological mobility depend largely on simplifications, condensations, popularizations, and even vulgarizations, a process accomplished frequently—though by no means invariably—through the technique of symbolization." Many authors, including Sutton, Lane, and Horowitz, emphasize the importance of persuasion in formulating and expressing ideological statements.

Function. Perhaps the most important current line of inquiry has to do with the functions of an ideology. Sometimes this refers to the *individual:* what does his ideology do for him? Erikson, Apter, and Kardiner take this line, often in connection with concepts of identity-formation. Sometimes the reference is to the functions of an ideology for some *social group:* common ideas help them to work together, define and achieve their purposes, maintain their group morale. For *societies* ideologies do the same thing but at a more fundamental level: they account for their histories, explain their special life styles, give moral purposes to their members, make their members want to do what they have to do.

The carriers of ideologies. If an ideology is defined as the characteristic thought patterns of some special society or culture, as in Cash's *The Mind of the South*, the vehicle for its passage is a people, or some segment thereof.

This is equally or even more true if the term is *political culture*, a concept which for some is equivalent to political ideology and practice. But for Lowenstein "the carriers of political ideologies ... in our mass society appear to be primarily the political parties." And for Marx, of course, the carriers of an ideology are social classes, modified by the phenomena of "false consciousness." More narrowly defined as the characteristic thought patterns of men occupying certain positions in society, the ideology is located in a set of "roles" and their host institutions (Sutton).

Individual or social. Most people agree with Adorno, Horowitz, and Lane that ideologies are best conceived of as shared beliefs, although Parsons speaks of the possibility of an ideology for a "sub-collectivity of one."

Ideology and personality. Glazer says, and Rokeach agrees, that "no study of the relation between attitude and personality has yet ... solved the problem of distinguishing ideology—the views that someone picks up—from character—the orientations that are basic to a person." Nevertheless, it is best to distinguish between idea-systems, with their special properties and modes of analysis, and personality systems. To confuse them is often to confuse cause and effect.

Compulsory belief. Parsons says: "To constitute an ideology there must exist the additional feature that there is some level of evaluative commitment to the belief as an aspect of membership in the collectivity." But, it is said by others (Jules Blanchet) that the competition of ideologies is a mark of modern society. Obviously, these authors have in mind somewhat different features of belief, a difference hinted at by the distinction between treason and deviance.

The Content of an Ideology or Belief System

The subject-matter referents of the term *ideology* are sometimes inclusive: "all forms of consciousness" (Marx) or "knowledge" (Mannheim) or any "coherent body of shared images, ideas, and ideals" (Erikson). Sometimes they are more selective, such as "vital aspects of a man's existence (Friedrich and Brzezinski), or "explanations" and "justifications" of the social order (Parsons, Billy). Sometimes the subject matter is related specifically to social institutions: "Ideologies and institutions are mutually interdependent and correlative" (Lowenstein). And a few authors limit ideology to political referents (Kim), while others speak of "political ideologies" as subordinate elements in a larger idea structure, perhaps breaking the fabric of the larger structure when torn out for specialized examination (Rokeach). Central to most discussions of ideology is the problem of authority, either as political authority (MacIver) or as authoritative knowledge (Rokeach). Whether or not authors specifically say so, they must also include certain, often latent, premises of a fundamental nature: metaphysical premises on the nature of cause and reality, epistemological premises on the nature of truth and knowledge, ethical premises on what is right and wrong. Some combinations of these things are embraced in Kluckhohn and Strodtbeck's concept of "value orientations," dealing with the goodness and plasticity of man, time focus, location of authority on a group, dominance of man over nature, and emphasis on "being" versus "doing."

Certain core dimensions of political thought have been employed to sort out and analyze political beliefs, among which the two most frequently cited are *equality versus hierarchy* and *order versus freedom*. Levinson, one of the authors of *The Authoritarian Personality*, says, "The concepts of autocracy and democracy are widely applicable and of fundamental importance in the analysis of ideology." In some ways each of these terms embraces one side of the equalitarian-hierarchy and order-freedom dimensions. Another psychologist, Sylvan Tomkins, says the domain of ideas may be divided on a basic left-right dimension, according to the answer to the following questions:

> Is man the measure, an end in himself, an active, creative, thinking, desiring, loving force in nature? Or must man realize himself, attain his full stature only through struggle toward, participation in, conformity to, a norm, a measure, an ideal essence basically independent of man?

Karl Lowenstein has given a useful list of historical themes in ideological discussion:

> 1. Absolutism, as monarchism; dynasticism; legitimism; or, with a more religious accent, as theocracy and Caesaro-Papism.
> 2. Constitutionalism, institutionalized in the ideologies of representative government; parliamentarianism; the rule of law (Rechtstaat) and democracy.
> 3. Individualism, in both its economic and political implications, as liberalism; free enterprise, capitalism; and humanism.
> 4. Social collectivism, as either democratic or proletarian socialism (communism); state capitalism; and the ideology of the service or welfare state.
> 5. Nationalism; imperialism; racism; internationalism; and universalism.
> 6. Elitist and organicist ideologies, such as aristocratism, agrarianism; managerialism; corporativism; and the modern variants of facism.

These themes are reflected in most contemporary texts on modern ideologies, e.g., Ebenstein's *Isms* and Michael Oakeshott's *The Social and Political Doctrines of Contemporary Europe*.

The Core Belief System

These several ways of classifying the content of political belief systems are useful if one wants to take them as evaluative-descriptive-prescriptive accounts of the political world. The values may be challenged; the descriptions may be proven wrong and the implied explanations falsified; the prescriptions may be shown to be based on false assumptions—but the utility of this kind of analysis has been demonstrated. Nevertheless, I think Lowenstein's account of historical themes misses some of the inner meanings of the accounts and hence loses the opportunity to show the source, the "functions," and the influence of a set of ideas. I will argue that at any given time in any given place all but a handful of intellectuals, reformers, and possibly statesmen (though that is by no means certain) develop their *political* beliefs by reference to an adaptation of certain core beliefs relevant to the political problem to which they must respond.

If this is true, we must map out these core beliefs and then inquire into the process of reference and adaptation. I think there are eight elements of core beliefs which are crucial in this inquiry, each of which will be briefly examined in due course for the light it can shed on a political belief system; and I would argue that the same is true for religious belief systems, economic belief systems, or beliefs dealing with health and sex, education, or other large areas of life. The eight areas of the core belief system are:

1. Beliefs about the self; concepts of identity; self-evaluation.
2. Beliefs about the world of "others," classification of human sets, concepts of human nature; beliefs about interpersonal relations.
3. Beliefs about authority, as a specially important set of interpersonal relations; beliefs about appropriate behavior in the face of authority; legitimacy, kinds of authority.
4. Desires, wants, needs, motives, goals—and the elaboration of beliefs about them. These elements are values, in one sense of the term.
5. Beliefs about the moral good; ethical systems; concepts of what people should desire contrasted to what they do desire.
6. Explanatory systems; concepts of causation, habits of causal inference.
7. Concepts of time, place, and nature, where nature is seen as the impersonal economy, the order of things, including the Divine order; metaphysics.
8. Concepts of knowledge, truth, evidence, and how to discover the truth; epistemology.

The ingredients of this core belief system help to guide religious thought through relating God, the church, its priests and fellow communicants to self, offering explanations that account for the way one's own life has turned out, giving evidence on whom to trust and what to consider real, good, authoritative, and true. The core belief system takes the material of religion, theology, and religious practice and gives it personal meanings; societies with similar core belief systems will by this process have similar theologies, even if the religious terminology differs.

In the same way the core belief system takes the materials of the political order—the questions asked of government, the demands made by government upon the individual and the demands by the individual upon his government—and works them into a meaningful political belief system. With much simplification we can create a paradigm from Lasswell's original definition of politics.[2] The political belief system, shaped by the core belief system, addresses itself to these questions:

Who gets what from whom, when, where, how, and why?
Who should get what from whom, when, where, how, and why?
What should be done about it? What shall I do about it?

Here we turn to an explication of the core belief system, in terms of the eight "ingredients" mentioned above.

BELIEFS ABOUT THE SELF

The most important "who" for each of us is the self. An ideology may be said to deal with "What should I get?" But we must start farther back and ask, for each individual, "Who is the 'I', the self?" We term the self-image, the sense of self, an *identity* and in common with many modern social observers believe it to be of crucial importance. Some of these observers, including many psychoanalysts, believe that the complexities of modern life and the conflicting codes of life presented to the urban dweller have created a kind of crisis of identity. Whereas the peasant and village dweller had a place given him in society at birth and consequently knew throughout life who he was and what was expected of him, the impersonal mobile society of today does not provide such clear instructions. Each must discover for himself who he is, what his identity is like.

An identity does a number of things for a person. Part of it, the social identity, tells him with whom he belongs, who his crowd is, what others he may regard as close and equal, who are strangers, who are above and below him. His class identification, that is, whether he thinks of himself as working class or middle class, is part of this social identity. Second, an identity determines for him an appropriate style of social encounter—confident and open for the person with a secure identity and a healthy self-esteem. Third, his identity tells him what his skills are, what part of himself he can rely on; nothing is more pathetic than the person who misreads his own talent, wasting it in some cases, constantly leading himself into failure in others. Fourth, it gives him knowledge of his needs and inner life so that he can move toward their satisfaction in a realistic fashion. Fifth, it helps him to understand others, for we all use ourselves as a reference in interpreting others. Some of this is projective thinking—imposing one's own conflicts and drives on others in violation of reality; some of it is simply generalizing from the experience one knows best, one's own experience.

It is obvious from this brief introduction to the idea of identity that a person's *political* belief system, particularly his primitive political ideas, will be heavily influenced by his identity. This would be most evident in several ways, some of them the political parallels of what I have just described.

In the first place, by telling something about the self it tells him about the scope and content of his self-interest. What gratifications do I want from government? Second, it will help to tell him what his role in political affairs "ought" to be, that is, what it is appropriate for him to do. If he conceives himself to be too lowly for anyone to pay much attention to him, too ignorant to be worthy of an audience, too lacking in social skills to make demands upon others, he will regard a political system which never consults him quite in order. Although this self-image is most characteristic of the traditional old-world peasant, there are many in America who take this view. Third, it tells him what benefits it is appropriate for him to receive or even to demand. Here again a sense of worth, his self-esteem, is crucial to his decision on this point, and his decision on this point is central to his conception of a just political system—the core of a political ideology. Fourth, by locating him in society, his identity will tell him whose political interests he shares, with what group he should combine to effect or resist a change. In whose name does he legitimately speak—the working class, the aristocracy, the Irish-Americans, the intelligentsia? And fifth, because, as we said, he uses himself as a resource in interpreting others, his identity will tell him whether or not political allies are trustworthy, whether people are capable of self-government, or whether he is fighting a one-against-all jungle fight in an asphalt jungle.

But "who," that is, the world of people, includes others as well as the self. These others must be classified and evaluated into categories or sets that the individual finds useful.

HUMAN SETS: THE WORLD OF OTHERS

In classifying people, men use such terms as Protestants and Catholics, Americans and foreigners, rich and poor, kin and stranger, members of my club, "they"—meaning the rulers of society—fellow Republicans, and so forth. On examination it turns out that the lines of cleavage for the most important human sets around the world are:

> family and lineage
> cliques and associates
> race
> region and place (including community)
> nationality or culture group
> occupation
> wealth
> belief: (a) religion (b) secular doctrine
> interest
> party

When these are hierarchically conceived as stratified sets, they produce several important new sets:

> estates, castes, and status groups
> social classes
> specialized elites and sub-elites

Each person carves a kind of private pattern of these sets out of the social categories his culture gives him. The rich may be remote and uninteresting; the Irish-American set may be the most important in his set-pattern and the best loved; the family may give way to the work and carousing clique at a given age. His pattern thus is a mixture of an approved culture pattern and an individually shaped design for his own life. He evaluates as he describes. Is the set legitimate? Is it for him or against him—friend, stranger, or enemy? Is it "high" or "low"? Is it powerful or weak?

Perhaps the two most important things to know about this picture of human sets found in men's minds are: (a) what is the relationship of the individual to his sets, and (b) what is the relationship between sets? The first question is important because it raises the issue of movement from one group to another, especially from one status group to another, and thus determines the social mobility of the individual. It is also important because it deals with the degree to which an individual is free to dissent from the views of his sets (family, work group, ethnic group, and so forth), with how much individualism there is in a given society. A society in which the people believe themselves to be loosely associated with a variety of sets, each having only a limited control over its members' acts and thoughts, approximates the conditions of modern industrial society. But within this framework there is the possibility of great variety. A society where the reverse is true, where there are relatively few relevant human sets for each individual and these are thought to be very influential, approximates a peasant or village society.

In addition to the individual's relationship to his sets there is, as mentioned above, the problem of the relationship between these sets. To define this is to define the lines of social status and social conflict in society. What sets rank above others and what is the significance of these ranks? Which sets are in conflict with others and what are the terms of the conflict? Marx, of course, thought that the social classes were the most important sets because they were most intimately related to the important differences in the way men got their living: profits and rents versus wages. He also thought that the relationship between these class sets was inevitably one of conflict; the economic system was one which encouraged this. For the Nazis the most important sets were racial ones, one of which, somehow labeled Aryan, was above others and properly at war with others. The democrat believes in a plurality of sets, none of them as important as either of those just named, and all of them in more or less friendly competition or antagonistic cooperation with each other. It is in this fashion that the delineation of human sets and their interrelationships gives answers to the two questions: "Who gets what?" and "Who should get what?"

AUTHORITY

There are authoritative commands, authoritative knowledge, persons who are endowed with authority to speak on behalf of a group, leaders who are authoritative models for behavior, roles whose incumbents carry authority regardless of their personal properties. The core belief system of an individual or, if shared, of a group or society not only designates what and whom is authoritative, it also guides a person in his behavior towards these several embodiments of authority. Should he be submissive, rebellious, critical, cooperative? If he has authority, over whom and what does his authority run? What is the appropriate way to exercise it? What will restrain him? Beliefs about authority apply to family situations, religious institutions, and occupational relationships and tend to be both general (for situations defined as somehow congruent) and specific according to definitions of legitimacy and a cosmic map of who can and should do what to whom.

At the heart of a political belief system are concepts of leadership, power, authority. They deal with who can legitimately command the resources of government to achieve his ends, who does command them, and who should. A political belief system must deal with the question: "Who shall rule?" A first approach to an answer to this question will focus on the means of choosing rulers, leaders, or authorities. In formal terms this method is dealt with by the *constitution*, and in the American Constitution it is provided that the people in their capacity as an electorate shall decide between candidates presented to them. Believing this, the people of Middletown also believe "that the voters, in the main, really control the operation of American government."[3] This is, so to speak, a primitive political belief in that it is unexamined and rarely challenged. But there are other primitive beliefs in America. Among the working men I interviewed in Eastport, an American industrial city, one says, "Big business is running this country today. There's nothing we can do about it, but they're running it."[4] Without knowing it, he is reporting a central theme in the Marxist ideologists' interpretation of political power in America. And, since it is not provided for in the Constitution, it suggests usurpation.

These are only beginning questions; beyond them lie the often half conscious views on the type of men who should rule: the rich and wellborn, the self-made man with a "log cabin" somewhere in his background, men of old American stock—the political notion of "availability" is based on just such concepts as these. Then, too, there are ideas about the propriety of certain careers as qualifications for office, and there are very important, though often vague, beliefs about the appropriate personalities of men in high political office. Out of a generous and broadly equalitarian tradition, we have tended to eliminate the authoritarian personality from powerful positions, and, by and large, with certain exceptions like Huey Long and William Jennings Bryan, we have been moderate in our search for the charismatic personality who will relieve us of our social burdens.

NEEDS, MOTIVES, AND VALUES

Beliefs about one's own needs and motives are likely to be rationalized versions of the real thing; human nature seems to want to beautify them for conscious thought either as they are summoned to the bar of one's own conscience or as they are presented to others: sex is love, aggression is self-defense, ambition is wrapped in the public interest. (Beliefs about others' motives are wrapped in a more transparent foil; self-interest is more apparent.) This tendency to disguise our needs and motives creates a special problem for our core belief systems because it misleads us to the extent that we are unaware of our most basic drives. Further it complicates the analysis of the way a core belief system shapes social thought.

Like dreams, social thought is motivated; hence the question, "Of what use to you are your political ideas?" But the candid and accurate answer to the question must be dragged from the limbo of unconsciousness.[5] Crucially important, the motivational system gives the energy and stimulus to thought; it is not itself embraced in thought, or at least not in a useful form. Instead, the needs and motives appear in the belief system in the language of values and goals.

The term *value* has two referents: what one desires, the object of a need or motive, and what one feels one *ought* to desire, that which may be said to be the desirable. In the next section we take up the second of these: concepts of the desirable as embraced in concepts of the good, or more broadly, of ethical systems. Here, let us consider values as reflections of needs and desires, the part of values people are likely to weave into belief systems. To illustrate the way in which needs are translated into values, here is a list of the needs I have said shaped social thinking,[6] coupled with their respective values:

Needs	*Values*
Cognitive needs	Self-orientation, knowledge, enlightenment
Consistency and balance	Emotional harmony, self-consistency
Social needs	Affection, friendship, love
Moral needs	Rectitude, honesty, trustworthiness
Self-esteem	Self-respect, respectability, status
Personality integration	Character, freedom from conflict, well-being

Expression and restraint of aggression and other impulses	Spontaneity and control
Autonomy and freedom	Autonomy and freedom
Self-actualization	Growth, development, maturation
Guides to reality	Security and safety; success as wealth, power, fame, respect

The list reflects how similar to each other needs and values can appear; sometimes they are covered by identical language. One can think of them as a parallel set of concepts, one referring to the property of the individual, the other to the thing he seeks; one of them serving as an impelling or pushing force, the other as an attracting or pulling and "magnetized" object. Further, as the term *goals* enters into this discussion, we may think of a goal as a value-impregnated event that a person seeks; although values are abstract and hard to "see," a goal can be concrete and tangible. A person can arrive at a goal; his possession of a value is never that final.

The values a person wants for himself, and for those he cares about, represent features of the core belief system that shape his thoughts about society and politics. We speak of politics as the authoritative allocation of values in society; hence in ascertaining "who gets what" and "who should get what" we are at the heart of political discourse. Would it be fair to say that the ideology of the aspiring colonels of a revolution-ridden Latin American country stressed the distribution (and concentration) of *power*; that the ideology of the "five-percenters" in post-war Washington stressed the distribution of *wealth*; that the ideology of the men annually scanning the honors list in Britain for their own names and those of friends features *respect*? Men want different things, value different things, and build into their critiques and visions of government the distribution of things they value.

The list of values emerging from our list of needs is by no means all-inclusive. Charles Morris has asked samples of Indian, Japanese, Chinese, Norwegian, and American students questions designed to find out their preferred ways of life. Do they like an active life designed to meet and conquer life's challenges? Do they prefer a contemplative life designed to give them philosophic insights into the great eternal questions? Is it a life of service which attracts them? Is it balance among these various ways? Through statistical devices he reduces the complexity of his thirteen "Ways" to a relatively few dimensions. Among his findings is that Americans, in contrast to others, prefer a many-sided active life, but they are rather less interested in social causes (but not civic duty) and rather more interested in gratifying their own personal pleasures. In general, it seems that values as preferred life styles in America tend to support the individualistic, entrepreneurial rationales embodied in the "official" democratic capitalistic ideologies of the American society.[7] (As the research on which these conclusions are based was done in the thirties and forties, the findings may not apply to contemporary youth.)

A third concept of value, embodied in a study by William A. Scott of some American value constellations, employs a set of categories which emerge from the way people talk about the qualities of other people they admire. Although it confuses moral with non-moral qualities (intelligence, happiness, honesty, and loyalty), the study is useful because it shows the variety of value constellations in different social groups. Among the general public in "Mountaintown," the picture "is suggestive of Riesman's 'other-directed' type of social character. The popular values in this town tend to be those which concern social relations rather than relations with oneself, values related to the present rather than to the past or future, and values of impulse restraint rather than hedonism or power."[8] In contrast to this, the students in "Fundamentalist College" emphasize religiousness, self-control, respect for authority, humility, and hard work. They also emphasize happiness, popularity, and social skills but do not stress what might be expected: generosity, love of others, genuineness. It seems that the values among this religious group combine the Protestant ethic and the YMCA glad-hander in that style of which Elmer Gantry was a caricature. As interpersonal styles affect preferred styles of international relations, these different American personal values are important for the framing of a political belief system.

One might ask about the balance between values distributed to the self and values distributed to the community, based on the so-called other-regarding attitudes that Wilson and Banfield have analyzed. Their findings suggest that Jews and what used to be called "Yankees" (Protestants with Western European origins) tend more than Catholics (from Southern and Eastern Europe) and Negroes to vote for bond issues that help the community but do not have immediate advantages for themselves.[9] Thus cultural background and personal experiences both affect concepts of value distribution as between self (or family) and community. In some ways, of course, this is a composite of *who* as well as *what* is valued. And it has to do with the other meaning of "value"—the concept of the desirable, of ethics, which is linked indissolubly with the problem of self versus others.[10]

ETHICAL VALUES AND BELIEFS ABOUT THE MORAL GOOD

All individuals, even so-called psychopathic personalities, and all societies have moral codes. Individuals need them to restrain and order the chaotic promptings of their impulses; societies need them to regulate and coordinate behavior, justify sacrifice, legitimize authority, and give meaning to life. The contents of these codes vary among individuals and societies; almost everywhere incest is bad and honesty good. Few would disagree with the generalities of the Boy Scout oath: "A scout (good man) is trustworthy, loyal, helpful, friendly, courteous, kind, cheerful, obedient, thrifty, brave, clean, and reverent," although the terms would have different meanings in

concrete situations and priorities would vary greatly. The interesting variations come often in the conflict of goods (rarely between good and evil). If a
student sees a friend cheating in an examination, should he (would you) report him to the authorities? Under these circumstances Stouffer found that
most students hedge, trying to preserve elements of both honesty (discouraging cheating) and loyalty (friendship, solidarity) values.[11]

Since ethical values are not subject to verification (one cannot convert
an "is" into an "ought"), there is, in the end, a tendency to treat them
relativistically, but this tendency is properly jeopardized by recent work on
normal development. In that work, initiated by Piaget and carried forward by
Lawrence Kohlberg and others, it appears that in all cultures there are stages
of moral reasoning as children grow older as well as differences between
more intelligent and less intelligent children. As children mature, they tend
first to give moral reasons based on hedonistic calculations and fear of
punishment, then to consider the opinions of others, and finally to reveal the
workings of an internal independent conscience or self-punishing moral code.
Further, increasingly they give arguments on questions of right and wrong
characterized by the following six properties: (a) A shift from moral judgment
based on the consequences of an act to moral judgment based on the *intentions* of the actor; (b) a growing capacity to see that moral problems look
different from the different perspectives of the people involved, an increased
relativism; (c) appreciation of the fact that *morality and sanctions are independent*, that punishment does not alter the moral status of an act; (d) increased sense of *reciprocity* (sacrifice by one party implies sacrifice by
another) and *empathy* for the other's position; (e) growing realization that
punishment should be regarded as a means of education and *reform, not
retribution*; (f) an understanding of the impersonal causes of misfortune, a
reduction of the tendency to blame. Furthermore, the more one explores the
conditions of moral development, the more it appears to be a cognitive
function, based on the capacity to generalize from and interpret experience.
Although it is hard to teach moral principles, under the right circumstances
moral reasoning can be taught.[12]

Inevitably, the core belief system includes a moral code shaped by moral
reasoning with more or less of the characteristics described. The moral
features of that belief system are then employed in social interpretation and
help to give content to a political belief system. But the content does not
simply well up from the conscience of the individual; society gives multiple
cues on what and how a political system should be justified or criticized, cues
from which the individual selects those which are congenial to him. Briefly,
let us look at the nature and sources of these social cues.

One of these sources is the persistence of an accepted regularized discrepancy between a practice and its ideal. Thus Middletown believes in
"being honest," but "that, human nature being what it is, there will always
be some graft in government."[13] The ideal is not expected to be put every-

where into practice. A second source, like the first, depends upon discrepancies in the belief system but involves two incompatible norms, both expressing expected behavior. Thus Middletown believes "that idleness and thriftlessness are only encouraged by making charity too easy," and "that it is a fine thing for rich people to be philanthropic." It is in the shift in the point of view that the discrepancy comes, and in this shift there is an opening for moral critique of social or governmental practice.

There is a third point of entry for moral judgment; it lies in the application of central ideological values or doctrine to the practices of a society. The ultimate moral justification of Marxist philosophy is made by reference to a few concepts: equality of status and rewards, rewards only for social functions performed (no unearned income), brotherhood of (working) man. The core value in the Catholic ideology which emerges from the social doctrine of the encyclicals and commentaries by authoritative spokesmen comes back to a single concept: discovering and doing the will of God. The democratic (capitalist or socialist) justification of a social situation is likely to depend upon the value placed upon individual free choice, the autonomous spirit. Discrepancy between doctrine and practice offer the political critic moral leverage.

A fourth source, confounding the others, lies in the moralization and rationalization of self-interest. One finds in cultural norms, in core values, some element that makes an interested act seem more moral: the working man eager for more wages speaks of "exploitation," his employer of the proper return to the stockholders, for, at least in Middletown, "capital is simply the accumulated savings of people with foresight," and such people should be well paid for their foresight and their abstinence. A moralized version of one's own interests and purposes (often carefully rehearsed until believed) gives one both concepts and motive for moral criticism of society.

As may be seen from these illustrations, it is not easy to sort out the evaluative from the explanatory or descriptive. Normative elements are embedded in definitions: "Property is theft," and "The democratic nature of public life is determined by whether this or that policy is carried out in the interests of the people."[14] Values are so woven into the explanatory argument that they become inseparable: "We must see this English experiment [that is, "socialism"] clearly because the plan by which England was sneaked into socialism is now being promoted in this country by a coalition of politicians and revolutionary crusaders who are the counterpart of the British Fabian Socialists."[15] Sufficiently elaborated, as with Proudhon, the communists, and John T. Flynn, these mixtures of fact and value become ideologies. Social discontinuities, role strains, and conflicts facilitate this ideologizing process.

WHY: AN EXPLANATION OF EVENTS

Not much is known about the explanatory principles in political or other discourse. Among the most familiar themes in social explanation are the following:

1. *Divine providence* and intervention. The Lynds say that the people of Middletown believe that God intervenes only in the large events of life, not in the day-to-day matters. They would agree with Theodore Roosevelt: "Fear God and take your own part." In Eastport prayer is a source of comfort, not a means of changing life's events.

2. *Fate.* The popular intellectual refers to "kismet," the Anglicized version of the Arabic *gismah*, meaning "portion" or "lot," and thinks he expresses the fatalism of the East. Actually this is a much more complicated notion, but it is true that in traditional society cause is more likely to be conceived in such terms—basically, the Will of Allah, the Will of God—but a God not so accessible as in the Protestant faith.

3. *Magic.* Magic, or sorcery, implies human intervention, often malevolent. By manipulating symbols and personal and social artifacts and by using analogical thinking, men conceive that the real world is also manipulated. Magic is the cradle of science; it is an experiment in causal theorizing.

4. *Great men* (heroes). Much of history is written as a kind of opera, where the social order is seen as infinitely manipulable in the hands of the great artist, the great hero. The ideology of charisma embodies such an explanatory principle.

5. *Organismic action.* Although Burke never actually used the term, preferring "methods of nature," he liked to think of social change as an organic process in which some kind of unfolding takes place and every event is so interrelated with every other event that the mind of man can never see the consequences of his actions.

6. *Natural law.* The idea of natural law has its empirical and its ethical components; as an empirical theory it embraced an explanatory principle, namely, the idea that men can only effect change as they first discover and then use some hidden principles of social interaction very like the principle of friction or momentum in physical science. Spencer, for all his modernity, based his argument on such an explanatory principle. There is a good deal of this in Marx. This principle is to be contrasted to the great-man theory, its virtual opposite.

7. *Science.* In the popular American mind there is at the same time a reverence for science in physical affairs and an attenuated belief that any man's opinion is as good as any other's in human affairs—the negation of scientific explanation. Nevertheless, the readiness with which the common men of Eastport used concepts of population pressure, colonial influence, ratio of men to resources, and demoralization of a population as explanations for wars and poverty suggest a readiness for scientific social explanations in contrast to conspiracy theories, great men, and Divine guidance. Science takes from natural law the principle that the world is orderly, from magic the idea that it is manipulable. Its heart is a principle of investigation, a method.

Talcott Parsons says that every ideology attempts to explain to the members of a community why they are in the situation they are in.[16] Marxism has a theory of history based on class conflict and a theory of capitalism based on the labor theory of value and exploitation, out of which emerged an explanation of the poverty of the nineteenth-century working classes. Nazism had a racial explanation of history and the then-current situation of Germany as a conspiracy of Jews. American democracy has an explanation for its prosperity based, among other things, on a theory of "the profit motive" and a therapy of "the unseen hand." In essence these theories represent first a simplistic psychological view of human acquisitiveness and second a serendipitous view of the results of self-seeking in a market situation. American historians explain America's free institutions by reference to the experience of the frontier, the protection of an ocean, and the lack of feudal institutions at an early stage of growth.

In all of these explanations one can perceive the employment of certain categories of events, certain properties of societies and their situations. Some men, like Charles Beard and Madison, emphasize the importance of the conflict among economic groups, the importance of economic institutions. Climate is important to such social interpreters as Montesquieu and some anthropologists; disease to Hans Zinsser, the author of *Rats, Lice and History*; geography to those who look at trade routes and insulation from the ravages of war; military and naval power to Admiral Mahan and General Haushofer. National character is employed by men as different as Aristotle, John Stuart Mill, and Charles McClelland; moral force and persuasion by Croce; communications by Daniel Lerner; cultural growth by Kroeber; religion by Sombart and Weber; science and technology by Whitehead and others; socialization practices by Kardiner and Mead; and colonialism (a combination of military, economic, and racial factors), by Lenin, Fanon, and most third-world historians. The precipitate of these learned views may be found in many core belief systems, sloganized, unsystematic, and sometimes passionately held.

These accounts of historical change refer to the larger explanations. But the explanatory principles also apply to more detailed matters: explanations of the origins and functioning of federal systems (or this federal system), explanations of why representatives look to the people for their guidance, explanations for the corruptibility or incorruptibility of judges. Political belief systems embody elements in their fine print along with the larger historical explanations, which provide the foundations for the important interpretations of how we got here and what we can expect from the future.

WHEN AND WHERE: THE SETTING FOR POLITICAL INTERPRETATION

Without knowing it, men are like clocks, their acts and expectations paced by some inner regulator. If they are lucky, their own sense of time and the prevailing sense of time around them will synchronize. As a political belief system involves demands and expectations, it is important to know how urgent they are. The possibilities for variety are great. In traditional society men tell time by the seasons; their daily life is regulated by the sun. When misery on earth is unendurable, men think of an afterlife and live in contemplation of it. In chiliastic codes the focus of attention may be upon an earthly renaissance some thousand years away; in utopian societies it may be the world of the grandchildren, as the communists used to say of their own utopian efforts. Bryce reported that in the 1890's Americans were characterized by "an intellectual impatience, and desire for quick and patent results," but the Lynds report that Middletown believes "change is slow."[17] In Eastport I found men focusing on events in the immediate and near future; their policy orientation, too, had this brief time span.

The Lynds say that Middletown is isolationist and local—or was some twenty-five years ago. Today, no doubt, it is less isolationist and, like most smaller cities, less local. A town may be "local" in opposition to the cosmopolitan universe that threatens it, as are the people of "Springdale" in Massachusetts and, to some extent, the sons of the middle border in Plainville, although they too have changed in this respect.[18] Contrast this kind of localism with that reported by Merton in Rovere, where men become "local" as a feature of growing up and going into business in that town, not as a reaction to the outside but as identification with a hometown.[19] In Eastport the common man tends to root such localism as he has in his extended family and his sense of the familiarity of place, not in public affairs. In this public sphere he has been "nationalized" by the media; he is much more interested in national than in local authorities, events, and elections. And each of these is a far cry from the parochial localism of the Balgat Chief, the traditional villager, that Daniel Lerner portrays in his *The Passing of Traditional Society*.[20]

Feelings about time and place are relevant to the political belief system because they provide boundaries to interests, define what is emotionally significant, point to important people, and give drama and drabness to the stages on which events are played. There is a quality of rootedness in some people's lives which is not present in others', and this anchors their politics; there is some sense of community for a few, but in modern times this sentiment is less frequent and less strong; there is a feeling of political leverage with local or state or national fulcrums; there is a map of the familiar and the strange and the hostile in the crannied minds of both ordinary and extraordinary men.

CONCEPTS OF KNOWLEDGE AND TRUTH

We might ask the same question about a piece of knowledge that we asked about a political idea: "Of what use to a man is some 'bit' of knowledge?" He may use it, as Karen Horney said some of her patients did, as a means of proving his status in a status-insecure society.[21] "Inside" information is evidence of being on the inside. Knowledge and information are counters in exchange to be traded, perhaps invested, in another cause. Knowledge provides orientation in a confusing world, safety if knowledge is relevant to danger, "intelligence" if it is useful in war and diplomacy. Knowledge is useful in meta-knowing; one piece illuminates another. As a guide to reality, it serves various life purposes, some as trivial as bargain hunting, some as important as professional advancement.[22] In a knowledgeable society the man of knowledge is king—well, an adviser to the king.

There are basic different ways men use knowledge which are important in the framing of a belief system. Some men use knowledge *defensively* to protect previously held ideas, giving them the security of the familiar world whose integrity they guard against attack. For them truth is ascertained by matching a statement against what they "know" and want to believe. Ideas are useful in defense of doctrine, dangerous if they do not serve that purpose. Such a posture leads men to be doctrinaire and dogmatic. Other men employ ideas *instrumentally* to know the world, to exploit it and explore it, and to extract both meaning and the satisfaction of purpose from it. The truth of an idea lies in its power to serve as a guide to reality and in its ability to withstand tests of falsehood, exaggeration, hyperbole. A third group finds a kind of *truth value* in an idea which escapes these tests of truth; the idea may have the capacity to amuse, delight, inspire, console. Reference to truth here is elliptical, for truth under these circumstances refers to resonance with human emotion; truth is consummatory and gratificatory. A moving account is a "true" story.

Like ethics there seems to be a "higher" and a "lower" form of knowledge, a dimension based in part on the sequential kinds of knowledge children reveal as their thinking matures, as they grow up. The dimension of this scale is from concrete to abstract, from taxic or stimulus-bound responses to a kind of parascientific mentality. At the lower end of the scale is a fixed or instinctual response to a given stimulus, like the phototropism of the moth and the cockroach. Such a posture robs a person of flexibility of choice, of rehearsal of alternative responses, of anticipation. In this sense neurosis is characterized by concrete thinking, for neurotic responses are choiceless responses.

At the other, abstract end of the scale there are certain qualities of thinking that may be characterized as follows. First, there is available, or ready for improvisation, a set of concepts which give meaning to information because they inform the knower what goes with what, what precedes what, what causes what. Second, the knower differentiates himself from the inner world of impulse and dream and is not subject to their promptings; at the same time he differentiates himself from his environment and as a separate person can employ a kind of detachment for purposes of appraisal. For him knowledge is neither hallucination, on the one hand, nor perception and sensation, on the other, but something else. Third, knowledge can be counter-factual, an imagined situation beyond experience and contrary to what the senses describe. Hence the capacity to rehearse alternatives and examine them before commitment. Fourth, knowledge is a synthesis of information from which a message is extracted: the point of a story, the key to a puzzle, the critical cause in an explanation. Knowledge is not the separate bits of information: it is their meaning derived for a purpose. Fifth, knowledge is hierarchical in the sense that subsumption is possible, inference is possible, generalization is possible. Finally, the truth value of a statement does not rest on the power or reputation of its author, for there are other methods of testing veridicality, probability, and plausibility.

In a discussion of the kinds of learning that prepare men for citizenship, *The Liberties of Wit* follows some of these steps of "higher" learning but sticks more closely to the axioms of a philosophy of science. Briefly these include: (1) an avoidance of the pitfalls of an idealistic metaphysics (concepts are somehow "out there"); (2) a close reading of historical and other explanations for their implicit reliance on unstated theories of social causation; (3) a parsimonious and informed use of taxonomies and classificatory systems; (4) appreciation of the relationship between language (symbols) and reality (interpretations of sensory experience); (5) knowledge of the ways to test or falsify generalizations; (6) sophistication regarding the processes implied in evaluative thought; (7) self-awareness on the uses of both fantasy and directed thought; and (8) ends-means rationality in all important matters. Of course this is a difficult order, but it suggests some of the elements of a core belief system as these touch on the problems of knowing and knowledge.[23]

Finally, we turn to the question of what *should* be known. In *Hasaan,* James Elroy Flecker speaks of the caravan to Samarkand as motivated by "the lust of knowing what should not be known." Although this was not a lust characteristic of the Middle East, the idea of forbidden knowledge may have started there in the Garden of Eden. In Eastport, although there is some forbidden knowledge dealing with religious heresy (matters on The Index), with Marxism, and with sex, the conditions are generally latitudinarian. Here are three suggestive inferences from interviews with working-class men in that industrial American city:

It is better to know what is true than what is good or what is beautiful. The "aesthetic continuum" that Northrup says is characteristic of the East gets short shrift in Eastport, where the idea of simply enjoying the messages of the senses and refining their discrimatory powers has no home. The senses are for work, not for enjoyment. Moreover, little time is spent defining or appreciating what is good or moral. Because there is so little conflict about the moral code, it remains unexamined. Perhaps for this reason:

Understanding external events and objects is more important than understanding "how I feel," or "how I should feel" about things. In this view it is true that the Anglo-American has an *epic* rather than a *tragic* sense. As a consequence the Eastport men tend to know themselves in the third person.

Understanding and knowing are tentative and progressive. Nothing can be known absolutely; people should be ready to change their minds as new information comes in; those who admit being wrong are more likely to be correct in the long run than those who take principled stands on things. Later information is always better than earlier information.

As these features of an epistemology and of concepts of what is true, how truth is to be tested, and what is worth knowing enter into the core belief system, they form a selective sieve that catches and holds some information and lets other information go. Further, they guide men in deciding who tells the truth as well as what the truth about society really is. If the truth will set men free, there must be many paths to freedom, for there are many concepts of what is true.

Notes

1. The authors and works referred to in this resume are: T. W. Adorno, Else Frenkel-Brunswik, Daniel J. Levinson, and R. Nevitt Sanford, *The Authoritarian Personality* (New York: Harper, 1950); David Apter (ed.), *Ideology and Discontent* (New York: Free Press, 1964); Daniel Bell, *The End of Ideology: On the Exhaustion of Political Ideas in the Fifties* (New York: Free Press of Glencoe, 1960); Jacques-Serge Billy, "Le Probleme de la Finalite des Societes Politiques et les Explication Ideologiques," Report of the Second International Congress of Political Science, 1952 (Karl Lowenstein, rapporteur), *International Social Science Bulletin*, 5 (1953), pp. 51–74; Jules Blanchet, "Ideologies et Transformation Sociales," in *Ibid.*; W. J. Cash, *The Mind of the South* (New York: Knopf, 1941); Erik Erikson, "The Problem of Ego Identity," *Journal of the American Psychoanalytic Association*, 4 (1950), pp. 56–121; Carl J. Friedrich and Zbigniew K. Brzezinski, *Totalitarian Dictatorship and Autocracy* (Cambridge: Harvard University Press, 1956); Nathan Glazer, "New Light on 'The Authoritarian Personality,'" *Commentary*, 17 (1954), pp. 289–297; Abram Kardiner and associates, *The Psychological Frontiers of Society* (New York: Columbia University Press, 1945); Young C. Kim, "The Functions of Political Orientations: A Typology," *World Politics*, 16 (1964), pp. 205–221; Robert E. Lane, *Political Ideology* (New York: Free Press, 1962); Harold Lasswell and Abraham Kaplan, *Power and Society* (New Haven: Yale University Press, 1950); Daniel J. Levinson, "Conservatism and Radicalism," *International Encyclopedia of the Social Sciences* (New York: Free Press, 1968), vol. 12, pp. 21–30; Karl Lowenstein, "Ideologies and Institutions: The Problem of their Circulation," *Western Political Quarterly*, 6 (1953), pp. 689–706; Robert MacIver, *The Web of Government* (New York: Macmillan, 1948); Karl Mannheim, *Ideology and Utopia*, trans. Louis Wirth and Edward Shils (London: Routledge and Kegan Paul, 1949); Talcott Parsons, *The Social System* (New York: Free Press of Glencoe, 1951); Milton Rokeach, *The Open and Closed Mind* (New York: Basic Books, 1960); Sutton and associates, *The American Business Creed* (Cambridge: Harvard University Press, 1956; Silvan Tomkins, "Left and Right: A Basic Dimension of Ideology and Personality," in Robert W. White (ed.), *The Study of Lives* (New York: Atherton, 1964), pp. 388–411.

2. Harold Lasswell, *Politics: Who Gets What, When, and How?* (New York: McGraw-Hill, 1936).

3. Here and in several references below to the beliefs of the people of Middletown, I am of course relying on Robert and Helen Lynd's interpretations. This reference is from *Middletown in Transition* (New York: Harcourt, Brace, 1937), p. 418.

4. The references to the opinions in Eastport rest in information in my *Political Ideology* (New York: Free Press, 1962).

5. The question about the uses to an individual of his political ideas serves as the basis of research in ideological self-analysis reported in my *Political Thinking and Consciousness* (Chicago: Markham, 1969). The last three chapters of that book deal with the problem of consciousness of one's own basic needs referred to in the preceding paragraph.

6. *Ibid.*, pp. 31–47.

7. Charles Morris, *Varieties of Human Value* (Chicago: University of Chicago Press, 1956), p. 50.

8. William A. Scott, "Empirical Assessment of Values and Ideologies," *American Sociological Review*, 24 (1959), pp. 304–305.

9. James Q. Wilson and Edward C. Banfield, "Public-Regardingness as a Value Premise in Voting Behavior," *American Political Science Review*, 58 (1964), pp. 876–887.

10. See Clyde Kluckhohn and others, "Values and Value-Orientations in the Theory of Action," in Talcott Parsons and Edward A. Shils (eds.), *Toward a General Theory of Action* (New York: Harper Torchbook, 1951), pp. 388–433.

11. Samuel A. Stouffer, "An Analysis of Conflicting Social Norms," *American Sociological Review*, 14 (1949), pp. 707–717.

12. Lawrence Kohlberg, "Development of Moral Character and Moral Ideology," in Martin L. Hoffman and L. W. Hoffman (eds.), *Child Development Research*, vol. 1 (New York: Russell Sage, 1964); Jean Piaget, *The Moral Judgment of the Child*, trans. Marjorie Gabain (New York: Free Press, 1965). The implications of these studies for political thought are developed in my *Political Thinking and Consciousness*, Chaps. 10 and 11.

13. See note 3 above.

14. Abridged from Georgi Aleksandrov, *The Pattern of Soviet Democracy*, quoted in Vernon Van Dyke, *Political Science, A Philosophical Analysis* (Stanford: Stanford University Press, 1960), p. 69.

15. John T. Flynn, *The Road Ahead, America's Creeping Revolution* (New York: Devin-Adair, 1949), p. 11.

16. Talcott Parsons, *The Social System*, p. 349.

17. Robert and Helen Lynd, *Middletown in Transition*, pp. 405, 419. Lord Bryce is quoted by the Lynds.

18. Arthur J. Vidich and Joseph Bensman, *Small Town in Mass Society* (Princeton: Princeton University Press, 1958); James West, *Plainville, U.S.A.* (New York: Columbia University Press, 1961).

19. Robert K. Merton, *Social Theory and Social Structure*, rev. ed. (New York: Columbia University Press, 1957), pp. 387–420.

20. (New York: Free Press of Glencoe, 1958).

21. Karen Horney, *The Neurotic Personality of Our Time* (New York: Norton, 1937).

22. Bernard Berelson provides an insightful interpretation of the uses of information of a special kind in his "What 'Missing the Newspaper' Means," reprinted in Daniel Katz and others (eds.), *Public Opinion and Propaganda* (New York: Dryden, 1954), pp. 263–271.

23. These points are discussed in chapter 8.

Chapter *11*
Core Beliefs and
the Agenda of History

As political problems differ in their demands upon belief systems, we here turn to see how it is that core beliefs such as those described might shape events and interact with the agenda of history. In *Political Thinking and Consciousness*[1] I analyzed in some detail the way personal needs influenced political thinking; here, by way of contrast, I focus on the interaction of core belief systems with history.

One feature of this explanation is the intrusion of a new set of considerations in the simple displacement hypothesis set forth by Harold Lasswell some thirty years ago. As reported in Chapter 1 above, he says:

> The most general formula which expresses the developmental facts about the fully developed political man reads thus: $p)d)r=P$, where "p" equals private motives; "d" equals displacement onto a public object; "r" equals rationalization in terms of public interest; "P" equals political man; and) equals transformed into.[2]

This formula, as well as other writings in which psychodynamic interpretations of personality are made to serve as the chief causal explanation for emerging political ideas, leaves out of account the two matters here at stake: the core belief system the individual has acquired as an instrument for interpreting the world and the political problems of a society. A man makes ideas out of other ideas, not simply out of needs and defense mechanisms. "The myth mediates between man and nature," says MacIver. "From the shelter of his myth he perceives and experiences the world. Inside his myth he is at home in his world."[3] The "myths" are the core belief system.

How then do the several features of men's philosophies, *weltanschauungen,*

Notes to this chapter will be found on pages 209–210

and political cultures engage the great problems that descend upon them? To tease the dogmatist, as well as to stress the problematic nature of the issues, I put the possible engagements in question form.

Questions of the Self in Historical Context

CONFLICTING CUES FOR EVALUATING THE SELF

Lack of self-esteem in the American Negro has sometimes been expressed in hedonism, criminality, and apathy;[4] perhaps one could judge that the rebellious spirit of the black power advocates and the slogan "black is beautiful" provide long-delayed and much-needed cues for restoring self-esteem to this oppressed group. Lucien Pye suggests how a small Eastern nation expresses ambiguous self-esteem *vis-a-vis* the West by unpredictable and sometimes self-defeating behavior in what he calls "The Spirit of Burmese Politics."[5] And Harold Lasswell has outlined how a person's *doubts* about his own strength or worth can lead to intense political activity in an effort to relieve those doubt.[6] In general, the problem of how to deal with outspoken critics and friends is a problem of political strategy with relatively straight-forward calculations of gains and losses, but the problem of how to deal with doubt and ambiguity, especially the internalized critic, the half-accepted denigration, engages elaborately disguised features of the core belief system. Thus:

> Will a nation-building political elite that feels superior to and well-esteemed by its own people but inferior to and patronized by the outside world express this ambivalence by identifying with the West and looking down on its own "ig-norant masses" or by heightening its nationalism and repudiating the "material-ism" of the West—or by using both strategies?
> Will the leaders of a group (like the American Negro today and the Italian-American forty years ago) that experiences social denigration at the same time that it is politically sought after and cultivated resolve this problem by a politics of self-advancement and accommodation to the national mores or by a politics of group advancement, using politics as a vehicle for the cause of the group members?
> Will the leaders of a nation like England, whose collective sense of esteem and pride was supported by a sense of world dominion, react to the loss of this support by clinging to dreams and myths of former glory or by a realistic shift in policy to the new "reduced circumstances?"

In each case the conflict is likely to be resolved by a rationale for policy that minimizes the blow to the self and at the same time provides the basis for more or less realistic power politics.

REPUTATION: THE MIRROR OF SELF-EVALUATION

In one sense, we always *do* see ourselves as others see us, but in different cultures and groups the bases for evaluation differ. Thus:

Will cultures in which heavy emphasis is put upon "face" (*lien*) develop political systems with elaborate formal rules, conflict masked (the term itself suggests "saving face") by courtesy, and depersonalized partisanship? In the light of the recent Chinese disturbances, should we conclude that reliance on these formalities to restrain aggression implies the lack of other restraining mechanisms when the concept of "face" loses its ethical force?

Where concepts of honor are strongly influenced by sensitivity to matters of virility and masculinity (*machismo*), is the show of violence more probable? Is a "spiritedness" or temper more likely to be indulged?

Where reputation is based on task skills, work performance, and achievement, is society more likely to be overly bureaucratized? Does conflict take on a colder, differently phased, more analytically based orientation?

Each of the hypotheses implied by the questions suggests that the way men earn their reputations influences the way conflicts are both generated and resolved.

Perhaps, however, there are differences in the degree to which self-esteem may be won in a society, some societies being better endowed with ways of giving esteem to all. Provisions for building self-esteem may be called, as they are in some psychoanalytic accounts, "narcissistic supplies." Would it be true, then, that where there is a less skewed and more generous distribution of these narcissistic supplies, (a) there will be more "matter of fact" and efficient policy-making processes (men are free to address themselves to social problems with less need to repair their own ego deficiencies) and (b) there will be less attention given to questions of "face," "honor," and "machismo" or other ego-protections in the political process?

CONSCIENCE: THE GROUNDS FOR SELF-DENIGRATION AND SELF-PUNISHMENT

The conscience is the internalized agent of society that makes an individual feel guilty and self-punitive for transgressing against someone, perhaps one's own better or higher self. Because the concepts of guilt and sin bring the individual to the bar of "justice," as he defines that term for himself, they affect the handling of justice in society.

To what extent are the alleged Russian ideas that *all* men are guilty of treasonable thoughts and that thoughts and deeds may be deemed equivalent related to Soviet practices of exemplary punishments by courts of law and the "confessions" of political criminals (who confuse their own guilty thoughts with guilty practices)?

To what extent does the idea of "paying a debt to society" reflect expiation for sin and therefore discharge guilt and release the prisoner (or individual fined) to transgress again? This interpretation of punishment may be characteristic of some Western prisoners; it is said to have frustrated, by encouraging recidivism, the introduction of Western law and courts by the British in Burma.

The Anglo-American concept of individualism underlying the idea of individual guilt (as contrasted to collective or symbolic guilt) can be said to find legal expression in the elaborate protection of due process in the court to assure that the guilty person and only the guilty person is punished. To what extent will this practice and set of concepts be undermined by the idea of social determination of individual acts? Does the resistance to this idea come from the belief lodged in each conscience that "I am responsible for my own acts"?

Generally speaking, one might suppose that the more specific the attachment of guilt to behavior (and not to thought or impulse): (a) the more likely the defendent is to be treated as an individual and not as a member of a class and (b) the more elaborate will be the concepts of "due process" and rules of evidence.

The Self and Others

SOCIAL IDENTITY: PLACING SELF IN A WORLD OF OTHERS

When one asks a person, "Who are you?" he may reply in terms of his name, some ideosyncratic property, or, very likely, he will refer either to group membership or to an occupation—an important choice. He will answer in terms of how he thinks about himself ("I am what I do" or "I am what my family is" or "I am what I believe") and also in terms of what is considered important in his circle, reading the meaning thus inferred into the original question. Inevitably these social placing concepts will direct the way groups divide, the lines of partisanship, and the solutions to problems of distributive justice in the society.

Will societies in which social identity means primarily status or ascribed group membership be more interested in distributive justice (who gets what) within the nation than societies marked by occupational identities, in which interest will focus on national performance and achievement?

Does the civil service minimize the influence of ascribed social identities while mass participation in politics tends at the same time to enhance it (with ethnic and familistic appeals predominating)? If this is true, does socialism serve to reduce familistic and ascriptive status (because there is a tendency towards official neutrality) or increase these kinds of familistic social identity (because the standards of performance required by the market are weakened and the traditional group loyalties are merely incorporated into the government service)?

Do nationalism and nationalistic foreign policies arise from social identities in which the nation is a primary referent, or do they emerge when people are uncertain of the importance of this referent, the nationalism serving to consolidate uncertain identifications?

INTERPERSONAL TRUST

The private belief system inevitably includes concepts of human nature and definitions of who can be trusted to do what. Such concepts will affect the quality of partisanship, attitudes towards "the opposition" and towards alternation of groups in power, the nature of representation, indeed, all political dealings. Furthermore, ideas of the trustworthiness of others will be projections of one's own sense of trustworthiness, as well as generalizations from experience and applications of cultural folk wisdom to particular cases.

Will a broadly held belief that people are generally predatory and "will take advantage of you" lead to placing faith in a distant, revered figure, "above politics" (like Hitler and Gandhi)?
Does the villager's suspicion of strangers and confidence in personal knowledge impede locally organized political conflict and orient conflict, instead, as existing between *us* (our village) and *them* (the metropolitan center)?
Does the "shared personality," said to be characteristic of the American character, lead to a greater trust in people, tolerance of an opposition, candor in politics?
Would the following be true? The more constricted the faith in strangers, (a) the larger is the number of political factions; (b) the more unstable are the coalitions in conciliar and popular organizations, and (c) the greater is the reliance on economic payoffs (corruption?) outside the family circle.

Here I would like to draw on interviews with working and lower middle class men in Eastport, an industrial city of about 150,000 in the eastern part of the United States. The interviews were made in the late fifties. Perhaps some of the ideas on appropriate interpersonal relations have changed since then, especially relations across ethnic lines; but as we are dealing with enduring values and beliefs, the change is probably slight. The statements set forth are to be read as my interpretations of these men's beliefs gleaned from some ten to fifteen hours with each of fifteen men; neither these men nor others in their position are able to articulate such fundamental beliefs without much help.[7] Of the beliefs of this group it may be said:
The proper relationship between people is mutual helpfulness, not intimacy; it is a warm handshake, not an embrace. Being friendly is important, doing things together is fun, but baring one's innermost thoughts to a close friend is embarrassing to both. The relationship should be mutual with an approximately even "balance of trade." It should be relaxed, not intense.

Individuals are more important than groups. Purposes are individual, not shared; groups dissolve as people move about and change jobs; even members of families (except for the Italian-Americans) tend to lose contact with each other. (Whereas in European literature one finds a *Forsyte Saga* or a *Buddenbrooks*, in America the literary epic deals typically with a single person or a single generation. The exceptions tend to deal with immigrant families, as does *Giants in the Earth*, or with the South, as does Faulkner's treatment of the Sartoris and Snopes families.)

The ideal group relationship is mutual independence modified by willingness to compromise. Political leaders are valued for their "independence," friendship is valued if it gives each friend "independence," ideas and opinions should be formed "independently"; yet they lose their value unless leaders and men are willing to adjust their differences, "give a little," work as a team. This is possible because the "independence" people value is not heterodoxy on fundamentals, but variations within a prescribed and tolerated field of values.

From these popular premises about interpersonal relations derive political relationships which are flexible, temperately partisan, accommodative within the limits of relatively conventional political positions.

Value Orientations: Man in Society

While the concepts of the self and of the world of others are crucial, they do not fully incorporate the additional ingredients of man's private belief sytem, his inarticulate philosophy, his ethos and *weltanschauung*. These additional features of the belief system undergird all phases of activity and belief without being stated or codified, making their influence felt through their consequences. Unstated, they are rarely directly challenged but change through erosion, insensibly, if at all. They are worth exploring and illustrating to make a vague concept more vivid.

It is said that among the Navaho the language and culture stress activity or doing, hence events rather than people are most often at the focus of attention.[8] F. S. C. Northrop also attempts to distinguish a "primary factor" in his treatment of "The Meaning of Eastern Civilization." For the Orient he says it is "the aesthetic continuum" which must constantly be interpreted and differentiated.[9] In a book on the *Making of the Mexican Mind*, it is said that "the dominant preconception on which Hispano-American culture rests is the *tragic* sense of life, and, in contrast, that on which the Anglo-American culture rests is the *epic* sense of life."[10] By this the author means that the Hispano-American is concerned with an inner struggle, an attempt to "conquer himself," while the Anglo-American is concerned with an attempt "endlessly to conquer obstacles external to himself." In this vein anthropologists, philosophers, observers of all kinds search for the premises of a culture, its operational codes, some central concepts by which to enter and order its life.

Here, let us draw again on the Eastport interviews, reconstructing some of the American ethos on nature and society.

Nature

The relationship between man and nature is one of uncertain but growing mastery. Man does not merely reflect the natural order, as Dorothy Lee says the Wintu believe,[11] or merely discover it so that he may adjust to it, as the eighteenth-century natural law philosophers seemed to imply. As a race he molds the natural order to his will, as an individual he feels mastery over its ingredients: he controls distance by television and rapid transportation; he controls weather by air-conditioning; he shapes materials through power tools; he controls illness, up to a point, through drugs. In Mexico "the Indian wishes to come to terms with the universe, the Mestizo to dominate it."[12] The Eastport common man, being Western, is like the Mestizo in this respect.

The world is not dangerous but worrisome. Not many years ago Frank Tannenbaum said of Mexican villagers, "They know that tragedy and death lurk around every corner."[13] An Eskimo spokesman said, "We do not believe; we fear." The Eastport man does not share this foreboding of tragedy; he does not fear, he worries. The order of magnitude of the troubles which may befall him is rarely catastrophic in the sense that they might embrace famine, violence, death, separation from wife or children. Indeed, one might say of Eastport that the lack of a tragic sense emerges from a situation in which men's troubles do not prompt a philosophic view; they merely prompt anxiety and worry, a concerned review of deprivations of one kind or another, plans and calculations thrown off, marginal purchases not necessary to life or even comfort made impossible, decrements of status, uncertainty—the ingredients of worry, not of philosophy, even street-corner philosophy.

The world is orderly and knowable. Eastport spends little time thinking about the ineffable, the unknowable, the infinite. Even in this predominantly Catholic group, there is little consideration of Divine intervention in men's affairs. The Divinity operates through regular laws; hence if one knows the laws, one need not know much more about the "mind of God." In this sense, and in some others, too, the world is secular.

What happens to people is their own doing. As the world is knowable and nature is not violent or cruel and can be mastered, those who come into conflict with nature must have erred. Their strategies of life were wrong. (They did not continue their education, they married the wrong persons, or they exposed themselves needlessly to some risk.) They are not so much blamed as held responsible in whatever accounting is made.

Society

The distribution of rewards in American society is generally just. Those who became rich must have been smarter than others; those who rise to political power "must have had something on the ball." Except for some negligible blue bloods, all status is considered achieved, not ascribed.

It is more important that the social order be efficient than moral. Men do not look for the moral basis of government or the economy or public policies; they look for its product in terms of *opportunities* for them to pursue their lives as they wish to and *security* against forces beyond their control.

The social order is benign; it is organized to promote everyone's welfare. If there are thieves in government, they do not intend major harm; if big business gets out of line, government will crack the whip. Therefore, the proper posture towards the going order is positive critical support. Only soreheads are bitter.

There is a true public interest which everyone should support. Therefore, class conflict, race conflict, geographic conflict stems from error, not fundamental and irreconcilable differences of interest. The game of life is not a zero sum game.

The churches, business corporations, governments, and media all work in "natural" ways, adjusting to each other as is best for society. As these institutions are functioning well enough, there is no need to examine their fundamental relations, ownership, power, or social contribution.

The common man in Eastport lives a busy life, often holding two jobs, sometimes raising five or six children, not infrequently hampered by sickness. The conservative tenor of these premises reflects this busyness and preoccupation; but it also reflects a deep and enduring trust, however overlaid with worry, in the going order. Politically this outlook implies an inattention to radical solutions, an incrementalist approach to change, a Burkian sense that practical men, not political philosophers, are the best guides for political reform. Under these circumstances it is little wonder that Americans are not confronted with a "Marxian" or even "socialist" party pitted against a "Christian" party, as is the case in much of the modern world.

The Agenda of History

The life calendar of an ordinary man will be marked by historic events to which he must respond. Unlike Lord Nelson high above Trafalgar Square, unmoved by the decline of empire, even a very ordinary but living man is part of change, whether it is featured in the news like a lost battle or whether it is incremental, like the rising power of the civil service or the growth of metropolitan centers. As history changes its agenda, the duties of political man are sharply altered, and the elements of his core belief system that are called into play are likely to differ according to the occasion. History will play upon him like an organ, but he can make music only with the pipes he has.

If we were to pursue a Marxian analysis, we might find clues to the historical agenda for which the citizen must prepare a response by ascertaining at which point of the materialist dialectic we now stand. The agenda would be different for those in the Asiatic mode of production and those in the feudal period, though we do not readily perceive the "Asiatics" welcoming colonialism and feudal relations with a hoarse cry, "Come on, let's get it over with." If we were followers of Auguste Comte, we would hasten the epistemological revolution, rushing through our religious phase to enter the metaphysical one, but only as commuters on the way to the scientific era. But we have no such grasp on certain historical development and no theory of historical inevitability to aid us. Rather, we have a set of problems in nation-building which seem to have some kinds of sequence, but the sequences vary, and although there is a model of "modernity" to guide the developing nations in their vision of the future, there is nothing manifest about that destiny. The modern nations are confronted with an even less precise goal, mopping up the residues of their past and hoping that "post-modernity" will emerge as something better. A rough sequence of problems will have to serve us as the agenda of history.

NATIONAL INDEPENDENCE: THE BIRTH OF A NATION

The demands upon political man in an age of national revolution make the strongest claim upon him at a time when he is least likely to be prepared for them. As a "citizen" he is called upon to be a "patriot" of a unit which up to that time may have had very little meaning for him. The very concepts "citizen" and "patriot" may be unfamiliar. His sense of national community, repressed, if it ever existed, during the colonial regime, is now called upon to justify sacrifice. Asked to shift allegiance from tribal or village loyalty to the nation unit, he may strain his sense of place and his horizon of concern beyond their elasticity.

His postures towards authority become contortions. Pursuant to the well-established order of things, he was obedient, if not almost reverent, to the foreign *Raj* and his local agents. Then, before and during the revolution, he is asked to disobey the established authority and follow some ragged partisan in the name of The Revolution. Once passive in the face of power he is now active in the pursuit of it. Next, there is a new authority in the place of the old, one which has not the magic of the old power, but in its stead has the magic of a leader who acquires charisma as something new, as a native who is a National Hero, an Emancipator.

The native culture whose mores, standards of beauty, ethical-legal codes were under the shadow of the Western culture now emerge sanctioned by "Negritude" or black power; but the folk-culturists wear an air of desperation that may not convince. They are caught in an agonizing conflict with the concepts of modernization. The old perspective synchronized with the harvest and hunting and life cycle is not in harmony with the demands for acceleration of time, the five-year plan, the eight-hour day.

New explanatory concepts of the social order are employed; The white foreigner was an exploiter, and the troubles of the nation are due to his extraction of its wealth and despoliation of its dignity. For nations who came to this struggle early, arguments were available about self-determination, taxation without representation, natural rights. For nations achieving independence at a later date, Marxist-Leninist arguments are more persuasive; they attribute the imperialist thrust to the colonialist need to shore up a crumbling capitalist system at home by exploiting the workers of other lands. Except for their implications for what to do when independence is achieved, these arguments come to the same thing: The colonial power is to be driven out and "we" are to control our own destinies. But what is there in the belief system of the newly freed citizen that will give conceptual content to these vague destinites? Most likely, the nearest concept at hand is the idea of more of what was wanted for the individual and his family before national liberation, an enlargement of old wants.

Independence promises so much, but rather than receiving a flow of new benefits, the newly independent citizen may find independence costly as well as disruptive. The language of freedom has been expansive, but new rules inhibit as much as the old. While the police are more acceptable because they are "ours" (unless, of course, they are officered by the wrong group), they may be less acceptable because more corrupt. In this phase of history freedom has more to do with collective self-determination (minimally, but importantly, "getting the foreigner off our back"), than with individual freedom of expression. But independence has one supreme gift: the opportunity for increased self-esteem. All core belief systems prize this opportunity. It is the basis for developing other values.

DEFINING THE BOUNDARIES OF A NATION

In *Saint Joan*, Shaw has Joan of Arc's accusers discuss in shocked tones her reference to "France," when previously there had been loyalties and obligations only to Burgundy, Anjou, Normandy, and other such fiefdoms. The coalescing of principalities, as in the unification of Germany and Italy in the nineteenth century, poses for the political man, as he was then and is under similar contemporary circumstances, problems of the definition of community. More often, for nations tenuously established, there are fissiparous tendencies to confuse national identity, as exemplified in the American Civil War, the division of imperial India into a Moslem state and a Hindu state, the break-up of the Mali Federation, and the Biafran secession. Each such coalescence and division poses for some men (Robert E. Lee was one) problems of loyalty and legitimate authority. What is it to be a patriot under these circumstances? Marginal men ask: Who can be counted on to provide the usual governmental indulgences and protections? Which of the divergent cultural themes (the agrarian South's or the industrial North's) are appropriately sanctified? Where do I belong?

The confused political man tries to lay down his core belief system on the torn political fabric, but the pattern is a patchwork. What is he to believe about himself, a Montenegrin in a partially alien Yugoslavia, an Alsatian after two world wars, a West Virginian in the Civil War—a traitor and patriot both? In a crisis no man does "enough"; someone always does more, hence the self-doubt, the guilt. It may be easy to divide the world into "we" and "they" when natives fight imperial troops, but when cousins fight each other, it is not so simple. The opponent may be not merely an enemy but a heretic; he is perfidious. Life goals get caught up in the struggle. Career patterns are broken. Moral guide-lines are confused—witness the black market, draft evasion, hoarding. Time is distorted, for the end of the conflict seems to promise and threaten so much. Place is distorted, for localisms may no longer serve; or by the involution of war they may become points of total reference—as was the case with the "locals" of Rovere, for whom the import of the Second World War was judged by its impact on Rovere.[14] The political belief system in a nation defining its nationhood reveals a strange version of core beliefs; while they guide men's thoughts they are themselves shaped by events, probably never to be the same again.

WHO SHALL RULE?

It is a rare government that does not rule in the name of the people, but the people do not rule. At best they choose among men with limited authority for limited terms who depend upon their constituencies for continuation in office. In a "new nation" this may be a new arrangement, difficult to learn, for it involves a friendly enmity with the opposition, and friendly enmity may be a new attitude for which there is no parallel in experience. For the rulers the concepts of "internalized restraint" against "abuse of power" may be unfamiliar in a world where restraint was predominantly external and exploitation of power was the mark of a man, to be made the most of while the occasion lasted. But the most likely situation in a new nation is one in which someone rules in the name of the people, creating political rules for them which are defined in a deceptive political language, in ambiguous, vaguely threatening, half honorific, half hypocritical terms. Under these circumstances, to know the political ropes is to know the power of flattery, *baksheesh*, connections, hedging against sudden change, obeisance—with some saving dignity where possible. The evocation of collective sacrifice for the national good combines with the practice of personal enrichment and privilege to confound morality and to compromise interpersonal trust, for the models are often bad. It is the purpose of the leaders to have their followers identify self and community; it is the tragic consequence of revolutionary and post-revolutionary situations that they tend to set self and community at war with each other.

As he applies his core belief system to the question of who shall rule, the citizen of a new country is guided by the old practices and the new rhetoric. He has internalized norms which may yet tell him that those who did rule should still rule, for by no means do all the citizens of the new nations reject the old rulers; the new unfamiliar colored faces seem "upstarts" to many. Ambivalence seizes them. But the rhetoric of nationalism, the slogans of independence, the promise of utopia, a "new birth of freedom," the elan of the first election, when they themselves out of the dust are addressed and entreated to support the new men—all these are persuasive. These appeals, even if spurious, give new dignity to the self. The partisan work of politics brings men together, fractious, unfamiliar with the give and take of politicking, impatient of the weary persuasion it takes to resolve differences, possessed of a time sense that does not allow for strategic defeat, they nevertheless become immersed in a communications net and in a process of action that changes their concepts of the world of others. If the immediate reaction is disgust and distrust, their ultimate achievement, if they can manage it, is a hope that a cooperative "we" can change things. Or this *might* occur (it rarely does) if ethnic rivalries do not become embittered (and politics embitters them), and the military is restrained, and the emancipating hero does not become infatuated with himself, and the radical intellectuals do not withdraw their support.

The old explanatory systems do not work in a modernizing state. Folk wisdom is challenged by the new agricultural experiment station; folk medicine is cast in shadow. Fate does not explain, nor do devils and the spirit world. But it is not in the nature of things for men to drop their explanatory patterns easily, and the new science often seems just as magical as the old magic. If one cannot see germs, they are no more plausible than unseen demons. The exorcism works in strange ways; in Trinidad the coming of electricity to the village of Mayaro was thought to have so charged the air as to make it uncomfortable to the women transformed at midnight into vampire "succiants."[15] But perhaps the presence of a District Medical Officer, the metereological reports on the weather, and standards of evidence in the local courts change the general concept of cause and effect and the relationship between the seen and unseen worlds as well. If so, the question of who should rule might turn as much on who gives good roads and medical services as who comes with the gift of grace. Political beliefs are cause and consequence of metaphysical and epistemological beliefs.

RELIGION, LANGUAGE, RACE

The agenda of history poses for every nation the struggles among those whose differences are marked by language, religion, race in a seemingly never ending quarrel for the symbols of esteem, the reality of power and place. The quarrels are bitter, for the goals are heavily moralized, encased in ancient scriptures, rights, heroes, traditions and handed down from father to son. They are hard to resolve because, unlike quarrels over money, religious and ethnic quarrels are not easily solved by fractional relief, a redivision of the pie. They are self-perpetuating because men live in religious, language, and racial ghettoes or provinces where there is endless rehearsal of the rights of "our" position and the wrongs of "theirs" and where that happy chance exchange of views across boundaries is not facilitated. Protestants fought Catholics in England, Germany, the Netherlands, and recently again in Northern Ireland. In India the Moslem-Hindu quarrel caused two nations to emerge where there might have been one. The disestablishment of the Church can also rouse tempers, as in Mexico, and the breach of the wall separating church and state can cause discomfort, as in the United States.

Language is the vehicle of culture, literature, saga and epic; it is branded on the tongue at an early age; it is the medium of memory; it binds men together in a web of communication. When, after centuries of living together, the Walloons and the Flemings of Belgium, the French and the English of Canada, even the archaic Welsh in Britain demand parity for their mother tongue, the force of linguistic ties is revealed.

Race is often compounded with religion and language, as with the overseas Chinese in Malaya, Singapore, Indonesia, and the Philippines; and the barriers between communities that must somehow work together are barbed at the top. Even without the language and religious barriers, as every American knows, the distinctions of race can become the single most important national problem. On the agenda of history, these matters often take priority; but without that priority they remain as old business, never quite resolved.

Politics is the art of alliance and coalition, as well as the art of "the possible," and alliances and coalitions are divisive on ethnic lines. Politics at the same time draws attention to these differences, reinforcing ethnic identities, and provides an opportunity and means of peaceful settlement. Thus the first task of political man, the definition of community, here draws a line around "we" and "they" that is more intimate than nationhood, and often more intensely felt; but it is also chartered by the political mores and through politics sometimes amenable to peaceful negotiations. Society has means for helping a man cope with national and ethnic identity: the balanced ticket (a Flemish President and Walloon Prime Minister). The Trinidadians have a Chinese Governor General, a Negro Prime Minister, a Moslem Minister of West Indian Affairs, and a Hindu Minister of Justice. The official doctrine of the comity of peoples, reinforced by homilies in every child's reader, probably helps; it provides an official standard against which the unofficial rumor and disparagement may be measured.

Shall he, the political man, give legitimacy to the authority of another race or religion or ethnicity? The device employed in the armed services comes to the rescue: he obeys the office, he salutes the insignia, not the man. Shall he work with the members of the contemned group? The rewards for alliances, for symbolic inclusion of "one of them" in our party are too great to ignore. Have they, the members of the other group, a right to claim inclusion in the national heritage? From every side the word comes down: the nation was built by a mixture of races and peoples. The Mayflower was only a little ship; those larger, later vessels, even those stopping at Ellis Island, brought talent as well as brawn: Carl Schurz, Andrew Carnegie, Joseph Kennedy, Enrico Fermi, Albert Einstein.

The strain on the core belief system is very great; often such strain serves more to continue the quarrel than to minimize it, but it has resources for both. A confident self is a better instrument for tolerating the dissonance of ethnic strain than a weak self, for it has been discovered that ethnocentrism is not only the dislike of this or that other group but a dislike and fear of other people generally and, more particularly, it is a dislike of and insecurity about one's own doubtful self. Thus the developing nations, whose members are only beginning to acquire self-confidence, are especially vulnerable to racial and religious and ethnic quarrels. The political belief system created by a person with self-esteem has scope for others, for the successes of others are not so threatening in a world less filled with danger and threat.

But if the world of others is less threatening, it must be classified and placed in human sets, some of them higher and some lower, some sets permeable and some closed. A man may choose to work in the familiar set of those like himself; it is reassuring. Lewin says of the ghetto Jew that he is more secure than the Jew who chooses to work in the outside world where he takes on that "restlessness" that makes for a creative, innovative, critical temperament.[16] But to take this step, especially in nineteenth-century Europe, was already to believe that the non-Jewish world was permeable. The meritocratic thesis of the modern world, the movement from status to contract, the death of *gemeinschaft* make this step less difficult; but this must be discovered anew by each group emerging in fear and anger from its ghetto, as the American Negro is only now tentatively beginning to discover.

Religious belief, language, and ethnicity, racial memberships, are so intensely associated with the self that they shape desire and give direction to lifetime strivings. Thus, in the core belief system they may give content to needs and motives and offer ready-made philosophies about why personal goals associated with Black Power or White Supremacy are better, more moral. They fuse the desired and the desirable into a bond that is further cemented by history, the history of "their people." Perhaps the solvent for this cement is individualism; the Japanese are finding that modernity brings increasing interest in self-development, one's own career, private success, and decreasing profession of idealistic group or national interest.[17]

In group quarreling there is a spurious explanatory system that infects concepts of cause and effect. It is the tendency to blame the other group for what goes wrong. As anti-Semitism is said to be the fool's socialism, so the natives of former colonies, perhaps influenced by Fanon, blame "the White Devil" for their difficulties in nation building, driving him out and with him the skills they need. The recently de-colonized person may be frightened by the new responsibilities; the explanations for his low status based on racial discrimination are easier for him to accept, and because they are historically true they are tempting to apply to "me" now in this situation, where they *may* no longer hold.

ECONOMIC DEVELOPMENT AND THE DISTRIBUTION OF WEALTH

If in the less developed nations this is the age of nationalism and nation-hood, in the developed world (as well as in the developing nations) this is the age in which history has placed three items on its agenda: the reduction of ethnic conflict, the elimination of poverty, and the appropriate division of wealth among the "social classes." The first of these was discussed above. On poverty and growth Keynes and Marx represent the two other items of the agenda, and they are curiously interrelated. As Marx seemed to capture the public conscience with his ideal of redistribution of wealth on a classless basis, Keynes and the economics he contributed to revealed a stronger engine for the elimination of poverty, namely the elimination of the business cycle and, by extension, the principle of a managed economy devoted to economic growth. It has been possible to organize popular movements dedicated to communism, for it provides an enemy, a sense of injustice, a carrier for the doctrine in class-based parties, an explanation of why things have not turned out well, and a vision of the future. One could hardly put together a better mix for a forensic and persuasive ideology, but the experience of the communist countries has been disillusioning for many a true believer.

Keynes—and here he represents a developed science of economics—has no enemy group; the faults of the system are due to false doctrine, not evil men. The carriers of "the true belief" are small groups of professional economists with their growing but sometimes skeptical business and profes-sional allies. In this view the poor are unjustly treated because of the failure to adjust savings and investment, consumption and inventory accumulation, interest rates and liquidity preference, and government deficit and the activity of the private sector. Of course they are also unjustly treated if the rich improve their positions more rapidly than do the poor, but as the proportion of the growing national income that has gone to the richest five per cent of the families in the United States has declined for over twenty years (1947 = 17%; 1968 = 14%); and as the richest countries are economically the most equalitarian, this does not seem to be the case. The "discovery" of economic growth is the most promising, intellectually stimulating social discovery of our time. But it functions without the *formal* apparatus of an ideology or social movement and is difficult to present as a polemical moral cause. This is particularly the case in view of the fact that communist countries can employ a market pricing system and can and do develop policies to accelerate national economic growth, with some assist from economic theories developed first within the confines of a capitalist system.

What is political man to make of these items on history's agenda? In the developing countries, where the division between the metropolitan rich and the urban poor or the landowners and peasants is so great, it is hard to define one's political community to embrace both. Political community is likely to be class based. Further, for the poor, "they," the rich, seem to have all the power. For the rich, it is hard not to be frightened by the masses of hungry poor. Authority is hard to share. Political roles are played with resources; the poor lack the connections, the money to buy indulgences, and the knowledge of the law. Their political roles are likely to be played in the streets, which they can control by force of number—hindered only by the military and the police. They are led to believe that whatever happens is willed by the seemingly omnipotent rich, or, if they live in a communist nation, the omnipotent government unchecked by an opposition. Poverty makes the self so overwhelmingly important that the community loses salience; the time is now, the focus is me and mine. In this perspective the intricacies of economic development are lost from view; they have no visceral appeal if the viscera are gnawed by hunger.

Nor is the core belief system of the new nations likely to provide an adequate template for the new developmental economics. From the perspective of the very poor, housing is better than "infrastructures" of roads and telephones—it hardly matters that housing is only a "durable consumption good." Pensions are better than docks and warehouses; clearly national wealth is increased by seizing the great refineries from the hated foreigner; the way to reduce unemployment is to put men on the government payroll. The overwhelming importance of the self now, the belief that we have a "right" to wealth on our soil and that "they" are intruders, the lack of experience in scheduling (postponing) wants, the popular focus on consumption goods and national dignity, the easy explanation of backwardness by foreign exploitation, and the simplistic epistemology that translates national economics into family budgetary experience all argue for Marx over Keynes.

In the developed Western countries it is different. Because the differences in wealth and particularly in life style between the rich and the poor are not so great (the matter of dress is especially imporant), it is possible to define political community in such a way as to embrace all nationals. The men of Eastport did not resent the rich; they felt that somehow the rich merited their wealth.[18] As authority is shared, and it is not impossible for a poor man's party to defeat the party of the rich and for a poor man to use the law against a rich man, the citizens of Western Nations may think of authority as accessible and diffused. Children see authority as hierarchical (the President tells the governors what to do and the governors tell the mayors), but most adults perceive, somewhat dimly perhaps, that there are domains of power with different authorities sitting over each. Hence, with a little leverage themselves and with chances for appeal they are less resentful. They do have resources for playing political roles. In the United States men believe they can combine to press for change, they can get their cousin who knows the mayor to do a favor, they can write to their congressman. Their own position in the social order is self-made; beyond that, the reason the social order is the way it is does not concern them. Unthinkingly, Americans are likely to believe that the Constitution they live under is the finest document ever written. While not community minded, Americans have a pride of place— nothing like the pride of place of the Englishman or the Frenchman, but still, they are "boosters" and not "knockers."

All of this is relevant for the working-class man's decisions in facing up to the problem of what to do about class exploitation, the condition of the poor, unemployment when the local factory shuts down, the high cost of illness, the tragedy of the ghetto. Given their definitions of themselves as successful political men, working-class men are not in the least disposed to join the mimeograph squad in the local socialist or communist backroom office. It has all been said before, but it is nevertheless true.

The core belief system is better prepared for economic technology than for Marxian polemics. If, as I said, "modern" men believe that they are responsible for their own destinies, especially their own successes, they can believe in an economic system that relies on individual decision to produce the goods. They are, as Tocqueville pointed out, anxious men but do not lack self confidence. Americans have a greater trust in others than the British, the British have more than the Germans, the Germans more than the Italians or the Mexicans.[19] Such trust makes market dealings both risky and easy; the easiness makes people impatient of price fixing and regulation. The greatest problem in a managed but free economy is the control of inflation; it is easy to have the government build up a deficit in times of underutilized resources but hard to impose the taxes that control inflation. To command the political power for such an unpopular act requires three things: a trust in the authorities, something which is an extension of trust in others generally; a belief in the epistemology of science, experts, economic doctrine; and a longer-run time span or mental calendar. As the core belief systems of the developed countries includes such a faith in the authorities and belief in science, it is possible to persuade the population, reluctantly and late, that higher taxes and credit controls are necessary and that in the long run (and when people are better off there is a longer run) they will be better off this way. I do not believe the evidence will show that these policies are possible in a country where the authorities are not trusted (and may not be trustworthy), where modes of thought are dominated by home economics, and where the long run is, indeed, the time when we shall all be dead.

The points have been made, but it may be useful to give a focus to the features of the political self-image and the core belief system which achieve greatest salience in each of the historical crises to which a nation is subject.

National independence and autonomy. Political man must somehow employ an inadequate belief system to redefine his concept of political community, change his allegiance to authority, redefine his political role to include "patriot," and adopt new explanations of the political order. He must sacrifice self to community in a new way during the struggle. Somehow from his range of identities he must manage a shift from a passive to a more active self, develop a new set of wants and desires associated with victory of the new nation, and enlarge concepts of time and place beyond the old village level.

Defining the boundaries of the new nation. In the core belief system there must be found (again) the basis for a shift in acceptance of authority from regional to national levels, giving up parochialism. National cultural norms that embrace other people and definitions of nation and community as one (but not the only one) must be supported. The core belief system is strained to give distant authority an appropriate but not exaggerated respect, to see the self as important by virtue of a national identity, to submerge old quarrels in the interest of the national good.

Who shall rule? Political man in a new nation is asked to learn political roles for which he has little experience. If the nation is called a democracy, he must learn complicated alternatives and procedures for which his experience has not trained him; he must place himself with others about whom he knows little; he must develop a strategy of extracting from the new government "his rights" and of defining himself *vis-à-vis* the community. For this his core belief system may be inadequate, for it may not give to men "like himself" the right to select among candidates; it may not provide for cooperation with disliked others; it may not allow explanations that give accountability in human terms.

Religion, language, race. Political man is ethnocentric, but politics provides a means of peaceful competition, rewarding coalition, and gives rules for conflict management. To learn these rules, to restrain the bitterness, to find rationales for cooperating with "the enemy," to accept authority more alien than the foreign ruler—these are the new tasks of citizenship in the new nations and the unfinished business of the old ones. If the core belief system has attenuated religion and introduced some relativistic perspective on ethnicity and race, a population is fortunate; otherwise its members risk civil war or communal strife. Individualism, the free-standing self, is an asset in this situation; trust in others and freedom of suspicion of strangers (the villagers' disease) are useful. So also are explanatory systems that give credence to impersonal causes (drought, glut in the world markets, technical deficiencies); otherwise the hated group is always to blame. To understand these causes, the epistemology of science is crucial. *Economic development and the distribution of wealth.* The core belief system in developing nations takes easily to the Marxian view. It gives him visible enemies, the appearance of immediate rewards from redistribution, a defined political role (if he should choose it—and most don't) as a partisan rebel, a simplistic account of his own and his nation's troubles, a solidarity with brothers in a moral cause, identification of self and community—until the revolution is won, when this and much else may turn sour. But for the developed nations, political man finds the Marxian task increasingly uncongenial as he becomes a settled member of the blue collar bourgeoisie.

Core belief systems of the modern working man will not accept the self-image of the downtrodden proletarian because he believes his fate (and success) is his own; he does not see the world in terms of rich and poor, but rather of himself now and himself later and his children still later, ever better off. (In any event, the world of others is divided ethnically more than economically.) Because he trusts others, he trusts authorities; he can accept their demands for sacrifices (grumbling all the while). To the extent that the moral good is the good of the self and family and to the extent that it is achievement-oriented, national achievement has resonance with his emotional life. He reveres science; this increases "cause" and reduces "blame" and accelerates remedial steps. There is a future, for the immediate present is not so pressing. He knows enough about knowledge to employ appropriate criteria for determining who is knowledgeable, or something approximating this. He is ready for Keynes.

Notes

1. Chicago: Markham, 1969.

2. *Psychopathology and Politics* (Chicago: University of Chicago Press, 1939), pp. 75–76.

3. Robert MacIver, *The Web of Government* (New York: Macmillan, 1948), p. 5.

4. Abram Kardiner and Lionel Ovesey, *The Mark of Oppression: A Psychosocial Study of the American Negro* (New York: Norton, 1951).

5. Lucien Pye, *Politics, Personality, and Nation Building* (New Haven: Yale University Press, 1962).

6. Harold Lasswell, *Power and Personality* (New York: Norton, 1948), p. 20.

7. For an account of the methods of this study and a report on other related findings, see *Political Ideology* (New York: Free Press, 1962).

8. Clyde Kluckhohn, "Values and Value-Orientation in the Theory of Action: An Exploration in Definition and Classification," in Talcott Parsons and Edward A. Shils (eds.) *Toward a General Theory of Action* (New York: Harper Torchbook, 1951).

9. F. S. C. Northrop, *The Meeting of East and West* (New York: Macmillan, 1946).

10. Patrick Romanell, *The Making of the Mexican Mind: A Study in Recent Mexican Thought* (Lincoln: University of Nebraska Press, 1952), p. 21.

11. Dorothy Lee, *Freedom and Culture* (New York: Spectrum, Prentice-Hall, 1959).

12. Romanell, *The Making of the Mexican Mind*, p. 16.

13. Frank Tannenbaum, *Mexico, The Struggle for Peace and Bread* (New York: Knopf, 1956), p. 19.

14. Robert K. Merton, "Locals and Cosmopolitans" in *Social Theory and Social Structure*, rev. ed. (New York: Free Press, 1957), pp. 387–420.

15. This chapter was written in Trinidad, where my friend and taxi driver, Ramnarine

Ramesar, expressed these views. Otherwise, in its drive towards independence and modernization Trinidad is an exception to much that is said in these pages.

16. Kurt Lewin, *Resolving Social Conflicts* (New York: Harper, 1948).

17. Akira Takahashi, "Development of Democratic Consciousness Among the Japanese People," *International Social Science Bulletin* (UNESCO), IV, no. 1 (1961), pp. 88–89.

18. *Political Ideology*, pp. 68 ff.

19. Gabriel Almond and Sidney Verba, *The Civic Culture* (Princeton: Princeton University Press, 1963).

PART IV

THE EFFECTS OF AFFLUENCE AND KNOWLEDGE ON BELIEF SYSTEMS

Introductory Note

The agenda of history includes ideological change, change produced, as Marx would say, by the altered material conditions of man, and, as Hegel would say, by the modification of ideas, especially (I think) ideas about ideas. The following two chapters present a portrait of a changing society characterized by an increasing agreement on social ends and a decline in the bitterness of social conflict. The two main facts arguing for this direction of change are (a) the effect of increasing affluence and welfare policy and (b) the effect of increasing knowledge and scientific methods of social analysis.

Now, but a few short years after the papers were written, it seems that history has falsified the analysis and that affluence and knowledge have *not* led to a decline in social conflict. Rather, the American society, like some other western societies (and most of the third-world nations), appears to be torn increasingly by conflict, much of it dealing with fundamentally different conceptions of how men should live together. We do not know whether this is merely a temporary disturbance in the trends towards "consensus" and greater reliance on knowledgeable experts; but, if the analysis in the chapters that follow has some merit (and I believe the facts were then as I described them), it is useful to speculate here on the sources of the discrepancies. Where did the analysis fail?

Let me present briefly the main thrust of the arguments of the two chapters. The chapter on "The Politics of Consensus in an Age of Affluence" argues that a combination of increasing per capital income, widely distributed, and welfare state policies is causally associated with certain observed changes in attitudes and behavior. These are (a) a popular increase in mutual trust, sense of personal effectiveness, hope for the future, and a decrease in social alienation; (b) a declining sense of alarm over the possible implementation of the policies of the main alternative political party and therefore a more flexible and less intensely felt political partisanship; (c) a declining importance of class-based politics and a general decline in the guidance given by class-awareness of political beliefs and choices; (d) a decline in the influence of religious institutions and a decline in religious prejudice (but a continuing use of religion as a set of cues for political choice); (e) a rise in racial conflict combined with a capacity to accommodate the demands of the radically oppressed minorities, hence the possibility of social accommodation and increasing equality of opportunity for the several races; and (f) a *rapprochement* between men and their government, in the sense that men will increasingly be willing to use political channels for peaceful change and will reduce their cynicism about governmental officials and policies.

The second chapter, dealing with the knowledgeable society, is a companion piece and hence, before turning to the specific statements mentioned above, let us set forth the main thrust of the arguments regarding the effect of our new knowledge and scientific epistemology on political ideas, behavior, and policy. The development of a knowledgeable society, it is claimed, rests first on our improved capacity to codify and transmit the lessons of ordinary human experiences, largely through the storage and retrieval of information. Second, unlike the arts, science (including social science) has a cumulative quality whereby knowledge grows and the capacity to handle increasingly complex problems develops on the basis of previous discovery. Science also has the means for disproving erroneous beliefs, ridding itself of error. Third, society has recognized the value of these efforts and provides resources for scientific inquiry out of all proportion to past investments for this purpose. Fourth, a broader understanding of the nature of concepts, theories, and evidence, taken together with an increased awareness of the difference between preference and reality and a licensing of imagination to consider ways of doing things and situations contrary to those established by convention, provides a better and broader base for social understanding and for acceptance of social change. Further, it is argued that more people receive the kind of education that leads them to accept dissonance and ambiguity and a metaphysics that does not provide an easy "escape" into mystical explanations. These epistemological and institutional changes, then, provide a basis for policy formation and policy acceptance grounded in something other than dogma, convention, and pure speculation. Further, with some agreement that poverty, disease, squalor, and group hatred now can and *should* be eradicated, knowledge of how to accomplish these aims will create intellectual and social pressure to do so.

The arguments in the second article link with those in the first in suggesting that there are certain humane social goals that will unify people, rather than divide them. By changing the focus of politics from partisan and ideological conflict to relatively less acrimonious disagreement over means, timing, and proportions, by introducing information and evidence to inform political discussion, and by devising successful solutions to social problems designed to alleviate the frustrations of our common life, political and social conflict will be less violent and less bitterly divisive.

It is an attractive picture, a Utopian one, contrasting sharply with the view of society that we see before us. Let me briefly identify some of the differences between the two pictures and try to say why my description was partly wrong.

In the discussion of social trends under the conditions of a decade of affluence, modified by a recession, I believe (without grounding in any further research) that people are, as stated, increasingly flexible in their party loyalties and decreasingly bitter in their partisanship, that the intensity of class-based politics is declining, that religious prejudice is declining and is a less important source of conflict, and that the increased racial conflict has produced (been associated with) increased social gains for racial minorities, gains that have decreased the "politics of despair." I suspect it is still true that an increasing number of people are gaining a sense of control over their own lives and destinies, but I am uncertain about the increased sense of mutual trust, and I doubt that there has been a decrease in social alienation. I also doubt that there is an increased sense of faith in government, or that there can be, as people are strongly divided on current issues. The score on the 1965 analysis and prediction (if my current conjectures are sound) is not good, but perhaps rather average as these predictive pieces go.

What is wrong, however, is less attributable to error on the matters discussed than to a failure to appreciate other kinds of conflict between other kinds of groups. Rather than class, religion, and party, the conflicts of our time might be characterized thus:

1. There is new conflict between generations based partly on the vested interest of (some of) the young in stopping the Viet Nam war because it threatens them with conscription and engagement in an enterprise of dubious moral standing, partly on the decline of authority in an age of rapid social, sexual, and technological change (the obsolescence of the old), and partly on the release of the young from the constraints of poverty that the affluent society (which I said would reduce conflict) has made possible.

2. The conflict between the exploited races (Blacks, Chicanos, Amerindians, Puerto Ricans) and the white majority, although predicted, has had an infectious influence and attendant violence that was not predicted. Guessing again, I believe that the mood of violence, the examples of violence—much of it unpunished—and the rationalization of violence associated with racial conflict has precipitated further violent conflict among the young, other minority groups, some anarchistic radicals, the "hard hats" in a "backlash," and the police. Perhaps the order should be reversed in some cases, when police violence has, finally, produced counter-violence by the Blacks.

3. The conflict between the knowledge institutions and the commercial and industrial institutions. The rise of the knowledge and educational industry has in some ways challenged the primacy of the commercial and

industrial centers; the universities have substantial resources, numbers, and status. Their ethos and cultural guidelines are different from those of the commercial world and hence challenge the conventional ways of looking at things among businessmen and their employees, inevitably producing a sense of strain and conflict.

4. Metropolitan cosmopolitan centers are in conflict with the small-town and rural populations; their members have different views on sex (abortion, contraception, sexual behavior, "pornography"), God and religion, interracial relations, patriotism, dress, and life style. The challenge of cosmopolitanism to "provincialism" creates a sense of malaise that is most disturbing; the counterattack threatens those enjoying (if that is the word) their new freedoms.

5. The conflict between the educated and the less educated draws lines overlapping those mentioned above, but it defines the conflicting parties and the issues a little differently. Education tends to make people more critical of convention, more ecumenical in religion, more universalistic in rule application (thus according Blacks more rights), more international and hence patriotic in a different sense, more tolerant of deviance, more trans-ethnic in their friendships and loyalties, less parochial in attention and interest, more concerned with arts, life style, the amenities of life. This outlook disturbs the half-educated and lays the more educated open to charges of effeteness, disloyalty, even immorality. Their relative preference for freedom over constraint leads to conflicts over the degree to which men should be inhibited by convention, dogma, and law.

None of these lines of conflict were envisaged in the discussion of the effect of affluence on consensus; yet with hindsight we can see that education, cosmopolitanism, and the encouragement of the exploited to take their places at the table of life are both the products of affluence and the sources of conflict and malaise. More particularly they are components and products of the rise of a more scientific epistemology and a philosophy of science that tends to denigrate the role of tradition, religion, and conventional myths justifying the hierarchical arrangements of class and race.

This brief review would not be adequate if it did not say something about the circumstances that encourage these conflicts. Some of these are transient, some are endemic to the affluent and knowledgeable society. As I see them, these circumstances include the following. First, we are losing a war, a fact that is bound to upset people; their very ambivalence about the war makes them uneasy about the impending loss. Second, if the constraints of poverty keep people quiescent, the loss of these constraints releases people for social action. Revolutions occur when people lose their sense of despair and their anticipations outrun their realizations. Third, ambiguous moral, especially sexual, standards create personal disturbances as people find their own consciences uncertainly reinforced by society. For their fear of their own lust or aggression, they blame others. Scapegoating is a form of conflict and leads to violence. Fourth, there is some evidence that congestion, high density, and the threat to one's own personal "territorial imperative" breeds aggression and antisocial behavior. Fifth, and related to density, the overstimulation of the human system through noise, light, excitement, lack of privacy, struggle for place on subway or bus breeds a state of mind congenial to vicarious violence, and perhaps to violent action. Sixth, the mobility of the labor force encouraged by modern society removes the constraints of community, for a personal knowledge of associates and personal consideration for them as people inhibits antisocial or otherwise divisive behavior. At the same time the anonymity of modern society provides concealment for acting out the antisocial impulses with which we are all endowed. Seventh, there is some evidence that familiarity, seeing things in the same way in the same place, with continuity and constant and recognizable cues for behavior, is a condition for peace of mind for many people. Social and technological change erodes the familiar, just as mobility, urban renewal, religious drift, and changed mores do. Eighth, one of the products of the combination of better social intelligence and social change is an accelerated calendar of proposed policy changes. The crowded agenda of reform that I once believed to have the effect of solving problems as they emerged is now seen as a problem in itself, a film run through the machine at a pace faster than the mind can grasp. Ninth, the relationship of affluence and full employment to inflation was imperfectly grasped by economists in 1965; inflation is a powerful engine for producing irritants and increasing demands, pitting union against management and consumer against "the system." Finally, the humane ideals taught in our schools, combined with the very idea of progress informing the two papers here under discussion, promised more than could be (or was) delivered. The difference between ideal and practice created the conditions for alienation and revolt.

In summary, affluence is associated with some forces that reduce conflict, especially as related to class, religion, and party, and it provides relatively favorable conditions for reducing racial inequities; but it produces or facilitates other kinds of conflict, especially those kinds associated with disturbances of mores and life style. Growing affluence creates many social disturbances of its own, among them an expectation that the incidence of affluence will fall equitably and generously on each concerned individual and group. Much of the conflict, not unnaturally, centers around the educational institutions, for it is often there that change and novelty and heterodoxy are born and frequently rehearsed. In the same way, the ingredients of a scientific philosophy, with its universalistic bias and its undermining of tradition, provide new sources of unhappiness and conflict. Yet it is also true, as stated in the chapter on the knowledgeable society, that science (including social science) provides the means for understanding the roots of unhappiness and, perhaps, the means for relieving it, even employing the very conflict that unhappiness generates to create a more humane society.

Chapter *12*
The Politics of Consensus in an Age of Affluence

Marx is surely right when he says that the ways men earn their living shape their relations to each other and to the state; but this is, of course, only the beginning. Aside from all the other non-economic factors which also have these effects, there is the matter of the *source* of income, the *level* of income, and, especially, the *security* of income. Moreover, each of these factors has both an individual effect, a set of influences apparent in the study of individual enrichment or immiseration, and a social effect, the influences which appear when whole societies become richer or more secure economically. So I am led to inquire into what is happening to men's political interests, behavior, and attitudes toward politics and government in an Age of Affluence, a period when men's economic security and income have increased and when, for the first time in history, it appears likely that the business cycle can now be controlled. Like Marx's, my interest is in change over time.

Quite candidly, this is a descriptive account of attitudinal change in recent years, portrayed against a background of economic change. Only argument supports the inference that it is the economic change—implied in the term "Age of Affluence" shortly to be explicated—that is accountable for much of the attitudinal change. It would take another paper with closer attention to subsections of the population and specific economic conditions to establish this argument on a firmer footing. In the meantime, perhaps these findings can help illuminate the more general problem of the relationship between economic development and stable and effective politics, as well as to help us to see where American politics is heading.

Reprinted from *The American Political Science Review*, 49 (1965), pp. 874–895. Also reprinted in Bernard Brown and John C. Wahlke (eds.), *The American Political System: Notes and Readings* (Homewood, Ill.: Dorsey Press, 1967), pp. 551–574.

Notes to this chapter will be found on pages 248–250

The elements of the economy which are most relevant to such an investigation are five-fold, and the term "affluent society"[1] or "Age of Affluence" refers here to more than higher per capita national income, though it includes that. The term embraces:

1. a relatively high per capita national income;
2. a relatively equalitarian distribution of income; ·
3. a "favorable" rate of growth of per capita Gross National Product (GNP);
4. provisions against the hazards of life—that is, against sickness, penury, unemployment, dependence in old age, squalor—the features now associated with the term "welfare state"; and
5. a "managed economy" in the sense of conscious and more or less successful governmental use of fiscal and monetary powers to smooth out the business cycle and avoid depressions, as well as to provide for the economic growth mentioned in point 3.

These five points include both economic conditions and governmental policies.

The appropriateness of the term "affluent society" or "Age of Affluence" rests upon intercultural and chronological comparisons; but in making these comparisons it is important to remember that an affluent society may still include a large number of very poor people: the average income of the poorests fifth of the families (consumer units) in the United States in 1962 was $1,662 and had to provide for a little over three people, on the average.[2] The term "affluence," however, is clearly relative both to other societies and previous periods. On the first point, comparison with other societies:

1. The United States ranked second (out of 122 countries) in GNP per capita (Kuwait was the first) in 1957, with no other country even a close competitor.[3]
2. According to one measure of "inequality of income distribution before taxes," the United States ranks about 7th in equality of income distribution. (Four British Commonwealth countries and India, for different reasons, are somewhat more equalitarian).[4]
3. Although until the last few years the annual increase of GNP was lower in the United States than in most developed and many developing countries (in Russett's volume, the United States is about 45th out of 68 countries), recently this has changed and the rate in the United States 1962–65 is about the same as in the Common Market countries.[5]
4. Although relatively less extensive than in most European countries, the American welfare programs, now that Medicare has been enacted, compare favorably in coverage and especially in absolute level of support with contemporary European programs.
5. With the possible exception of Italy, no European or developed Commonwealth country has suffered a recession (after the postwar reconstruction period) with anything like the depth or duration of the depressions of the twenties and thirties. This is also true of the United States, as we shall see.

But our main interest here lies, not in comparative economics and politics, but in changing patterns in the United States. Were we not always an *Affluent Society, a People of Plenty*,[6] bothered by the question *"Abundance for What?"*[7] Relative to other nations, perhaps! But the modern era is different from previous eras in several important and relevant ways. It will be convenient to designate four economic time periods in the United States, of which only the last three are of current interest to us (and only the latter part of the earliest of these). The periods are: Agricultural State of Nature (1789–1869), Industrial State of Nature (1870–1929), Period of Economic Crisis (1930–1941), and Age of Affluence (marked by a preliminary uncertain period, 1946–50, and beginning to take on its central characteristics in 1951 and then continuing through the present). Inevitably, since we are dealing with more or less continuous change, the margins of the periods blur into each other. Each leaves its historical "deposit" in the milieu of the next, so that—as with countries still struggling with the remnants of the feudal order in the modern period—we have with us today substantial economic characteristics of the Agricultural State of Nature (not to mention the political and cultural residues of that period).

But since periods must have boundaries, let us mention our reasons for selecting these. The Industrial State of Nature began in 1870 when the society became more than half industrial and commercial, as indicated by the decline below the 50 per cent mark in value added to the national product by agriculture. During this industrial period, and prior to the great economic crisis of the 1930s, we find a decelerating rate of development, as indicated by the number of years required for the GNP to double (in constant prices): 13 years, then 18 years, then 21 years—taking us up to the mid-twenties. But we are concerned with more than economic performances; we are interested in government policy as well. "Reform" during this period focused upon the regulation of "natural monopolies," such as railroads, grain elevators, and the like; pure food and drug laws; and policing certain trade practices. There was no concept of a welfare state, and the nearest thing to an argument over a "managed economy" was the chronic debate over "easy" versus "hard" money.

The period of Economic Crisis (1930–1941) was, of course, marked by economic depression, the most extended and severe in our history. In this period GNP (in constant dollars) remained below the 1929 figure until 1939; investment fell off drastically, and widespread unemployment and suffering ensued. The period defines itself by these facts of economic life *plus* two things: first, the advent of welfare state policies (especially social security, unemployment insurance, extended home and work relief, and a variety of agricultural policies designed to relieve the insecurities and penury of farm life); and second, the early beginnings of a fiscal and monetary policy (pump priming, inflationary monetary policies) designed to eliminate the troughs of the business cycle. These policies, of course, were extremely controversial, but—if we omit the war years—one might say that the passage of the Employment Act of 1946 represented a turning point in governmental (but not business) acceptance of responsibility for a "managed economy" in this special moderate sense. Specific policies to implement this concept remained controversial in many circles for a long time thereafter.

The 1940s represent an anomalous period, partly because of the war, and partly because per capita GNP (hovering around $2,000 in constant 1954 dollars) scarcely changed during the reconversion period, with its widespread shortages and rapidly rising prices, from 1946 into 1950. People were much better off than in the 1930s, but civilians generally were not much better off (economically) than they had been in the first half of the decade. Although there were no recessions as serious as the 1920–21 recession, yet both 1947 and 1949 were difficult years. As a consequence the annual rate of growth of GNP was low (1.8 per cent from 1946 to 1950), and, moreover, this period, like all postwar periods, was marked by high industrial strife. Yet there was an important difference, compared to 1929, and also compared to 1935–36; the share of income going to the very rich, the top 5 per cent, declined substantially (1929 = 30 per cent, 1935–36 = 26.5 per cent, 1946–50 = c.21 per cent). From 1950 on, this proportion going to the richest 5 per cent scarcely changed, drifting down a percentage point or two, for the next fifteen years. Aside from this last feature, however, the period of the forties seems to have been characterized by some of the economic elements of earlier periods; but at the same time, the basic welfare state measures provided assistance for the very poor, the economically insecure, and for the unemployed—rapidly increasing in 1949 and 1950.

The Age of Affluence, after its poor beginning in the 1940s, may be said (for analytical purposes) to commence in the 1950s, especially after the Korean fighting had stopped. From that time on, although three recessions have occurred, only the one in 1957–58 involved any decline at all in per capita GNP in real terms. The rate of growth improved substantially: from 1950 to 1961 the annual rate of growth was 3.1 per cent in constant dollars. Industrial strife declined; prices were more stable, and in this decade available spending money rose dramatically (50 per cent increase in disposable income—current dollars) with goods to spend it on.

While the 1950s began to resemble a period appropriately termed an "Age of Affluence" (except for the unemployment), the 1960s look even better. From early 1961 into 1966 there have been *no* recessions, the longest continuous period of prosperity in our history. The annual rate of increase of GNP in constant dollars is about 4.2 per cent in real terms. Unemployment has declined somewhat, though it remains a "spot" on the affluent portrait. Equally important, the Kennedy and Johnson administrations have made an explicit point of their use of fiscal policies, especially tax policies, to reduce or eliminate depressions and to encourage growth. Finally, in 1964 certain anti-poverty programs were instituted to attack unemployment, poverty and squalor with more precise instruments; and in 1965, for the first time in 20 years, major new advances were scored toward the realization of the welfare state, especially medicare and extension of social security coverage; and a "breakthrough" was made on federal aid to education.

This long (but too brief) review of the economic and policy characteristics of recent times shows, then, a profile of increasing per capita income but decreasing economic effectiveness in the period of Industrial State of Nature (1870–1929); a period of Economic Crisis (1930–1941) with low income and no growth; an anomalous decade in the forties; and then an accelerating economy in the Age of Affluence. No doubt the implications as drawn seem overly optimistic, but I see no reason to anticipate a reversal of any of the major trends (unless there is a war), though a slowing down of growth may take place. The question, then, is how these changes relate to political behavior and attitudes, especially in the contemporary period.

Politics and Civics in an Age of Affluence

The relationships between individual affluence and political attitudes are comparatively well known, but the relationships between communal affluence and political behavior are somewhat obscure. Even more obscure are the relationships between *change* in affluence and *change* in politics. Consider the following plausible hypotheses:

One might expect an increased conservatism in the Age of Affluence, on the ground that as people become more prosperous they take on the known attitudes of prosperous individuals in an earlier period. Or, to the contrary, one might expect increasing support for the kinds of measures which have worked successfully in the past in helping to bring about the Age of Affluence, i.e., support for an extension of the welfare state.

One might expect a declining urgency of political concern, on the ground that when men are more satisfied with their lot in life they become less desperate for political help. Or, one might expect increased political interest and concern because these attitudes are generally related to higher income and an improved capacity to take an interest in matters other than immediate day-to-day breadwinning problems.

One might expect a shift in political cleavage from social class to religious and ethnic bases on the ground that economic issues would become less important, thereby releasing men's attention for other submerged conflicts. Or, one might argue that because religious and ethnic cleavages are nourished by economic insecurity and poverty, growing affluence and security would weaken the intensity of these conflicts too.

Finally, one might expect a decline in political partisanship, i.e., the extent and intensity of identification with a political party, on the ground that both parties are likely to accept the policies of the welfare state and the managed economy, thus depriving party differences of much of their meaning. Or, one might argue that since social class is likely to lose its cuing function in elections, parties will remain important, or even become stronger, as intellectual and emotional "props" in electoral decisions.

The fact is that, as usual, both "theory" and common sense lead in diverse incompatible directions, and only evidence will help. The evidence to be presented here suggests a lessening of hostility between parties and religious groups and a *rapprochement* between men and their government—a combination of changes which I cover in the term "politics of consensus." This does not imply that there are no sharp, intensely felt, hostile cleavages in society, but rather that these have (a) lost most of their political and emotional impact for most people (but not for Civil Rights workers) and (b) changed from cleavages in which the public was more or less evenly divided, to cleavages between a main body of opinion and a small and dwindling group. Specifically, the thesis has six themes. In the Age of Affluence:

1. People will come increasingly to trust each other, to feel less at the mercy of chance and more in control of their lives, and so to be more optimistic regarding the future. These changes, in turn will help to promote others:

2. People will slowly lose their sense of high national, personal, and group stakes in elections; political partisanship, while not changing on the surface, will change its meaning.

3. People will slowly change their class awareness and consciousness, so that the relationship between ideology and class status will change; but occupation and class will continue to influence electoral choice—even as the electoral "pivot" shifts.

4. Religious institutions and dogmas will slowly lose their influence over men's secular thought, interfaith hostility will decline, but religious community identification may retain a constant political "cuing" function.

5. The struggle for racial equality will be facilitated by affluence and its associated attitudes, but the sense of crisis and strife in this arena will continue or grow for an indefinite period.

6. There will be a *rapprochement* between men and their government and a decline of political alienation.

We cannot explore (for want of time and survey data) these changes in the earlier periods, so we will focus upon recent changes. The reader will understand the difficulties of relying on survey materials, with their different questions, eclectic timing, and, hence, ambiguous inference. He will, I hope, further understand that the nature of the changes we are considering are glacial in their slow movements, interrupted by dramatic events abroad and influenced by changing leadership appeals at home. One can, moreover, write interpretative historical essays without data, or more closely controlled and specific studies well documented by data, and both seem equally immune from criticism. This paper lies in between; it is a speculative historical study making use of such data as come to hand.[8]

Trust, Optimism, and Alienation

1. *In an Age of Affluence, people will come increasingly to trust each other more, to feel more in control of their lives, and to be more hopeful regarding the future. Social alienation will decline.*

Greater economic security and protection against life's hazards should, one would imagine, increase people's sense of well-being or happiness, and occasion a decline in various kinds of anxiety. In some ways, this seems to be the case, while in other respects it is not. Over the years, both in the United States and abroad, survey organizations have asked people "In general, how happy would you say you are—very happy, fairly happy, or not very happy?" (AIPO). The question, in spite of its superficial naivete, has been found to be related to many concrete symptoms of adjustment and happiness and thus to have a promise of some validity.[9] Comparatively speaking, by this test, the United States was in 1949 the third happiest nation (this statement sometimes amuses one's friends), with Australia by far the happiest and France the unhappiest.[10] But over time, it would be impossible to conclude that the evidence suggests that Americans have become "happier" in the Age of Affluence. In the three-year period 1946 to 1949 there seemed to be a drift in this direction (from 39 per cent "very happy" to 43 per cent), but, when in 1957 the Survey Research Center asked an almost identical question of a national sample ("Taking all things together, how would you say things are these days—would you say you're *very happy, pretty happy,* or *not too happy* these days?"), only 35 per cent reported themselves to be "very happy."[11] Since happiness, as the reader might suspect, is strongly related to education and income and since both education and income have been increasing, the findings are puzzling and suggest further inquiry.

But there is other evidence to suggest the kind of basic changes in orientation predicted in the Age of Affluence. One of the fundamental attitudinal ingredients of successful democracies is a relatively widespread sense of interpersonal trust.[12] It is a correlate of several important democratic attitudes[13] and, I believe, an ingredient in economic development itself, since this requires cooperation, responsibility and integrity to facilitate the working out of informal agreements.[14] Comparatively, the United States is a "trusting" nation, perhaps the most trusting; but we may not always have been that way. In Table 12-1 (a) there is some suggestion that interpersonal trust has increased since the war and the immediate postwar period. If this is true it would provide the strongest attitudinal foundation for some of the political changes we shall examine shortly.

While the sense of current happiness does not seem to have grown in the

Age of Affluence, nevertheless an important change has occurred in attitudes about the past, present, and future chances for happiness or life satisfaction. In Table 12-1 (b) we see a very strong suggestion that, compared to people in the later phases of the Period of Economic Crisis, people today believe that their lives provide greater satisfaction than their parents or grandparents had. The nostalgia of the thirties for an earlier, possibly "village" America, seems to have declined, in spite of the resurgence of these attitudes said to be characteristics of the Goldwater campaign. If this is a measure of an emotional traditionalism, this change, too, is important.

Looking toward the future as a period offering greater promise of a happier life, could imply some dissatisfaction with the current state of things; but, on the contrary, it seems to me to imply exactly the opposite view, namely, that the present is full of hope, carrying within it the seeds of fruitful change. In any event, the increase in the past ten years of faith in the future compared to a plateau of relatively lower hope during the previous 13 years (Table 12-1 (c)) seems to me to reflect exactly that sense of security in the future which one might expect from the protective arm of the welfare state and newly acquired control over the ravages of the business cycle.[15]

This theme is further reflected and more directly stated in a question on the carrying out of plans, shown in Table 12-1 (d). Here, unfortunately, the time span between measures is short (1958 to 1964), and the change in attitudes relatively small. Moreover, the first measure is taken in a period of recovery from the only important recession in the Age of Affluence. Nevertheless it is suggestive that a growing sense of mastery over fate emerges—the very antithesis of the traditionalist orientation suggesting that one is the helpless object of forces beyond human control.

Finally, we must note in Table 12-1 (e) a somewhat larger increase in the belief that one is, in some sense, the child of fortune, blessed with better than the average share of good luck. Again we are dealing with "late" (for us) changes in the Age of Affluence, but the halving of the proportion of those who think of themselves as dogged by bad luck is surely significant. The implication is twofold: men feel more in control of their lives, as we said before, and "nature" or "the fates" or even "society" is less malevolent— perhaps even benign.

Table 12-1. Trust in Others; Perceptions of Life Now, Earlier, and Later; Control Over One's Own Life, and Share of Good Luck

(a) "Do you think most people can be trusted?" (OPOR, March 26, 1942; NORC, Aug. 1, 1948; Jan. 1964)[a]

	1942	1948	1964
	(%)	(%)	(%)
Yes	66	66	77
No	25	30	21
No opinion	9*	4	2

* includes 5% qualified answers

(b) "Do you think Americans were happier and more contented thirty years ago than they are now?" (AIPO, Mar. 8, 1939).[a] "Do you think the average man gets more satisfaction out of life these days or do you think he got more out of life 50 years ago?" (SRC, Nov. 1964)[b]

	1939 (%)	1964 (%)
In earlier period people were happier; got more satisfaction out of life	61	34
Not happier in earlier period; get more satisfaction out of life these days	23	59
Other, it depends, no opinion	16	7

(c) "Ten years from now, do you believe Americans will generally be happier than they are today?" (AIPO, May 18, 1939). "As you look to the future, do you think life for people generally will get better—or will it get worse?" (AIPO, March 15, 1952; Aug. 29, 1962)[a]

	1939 (%)	1952 (%)	1962 (%)
Better (happier)	42	42	55
Worse (not happier)	35	34	23
No difference		13	12
No opinion	23	11	10

(d) "When you make plans ahead, do you usually get to carry out things the way you expected, or do things usually come up to make you change your plans?" (SRC, Nov. 1958; Nov. 1964)[b]

	1958 (%)	1964 (%)
Things work out as expected	52	59
Depends, other	1	4
Have to change plans	42	36
Don't know and NA	4	1
No. of cases	(1822)	(1450)

(e) "Do you feel that you are the kind of person that gets his share of bad luck, or do you feel that you have mostly good luck?" (SRC, Nov. 1958; Nov. 1964).[b]

	1958 (%)	1964 (%)
Mostly good luck	63	75
Pro-con; it depends	5	10
Bad luck	29	14
Don't know and NA	4	1
No. of cases	(1822)	(1450)

[a]Erskine, *POQ*, pp. 517, 523, 525. AIPO refers to American Institute of Public Opinion; OPOR to Office of Public Opinion Research; and NORC to National Opinion Research; Corp.
[b] Inter-University Consortium for Political Research, Codebook for 1964 Survey Research Center Election Study. These sources will hereafter be abbreviated as "Consortium Codebook" and the initials SRC will be used for the Survey Research Center (University of Michigan).

In review, in spite of the findings on "happiness," one can only conclude that during this period the direction of changing personal orientation has been toward a sense that life is better than it was, and will get still better; that people are more trustworthy; that events are more under control and fate is kinder. There is a group of intellectuals who have, in one sense, inherited the place once held by the proponents of Marx's immiseration theory of capitalism. With tongue in cheek, we may refer to them as "alienists," for their apostle is a psychoanalyst, Erich Fromm, and their theme is the increasing alienation of men from work, society, and government. I have long suspected that they reflected their own discontent with society rather more than any mass discontent—some, like C. Wright Mills, have said as much.[16] Partly too, I think, their views reflect their own alienation from the field of endeavor where there is a true *elan*, the field of science. Whatever the reason, and somewhat apart from the main argument of this piece, I suggest that these data cast doubt upon the principal themes of these alienist thinkers.

Political Partisanship

2. *In an Age of Affluence, the sense of crisis and of high national, personal, and group stakes in national elections declines; political partisanship takes on a new meaning.*

This change in "sense of crisis" is, perhaps, the most important attitudinal change from the Period of Economic Crisis to the Age of Affluence, and it is the most difficult to substantiate with really good evidence. The argument, however, is straightforward.

In an Age of Affluence an increasing proportion of the working class achieve sufficient income and security to adopt middle class social and political patterns—but they nevertheless are likely to remain Democrats. At the same time, the middle class will associate its own increasing welfare and security with the policies of the welfare state, including flexible fiscal policies, and will be in no mood for change. Many will become Democrats; others will be liberal Republicans. Many industrialists and businessmen will come increasingly to perceive that the fight against a limited management of the economy is not in their interests because these "liberal" policies provide the basis for the prosperity and growth in which they share. It is certainly not true that the more prosperous a person becomes, the less likely he is to be alarmed about political events. But, generally, I think it is true that the more secure he is about his income, and the more it appears to him that the government will not jeopardize that income, the less intense he is likely to feel about political decisions in the realm of economic affairs.

Before turning to time comparisons in the United States, something may be learned from cross-cultural comparisons of attitudes toward victory by opposition parties. From the data in Table 12-2, one learns that the sense of electoral crisis is lower in the United States than elsewhere. This is enormously significant for the smooth functioning of democratic institutions, not only because it makes transition easier from one administration to another, but also because it reduces antagonism and hostility in electoral campaigns. The data also show a sensitivity in these foreign nations to real dangers; but for our purposes, let us note only one other point. In every country except Mexico the more conservative party is in power, but only in the United States—and there only in a minor way—is a larger proportion fearful of the conservative party policies than of the more liberal party. So much has the welfare state been accepted here that its mild opponents, even when in power, were considered more threatening than its apostles. This was true in 1960— perhaps the 1964 election may be interpreted as further confirmation of this point.

Not infrequently the American experience is taken by (American) scholars to represent a kind of prototype for modernizing societies, a model of what is to become of them. If that interpretation is true, it implies that we have passed through some of the phases of economics and politics which these

Table 12-2. Sense of Alarm Over the Victory of an Opposition Party, in Five Nations

"The Republican Party now controls the administration in Washington. Do you think that its policies and activities would ever seriously endanger the country's welfare? Do you think that this *probably* would happen, that it *might* happen, or that it *probably wouldn't* happen?"*
"If the Democratic Party were to take control of the government, how likely is it that it would seriously endanger the country's welfare? Do you think that this would *probably* happen, that it *might* happen, or that it *probably wouldn't* happen?*"

Country	Response	Per Cent "Probably Would Happen," of total sample
United States		(%)
Republicans probably endanger welfare		5
Democrats probably endanger welfare		3
Great Britain		
Conservatives probably endanger welfare		7
Labour probably endangers welfare		17
Germany		
Christian Democrats probably endanger welfare		7
Socialists (SPD) probably endangers welfare		12
Right wing (DRP) probably endanger welfare		35
Italy		
Christian Democrats probably endanger welfare		10
Communists (PCI) probably endanger welfare		60
Socialists (PSI) probably endanger welfare		43
Socialists (PSDI) probably endanger welfare		23
Right Wing party like MSI probably endangers welfare		41
Mexico		
Party of Revolutionary Institutions (PRI) probably endangers welfare		13
PAN (minor party) probably endangers welfare		18
PP (minor party) probably endangers welfare		37

* Appropriate changes in wording, of course, for each nation.
Source: Almond-Verba five-nation study; *Consortium codebooks.* The major report on these surveys is made in Gabriel A. Almond and Sidney Verba, *The Civic Culture, op. cit.* The number of cases for each country is about a thousand; U.S. survey was made in March 1960, others in June and July 1959.

other nations are now experiencing—a hypothesis which runs counter to the notion of American uniqueness, and runs counter to much common sense as well. Nevertheless, the implication of Table 12-2 is in line with our major theme: the decline of a sense of high stakes involved in national electoral decisions.

These stakes might be national stakes, where the welfare of the *country* is somehow "risked," as implied by the question eliciting the Almond-Verba data; or the stakes might be more personal, turning on *one's own economic condition*; or they might refer to the welfare of the *group* to which one belongs. Changing attitudes toward these three kinds of stakes are reflected in Tables 12-3 and 12-4.

The argument for a declining sense of national urgency in electoral outcomes must rest on two comparisons over time, the only comparable ones I could find (Table 12-3). One is a comparison of the responses to two similar questions: how much difference it makes which party wins in 1946, and how much difference it makes which party runs the country nineteen years later in May, 1965. Note that the latter time follows by only several months an election in which the candidates were thought to have sharply different views on domestic and foreign policy. The decline in those believing partisan victory or partisan government of one kind or another makes "a great deal of difference" is suggestive of the process of consensus revealed in Table 12-2 and anticipated in our argument. The other comparison is between attitudes directly mentioning "difference to the country" or "important to the country" in 1944 and in 1952—the beginning of the politics of consensus. Fortunately, in 1952 the question was asked twice, once before the election—mentioning only parties—and again after the election, mentioning the candidates' names. The lack of difference between these two times and wordings gives us a sense of the reliability of the attitudes involved. And the magnitude of the apparent change in attitude over this 8-year period suggests that chance or sampling error or minor differences in wording could not account for the change. But perhaps it is the difference between a war election and a peacetime election, rather than any between an election colored by the politics of the Period of Economic Crisis compared to the politics of consensus in the Age of Affluence? This would be a more plausible construct were it not for a previous (AIPO) poll in (August) 1942 asking people whether they thought the outcome of the election would "make *any* difference in the war effort"; only 30 per cent thought—correctly, as the election consequences for domestic mobilization programs showed—that it would make any difference in this particular respect, compared to 88 per cent seeing some unspecified difference in 1944. The implication is clear: people were carrying into the 1944 election—when postwar reconversion anxieties loomed—their sense of partisan alarm learned in the 1930s. In 1952, with a war in the Far East still unresolved, and the cold war in full swing, the sense that the country's welfare hinged on the election nevertheless dwindled drastically and the conditions were prepared for the very low sense of partisan alarmism seen in the 1960 Almond-Verba data presented above.

Table 12-3. Does It Make Much Difference to the Country Which Party Wins?

(a) "Do you think it makes much difference or only a little difference which party wins the elections for Congress this fall?" (AIPO, Sept. 1946)[a]
"Do you think it makes a great deal of difference or just a little difference which political party runs the country?" (AIPO, May 1965)[b]

	1946	1965
	(%)	(%)
Great deal of difference	49	39
Little difference	31	40
No difference	11	14
Don't know	9	6

(b) "Which one of these ideas comes closest to the way you feel about this election: It is very important to the country that Roosevelt be elected; the country will be better off if Roosevelt is elected; the country will be better off if Dewey is elected; it is very important to the country that Dewey be elected?" (NORC, Oct. 2, 1944)[a]
"Do you think it will make a good deal of difference to the country whether the Democrats or the Republicans win the election this November or that it won't make much difference which side wins?" (SRC, Oct. 1952)[c]
"Do you think it will make a good deal of difference to the country that Eisenhower won instead of Stevenson, or don't you think it will make much difference?" (SRC, Nov. 1952)[c]

	1944	1952	
		October	November
Very important to the country;	(%)	(%)	(%)
good deal of difference	54	21	20
Country will be better off;			
some difference; it depends	34	40	42
Won't make much difference;			
no difference	9	32	31

[a] Hadley Cantril and Mildred Strunk, *Public Opinion, 1936–1945* (Princeton University Press, 1951).
[b] AIPO release, May 1965.
[c] *Consortium Codebook.*

Part of the political style of the period of transition to the welfare state—and, we must add, its brief resurgence in 1964—is the hostile posture of each partisan toward his opponents, something which follows naturally from the view that a great deal is at stake in the political contest. Not infrequently in such a strained atmosphere, the election seems more of an effort to keep the other man out, rather than to elect one's own candidate. The evidence (not presented here) suggests that the intensity of opposition—except on the extreme fringes—is greater among the *defenders* of the liberal established order; the threat of deprivation of the welfare state is apparently felt more intensely than the threat which the welfare state, once established, implies to its opponents. In any event, it is our thesis that the politics of consensus is also the politics of support, rather than the politics of opposition. There is some evidence for this in the responses of three national samples to questions almost identically worded asking "would you say you are voting mostly to get one man into office (for 'R's candidate'), or mostly to keep the other man out (against 'opposing candidate')?" In 1944 the oppositional vote was 25 per cent, and in 1964, with the return of anti-welfare state politics, it was 21 per cent. By contrast, in the 1960 election—marked by some anti-Catholic voting, but not by threats to the welfare state and a managed economy, and basically in the consensual style—oppositional voting was only 10 per cent, less than half as large.[17]

Table 12-4. Does It Make Much Difference to a Person's or a Group's Welfare Which Party Wins?

(a) "Do you think it will make any important difference in how you and your family get along financially whether the Democrats or the Republicans win? How is that?" (SRC, Oct. or Nov. of years indicated)[a]

	Per Cent Saying "No Difference" or Unable To Think of Any Difference (Don't Know)					
	1952	1954	1956	1958	1960	1964
	(%)	(%)	(%)	(%)	(%)	(%)
Presidential elections	53		66		66	66
Congressional ("off year") elections		65		72		
No. of cases	(1799)	(1139)	(1762)	(1822)	(1954)	(1571)

(b) "As of today, which political party—the Democratic or the Republican—do you think serves the interests of the following groups best: Business and professional people? White collar workers? Farmers? Skilled workers? Unskilled workers?" (AIPO, months uncertain, years as indicated)[b]

	Per Cent Saying "No Difference"		
	1952	1960	1964
Responses referring to own group (business and professional people referring to the interests of business and professional people, etc.)	(%)	(%)	(%)
Middle groups (less class conscious)			
White collar	12	15	17
Skilled workers	13	14	16
Farmers	10	16	17
Extreme groups (more class conscious)			
Business and professional	11	15	12
Unskilled workers	11	13	12

[a] *Consortium Codebooks* for election studies of years indicated.
[b] AIPO release, Feb. 28, 1965.

These findings and arguments deal essentially with the question of national stakes and concerns, but one might well argue that political life more directly reflects a person's own perceived self interest—at least Campbell, Converse, Miller, and Stokes do seem to take this position.[18] This is a fundamental question, for the heart of my argument rests on the view that the Age of Affluence produces, with occasional regression, political contests which do not jeopardize a person's income or economic security. Unfortunately, here, the time series goes back only to 1952, and hence the comparison must rely upon trends within the later era. My thesis, as it turns out, is only partially supported by the evidence, as may be seen in Table 12-4 (a). Where, according to the argument, a slowly growing number of persons should emerge who do not believe that their own income will be greatly affected by the outcome of an election, we find instead, for the Presidential election years, a marked increase in this sense of "indifference" only between 1952 and 1956— followed by no change at all, a plateau. For the congressional years, a crucial datum is missing for 1962, but the change from 1954 to 1958 is in the expected direction. There are, of course, natural limits to the rise of this "indifference curve" and a counter-tendency in the increased level of education in the population, for the more educated are more likely to see the links between their economic well-being and governmental policy. Nevertheless, if one might project these figures backward into time, one would infer, albeit somewhat hesitantly, a lower sense of indifference in the politics of the Period of Economic Crisis to correspond to the greater sense of national stakes we discovered in the earlier data.

Finally, there is the question of perceived group or class stakes in a national election. As has often been said, politics is a group process, men often take their cue for party identification by some simple phrase such as "party of the business man" or "party of the working man." Where issues are obscure, categoric group tradition and alignment, mediated through primary groups, is central. The measure for this perception of group stakes in politics, as seen in Table 12-4 (b), is the response to a question on the party which best serves the interests of each of five groups, classified by the group membership of the respondent. Here I have omitted some data in 1962, since congressional years are different in most series from Presidential years (these data suggest an acceleration of the indifference effect prior to the 1964 election), and I have grouped the socio-economic classes in two divisions: the more flexible middle group and the more extreme and usually more class-conscious group. The evidence, again rather tenuous, suggests that within the middle groups whose class identifications are likely to be less clear, there is a slowly growing sense that neither party will jeopardize the interests of one's own particular class. Even among the unskilled workers who have been the most partisan of any of these groups, this sense of indifference seemed waxing in 1962 (when the "no difference" responses were 19 per cent, a gain of 6 points in two years), only to be sharply cut back in 1964. Since the 1964 election was, as I have mentioned, a return to welfare state issues, the fact that the sense of "no difference" continued to grow at all, compared to 1956, for these three middle groups is a tribute to the strength of this attitude.

The importance of this measure of sense of indifference is, I think, much greater than is indicated by the small size of the groups involved. For if, at this extreme, the group is slowly growing which claims that there are no important group stakes in an election, then, for a much larger group, there must be doubts, inarticulate mood changes, and declining intensity of conviction.

Before closing this section on the declining sense of crisis, declining perception of threatened policies that might endanger the country, and declining belief that personal or group welfare is involved in an electoral decision, let us note two implied consequences which do *not*, in fact, take place. One implication is that people are becoming less interested in politics. Two extensive series of questions have been asked over time, inquiring into people's interest in the elections, and neither of them shows any decline; indeed, the SRC series catching every national election from 1952 to 1964 (except 1954) shows with some variation over the years a peak interest in 1964 (41 per cent "very much interested") and a marked increase from 1958 to 1962 (from 26 per cent to 36 per cent "very much interested")—suggesting, if anything, an increased interest in this time period.

Moreover, rather paradoxically, no decline has been reported in the strength of party identification. That is, the proportion reporting that they are "strong Democrats" and "strong Republicans" has remained remarkably constant (with a slight increase in "strong Democrats" in 1964). Furthermore, although the proportion of people reporting themselves "independent" has increased slightly—from around 20 per cent in the 1930s and 1940s, to between 21 and 24 per cent in the 1950s and 1960s—the change is very moderate indeed.[19]

The consequent pattern emerging, therefore, is of the interested, party-identified citizen, following politics at least as closely as he did in the days of the great intense clashes when the welfare state was first launched and when men were harassed by insecurity and poverty; voting more regularly and, indeed, "personally caring" about the outcome as before; but believing that the national and personal stakes involved were not so great. People need their party identification as a cue for voting decisions. For most voters, these identifications are the most significant means of orientation in politics. Hence, people will not give them up easily, and if they did, they would have to find others, such as race, or class, or religion, or charismatic leadership. But people are changing the meanings assigned to their party membership and increasingly believe that the opposition is not so dangerous after all.

We can apply one test to this theory of the politics of consensus. If partisanship has lost some of its "bite" and acrimony, one would expect the views of partisans of both parties on the way in which the President is conducting his business to vary more or less together. Approval of the way the President is "handling his job as President" has usually been higher than the partisan vote for the President, in any case. But if we could show that the difference between the approval of members of his own and of the opposition party (Republicans for Roosevelt, Truman, Kennedy and Johnson; Democrats for Eisenhower) was less in the Age of Affluence than in the Period of

Economic Crisis (including the ambiguous 1940s), our case for historical change would be that much stronger. Since approval and disapproval fluctuate within Presidential terms, an ideal measure would take each President at the beginning of his term; but we are forced here to employ the time periods in which the data are given by party breakdown as shown in Table 12-5. Subtracting the per cent of the opposition party approving the President's handling of his job from the per cent of his own party so approving, we have a measure of partisanship.

Table 12-5. Political Partisanship and Approval of the President's Course

"Do you approve or disapprove of the way (name of President) is handling his job as President?" (AIPO)

Time	President	% Support by Pres.' Own Party	% Support by Opposition Party	Partisanship of Support: Pres. Party Less Opp. Party	Average Partisanship Difference
A. Presidents Associated with Conflict over Welfare State					
		(%)	(%)		
Feb. 1941	Roosevelt	90	40	50	
Feb. 1947	Truman	59	41	18	36.3
Oct. 1952	Truman	50	9	41	
B. Presidents in the Age of Affluence (Post-Transition)					
Jan. 1953	Eisenhower	90	70	20	
Jan. 1957	Eisenhower	95	66	29	
Feb. 1960	Kennedy	84	55	29	27.5
Jan. 1964	Johnson	85	74	11	
May 1965	Johnson	77	51	26	

As may be observed (Table 12-5) from the average figures for the two periods, a substantial decline occurred in the partisanship of judgment, the degree to which the judgments reflect partisan divisions. Moreover, except for the special tragic circumstances bringing Johnson into power—circumstances which produced a burst of sympathetic good will toward the new incumbent—the variation in partisanship in this period is rather slight. It seems to have stabilized (to the extent that any set of attitudes at the mercy of historical events may be so described) in a modest 20 to 29 per cent range. In short, our expectations of the consequences of a consensual politics are generally confirmed.

Social Class

3. *In an Age of Affluence, (a) people slowly lose (or relax) their class awareness, (b) the link between social class and ideology changes; but, (c) in spite of their security and prosperity, people do not increasingly think of themselves*

as middle class, and (d) social class does not (after a transition period) lose its link to partisan political choice, although the changing political "pivot" diminishes the importance of class voting in many electoral districts.

The absence in American history of a feudal structure or a landed class—and therefore of a peasant class—has given it a unique lack of class consciousness, as so many observers have noted. Yet American society has always been stratified and important differences in life chances, honor, and distribution of rewards inevitably enter into the experience of Americans, like others, and have been historically associated with political choice as well as many other attitudes towards society. Different social strata have always been the vehicles or *milieux* for different social movements, social ideas, and political parties. In the Age of Affluence, we would expect a continuation of past behavior and opinion modified very slowly by new feelings of security, life syles, and perspectives. I stress the slowness because social class, unlike political party, refers to the basic pattern of life experiences, learned early, reinforced daily, and inevitably loaded with emotion.

First, one wants to know both the nature of objective social change and the nature of subjective responses. Briefly, the proportion of white-collar workers has increased by an average of a little less than five percentage points in every decade for fifty years, with a much smaller increase during the Period of Economic Crisis and a larger increase in subsequent years (1940 to 1960). In 1960 43.2 per cent of the employed persons were in white-collar occupations (professional, technical, managerial, clerical, and sales).

But, of course, there is a great deal of slippage between objective and subjective class identifications (some estimates indicate that self-misclassification is as large as 25 per cent), and, hence the objective occupational change is not a very good immediate indication of how people will see themselves over time. Measures on this go back to 1945[20] and 1946[21] and, after 1952 continue in rather orderly fashion to 1964.[22] Any expectation that the increasing proportion of workers engaged in white-collar jobs, and the general levelling up of economic security and income, would, produce an increased middle class identification, would turn out to have been wrong; about 40 per cent thought of themselves as middle or upper in 1946, and about 40 per cent again in 1964. In between, the decline in middle class identification noted by Converse in his comparison of 1945 data with 1952 and 1956 data has subsequently been reversed[23] and, without finer examination of special groups, one can only conclude in 1965 that this aspect of "bourgeoisification" of society has not taken place. Men appear to be as willing today as they were about twenty years ago to see themselves as members of "the working class." As a nation we are certainly not "putting on airs."

But, as with party identification, it may be that class identification is slowly assuming a new meaning, a lack of intensity, a different reference. Here the SRC series shown in Table 12-6 (a) gives us some clues, though rather slight ones. We would not—particularly just before the 1964 election—

have expected much change, in any event; but we would expect a drifting decline in class awareness or consciousness in the sense of "thinking of oneself as belonging to a social class," partly because of the erosion of the intense feelings evoked by the experience of the 1930s, and partly through a change in age cohorts (in 1956 people in their fifties were the most class-conscious age group).[24] The time period is short, one of the figures is anomalous and is omitted from the table (in 1960 the comparable figure was 25 per cent), but after grouping contiguous years and thus doubling the sample sizes, a slow increase does appear in the proportion of people for whom social class is not a conscious reference. And if this is overtly true of this third of the population or so, one suspects that the meaning of class is *changing* for the other two-thirds, as well.

Converse, in neat analysis, has already given a strong indication that this is probably the case. He relates, for each of the two periods, class identification and certain social opinions dealing with the government's responsibility for employment, medical care, and housing and electricity; and finds that the correlations between class and opinions decline markedly in each case. Moreover, this is true of both objective status and subjective class identification.[25] This is strong evidence for a changed meaning of class identification so far as government policy is concerned. After all, government is increasingly seen as the agent for improving *everyone's* prosperity.

But would this also be true of attitudes toward unions, organizations which do not have this trans-class role and which, indeed, are often seen as (and are) the agents of class conflict? From 1936 to 1963 the Gallup polls have asked national samples about their attitudes toward unions: "Are you in favor of labor unions?" and "In general do you approve or disapprove of labor unions?" (Responses in contiguous years to these different questions indicate no difference in response patterns.) Three things are most notable about these responses. First, in this 26-year period, some fluctuation has occurred (from 58 per cent approve in 1938 to 76 per cent in February, 1957), with increased disapproval following severe strikes or critical investigations (like McClellan's in 1957), but no long term decline or increase in public criticism or support. Second, at no time has a majority of any group, including the business and professional group, failed to approve of unions. And third, and most important for our purposes, the discrepancy between working class and middle class support of unions seems to be growing, as may be seen in Table 12-6 (b). Moreover, in the eleven years between 1950 and 1961, a modest increase has occurred in the proportion of business and professional and of white collar workers—but *not* of manual workers—who believe that the laws regulating labor unions are "not strict enough" (Table 12-6 (c). Such evidence, running contrary to my main thesis (the weakening effect of socio-economic status upon "ideology") suggests that there may be two themes here instead of one. Social class (objective and subjective) may have a weakening relationship to opinions about welfare state policies but not to opinions about labor unions. Perhaps, in a period when attention turns to questions of productivity and growth, rather than social justice and equality, and when the government, rather than unions, is the main agent of economic protection—especially for the underdog—unions will seem somewhat different to middle class and working class people. If this were the case, it would give us a better understanding of why it is that just at the time when the relationship between class and opinion on the welfare state is (in

Table 12-6. Changing Patterns of Class Consciousness and Class Ideology

(a) "There's quite a bit of talk these days about different social classes. Most people say they belong either to the middle class or to the working class. Do you ever think of yourself as being in one of these classes?" (SRC, Oct., Nov. years indicated)[a]

	The Late 1950s (Average for 1956 and 1958)		The Early 1960s (Average for 1962 and 1964)	
	(%)	(N)	(%)	(N)
No, never thinks of self as being in a social class	34.6	(1241)	37.6	(1078)
Yes, thinks of self as being in a social class	64.2	(2302)	60.8	(1744)
Don't know and other	1.1	(41)	1.6	(46)
Total	99.9	(3584)	100.0	(2868)

(b) "Are you in favor of labor unions?" (AIPO, Oct. 26, 1941). "In general do you approve or disapprove of labor unions?" (AIPO, Feb. 19, 1949; Nov. 11, 1953; Feb. 8, May 1, 1957; Feb. 8, 1959; Feb. 15, May 26, 1961; Jan. 30, 1963)[b]

	Per Cent Approve			Index of Unlikeness	
	Manual Workers	Business & Professional	White Collar	Manual Wkrs. Minus Bus. & Prof.	Manual Wkrs. Minus White. collar
	(%)	(%)	(%)		
1941 (October)	73	—	69		4
1949 (February)	67	65	63	2	4
1953 (November)	81	70	75	11	6
1957 (February)	83	73	77	10	6
1961 (February)	77	64	65	13	12
1963 (January)	75	61	67	14	8

(c) "As things stand today, do you think the laws governing labor unions are too strict or not strict enough?" (AIPO, Jan. 15, 1960). "Do you think the laws regulating labor unions are too strict, or not strict enough?" (AIPO, Oct. 22, 1961)[b]

	Per Cent "Not Strict Enough"	
	1950	1961
	(%)	(%)
Business and Professional	54	60
White collar	43	48
Manual workers	34	35

[a] *Consortium codebooks.*
[b] Erskine, *POQ*, Vol. 26 (1962), pp. 284, 288 (and AIPO release, Jan. 30, 1963).

Converse's measure) weakening, the relationship between class and attitudes toward unions is growing stronger.

But political choices, as we know, are only loosely related to ideology. The facts seem to be as follows: the relationship between social status or class membership and political choice ("status polarization" or "class voting") tended to become closer, as one might expect in Presidential elections during the Period of Economic Crisis, at least from 1936 to 1940; then, after a depressed relationship in 1944 due to attention to war issues, the correlation reached a peak in 1948, whereupon it declined in 1952 and again in 1956. At this point it reached a plateau and remained at about the 1956 level in 1960 and, surprisingly, in 1964.[26] By Alford's measure (a variation of Rice's "index of likeness")[27] this 1956–64 plateau is at about the same level as the starting point of the series in 1936, suggesting that class voting has a kind of "natural level" for a given country in a given period, altered only occasionally by certain "critical elections."

But, while the measure of likeness (or, actually, "unlikeness") which Alford uses and which I have employed elsewhere in this paper, is useful in indicating some elements of similarity, it does not take into account the *level* at which these similarities and discrepancies occur. For example, a situation where 60 per cent of the manual workers and 40 per cent of the non-manual workers vote Democratic (index = 20) and another situation where 80 per cent of the manual workers and 60 per cent of the non-manual workers vote Democratic (index = 20) are scored alike. Yet in the first instance, a majority of the manual workers is on one side of the political division and a majority of the white collar and business and professional workers is on the other, whereas in the second case, a majority of both groups is on the same side.

Let us suppose that the party responsible for innovative institution of welfare state measures and fiscal and monetary measures designed to level out the business cycle and promote growth gradually extends its following in the Age of Affluence so that it becomes overwhelmingly the dominant party. This is done partly by a gradual shift in the middle "white collar" groups so that they see the more liberal party as appropriately "their own", and by some defection of business and professional groups, especially among Catholic and Jewish communicants. Our measure of political likeness does not change, but the pivot changes and we have a situation where class voting differences, with their winner-take-all payoff, become less important.

The evidence that this is the case is strong. A majority of the skilled and unskilled workers have been Democrats at least since 1928 and probably before,[28] with a variable minority occasionally voting outside the party (especially in 1952 and 1956). Even these defectors, however, tended to identify with the Democratic party throughout. On the other hand, historically the business and professional groups, the white collar groups, and usually the farmers, have identified with the Republican party, occasionally voting for Democratic candidates, but then returning to the fold—though returning in decreasing numbers. The consequence was that in terms of party identification at the end of the Period of Economic Crisis both parties started about even: In 1940 some 42 per cent of the population said they were Democrats, 38 per cent Republicans, and 20 per cent claimed to be Independents. By July 1964, just prior to the nomination of Barry Goldwater, the count was 53 per cent Democrats, 25 per cent Republicans and, 22 per cent Independents. And the shift seemed to be accelerating: between 1960 and 1964 all major groups became more Democratic, with the business and professional group moving a little faster than average (7 per cent shift compared to an average of 6 per cent) and thus becoming more Democratic than Republican for the first time.[29] Thus, as far as party identification goes, all groups have Democratic pluralities, and although proportions differ between social classes, majorities tend to agree.

The difference between the kind of situation where majorities of all major social groups (business and professional, farmers, manual workers, etc.) agree, compared to a situation where the majority of one group is for one party and the majority of an opposing group is for another, is illustrated by the 1964 election. In such an election, business and union spokesmen (like Henry Ford, and Walter Reuther) support the same candidate; the candidate of the dominant coalition assumes a moderating "national unity" tone and his opponent sounds "shrill"; references to class-linked slogans such as "union bosses" and "economic royalists" are muted in the dominant party. In short, the shifting "pivot" of class allegiance implies a very different kind of "democratic class conflict"—even though the index of unlikeness or of "class voting" may remain constant. Within the dominant party, the politics of consensus takes over, while the minority party occasionally reverts to the older politics of economic crisis.

Religion

4. *In the Age of Affluence, religious institutions slowly lose their influence over men's thought and behavior; religious prejudices and hostilities decline; but the influence of religious identification upon partisan political choice is among the slowest influences to change.*

It may be argued that class divisions in politics and the influence of status upon social and political opinion are "healthier" for a society than are religious divisions and influences. They are less likely to be "moralized," therefore less likely to be intransigent; conflicts are more easily solved by economic growth and economic change; compromise is easier because the stakes are often divisible and allocable by small units; the controversies are increasingly subject to empirical proof, referring, as they do, to cause and effect in *this* world. Therefore, whatever one's feelings about religion in its own sphere, a declining influence of dogmatic religion (as contrasted to some Judeo-Christian ethics) on social thought and of religious affiliation on political choice might be seen as a step toward a more healthy polity.

Since space is brief, let us, for the record, summarize some evidence pointing generally, with some exceptions, in this direction. The basic facts on religious affiliation and church attendance are these: The proportion of the population with some kind of religious affiliation increased in the 1920s, remained constant in the 1930s, increased substantially in the 1940s, increased very moderately in the 1950s, and from 1959 to 1962 (the latest date on which I have figures) increased not at all. Church attendance (as contrasted to affiliation) increased in the late 1940s and early 1950s to a peak average attendance of 49 per cent in 1958 and from that time decreased slowly but steadily to 45 per cent in 1964, with Protestants and Catholics moving in the same direction.[30] Since affiliation and church attendance have been higher among white collar than blue collar groups and among better-educated than less-well educated groups, this levelling off and decline are, so to speak, "bucking" the educational and occupational trend. Some perception of this tendency seems to have entered the public consciousness. Asked whether religion is "increasing or losing its influence on American life," the proportion seeing religion losing its influence has recently grown: 1957: 14 per cent; 1962: 31 per cent; 1965; 45 per cent.[31] These changes are late in the Age of Affluence; their political and ideological effects would not be expected to appear for some time.

Such observations refer to the theological or institutional aspects of religion, but the community effect, the identification with co-religionists, is something else.[32] This can take a variety of forms, but briefly, identification with co-religionists in recent years seems to include a declining element of suspicion and declining ideological component. The evidence for this is partly in the changes among Catholics (but not so much among Protestants) indicating greater hope for *rapprochement* of the Christian religions—ecumenism.[33] Among Protestants, on the other hand, there is increasing support for federal aid to religious schools, thus almost eliminating one of the major bones of contention between communicants of the two religions. National resistance to voting for "a well qualified man who happened to be a Catholic," decreasing over the years, collapsed with Kennedy's term in office (Table 12-7 (a)). Attitudes towards Jews, as measured by the same question, willingness to vote for a "well-qualified person who happens to be Jewish," have continuously been more accepting (Table 12-7 (b)). And Jews themselves, a declining proportion of the population, indicate, in a brief series (1956, 1958, 1960) a modestly declining sense of greater "feelings of closeness" to other Jews, compared to closeness to non-Jews.[34] The evidence is strong that ideological divisions, suspicion, prejudice, and sense of difference, especially as these relate to political matters, are declining.

But not, apparently, the influence of religious identification on political choice. Employing, once again, the "index of unlikeness" (per cent of Catholics voting Democratic, less the per cent of all Protestants so voting), the series is as follows: 1948: 19; 1952: 19; 1956: 14; 1960: 40; 1964: 21.[35] The decline of the relationship between religion and vote predicted by Berelson on the basis of age-group differences in 1948 has not materialized, at least at this gross level.[36] But, as the above attitudinal evidence indicates, the meaning has changed; and as the above trends in affiliation and attendance portend, the institutional reinforcements is likely to decline.

Race

5. *In an Age of Affluence, the struggle for equality by a deprived racial group will be facilitated by the expanding economy, the availability of governmental resources for special assistance, and the relative security of otherwise challenged and more hostile "opposition" groups. These conflicts will be expressed by the increased militance of the deprived minority group, and the vacillating, often reluctant, sometimes idealistic acceptance of these claims by the more affluent majority.*

Racial cleavage and politics are different from class politics in the United States and, indeed, everywhere. Mobility ("passing"), intermarriage, ecological scattering, and intergroup communication are much more difficult across race (caste) lines than across class lines; the middle groups identifying now with one side, now with the other are smaller; the role of property and

Table 12-7. Indications of Declining Religious Hostility in Politics

(a) "If your party nominated a generally well-qualified man for President, and he happened to be a Catholic, would you vote for him?" (AIPO, Oct. 4, 1963)

Year	Yes	No	Undecided
	(%)	(%)	(%)
1940	62	31	7
1958	68	25	7
1959	69	20	11
1960	71	20	9
1961	82	13	5
1963	84	13	3

(b) "Would you vote for a Jew for President?" (AIPO, Feb. 8, 1937). "If your party nominated a generally well-qualified man for President, and he happened to be a Jew, would you vote for him?" (AIPO, Oct. 23, 1963)

Year	Yes	No	No Opinion
	(%)	(%)	(%)
1937*	49	51	(excluded)
1958	62	28	10
1960	72	22	6
1963	77	17	6

* Data for this year are from Cantril and Strunk, *Public Opinion.*

relations of the different groups to the means of production are different; visibility and, hence, treatment by the dominant group are different. Changing group proportions are not induced by technology and the demand for new and different services; rather they are a matter of birth and mortality rates. And, most important, in the United States there are only 22 million Negroes, about half of them still in the South. As a consequence, there cannot be a Negro party and a white party, except in some Southern communities; but for a national or a state contest, current trends suggest a division between one party regarded as more friendly to the Negro, made up of Negroes *and whites* pitted against a predominantly all-white party. These trends rest in large measure on the wholesale northward migration of Negroes, stemming initially from wartime conditions of extreme manpower shortages and consequent job opportunities, and the repercussions of the migration in the South as well as the North. Under these circumstances, how have the Age of Affluence and the politics of consensus affected the situation?

In the first place, one needs to know whether or not the non-white population has shared in the affluent society. The answer, of course, is that they are still faring very badly, economically, educationally, and socially:

The median income of the non-white population is about half the median income of the white population (1962).

The median school years completed for non-whites is 8.2; for whites it is 10.9 (1960). This understates the difference, for the caliber of education in most non-white schools is notoriously poorer.

The proportion of non-whites in white collar jobs is 17.7 per cent; for whites it is 46.9 per cent (1963).

When, however, we turn to recent rates of change, the picture is a little better, for the Negro rate of increase in median income is about half again as high as for whites in recent years (1959–1962) and also in the war period. Similarly, in the past decade and a half the proportion of workers in white-collar jobs has increased about three and a half times as fast among Negroes as among whites. But in terms of education, there is little difference in rate of change; indeed, most recently it seems the white rate of increase has been greater than the Negro rate. On balance, the Negro has participated increasingly in some of the rewarding aspects of affluence, but for him the term "affluence," comparatively speaking, is anomalous: aspirations are running much beyond achievement, and the current *level* seems to belie the hopes for full equality.

I know of no available series of questions asked of Negroes over time to indicate whether or not they experience a greater or lesser sense of deprivation today compared to some previous time, whether their anger at the white community is greater or less, whether the frustration expressed in recent riots is greater or less than it was when anger and frustration may have been differently expressed, whether a sense of special community among Negroes is growing or declining, and whether or not whites are more easily embraced in this community than they once were.[37] But, perhaps these are straws in the wind:

1. Electoral participation in the South has been increasing for the past 15 years and will now (1965 and 1966) increase dramatically in certain places with federal voting registrars. It has always been high (education and income held constant) in the Northern cities. Where non-voting indicates coercion, the lifting of this coercive force may remove some sources of hostility; where it indicates apathy and withdrawal, the change may mean a decline of these symptoms.

2. In 1960 a set of extended interviews (by a Negro) of working-class Negroes in New Haven revealed, in the midst of hostility and frustration, a kind of non-alienated faith in "Washington" as a reliable (indeed, almost omnipotent) source of help.

3. Two AIPO surveys in August 1963 and May 1965 revealed in the South (but not in the North) an increase of about 20 percentage points in the Negro group believing that Negroes were treated "the same as whites."[38]

I put little stock in these indicators. I suspect the fact that about the same proportion of Negroes in 1946 and 1965 (roughly 70 per cent) believed that the Negro was "unfairly treated" or "treated less well than whites" in his community is a better measure of resentment.[39] At the same time, I would expect a substantial change in the quality of this resentment: fear, apathy, self-hatred, and latent hostility in the 1940s and earlier; disappointment, frustration, manifest hostility, ambivalence, and qualified hope in the later period. One indication of this last quality, hope, lies in the growing support among Southern Negroes for integrated schools and the high proportion (70 per cent in 1956) of Southern Negroes who believe that "the day will come in the South when whites and Negroes will be going to the same schools, eating in the same restaurants, and generally sharing the same public accommodations."[40]

The survey evidence is substantial that for the white community, nationally, there is a growing sense that integration in schools (without bussing), residential neighborhoods, and in public accommodations is inevitable, socially desirable, and, with many reservations, personally acceptable. These data are presented in Table 12-8. The rate of change is slow, and there are setbacks, now and then; but the series reveals a growing willingness to accommodate to the demands for change of a deprived group. At the same time, variable tensions emerge over the actual implementation of these demands by governmental action (or, probably, over any action by any agency). Thus, when asked "Do you think the Kennedy (Johnson) administration is pushing integration too fast, or not fast enough?" from 36 to 50 per cent have said "too fast." This is a measure of resistance to change, a measure of the lack of strength or salience of the ideal and of the discrepancy between

Table 12-8. Changing Attitudes toward Integration

(a) "Would you, yourself, have any objection to sending your children to a school where a few of the children are colored? Where half of the children are colored?" (AIPO)

Per Cent "Yes"

	WHERE A FEW CHILDREN ARE COLORED		WHERE HALF OF CHILDREN ARE COLORED	
	Outside South	South	Outside South	South
	(%)	(%)	(%)	(%)
1958	13	72	39	81
1959	7	72	34	83
1963 (June)	10	61	33	78
1965 (May)	7	37	28	68

(b) "Do you think the day will ever come in the South when whites and Negroes will be going to the same schools, eating in the same restaurants, and generally sharing the same public accommodations?" (AIPO)

SOUTH ONLY

	Yes	No	Uncertain
	(%)	(%)	(%)
1957 (August)	45	33	22
1958 (October)	53	31	16
1961 (January)	76	19	5
1963 (July)	83	13	4

Sources: Erskine, *POQ*, Vol. 26 (1962), pp. 138, 141; AIPO releases, July 19, 1963 and May 23, 1965.

verbal and behavioral support. Perhaps, too, it indicates a response to style or manner of "pushing"—consensual or argumentative and coercive; Johnson has fared better than Kennedy in this respect. In any event, this apparent ambivalence and reluctant acceptance indicates exactly those attitudes which, in an insecure, depression-ridden, stagnant society might easily become violent hostility and implacable opposition. The lower-income and less well educated people are more resistant than others to integration. What would their responses be if they were fearful of unemployment, less hopeful of the future, more suspicious of people generally, and feeling victimized by fate; if, in short, they had the attitudes which we saw had changed with growing affluence in recent years?

How then has the Age of Affluence, shaped for the Negro by a partially sympathetic dominant white majority, affected his politics? In one sense "consensus" describes two aspects of the situation. First, Negroes have, ever since the New Deal, become partisan advocates of welfare state policies. Ideologically, in this sense, they are in tune with the dominant political theme of the times. Second, their partisan party preference has gradually, and with some reversals of direction in the 1950s, shifted toward the Democratic camp so that they are now more partisan than any other major group. In 1964, only 6 per cent voted Republican; nine months later only 9 per cent identified with the Republican party.[41] Since there are about twice as many Democrats as Republicans in the United States, again, it seems, the Negro community has adopted the "in" party; in this respect they are in agreement with majorities in almost all other major demographic groups.

On the other hand, this dramatic increase (and it might be viewed with caution, since, in the past, the Negro vote has been more volatile than others —more volatile than the manual-worker vote, for example), has meant, according to the index of unlikeness, an increase in racial voting and partisanship, at least in 1964 and 1965. In one sense, this *is* a measure of hostile cleavage, since it reflects the partisan politics and policies of recent years. Moreover, the Republican party, having lost almost all of its Negro following, may come to believe that it is in its interest to stress "states rights," "law and order in the streets," and "voluntarism in school assignments," and other themes with barely disguised white racial appeal; in which case there will be a re-sorting, not of the Negroes, but of some village traditionalists, many Southerners, and some alienated and marginal Northern and Western urban dwellers. The Goldwater trial run for these themes was not encouraging in the North, but feelings on such matters run deep for an uncertain number of people, and the search for a winning theme may lead the Republican leadership in this direction. Then, racial voting, unlike class voting, will take on a new intensity and move away from the politics of consensus.

But, probably, for most white people, neither the Negro's problem nor the "threat" of integration in their own communities (and certainly not elsewhere) is sufficiently important to determine partisan choice. The politics of consensus can go on around this "American dilemma," within sound of the battle but relatively undisturbed by it.

Political Alienation

6. *In the Age of Affluence, there will be a rapprochement between men and their government and a decline in political alienation.*

It is easier to make the argument that political alienation should decline than to find the evidence to support this view. The argument, again, is simple: the declining intensity of partisanship implies a decline in hostility toward government on the part of the "out" group—with, perhaps, a reverse effect and embitterment on the "far out" right. Politics, then, deals less with moral absolutes and becomes more a discussion of means than ends—its ideological component declines. Since everyone is "doing better" year by year, though with different rates of improvement, the stakes are not so much in terms of gain or loss, but in terms of size of gain—giving government more clearly the image of a rewarding rather than a punishing instrument. Taxes, while primarily the instrument for financing government, now also may be seen

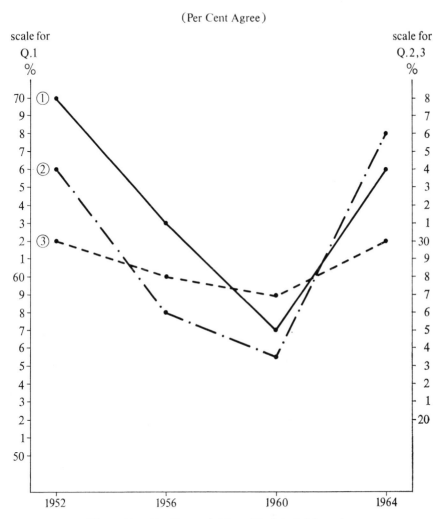

Figure 12-1. Decline and Rise of Political Alienation

Q.1. "Sometimes politics and government seem so complicated that a person like me can't really understand what's going on."

Q.2. "I don't think public officials care what people like me think."

Q.3. "People like me don't have any say about what the government does."

Source: SRC questions in election studies of years indicated, reported in *Consortium code-books.*

as instruments for maintaining prosperity and financing benefits for all rather than for redistributing income.

The difficulty with the use of some evidence supporting this is that I seem to have adopted a "heads I win, tails you lose" strategy with respect to the main source of recent data, the 1964 surveys. If these data show a decline in symptoms of alienation, they seem to support the argument that historical trends are thus revealing themselves. If they show an increase in alienation symptoms, they support the argument that the 1964 election was a regression to the politics of crisis. If we had a long enough time series, this dilemma of ambivalence could be avoided by showing a decline in alienation symptoms up to 1964, with a rise at that time.

In one series we do have exactly this pattern. Figure 12-1 shows a decline from 1952 to 1960 and then a rise in the proportion of (a) people who feel that public officials are indifferent to what "people like me think," and (b) those who believe "people like me don't have any say about what the government does," and (c) those for whom politics and government are "too complicated" to understand. The trouble is that I can see no very plausible reason why the themes or personalities of the 1964 election should occasion these particular changes. That particular election might well have increased the crisis atmosphere; it might (and apparently did) increase the salience of "corruption in politics" themes;[42] it might have created new cleavages in society and thus have disrupted the politics of consensus. But why this campaign, at least compared to 1956 and 1960, should encourage a sense of ineffectiveness and lack of responsiveness in government is obscure. Therefore, in spite of the appearance of a confirming pattern, we must leave this evidence as anomalous.

Nevertheless, as may be seen in Table 12-9, some evidence exists for believing that in certain ways there has been a *rapprochement* between men and their government and a decline in political alienation. In the first place, the increase in the proportion of the public who would like to see their sons (if they had any) enter politics as a career, is, I think symptomatic of a growing attitude that political life is both rewarding and honorable. One reason for interpreting this series in this way is the sharp decline in the proportion of arguments against such a career which refer to corruption: from 30 per cent in 1946 to 17 per cent in 1965.[43]

On the other side of politics, the voter side, note the marked increase in the sense that one "ought" to vote under various more or less discouraging circumstances. These items, taken together, have been called a "citizen duty" scale and one may interpret these data as indicating a reinforced or growing belief that good citizenship means a politically more active citizen. From 1952 to 1960, in the eight possible comparisons over time in Table 12-9 (b), each shows a growth of the sense of citizen duty.

In the argument set forth above, I suggested that attitudes toward taxation should change. The AIPO question, "Do you consider the amount of income

Table 12-9. Rapprochement between Men and Politics: Politics as a Career, Elections as a Duty, and Taxes as a Burden

a) "If you had a son just getting out of school would you like to see him go into politics as a life-work?" (NORC, Nov. '43, Nov. '45). "If you had a son would you like to see him go into politics as a life's work when he gets out of school" (AIPO, Dec. 28, 1944). "If you had a son, would you like to see him go into politics as a life's work?" (AIPO, July 20, 1953; March 5, 1955; March 3, 1965)[a]

	Yes	No	No Opinion
	(%)	(%)	(%)
1943 (Nov.)	18	69	13
1944 (Dec.)	21	68	11
1945 (Nov.)	24	65	11
1953 (July)	20	70	10
1955 (March)	27	60	13
1965 (March)	36	54	10

(b) The duty to vote in elections: 1952, 1956, 1960.[b]

	Per Cent Agree		
	1952	1956	1960
	(%)	(%)	(%)
"If a person doesn't care how an election comes out he shouldn't vote in it."	53	45	43
"A good many local elections aren't important enough to bother with."	17	13	12
"It isn't so important to vote when you know your party doesn't have any chance to win."	11	9	7
"So many other people vote in the national elections that it doesn't matter to me whether I vote or not."	12	10	8
No. of cases	(1799)	(1762)	(1954)

(c) "Do you consider the amount of income tax which you (your husband) (had, have) to pay as too high, too low, or about right?" (AIPO)[c]

PER CENT SAYING "TOO HIGH"

Year	Prof. & Bus.	White Collar	Farmers	Manual Workers
	(%)	(%)	(%)	(%)
1952 (March 12)	74	73	63	72
1953 (March 8)	61	61	55	59
1957 (April 24)	63	69	51	62*
1959 (April 15)	50	51	51	51*
1961 (March 8)	42	50	47	49
1962 (March 11)	50	49	36	51

* Skilled workers only; in 1957 unskilled workers were 65%, in 1959, 58% saying "too high."
[a] Cantril and Strunk, *Public Opinion*, p. 534; AIPO releases as indicated for 1953, 1955, 1965.
[b] *Consortium codebooks;* SRC election studies, October or November of years indicated. These questions were not asked in 1964.
[c] Erskine, *POQ*, Vol. 28 (1964), p. 161.

tax which you (your husband) (had, have) to pay as too high, too low, or about right?" has been asked many times since 1947. The earlier years are non-comparable for several reasons, and show great variability, but we have data from 1952 to 1962 not only by national totals, but also by major occupational groups (Table 12-9 (c)). The data reveal two things, especially: first, the lack of any substantial association between occupational status and attitudes toward taxation. We have known for some time that working class attitudes toward taxation did not fit into conventional concepts of "liberalism" (high taxes and high welfare payments); this is only further illumination of that point. And second—the point to be made here—is the general decline in a sense of taxation as too burdensome. (These findings, it will be observed, do not include the period of great discussion and final legislative action on tax reduction to improve the state of the economy.) Since opposition to "tax-eaters" and the burdens of taxation have traditionally been symptomatic of alienation from government, I think we may quite appropriately see this set of changing attitudes as a part of the *rapprochement* between men and their governments.

In spite of certain anomalies associated with 1964 data, including a constant state of "trust in government" from 1958 to 1964,[44] I am persuaded that there has been a growing state of confidence between men and government, perhaps especially men and politics, during the Age of Affluence. This argument takes on weight when it is placed against the increased life satisfactions and self-confidence examined earlier, the decline in sense of crisis in elections, the changed meaning of class cleavages, the slow drift toward religious harmony, and even the reluctant yielding to the demands for racial equality. The headlines will not show this consensus, nor will the demonstrations at city hall or on the campus, but the ordinary man in the Age of Affluence is beginning to find some greater sense of hope and peace and self-assurance expressed in a less acrimonious political style.

Notes

1. John K. Galbraith, *The Affluent Society* (Boston: Houghton Mifflin, 1958).

2. These data and the economic and social statistics to follow are taken (or derived) from three main sources, all by the U.S. Bureau of the Census: *Historical Statistics of the United States, Colonial Times to 1957* (Washington, D.C., 1960) and its *Continuation to 1962 and Revisions* (1965), and the *Statistical Abstract of the United States, 1964* (85th ed., Washington, D.C., 1964).

3. Bruce M. Russett and associates, *World Handbook of Political and Social Indicators* (New Haven and London: Yale University Press, 1964), p. 155.

4. *Ibid.*, p. 245.

5. *Ibid.*, pp. 160–161; also First National City Bank, *Monthly Economic Letter*, August 1965, p. 89.

6. David M. Potter (Chicago: University of Chicago Press, 1954).

7. David Riesman (Garden City, N.Y.: Doubleday, 1964).

8. The difficulties of showing change through survey data are substantial. Sampling error may often account for the differences (though it should be recalled that most comparisons are between a proportion in one survey, with a sample usually of about 1600 subjects, and a proportion in another; not, as is more familiar, proportions of subgroups in only one survey). Great differences such as one hopes for in correlational analysis

would here imply some rather unstable attitudes and hence indicate the influence of transient events rather than historical change. The most solid evidence is provided, rather rarely, by many observed changes in the same direction over a long-period. Unfortunately, the data for this paper often come from sources which do not give the size of the sample, eliminating the possibility of significance tests or correlational tests. Wherever possible [Tables 12-1(d), 12-1(e), 12-4(a), 12-6(a), and 12-9(b)], I have tested the significance of the distributions by the method of difference of proportions (Z). The dichotomized differences are all significant beyond the .01 level. I wish to thank Mary Frase for these computations.

9. See Norman M. Bradburn and David Caplovitz, *Reports of Happiness* (Chicago: Aldine, 1965).

10. See compilation of survey material by Hazel Gaudet Erskine in *Public Opinion Quarterly*, 28 (1964), p. 519. Future reference to these compilations will be as follows: Erskine, POQ.

11. Gerald Gurin, Joseph Veroff, and Sheila Feld, *Americans View Their Mental Health* (New York: Basic Books, 1960), p. 22.

12. See Gabriel A. Almond and Sidney Verba, *The Civic Culture* (Princeton, N.J.: Princeton University Press, 1963), pp. 266–268.

13. Morris Rosenberg, "Misanthropy and Political Ideology," *American Sociological Review*, 21 (1956), pp. 690–695.

14. This is the implication in David McClelland's discussion of other-directedness. See his *The Achieving Society* (New York: Free Press, 1961), pp. 190–203.

15. Candor compels me to note here that between 1937 and 1964 there was virtually no change in the belief that we will never do away with poverty in this country: in both 1937 and 1964 some 83 per cent said "no," we will never do it. Erskine, POQ, p. 526.

16. See Erich Fromm, *The Sane Society* (New York, 1955); C. Wright Mills, *The Sociological Imagination* (New York: Oxford University Press, 1959), esp. pp. 165–176.

17. *Consortium Codebooks*, NORC 1944 election study and SRC 1960 and 1964 studies.

18. Angus Campbell, Philip E. Converse, Warren E. Miller, and Donald E. Stokes, *The American Voter* (New York: Wiley, 1960), pp. 205–207.

19. These findings on "interest," "personal caring" and partisanship are from the *Consortium Codebooks* of the relevant years.

20. Richard Centers, *The Psychology of Social Classes* (Princeton, N.J.: Princeton University Press, 1949).

21. Hadley Cantril and Mildred Strunk, *Public Opinion, 1936–1945*, cited in Table 12-3.

22. *Consortium Codebooks* (SRC).

23. Philip Converse, "The Shifting Role of Class in Political Attitudes and Behavior," in E. E. Maccoby, T. M. Newcomb, and E. Hartley, *Readings in Social Psychology* (New York: Holt, Rinehart & Winston, 1958), pp. 388–399. The consortium codebooks show the following proportions of national samples reporting themselves as "middle class": 1952: 37 per cent; 1956: 36 per cent; 1960: 31 per cent; 1964: 40 per cent. The 1952 figure includes "upper class."

24. Campbell and associates, *The American Voter*, p. 357.

25. P. Converse, "The Shifting Role of Class," pp. 391–393.

26. The 1944–56 changes are documented in Converse, *ibid.*; these and the 1936, 1940, and 1960 data are reported in the most extensive available study of "class voting," Robert Alford's *Party and Society* (Chicago: Rand McNally, 1963), pp. 103, 352–353. The 1964 figures are based upon AIPO release, December 13, 1964.

27. See Stuart A. Rice, *Quantitative Methods in Politics* (New York: 1928), pp. 210–211.

28. See Alford, *Party and Society*, pp. 225–231.

29. AIPO releases, Feb. 21, 1960 and July 5, 1964.

30. The U.S. Bureau of the Census, *Historical Statistics*, give the basic data on affiliation; The American Institute of Public Opinion conducts surveys every year on church atten-

dance. The percentages given above are averages based on several surveys a year. Erskine, POQ, Vol. 28 (1964), pp. 671–675.

31. AIPO release, April 18, 1965.

32. See, for example, Gerhard Lenski, *The Religious Factor* (Garden City, N.Y.: Anchor Doubleday, 1963).

33. AIPO release, April 21, 1965.

34. *Consortium Codebooks*; SRC data from election studies for years indicated.

35. The 1948 data are computed from Angus Campbell, Gerald Gurin, and Warren Miller, *The Voter Decides* (Evanston, Ill.: Row, Peterson, 1954), p. 71; the data for the other dates are based on AIPO release, Dec. 13, 1964.

36. See Bernard R. Berelson, Paul F. Lazarsfeld, and William N. McPhee, *Voting* (Chicago: University of Chicago Press, 1954), p. 70. On the cognate matter of ethnic influences, see Raymond E. Wolfinger and Joan Heifetz, "The Development and Persistence of Ethnic Voting," in *American Political Science Review*, 54 (1965), pp. 896–908.

37. Some of these data are available and are increasingly accessible both at the Roper Center, Williamstown, Mass., and Inter-university Consortium for Political Research, University of Michigan, Ann Arbor. Further exploration of these data is needed.

38. AIPO release, May 5, 1965.

39. NORC, May 1946, reported in Erskine, POQ, Vol. 26 (1962), p. 139; AIPO release, May 5, 1965.

40. AIPO release, March 1, 1956.

41. AIPO releases, Dec. 13, 1964 and Aug. 15, 1965.

42. This evidence, based on a comparison between SRC 1958 and 1964 findings, runs contrary to my main argument regarding the increasingly favorable view of men toward government in the Age of Affluence, but supports the minor theme: 1964 as a return to the politics of crisis and alienation. Actually, I think it is a more or less ephemeral response to discussion about corruption in the Bobby Baker case and the Johnson administration more generally. Compare reasons for not wanting one's son to enter politics, reported below.

43. AIPO release, March 3, 1965.

44. The SRC 1958 and 1964 election studies asked, "How much of the time do you think you can trust the government in Washington to do what is right—just about always, most of the time, or only some of the time?" Proportions in each category are nearly constant. I interpret this as a long run increase in trust equalized by an election which stirred up (short term) doubts on the matter. But perhaps it is better to leave it uninterpreted for now.

Chapter *13*
The Decline of Politics and Ideology in a Knowledgeable Society

It has been a common thing to speak of a "democratic society," and recently of an "affluent society." Could one, in some analogous sense, speak of a "knowledgeable society," or perhaps historically of an "age of knowledge?" Good scholars are likely to be so aware of what they do not know to regard the term as pretentious, yet they are familiar with, and perhaps accept the implications of conventional statements on the "scientific age." The purpose of this piece is to explore the concept of a knowledgeable society, and to examine some of its political implications.

The strands of thinking which may be woven into such a conceptual fabric are many and varied and curiously isolated from one another. There are, in the first place, certain early sociological and anthropological thinkers, each with a somewhat different interpretation of the stages of development of knowledge.[1] The Marxian dialectic offers a further developmental analysis, in the tradition of the sociology of knowledge.[2] Students of social change,[3] historians of science,[4] and philosophers of sciences[5] add to the picture. Knowledge is cognition—psychologists dealing with cognitive processes and concept formation and thinking illuminate the microprocesses given greater emphasis in an age of knowledge.[6] Even economists have recently dealt with knowledge.[7] The organization and professionalization of knowledge is analyzed in the works of contemporary sociologists.[8] The relationship of science to government has many contemporary students, some of them

Reprinted from *American Sociological Review*, 31 (1966), pp. 694–662. Also reprinted in Edward C. McDonagh and John E. Simpson (eds.), *Social Problems: Persistent Challenges*, 2nd ed. (New York: Holt, Rinehart and Winston, 1969), pp. 602–616; Edgar Litt (ed.), *The New Politics of American Policy* (New York: Holt, Rinehart and Winston, 1969), pp. 50–69.

Notes to this chapter will be found on pages 268–271

gathered together in a recent collection.[9] Finally, the current controversies dealing with the "end of ideology" on the one hand and the place of the intellectual in modern society on the other, bear on the matter.[10] Obviously the scope of the problem is large, the complexity great, and the various treatments disparate. Nevertheless in discussing the concept of a knowledgeable society, we have the help of many others.

"Knowledge," of course is a broad term, and I mean to use it broadly. It includes both "the known" and "the state of knowing."[11] Thus a knowledgeable society would be one where there is much knowledge, and where many people go about the business of knowing in a proper fashion. As a first approximation to a definition, the knowledgeable society is one in which, more than in other societies, its members: (a) inquire into the basis of their beliefs about man, nature, and society; (b) are guided (perhaps unconsciously) by objective standards of veridical truth and, at the upper levels of education, follow scientific rules of evidence and inference in inquiry; (c) devote considerable resources to this inquiry and thus have a large store of knowledge; (d) collect, organize, and interpret their knowledge in a constant effort to extract further meaning from it for the purposes at hand; (e) employ this knowledge to illuminate (and perhaps modify) their values and goals as well as to advance them. Just as the "democratic society" has a foundation in governmental and interpersonal relations, and "the affluent society" a foundation in economics, so the knowledgeable society has its roots in epistemology and the logic of inquiry.

In order to support such an epistemological effort, a society must be open, i.e., free discussion must be allowed on every topic, with the outer limit posed not by threats of social change, but by concern for survival as a society. It must be stable enough to maintain the order necessary for the process of inquiry, trusting enough to encourage cooperative effort and acceptance of each other's "findings,"[12] rich enough to educate its population in the modes of inquiry, dissatisfied or curious enough to want to know more.

Obviously this definition and these conditions raise more questions than can be answered easily: Who are these paragons? What power have they? What standards of knowledge qualify a man or a group or a society? How shall we deal with mystical and religious knowledge? With political and artistic knowledge? What about the basis for the epistemology itself—is not this the crudest act of faith? This is only an approximate definition of a model of a "knowledgeable society." The elements are present in some degree in every society; in the knowledgeable society they are present to the greatest degree.

Comments on the Development of the Knowledgeable Society

I have defined the knowledgeable society in terms of an epistemology, a search for and quantity of knowledge, and a pattern of use of that knowledge. Any effort to examine in detail how such a society developed leads into theories of social change. Let us briefly consider the problem of development, partly as a means of showing, for contrast, what the knowledgeable society is not.

The growth and communication of experience. Malinowski gives us a starting point: "every primitive community is in possession of a considerable store or knowledge, based on experience and fashion by reason."[13] He is here arguing against the view that primitive men are irrational and mystical; his argument takes the form of identifying the "profane" domain of life where cause and effect and the effectiveness of skill and reason are clearly perceived, in short, where "scientific thought" is dominant. Wherever the relationships between action and results are obscure, magic and religion have their domain, but the two may be kept separate and the latter need not dominate the former.[14] The knowledgeable society develops by an extension of an understanding of the cause-and-effect relationships in everyday experience and the withering away of the supernatural. Two further points can be made. Following Sumner part way,[15] we propose that philosophy and ethics, and perhaps a kind of low-level science, come to be the generalized and rationalized versions of everyday experience. To some extent they are emergent from and dependent upon the codification of everyday experience. The interaction between science, or at least technology, and philosophy and religion is an interaction between experience of the mass and the reflections of the elite. In making experience conscious, modern society may, quite apart from the apparatus of science, increase the knowledge applied to everyday acts and decrease their magical and religious components. When experience is "lost" or when it is unconscious and traditional, the opportunities to build a knowledgeable society at this level are wasted.

The growth of culture and science. In *Configurations of Culture Growth*,[16] Kroeber employs the notion of episodic cultural "flowering," of typical phases of early growth, pause, maturity, perhaps revival, and then exhaustion. The reference is to all phases of culture—art, music, architecture, and philosophy, as well as science and invention. The flowering of one field of culture is, according to Kroeber, likely to be accompanied by the flowering of others, but there are no necessary associations. "Flowering" and "growth" identified by historical recognition of excellence, represent the selection of a dominant "pattern," reinforced (or at least not opposed) by other social forces or areas and selectively exploited until the possibilities of this particular specialized way of looking at things is exhausted, ending either in repetition or in rebellion, perhaps with an occasional revival.[17] Science, it seems, is no different. "It is ... specifically to be noted that continuity is a proper quality only of the results of scientific activity. The activity itself is discontinuous." Following[18] Kroeber's line of thought on general culture growth, a knowledgeable society might be in a period of special "flowering," to be followed by decline; there have been many such in history. But since we are interested in exactly those areas of knowledge that are cumulative (and we have reason to believe that the policy sciences are beginning to show this property) we consider a trend to be more reasonable than a cycle.

The concept of growth in knowledge together with irregular scientific "flowering" is partly at odds with Ogburn's concept of an exponential growth of invention, due to the over-expanding number of "elements" in a culture. Invention, for Ogburn, is the recombination of these elements into a new pattern. Since the invention of printing, "elements" are unlikely to be lost, and the communication process promotes increased diffusion; the possibility of new combinations is cumulative, and restrained only by friction, lag and disturbance. Ogburn seems less concerned with the "quality" of the invention, a property central to Kroeber's ideas, than with the quantity and the accelerated rate of innovations of all kinds, and with their capacity for creating social change and social strain.[19] Thus, the knowledgeable society is a strained society.

Derek Price has made some relevant observations by considering the numbers of scientific journals, abstracts in specific sciences, and trained scientists, over time. Price finds something similar to Ogburn's cumulative curve. He says:

> It must be recognized that the growth of science is something very much more active, much faster in its problems, than any other sort of growth happening in the world today. For one thing, it has been going on for a longer time and more steadily than most other things. More important, it is growing much more rapidly than anything else. All other things in population, economics, nonscientific culture, are growing so as to double in roughly every human generation or say thirty to fifty years. Science in America is growing so as to double in only ten years. . . . If you care to regard it this way, the density of science in our culture is quadrupling during each generation.[20]

But Price is explicit about the inhibition of science. Clearly such exponential growth cannot continue: "To go beyond the bounds of absurdity, another couple of centuries of normal growth of science would give us dozens of scientists per man, woman, child and dog of world population."[21]

According to Price, the curve of development is logistic in shape and we are nearing the point of deceleration of growth. One could then, at least on this quantitative basis, differentiate perhaps three periods: (a) accelerating rate of growth; (b) some intermediate constant rate; and (c) decelerating rate of growth. But this is still quantitative growth; it is at least possible that Kroeber's comments on "bursts" of greatness or eminence or quality apply. Nevertheless Kroeber's view that "there is no clear evidence of a tendency toward acceleration of growth as we pass from ancient to modern times"[22] seems to require reservations with respect to science.

Machlup is concerned with yet another kind of relevant data: the increase in personnel and expenditure on knowledge, and the implicit evaluation of worth by society relative to other pursuits. Machlup's concept of "the knowledge industry" is much broader than the focus on "science" or even "culture"; it includes those who distribute knowledge (in education and teaching) as well as those who produce it. He finds that knowledge-producing occupations have grown much more rapidly than others and that the salaries of knowledge producers and distributors, relative to other occupations with equal education, have tended to increase. He also observes a changing emphasis within the knowledge industry: "While in the first part of this century growth was fastest in the clerical occupations, the lead was then taken by managerial and executive occupations, and more recently by professional and technical personnel."[23] The knowledgeable society encourages and rewards the "men of knowledge," compared to the "men of affairs."

The United States has been slow to recognize the importance of scientific knowledge, partly, as Machlup says, because of the "American idiosyncrasy in favor of the immediately practical and against the general-theoretical."[24] Although, in some ways, science grows out of technology,[25] it is often the other way around; even in technology the United States in the nineteenth century tended to lag behind Europe.[26]

This is no longer so. Consider the following data on current American expansion in the sciences: (1) From 1940 to 1957, Federal government expenditures for research and development (excluding military pay) increased from $74 million to $2,835 million; from 1953 to 1963, total Federal ependitures for these purposes increased from $3 billion to $10 billion.[27] (2) in the ten-year period from 1953 to 1963, expenditures for research and development by colleges and universities increased from $420 million to $1,700 million.[28] (3) In the seven-year period from 1957 to 1964, the number of Ph.D.'s conferred annually increased as follows:[29] from 1,634 to 2,320 in the Life sciences; from 2,535 to 4,980 in the physical sciences; and from 1,824 to 2,860 in the social sciences. (4) In the period from 1950 to 1964 books in "science" published annually in the United States increased from 705 to 2,738 and books in "sociology, economics" from 515 to 3,272.[30]

The prodigious and increasing resources poured into research, the large and increasing numbers of trained people working on various natural and social "problems," and the expanding productivity resulting from this work make up, at lease in size, a new factor in social and (I shall argue) political life. This "second scientific revolution," as it is sometimes called, reflects both a new appreciation of the role of scientific knowledge and a new merger of western organizational and scientific skills.[31]

The knowledgeable society is a modern phenomenon; it has inherited a body of knowledge of man, nature, and society which has been continually created and reversed throughout a history of accelerating attention to systematic investigation, despite the irregularity of the production of "great" ideas. The scientific and technological component of culture is different from all other cultural products. Unlike "schools of art and literature" or religious or political movements with their regional incidence, it is a world-wide phenomenon, with demonstrable success in implementing whatever purposes it is applied to.[32] All countries are devoting increasing resources to scientific investigation, and part of this increase is in the social or behavioral sciences. Like the rest of the "knowledge industry," to use Machlup's term, the social knowledge industry is expanding.

The Thoughtways of a Knowledgeable Society

The knowledgeable society is characterized by a relative emphasis upon certain ways of thinking, a certain epistemology, or, at the very least, a certain knowledge about knowledge. Is this epistemological skill more characteristic of modern, particularly American, society than of societies in previous periods? It is possible to speak of the development of episte-mology somewhat as one speaks of economic and political development and to construct a sketch of the "thoughtways" of a knowledgeable society. The view that these qualities are more widely distributed today than ever before (one of the themes of Whitehead's *Science and the Modern World*) and are more thoroughly understood by a governing elite of professionals and managers is reinforced by research showing the impact of modern education upon thinking processes.[33]

Anthropomorphic and analogical thinking. The first stage of thought is labelling, i.e., assigning things to classes—a more complicated process than at first appears.[34] Durkheim and Mauss argue that primitive classification was first developed according to social categories: "the first classes of things were classes of men, into which things were integrated. It was because men were grouped, and thought of themselves in the form of groups, that in their ideas they grouped other things, and in the beginning the two modes of grouping were merged to the point of being indistinct," So, also, "the unity of knowledge is nothing else than the very unity of the collectivity. ... Logical relations are thus, in a sense, domestic relations."[35] This view has been criticized in detail,[36] but the general point, seen in animistic thought everywhere, is valid: Men classified the unfamiliar terms of the homely, familiar concepts developed in daily living. Even in the history of science the use of familiar analogies dominated thought. For example, it is said that Aristotle thought of causal effects in terms of a horse drawing a cart and that Galileo thought of heavenly bodies as something like ships moving in an ocean without friction.[37] The knowledgeable society is one where, by succes-sive approximation, categories and classes of things move from the immediate, personal, and familiar, to more abstract concepts with a better fit (more adequate to account for the properties of the phenomena observed).

Differentiation of ego from inner world and from environment. The more a person responds "unselfconsciously" to his inner moods and fantasy life, without conscious thought, or to the stimuli of his environment, reactively, the less able he is either to schedule his drives and maximize his purposes or to master and control the environment. Somehow, he must be "separate" from his inner world and his outer world; he must have ego strength to think through his problems, synthesize his desires and control his behavior. These qualities are said to be lacking in primitive man, as they are demonstrably lacking in a child. Indeed as one ascends the phylogenetic scale, the separation of ego from inner and outer worlds becomes more and more marked.[38] This is sometimes mistaken for alienation; in reality it is a necessary element in thought and a necessary ingredient of the knowledgeable society.

Imagining situations contrary to fact or beyond experience. In *The Passing of Traditional Society*, Daniel Lerner reports on surveys where Middle Eastern subjects are asked to imagine themselves as an editor of a newspaper, Governor or President of their society, or a resident in a foreign country. Those with the most limited experience and the most parochial orientations cannot do this; they boggle at the very thought. Lerner refers to this imagination of the self in the place of another as "empathy."[39] A more general notion is the "assumption of a mental set willfully and consciously,"—as distinguished from a capacity to respond only in terms of a given and familiar state of affairs and an inability to manipulate concepts in the mind so as to reconstruct them in an ungiven manner.[40] Any society which relies upon widely distributed initiative, ambition, and innovation must encourage these qualities of imagination: Men must think of themselves and of elements of their situation as other than they are.

Holding simultaneously in mind various aspects of a situation. Primitive and uneducated people can learn a task, a creed, a message, a set of conventions, but it takes special qualities to grasp the "essential" parts, to see how they are put together, to compare them, in short to analyze them. Comparison and contrast imply holding and bringing together at least two things at once.[41] Rote learning, as in many traditional schools, does not develop these special analytical qualities; it teaches only parts or, perhaps, sequences. To analyze is to question, and questioning is regarded as dangerous.

The reflective abstraction of common properties and the formation of hierarchic concepts. The capacity to compare and analyze, to disintegrate a whole, is usually paired with the more difficult task of integrating and organizing parts into a new pattern: analysis and synthesis. In the most primitive societies, the concept of abstract numbers, in contrast to concrete instances, is sometimes missing.[42] Once possessed of the idea of say, "five-ness" it is not difficult to assign groups with five discrete elements to this class; but to invent, from a multiplicity of objects, the concept of "five" or any other abstract number is the act of genius. The knowledgeable society is not only endowed with a great variety of useful concepts, it actively encourages concept formation to create classes and relationships which give a better account of observable phenomena. The pre-knowledgeable society employs the concepts given by tradition.

The qualities discussed above fall along a dimension of concreteness-abstraction. The concrete style of thinking is stimulus-bound, unreflective, unanalytic, unsynthetic, and unimaginative. Present in all societies, it is most evident in primitive societies. Harvey, Hunt, and Schroder believe it has social consequences, which can be summarized in these ways:[43] Greater concreteness tends to be accompanied by absolutism, categorical thinking, and stereotyping; it is likely to be expressed in attribution of external causality and "oughtness" to rules; it disposes toward catechisms and word magic; it tends to be accompanied by negativism and resistance to suggestion; and it encourages ritualism. In these ways, as readers of *The Authoritarian Personality* and of *The Open and Closed Mind* will recognize, the dimension of concreteness-abstraction has political and social implications: concreteness is related to authoritarianism and to dogmatic, rigid, and opinionated thinking;[44] The democratic society in contrast is marked by abstract thinking.

Employment of objective truth criteria. A knowledgeable society is not only one where more people value knowledge, but one where knowledge is more likely to be valued if it can be shown to be true by certain objective criteria. In the words of Ithiel Pool:

> To evaluate assertions primarily by a criterion of objective truth is not a natural human way of doing things; it is one of the peculiar features of the Graeco-Roman-Western tradition. . . . The Western criterion of truth-value . . . assumes that a statement has a validity or lack of it inherent in itself and quite independent of who says it and why. . . . In most societies facts must be validated by an in-group authority before they can be considered credible.[45]

In most societies, statements are true according to whether the spokesman is powerful and likely to dominate others, whether he is "one of us," whether it is expressed with appropriate politeness, and so forth. Moreover, in Eastern philosophies a thing can be both true and not true at the same time; there is no rule of the undistributed middle.[46]

In a sense, this is a facet of a much larger problem analyzed by Rokeach: the processing of information according to its "intrinsic merits." In his discussion of the open and closed mind, he says that the "basic characteristic that defines the extent to which a person's system is open or closed" is "the extent to which the person can receive, evaluate, and act on relevant information received from the outside on its own intrinsic merits, unencumbered by irrelevant factors in the situation arising from within the person or from the outside." By irrelevant internal pressures Rokeach means unconscious intruding habits and poses, irrational power needs or needs for self-aggrandizement, the need to allay anxiety, to create an impression, and so forth. The irrelevant outside factors are attitudes of dislike towards the source, conformity pressures, the rewards and punishments implied by acceptance and rejection.[47] The knowledgeable society screens out more of the irrelevant internal and external factors for more people.

Tolerance of dissonance and ambiguity. The authoritarian personality, according to Else Frenkel-Brunswik, is intolerant of ambiguous stimuli; he needs quick, sharp resolution of his doubts. Thus he likes sharply defined art, quick (and usually easy) answers, people who are decisive.[48] The person with a closed mind, according to Rokeach, does not bring together conflicting elements of his belief system; rather he compartmentalizes them, linking them only through the authority of the dogma or the party line or the dominant spokesmen's view.[49] Similarly the capacity and inclination to hold simultaneously in view opinions or attitudes each of which "implies" the reverse of the other (a favored message from a hated source) varies greatly in the population and generally forces various kinds of reconceptualization to reestablish a consonant emotional posture.[50] More than others, the members of a knowledgeable society are endowed with the capacity to tolerate ambiguity, conflict, and dissonance.

Changed views of metaphysics and religion. Comte, writing in the early nineteenth century, held that social progress was produced by a changing epistemology and metaphysics. Societies pass (necessarily, he thought) through certain stages marked by the dominance in modes of thought and emphasis, first of theology, then of metaphysics, and finally of science associated with industrial development, centrally planned and controlled with the help of extensive sociological studies which give the controllers knowledge of the laws of society.[51] The agency of change is, however, unclear; there is no epistemological dialectic. Yet one can at least accept the idea that in the knowledgeable society theological and metaphysical modes of thought shrink in contrast to scientific modes.

Within this framework, however, certain kinds of religious thought seem to have encouraged the growth of science. Merton expressed his position as follows: "It is the thesis of this study that the Puritan ethic, as an ideal-typical expression of the value-attitudes basic to ascetic Protestantism generally, so canalized the interests of seventeenth-century Englishmen as to constitute one important *element* in the enhanced cultivation of science. The religious *interests* of the day demanded in their forceful implications the systematic, rational, and empirical study of Nature for the glorification of God in His works and for the control of the corrupt world."[52] A knowledgeable society, then, emerges from and is reinforced by religious beliefs which, however, framed, focus attention upon this world and allow for or encourage a scientific epistemology. Today, scientists and professional people are much less likely to be religious or believe in God than businessmen, bankers, and lawyers.[53]

Changed philosophy of knowledge. The mind vs. matter problem appears in many guises: as the contrast between "words and things," as rationalism vs. empiricism, as idealism vs. nominalism, and so forth. Whitehead considered that the great difference between the modern scientific age and all other periods was the wedding together of speculative and theoretical modes of thought with empirical and systematic modes of investigation.[54] Similarly Reichenbach has argued that the rise of scientific philosophy is grounded in a shift from "*transcendental* conception of knowledge, according to which knowledge transcends the observable things and depends upon the use of other sources than sense perception," to a "*functional* conception of knowledge, which regards knowledge as an instrument of prediction and for which sense observation is the only admissible criterion of nonempty truth."[55] There are not two worlds, an ideal and a real one, but one integrated world of thought and experience. The knowledgeable society is marked by an increased acceptance of this view. "The opium of the intellectuals" is not so much, as Raymond Aron thinks, Marxism,[56] as it is philosophical idealism.

One facet of this changed concept of knowledge has been an emphasis upon operationalism, *i.e.*, the position that concepts are related, however indirectly, to the operations which measure them, and by intersubjective testability. Knowledge in the knowledgeable society must be public, its sources indicated and its conceptual boundaries marked by something other than incommunicable experience.

From symptomatology to taxonomy to explanation. The history of the biological and behavioral sciences reveals a tendency first to report observations on phenomena (the naturalist and the journalist), then, with greater care, to group these observations into classes and syndromes, and then, with experimental or controlled observational techniques, to attempt to understand causal relationships, to explain why the phenomena change as they do. When this latter phase is successful, control is more feasible and social policy is likely to be more adequate to the situation. In the knowledgeable society, the intellectual emphasis is more likely to be upon laws of behavior, change, and control. Attaching metrics to phenomena often improves our understanding and our control. The knowledgeable society increasingly employs mathematical modes of expression and thought.

The contribution of the philosophy of science. We have been discussing the complex of attitudes and skills which equip men to deal realistically with the events which impinge upon their lives—policy-formation at the micro-level. This is related to but separate from the ways of thinking of scientists and philosophers who are interested in social policy. This history of social thought reveals the importance of analogical thinking: If geometry yields results from axiomatic methods, so should sociology; in an age of mechanics the model may be clockworks or hydraulics to some (cf. Freud); organismic theories dominate certain periods: a primitive set of anatomical analogies seems to have been prevalent in the Middle Ages.[57]

It seems to me that the emergence of a coherent philosophy of science or logic of inquiry represents a crucial change in this groping toward a method of studying society, particularly as it has matured and increased the scope given to imagination. If one goes back no further than the beginning of this century, with the rise of analytic philosophy in Austria (the Vienna Circle) and in England, the development of the "unified science" group at Chicago, perhaps the general systems theorists, and the widespread teaching of the philosophy of science today, a change in the intellectual posture toward man and society so great as to represent a watershed is evident. Other knowledgeable societies, marked by Kroeber's "bursts" of culture growth, have not sustained their performance. I believe the development and widespread acceptance of the philosophy of science as a basis for social inquiry represents a "take-off" phenomenon in social science, promising sustained growth in social interpretation.

Professionalism and the "Pre-Formulation" of Policy

The discussion so far has sought to illuminate the development of the knowledgeable society, and to show its characteristic thoughtways. Now we turn to the application of this knowledge to public policy. The people who make this application are, in the first instance the professionals, organized in their own associations, governing and staffing institutions devised to develop and teach the new knowledge and apply it to current problems. Within the professions there are tendencies to allocate responsibility for knowledge domains and hence responsibilities for working out "solutions" of social problems relevant to these domains. One aspect of professionalization is the establishment of standards of performance well above actual performance. The gap between the actual and the idea creates within the profession a kind of strain towards remedial action. The consciousness of meeting or failing to meet standards enlists professional ambition, reputation, credit and blame. Staff conferences, annual meetings, and new research studies set up strains for better performance, better instruments, better laws, and new agencies to meet the new standards. In the knowledgeable society, much policy is made first through professional intercourse concerning what solutions to press upon the government and what men to advance to positions of influence as well as what standards to impose. In some ways this is only a change of venue for political maneuvering, but in an important sense it implies a change in criteria for decision-makers from immediate political advantage to something within the professionalized domain of knowledge.

Knowledge Is Encroaching on Politics

If one thinks of a domain of "pure politics" where decisions are determined by calculations of influence, power, or electoral advantage and a domain of "pure knowledge" where decisions are determined by calculations of how to implement agreed-upon values with rationality and efficiency, it appears to me that the political domain is shrinking and the knowledge domain is growing, in terms of criteria for decisions, kinds of counsel sought, evidence adduced, and nature of the "rationally" employed. Some of the evidence for this direction of change may be suggested in the following sampling of recent events:

1. With due allowance for political slippage, there has been a gradual expansion of the civil service based on competitive examinations from 23 per cent of personnel employed in the executive branch of the Federal government in 1891 to 87 per cent in 1962.

2. The General Accounting Office, established in 1921, and the General Service Administration, established in 1949, supervise government business operations so as to encourage economic rather than political criteria.

3. The Council of Economic Advisers was set up in 1946, symbolizing the introduction of economic criteria into the monetary and fiscal operations of government.

4. The professionalization of the attack on poverty is illustrated by the contrast between the methods and programs of the Works Progress Administration (1933) and the Office of Economic Opportunity (1965).

5. The growing use of extra-governmental organizations, like Rand and the university research centers, to study social and technical problems and formulate policy proposals introduces a variety of less political (if not value-free) criteria for policy-making.

6. Similarly, the growing employment of Presidential Commissions and Committees and White House Conferences changes the nature of the criteria employed in policymaking.

7. An enlarged governmental apparatus has been created to enlist scientific advice on a variety of topics (not just what is coming to be called the management of "science affairs"), as seen in the President's Scientific Advisory Committee and the Office of Science and Technology, and even the office of Science Adviser to the Secretary of State.[58]

Moreover, the dominant scholarly interpretation of policy-making processes has changed in the direction of emphasizing the greater autonomy of political leaders and legislators: with respect to the role of pressure groups,[59] the power elite,[60] and the electorate.[61] If leaders and other legislators are less bound by the domain of pure politics than we had thought, then they are freer to be guided by the promptings of scientists and findings from the domain of knowledge.

Studies of the legislative process reinforce this view. A massive literature documents four relevant points: (a) The rising influence of the bureaucracy is based in large part on bureaucratic command over the sources of knowledge; (b) state and national legislators respond to the growing importance of technical knowledge both with increased standards for their own mastery of subject-matter fields and with demands for greater staff resources to help them meet the challenge; (c) there is an increased reliance on the kind of professional help enlisted by the executive; and (d) the power of the lobby is less likely to be based on electoral sanctions than upon specialized information helpful (however self-interested) in formulating policy change.[62]

The Changed Approach to Problems

Of course there will always be politics; there will always be rationalized self-interest, mobilized by interest groups and articulated in political parties. But if political criteria decline in importance relative to more universalistic scientific criteria and if the professional problem-oriented scientists rather than laymen come to have more to say about social policy, the shift in perspective is likely to occasion some differences in policy itself. What would these be?

In the first place there is the question of the very *consciousness* of a problem. The man in the middle of the problem (sickness, poverty, waste, and especially ignorance) often does not know there is anything problematic about his state. He may accept his condition as embodying the costs of living: If one accepts his lot in life, one accepts lesions, hunger, overwork, and unemployment. For this reason such people are often hard to reach. As Harrington says, "First and foremost, any attempt to abolish poverty in the United States must seek to destroy the pessimism and fatalism that flourish in the other America," the America of the poor.[63] Often it takes years of dedicated agitation to make people aware that they live in the midst of a problem. The curious thing about modern times is the degree to which government itself undertakes to do what, in the past, has so often been the task of the agitator. The New Deal helped to organize labor, and the New Frontier and the Great Society help Negroes to demand more of society and help organize the poor to pursue their own interests. Admittedly there are political benefits in these acts, and they can be attributed only in minor part to the growing insights into the nature of poverty and apathy. Yet consciousness of a problem may come *first* to the authorities, scientific and governmental. People may have to be told not that they are miserable, but that the conditions of their lives are, in some sense, remediable.

Beyond consciousness is something else, the analysis of the nature of the trouble, its causes, and what should be done about it. Here the main point is the environmentalism of the authoritative scientific or governmental view, in contrast to the personalism of the man involved. The problem as it presents itself to those two attentive persons is in each case different. For the unemployed worker, his problem is to find a job; for the economist, the problem is to analyze the causes of unemployment and sometimes to suggest remedial action. To the worker the "cause" of his plight is that he was let go; to the economist, the cause of the worker's plight may be insufficiency of

demand due to higher interest rates and a budgetary surplus. What is cause to
to the worker is to the economist only a symptom, so different are their perspectives.

The view of a problem by scientific or governmental authorities is very often
an analysis of the environment in which it occurs; the causes for the scientist
are the factors which make the "problem" for the individual. In consequence,
the political demands of the affected group and the demands of the professionals interested in the group's condition may lead in different directions.

For people within a system (hospital, market, watershed, communication
network), the boundaries and budgets seem fixed; they bargain for limited
resources and more for them seems necessarily to imply less for someone
else. An authoritative overview can change that perspective by introducing
the possibility not of reallocating limited values but of generating an increase
in values. Thus an economist today considers the problems of equity and
efficiency in distribution in conjunction with the problem of growth. For the
medical sociologist, the problem of the distribution of hospital facilities is
paired with the problem of more and better facilities and better health; he is
unsatisfied simply with a redistribution of untreated illness in a more equitable
fashion. Political scientists have failed to understand this point, because their
attention to "the authoritative allocation of values" has tended to obscure
another facet of government, the generation of values.

Knowledge Is Encroaching on Ideology

If we employ the term "ideology" to mean a comprehensive, passionately
believed, self-activating view of society, usually organized as a social movement, rather than a latent half-conscious belief system,[64] it makes sense to
think of a domain of knowledge distinguishable from a domain of ideology,
despite the extent to which they may overlap. Since knowledge and ideology
serve somewhat as functional equivalents in orienting a person towards the
problems he must face and the policies he must select, the growth of the
domain of knowledge causes it to impinge on the domain of ideology.

Silvan Tomkins has developed a theory of a basic ideological left-right
dimension in virtually all domains of life, turning on the questions, "Is man
the measure, an end in himself, an active, creative, thinking, desiring, loving,
force in nature? Or must man realize himself, attain his full stature only
through struggle toward, participation in, conformity to, a norm, a measure,
an ideal essence basically independent of man?"[65] He believes that arguments
along these lines develop in passionate forms (in philosophy, mathematics,
jurisprudence, etc., as well as in politics) wherever men are least certain of
their ground. These arguments thrive on uncertainty and ignorance. "When
the same ideas (that men have been arguing over in these ideological terms)
are firmly established and incorporated into the fabric of a science or tested

and found wanting, they cease to constitute an ideology in the sense in which we are using the term. At the growing edge of the frontier of all sciences there necessarily is a maximum of uncertainty, and what is lacking in evidence is filled by passion and faith and by hatred and scorn for the disbelievers. Science will never be free of ideology, though yestereday's ideology is today's fact or fiction."[66] The theory, then, is of an "ideo-affective" orientation toward the world directed towards subjects about which there is doubt. If the doubt is clarified by knowledge, this ideological orientation moves on to some other marginal and uncertain area. Increasing knowledge about man, nature, and society can be said to reduce the target area for ideological thinking.

A second way in which the characteristics of a knowledgeable society may be thought to reduce ideological thinking is through the reduction of dogmatic thinking. Following Rokeach, we may conceive of dogmatic thinking as a selection and interpretation of information so as to reinforce a previously established creed, dogma, or political ideology. Information is used not so much to understand the world as it really is, but as a means of defending against conflict and uncertainty.[67] The knowledgeable society is marked by a relatively greater stress on the use of information veridically, relying on its truth value and not on any adventitious defense, popularity, or reinforcement value. This should be associated with a decline in dogmatic thinking. The decline of dogmatism implies the decline of ideology, in the narrower sense of the term used here.

In the third place, consider the way in which knowledge may limit Mannheim's thesis that political thinking is inevitably biased. He says "all knowledge which is either political or which involves a world view is inevitably partisan"; and later "at the point where what is properly political begins, the evaluative element cannot easily be separated out"; and still later, "the peculiar nature of political knowledge, as contrasted to the 'exact' sciences, arises out of the inseparability, in this realm, of knowledge from interest and motivation."[68] Mannheim has in view only the thinking of those who are themselves engaged in political strife; he does not envisage the possibility of such studies as *The Legislative System* and *The American Voter*,[69] which, although evaluative in many ways, nevertheless narrow the range of partisan, irrational, and evaluative thought. Granting that interested parties form their ideas about politics into ideological constructs, it seems likely that knowledge may constrict the scope of their ideology.

This narrowing effect was, in fact, experienced by the participants at the conference of the Congress for Cultural Freedom in Milan in 1955 out of which the theme of "the end of ideology" developed. Those scholars and scientists came expecting, indeed, inviting, a great confrontation of world views. Under the pressure of economic and social knowledge, a growing body of research, and the codified experience of society, ideological argument tended to give way to technical argument, apparently to the disappointment of some.[70] The debate remained evaluative and partisan, but the domain of ideology was shrunken by the dominance of knowledge.

Knowledge as Disequilibrium

What happens when the scientific apparatus of the knowledgeable society produces some important findings: existential, causal, remedial, or whatever? Here are some examples from the social sciences:

> Among the nations of the world, the United States ranked 16th in rate of infant mortality in 1961.[71]
>
> To raise every individual and family in the nation now below a subsistence income to the subsistence level would cost about $10 billion a year. This is less than 2 per cent of the gross national product. It is less than 10 per cent of tax revenues. It is about one-fifth of the cost of national defense.[72]
>
> The reinforcing experience for convicted criminals while in jail results in high rates of recidivism: about three-fourths of those entering jail have been there before. And the younger the person at the time of first offense, the higher the rate of recidivism and the sooner it occurs.[73]
>
> Today, more American school children die of cancer than from any other disease. So serious has this situation become that Boston has established the first hospital in the United States devoted exclusively to the treatment of children with cancer. . . . One of the earliest pesticides associated with cancer is arsenic. . . . In the United States the arsenic-drenched soils of tobacco plantations, of many orchards in the Northwest, and of blueberry lands in the East easily lead to pollution of water supplies.[74]
>
> The more an individual engages in personal interaction with persons of different race, religious, or national background, the lower is his general level of prejudice. This result holds not only for majority group prejudices but also for minority prejudices against the majority group and other minorities. It is true of youths as well as their elders. It has been confirmed in 14 different samples, involving about 6000 persons.[75]

Such knowledge—discovered, organized, and communicated by professional men—creates a pressure for policy change with a force all its own. Knowledge (and what is regarded as knowledge) is pressure even without pressure groups, and without reference to an articulated forensic ideology. If the reader of these statements experiences some kind of policy-oriented speculation, so, I believe, do policy-making officials. The source of the tension is not difficult to discover. In skeleton form, the sequence may be as follows:

1. A state of affairs is presented, conveying new or more precise information than that previously known (infants and children are dying at a "high" rate; poverty could be eliminated).

2. A value is engaged (early death is bad; poverty is worse than prosperity).

3. In some cases the information applies to particular groups whose needs and values are especially significant to an observer (Northwest apple growers, Southern Negroes and whites, delinquent youth).

4. Remedial action may be suggested (subsidies to the poor, policing of pesticides, enforced integration).

5. Social, economic, and political costs are implied (taxation for subsidies to the poor, expensive re-education for prisoners, the opposition of tobacco growers).

7. Certain "pre-political ideological" positions on man and society are enlisted (Can man control his own fate? Is poverty "necessary"? Is human nature a constant?).

8. Certain ideological postures toward the business of government are enlisted (Is every increment of government a bad policy in itself? Is government too corrupt an instrument to employ in changing conditions? Are tax dollars better spent by private organizations and individuals?).

Let us suppose, as seems likely, that knowledge like that presented above sets up a kind of "disequilibrium" in a person's mind. The restoration of equilibrium, then, is the problem-solving process, perhaps by questioning the data or the source, perhaps by changing one's own priorities of action, perhaps by selective inattention, perhaps by delegation (real or symbolic), perhaps by purely expressive as opposed to instrumental behavior, perhaps by rationalization, perhaps by scapegoating, perhaps by advocating simplistic solutions, and so forth.[76] But the point is that knowledge, with little more, often sets up a disequilibrium or pressure which requires compensating thought or action.

Summary

In this article I have tried, first, to develop the idea of a knowledgeable society, with special attention to questions of growth and epistemology. Then, assuming that the concept applies to modern American society, I have suggested that the professionals and their associations have a role in the preformulation of policy, not all good, but generally responsive to the needs of society. Further, in comparing two "pure" domains, that of politics and that of knowledge, I have suggested that the criteria and scope of politics are shrinking while those of knowledge are growing. This has created a difference in perspectives of policy-makers: a different kind of consciousness, an environmentalist approach, and a concept of the generation of values. Like politics, ideology is declining as a *necessary* ingredient in change, partly because, given present values, knowledge sets up a powerful kind of attitudinal disequilibrium all its own.

Notes

1. See Auguste Comte, *A General View of Positivism*, trans. by J. H. Bridges (Stanford: Academic Reprints, 1958), and comments in Howard Becker and Harry Elmer Barnes, *Social Thought from Lore to Science* (New York: Dover, 1961), 3rd ed., Vol. 2, pp. 573–574; Emile Durkheim and Marcel Mauss, *Primitive Classification*, trans. by Rodney Needham (Chicago: University of Chicago Press, 1963); Bronislaw Malinowki, *Magic, Science and Religion* (Garden City, N.Y.: Doubleday Anchor, 1955); A. L. Kroeber, *Configurations of Culture Growth* (Berkeley: University of California Press, 1944).

2. See Marx's discussion of consciousness and of ideas as superstructures in his "Economic and Philosophical Manuscripts" and "German Ideology," in *Marx's Concept of Man*, Erich Fromm (ed.) (New York: Ungar, 1961); Karl Mannheim, *Ideology and Utopia*, trans. by Louis Wirth and Edward Shils (London: Routledge & Kegan Paul, 1949); Robert K. Merton, *Social Theory and Social Structure* (New York: Free Press of Glencoe, 1957), rev. ed., Parts 3 and 4.

3. See, especially, "Social Evolution Reconsidered" (1950), in *William F. Ogburn On Culture and Social Change*, Otis D. Duncan (ed.) (Chicago: University of Chicago Press, 1964).

4. Derek J. de Sola Price, *Science Since Babylon* (New Haven: Yale University Press, 1961); Herbert Butterfield, *The Origins of Modern Science* (New York: Macmillan, 1961), rev. ed.

5. Alfred N. Whitehead, *Science and the Modern World* (Cambridge: Cambridge University Press, 1933); Carl G. Hempel, *Fundamentals of Concept Formation* (Chicago: University of Chicago Press, 1952), Vol. 2, No. 7 of the *International Encyclopedia of Unified Science*; Hans Reichenbach, *The Rise of Scientific Philosophy* (Berkeley: University of California Press, 1953).

6. For a general overview, see D. E. Berlyne, *Structure and Direction in Thinking* (New York: Wiley, 1965); a developmental (individual and social) view is presented in O. J. Harvey, D. E. Hunt, and H. M. Schroder, *Conceptual Systems and Personality Organization* (New York: Wiley, 1961); I have found Milton Rokeach's especially helpful. *The Open and Closed Mind* (New York: Basic Books, 1960).

7. Fritz Machlup, *The Production and Distribution of Knowledge in the United States* (Princeton: Princeton University Press, 1962).

8. Bernard Barber, *Science and the Social Order* (Glencoe, Ill.: Free Press, 1952); Florian Znaniecki, *The Social Role of the Man of Knowledge* (New York: Columbia University Press, 1940); Everett C. Hughes, *Men and their Work* (Glencoe, Ill.: Free Press, 1958); T. H. Marshall, *Class Citizenship and Social Development*, especially Ch. VI (Garden City, N.Y.: Doubleday, 1964); H. L. Wilensky, "The Professionalization of Everyone?" *American Journal of Sociology*, 70 (1964), pp. 137–158.

9. Robert Gilpin and Christopher Wright (eds.), *Scientists and National Policy Making* (New York: Columbia University Press, 1964); Don K. Price, *Government and Science* (New York: New York University Press, 1954).

10. Daniel Bell, "The End of Ideology in the West" in *The End of Ideology* (Glencoe, Ill.: Free Press, 1960); Edward Shils, "The End of Ideology?" *Encounter*, 5 (November, 1955), pp. 52–58; S. M. Lipset, "The End of Ideology?" in *Political Man* (Garden City, N.Y.: Doubleday, 1960).

11. Machlup, *op. cit.*, p. 13.

12. Ithiel Pool holds that acceptance of statements on grounds other than the status of the source implies "an unusually high degree of mutual trust in interpersonal relations." See "The Mass Media and Politics in the Modernization Process," in Lucien Pye (ed.), *Communications and Political Development* (Princeton: Princeton University Press, 1963), p. 242.

13. Malinowski, *op. cit.*, p. 26.

14. *Ibid.*, pp. 26–36.

15. William Graham Sumner, *Folkways* (Boston: Ginn & Co., 1940), pp. 1–74.

16. See note 1 above. For a cyclical theory of cultural change, see P. A. Sorokin, *Social and Cultural Dynamics* (New York: American Book, 1937, 1941), Vols. I–IV.

17. Kroeber, *op. cit.*, pp. 762–777.

18. *Ibid.*, p. 204.

19. Ogburn, *op. cit.*, pp. 17–32.

20. Price, *op. cit.*, pp. 107–108.

21. *Ibid.*, p. 113.

22. Kroeber, *op. cit.*, p. 842.

23. Machlup, *op. cit.*, p. 396.

24. *Ibid.*, p. 202.

25. See Derek Price's discussion of "Renaissance Roots of Yankee Ingenuity" in his *Science Since Babylon, op. cit.*, pp. 45–67.

26. Eugene Ayres, "Social Attitudes Toward Invention," *American Scientist*, 43 (1955), pp. 533–535; quoted in Machlup, *op. cit.*, p. 202.

27. U.S. Bureau of the Census, *Historical Statistics of the United States, Colonial Times to 1957* and *Continuation to 1962 and Revisions* (Washington, D.C.: U.S. Government Printing Office, 1960 and 1965), Series W 79, 80.

28. U.S. Bureau of the Census, *Statistical Abstract for the United States: 1965* (Washington, D.C.: 1965), p. 545.

29. *Ibid.*, p. 551.

30. *Ibid.*, p. 527.

31. See John J. Beer and W. David Lewis, "Aspects of the Professionalization of Science," *Daedalus*, 92 (1963), No. 4, pp. 764–784.

32. "The Reformation, for all its importance, may be considered as a domestic affair of the European races. . . . Modern science was born in Europe, but its home is the whole world." A. N. Whitehead, *Science and the Modern World*, p. 304.

33. See Harold Webster, Mervin B. Friedman, and Paul Heist, "Personality Changes in College Students," in Nevitt Sanford (ed.), *The American College* (New York: Wiley, 1962), pp. 811–846.

34. See the discussion of "concept attainment" in Jerome S. Bruner, Jacqueline J. Goodnow, and George A. Austin, *A Study of Thinking* (New York: Wiley, 1956).

35. *Primitive Classification*, pp. 82–84.

36. See Rodney Needham's excellent introduction to Durkheim and Mauss, *ibid.*, pp. vii-xlviii.

37. Stephen Toulmin, *Foresight and Understanding* (New York: Harper Torchbook, 1961), pp. 52, 54.

38. This point and several following are derived from Harvey, Hunt, and Schroder's explication and development of Goldstein and Scheerer's concept of a concrete-abstractness dimension of thought, originating from studies of children and brain-damaged patients. See Harvey et al., *Conceptual Systems*, pp. 24–49.

39. *The Passing of Traditional Society* (New York: Free Press of Glencoe, 1958), pp. 47–52.

40. Harvey et al., *Conceptual Systems*, p. 29.

41. See the discussion of "conceptualizing in political discourse," in my *Political Ideology* (New York: Free Press, 1962), pp. 346–363.

42. H. Werner, *Comparative Psychology of Mental Development* (New York: International Universities Press, 1957), rev. ed., quoted in Harvey et al., *Conceptual Systems*, p. 33.

43. Harvey et al., *ibid.*, pp. 36–46.

44. T. W. Adorno, Else Frenkel-Brunswik, Daniel J. Levinson, and R. Nevitt Sanform, *The Authoritarian Personality* (New York: Harper, 1950); Rokeach, see note 6.

45. "The Mass Media and Politics," p. 242.

46. *Ibid.*, pp. 242–244.

47. Rokeach, *The Open and Closed Mind*, p. 57.

48. "Intolerance of Ambiguity as an Emotional and Perceptual Variable," *Journal of Personality*, 18 (1949), pp. 108–143.

49. Rokeach, *The Open and Closed Mind*, pp. 67–97.

50. I think the most useful short account of the general phenomenon of cognitive dissonance and cognitive balancing is in Milton Rosenberg and others, *Attitude Organization and Change* (New Haven: Yale University Press, 1960), pp. 112–163.

51. *A General View of Positivism, passim.*

52. *Social Theory and Social Structure*, pp. 574–575 (Merton's emphasis).

53. S. M. Lipset, *Political Man*, p. 314.

54. *Science and the Modern World*, p. 3.

55. *The Rise of Scientific Philosophy*, p. 252.

56. *The Opium of the Intellectuals*, trans. by T. Kilmartin (New York: Norton, 1957).

57. Karl Deutsch has an interesting discussion of these analogies in his *The Nerves of Government* (New York: Free Press, 1963), pp. 24–38; The anatomical metaphor in medieval political thought is most explicit in Otto Gierke, *Political Theories of the Middle Ages*, trans. by F. W. Maitland (Boston: Beacon, 1958).

58. Much of this is reported and commented upon in Gilpin and Wright, *Scientists and National Policy Making*. Here (on p. 109) one will find Wallace Sayre making the point that "politics is inescapable." Nothing in this section should be read as implying anything contrary to this maxim.

59. E. E. Schattschneider, *Politics, Pressures and the Tariff* (New York: Prentice-Hall, 1935); Peter H. Odegard, *Pressure Politics* (New York: Columbia University Press, 1928); Raymond A. Bauer, Ithiel de S. Pool, and L. A. Dexter, *American Business and Public Policy* (New York: Atherton, 1963).

60. Floyd Hunter, *Community Power Structure* (Chapel Hill: University of North Carolina Press, 1953); Robert A. Dahl, *Who Governs?* (New Haven: Yale University Press, 1961).

61. "Toward a More Responsible Two-Party System," Supplement to *American Political Science Review*, XLIV (1950), No. 3; and see, for example, Warren E. Miller and Donald E. Stokes, "Constituency Influence in Congress," *American Political Science Review*, LVII (1963), pp. 45–56.

62. See, for example, John Wahlke, Heinz Eulau and others, *The Legislative System* (New York: Wiley, 1962); James D. Barber, *The Lawmaker* (New Haven: Yale University Press, 1965); Bauer, Pool, and Dexter, *American Business and Public Policy*; Robert L. Peabody and Nelson W. Polsby (eds.), *New Perspectives on the House of Representatives* (Chicago: Rand McNally, 1963); Donald R. Matthews, *U.S. Senators and Their World* (New York: Random House Vintage, 1960).

63. Michael Harrington, *The Other America* (New York: Macmillan, 1963), p. 163.

64. See my *Political Ideology*, pp. 13–16; also note 10. Of course there are many definitions of ideology referring to a wider range of "mental products."

65. "Left and Right: A Basic Dimension of Ideology and Personality," in Robert W. White (ed.), *The Study of Lives* (New York: Atherton, 1963), pp. 391–392.

66. *Ibid.*, p. 389.

67. See note 49 above.

68. "The Prospects of Scientific Politics," in *Ideology and Utopia*, pp. 132, 168, 170.

69. Angus Campbell, Philip E. Converse, Warren E. Miller, and Donald E. Stokes, *The American Voter* (New York: Wiley, 1960).

70. See note 10 above.

71. *United Nations Statistical Yearbook*, *1962* (New York: United Nations, 1963), p. 50.

72. James N. Morgan et al., *Income and Welfare in the United States* (New York: McGraw-Hill, 1962), pp. 3–4.

73. Bernard Berelson and Gary Steiner, *Human Behavior* (New York: Harcourt, Brace, 1964), p. 630.

74. Rachel Carson, *Silent Spring* (Boston: Houghton Mifflin, 1962), pp. 221–223.

75. Robin M. Williams, quoted in Berelson and Steiner, *op. cit.*, p. 519.

76. Dan Berlyne's *Structure and Direction in Thinking* illuminates the processes of "problematicity" and problem-solving, especially pp. 236–293 (see note 6).

PART V

THE GOOD CITIZEN

Introductory Note

Prevalent concepts of citizenship embrace two rather different phases of human activity and thought. On the one hand, they have to do with active participation in the political and social life of the community, and on the other hand they deal with a person's response to the constraints placed upon him by society, his obedience to the laws and norms of society. Because these two phases of social life are interrelated, though often treated in isolation from each other, I have included two papers on the active participant citizen and two papers on the constrained citizen in this section. The problems discussed in these papers offer a brief opportunity for examining these two aspects of citizenship in the contest of three social themes that characterize modern society: the decline of community, role strain, and rapid social change.

The decline of community. The small society with its intimacy, its ascribed status, its static if diffused roles, its warmth has given away to the great society demanding a different kind of citizenship and creating for the individual a set of man-state relationships of a new order. Under these circumstances several things happen. The first is that the duty to participate is based more upon abstract and symbolic values than upon the old personal loyalties and the network of social ties. Consequently, men must think about citizen duty and define it for themselves, whereas previously the concept and its duties were given. In a figurative sense "citizenship" has to be earned and thus poses for the individuals concerned questions about the worth of these duties, the costs to themselves of performing these duties, the moral sanctions attaching to the duties, and the counter-claims which dutiful performance entitles them to. As these concepts and duties are nowhere easily or readily defined for them, the effort on the part of each citizen is painful, and the

273

resolution of the conflicts involved, like all conflict resolution in ambiguous situations, reflects the personal problems of each individual engaged in the task. Chapter 14 gives some indication of how this resolution is achieved, while Chapter 15 elaborates on the calculations employed in defining for oneself the proper investment of self in social participation. They should be read as contrasting approaches—the first stressing the part played by personality differences and the second dealing with a model of rational calculation.

Furthermore, the decline of community with all of its "givens" requires each person to think about the nature of his obligation to obey the laws as well as his duty to participate. In the small society this was not a matter for much thought; in the social contract theories the decision to obey is made once, when one enters society. But in the large, modern society nothing is taken for granted, and the calculation of risk and loss in disobeying the laws versus the probability of gain from such illegality is at least marginally encouraged by the ethos of the times. If society is contractual, then each "contract" with the state must be examined. Of course the ordinary man makes these calculations only in minor ways, but today's average businessman, both because of his familiarity with the economic calculus and because of the more self-evident gains in illegality, may have occasion to rethink his obligations to society on many occasions.

Two other points bearing on the decline of community emerge from the evidence of the studies that follow. One of them has to do with the learned social detachment in the great society, a detachment that applies to smaller social groups as well as to the society as a whole. On the one hand this has the effect, or so we shall argue, of loosening the bonds of patriotism, as attachment to family, union, church, and other groups implies a mode of relating to groups that is transferred to man-nation relationships. It makes the claims of citizenly duties less self-evident. On the other hand the commands of an overriding patriotism could make citizenly participation and obedience to law a matter of course.

The other point has to do with the concept of "differential association," that is, the differences in intensity and frequency of association within one social group as contrasted to another. In the *gemeinschaft* community, of course, such differential association took place, but the loyalty to the totality was not thereby diluted; the architecture of group loyalties was cumulative, not selective or competitive. Again the impact of this change in the relationship of subgroup loyalties to the individual's loyalty to the whole has two consequences. On the one hand, he must select from among several competing models of citizenly norms. This forced choice then creates for him one source of the strains we will examine. On the other hand, he may be guided into defiance of the laws by his selective association with those who hold the laws to be illegitimate, or contrary to the norms that he believes to be moral. We may be witnessing something of this kind of differential association in the ghettos of the great society.

Role strain. One could read the problems of role strain into the discussion of the decline of community; it follows from the specificity of roles in the great society and from the conflicting references that individuals employ for role guidance. In previous chapters I have referred to the ways ideologies are devised to relieve role strain by rationalizing hard choices among competing ethical norms and giving moral standing to the role occupant: businessman, or foreman, or whoever he may be. Here let us discuss some features of the role strains that emerge when men must *choose* their citizen roles, both as active participants in the polity and as the subjects of rules and regulations.

Ordinary citizens define the concept of "good citizen" in many different ways, a fact that suggests the plurality of norms competing for ascendance in that role. They see him (the good citizen) as a moral man, honest, kind, and tolerant of others; as a good family man; as a good member of the community in the sense that is sociable and charitable; and as a good member of the polity, that is, informed, voting, paying taxes, and obeying the laws. Each person, as we shall see in Chapter 14, defines a different mix of these qualities as his ideal. But, of course, no one can achieve such an ideal, and the discrepancy between how he perceives himself and how he defines the role produces some strain. The consequence, inevitably, is that he searches for devices that will help reduce the strain: restricting the definition of citizen, placing more reliance on good thoughts than on time-consuming action, purging his guilt through symbolic acts of voting or by working for the Little League. In the process, of course, he redefines the citizen role and hence his concepts of democracy so as to bring them into line with his own self-image.

Role strain in general brings out the personal dispositions of the individual and, as explained in Chapter 14, the conflicts within the person find expression in the development of both shared and idiosyncratic belief systems.

Social change. Social change takes place in the small society and in the great society; the difference lies in the rapidity of change in the great society and the consequently greater difficulty of adjustment. This problem of adjustment to rapid social change, with its concomitant shifting agenda for participation, shifting policies requiring support, and shifting nature of laws demanding obedience, is reflected in the two articles in this section. Take, for example, the problems of "scanning" the news in conformity to the norm of being an "informed" citizen. This is preliminary to social interpretation, as explained in Chapter 15, but intelligent scanning implies sufficient familiarity with a problem to see what is important or relevant to one's own self-interest, however defined. The consequence of a rapidly shifting set of policy issues is that men may retreat from the effort at comprehension, settling for catchwords and slogans that provide only the illusion of understanding. What I have in mind is the shift from a focus on wages and hours legislation in the thirties, to urban redevelopment legislation in the late forties and fifties, to medicare and health legislation in the late fifties and early sixties, to civil rights legislation, to environmental and pollution poblems, to consumer protection in current policy discussions. The agenda moves more rapidly than comprehension or capacity to assimilate and understand, and the strain on the citizen role is substantial. For businessmen, who are intimately involved in meeting the new regulatory requirements, the attention is greater than for others, but the moral commitment and understanding lags at a perceptible distance behind the law.

In the chapters that follow, this problem of coping with the rapidity of social change is reflected in several ways. In Chapter 15 it enters into several terms of the formula for appraising the costs of active participation, especially (a) "cost of following and understanding the news," (b) "cost of modifying one's own situation according to an estimate of the impact of an event on the self," and (c) "cost of any indicated effort to alter the course of history." These costs are multiplied by the uncertainty consequent to rapid social change. Further, the problems for businessmen of keeping informed on the changing regulations, of altering established calculuses of gain and loss because of non-market considerations, of adjusting to the new ideologies of "socialism" or "welfare-statism," and of bringing discrepancies in culture or circumstance of a market or business to the attention of the regulators are all most obviously exaggerated by the rapidity of social change after World War II. That men do learn is shown by the adjustment to regulation in the United States as well as England and by the fact that, once convicted of an offense, there is very little recidivism in this world of "white-collar crime."

The difficulty of rapid social change, as with role strain and the decline of community, tends to bring out the strains and conflicts within a personality. These personalistic responses, apparent in the definitions of citizenship and the development of belief systems to cope with the strains, reveal from another facet the intimate and complex relationships of person and polity.

Chapter 14
The Tense Citizen
and the Casual Patriot:
Role Confusion
in American Politics

I. The Tension of Citizenship

> As a city is a collective body, and, like other wholes, composed of many parts, it is evident our first inquiry must be, what a citizen is: for a city is a certain number of citizens.... For he who has a right to share in the judicial and executive part of government in any city, him we call a citizen of that place; and a city, in one word, is a collective body of such persons sufficient in themselves to all the purposes of life.
>
> Aristotle's *Politics*
> (Everyman) pp. 67, 68.

In a recent book by Mark Roelofs entitled *The Tension of Citizenship*, the concept of citizenship is conceived to include three attitudes and ways of behaving: pride and a participation in public events; defiance toward authority and insistence upon the right to a private life; and loyalty and willingness to serve and sacrifice for the common good. These elements, in turn, through some little historical juggling, are related respectively to the Greek tradition of pride and participation; to the Hebraic pattern of community values, including loyalty and sacrifice; and to what is called the Roman-Christian heritage of "defiance and privacy."[1] C. E. Merriam, in a review of interlocking studies on citizenship training in a variety of countries, finds that in

Reprinted from *The Journal of Politics*, 27 (1965), pp. 735–760.

277

Notes to this chapter will be found on pages 297–298

the great diversity of qualities associated with the term "citizenship," the following are important features in almost every country:

Patriotism and loyalty
Obedience to the laws of society
Respect for officials and government
Recognition of the obligations of political life
Some minimum degree of self-control
Response to community needs in times of stress
Ordinary honesty in social relations
Knowledge of and agreement with the ideology forming the rationale for the prevailing form of government and the maintenance of limits on the criticism of this rationale
And, often, special beliefs in the qualities of one's own people compared to others.[2]

Almond and Verba, carrying on the inquiry into the qualities of the good citizen, stress his obligations to perform his economic and family duties along with his political ones. "It is only when the individual thinks of his family's advantage as the only goal to pursue, or conceives of his role in the political system in familistic terms, that he is is . . . not also a good citizen."[3] But beyond this, the whole theme of the book is that certain qualities of citizenship are necessary features of a "civic culture," that is, a political culture conducive to stable and responsive democracy. Among these qualities are trust in others, pride in an allegiance to the institutions of the country, a sense of being able to shape political events, and an activist "out-going" orientation.

THE DEFINITION OF THE CONCEPT IN EASTPORT

So far as I know, there has been little effort to discover how the ordinary citizen views this concept of a role which he himself occupies with greater or less success. In a set of extended interviews (averaging twelve hours each) with fifteen working and lower middle class men in Eastport, an Eastern industrial city, an effort was made to explore these men's views on this matter, and on the related concept of "patriot," reported in Part II of this article. The interpretation of other facets of these interviews has been developed in my *Political Ideology: Why the American Common Man Believes What He Does*,[4] but recent concern with "education for citizenship" and with the problem of nationalism, both here and abroad, suggests the usefulness of this further exploration. The composition of the sample, randomly selected from residents in a housing development, is given in Note 5. The interviews were held in 1957–58; they were relaxed, conversational, loosely structured; they were taped with the men's permission, transcribed, and analyzed, as time permitted, over the succeeding years.

When the men of Eastport turn to the question of citizenship, something of the scholarly views reported above appears—but not very much. They do not pay much attention to the concepts of loyalty and patriotism in their associative thinking on citizenship. These concepts belong to a different category of things, a category we shall turn to in a later discussion. Only one referred to military duty as in any way connected with citizenship; certainly they did not think of eligibility for office or jury duty as important. Further, referring to the last of Merriam's items associated with civic training and citizenship in other countries (and perhaps in our own), there was only the slightest trace of jingo sentiments, no feeling of manifest destiny, no patronizing of other races and nations—indeed, almost no sense in which the idea of citizenship seemed to have any bearing on national identity.

Yet, other features were clearly recognizable: the elements of local pride and participation; the notion of obedience to the laws; and the concepts of duty to others, self-control, and morality—and sometimes, orthodoxy. These factors were apparent in the manner in which the Eastport men discussed their ideas of the properties of citizenship, or, more precisely, their concepts of the good citizen. The idea of picturing the good citizen produced ready responses. It was not, like some questions, followed by a series of "what do you mean?" remarks; in this case only one person had trouble deciding what was being looked for. The concepts were not cliches; they were such that they might guide behavior.

The most notable feature of these views, however, was the great variation in types of response. Woodside, a railroad guard, speaks of a good citizen as "a good provider," a good neighbor, a person who takes an interest in the community, one who voices his opinions. Rapuano, a packing house checker, conceives of a good citizen as a person interested in "who's going to run things in the city," a voter, a person who "stays out of trouble," and a taxpayer; and he mentions his own military service as evidence of his own good citizenship. For Farrel, our "overeducated" apprentice social worker, it is "goodwill, in the sense of (being) willing to live and let live, keep informed and acting on his best information." It is this very diversity of images and concepts which leads us to the first of those social and personal problems which we term "the tension of citizenship."

THE TENSIONS OF A DEMANDING BUT AMBIGUOUS ROLE

Questions on role behavior, evoking a wide variety of responses and even conflicting frames of reference, indicate a kind of social "role diffusion," a social version of identity diffusion. This is, of course, very different from the situations where there are *partisan* opinions on role interpretation, organized on the basis of some social groupings with different interests or positions.[6]

The ambiguity of the concept "good citizen" is revealed even when the answers have been classified, thereby reducing considerably the idiosyncratic nature of each man's concepts. Consider, if you will, the following points of reference emerging from the discussion:

> The idea of moral man: living a good life and being unselfish, pious, honest, kind, altruistic, charitable, obedient to duty, cheerful, tolerant, self-improving.
>
> The idea of a good family man: being a good provider, procreating and rearing children, raising family standards of living, looking out for family welfare.
>
> The idea of a good community member: helping the unfortunate in the neighborhood, being sociable, avoiding appearance of snobbishness, going to church, positively supporting improvements, giving blood, giving funds to charity.
>
> The idea of a good member of a political community: keeping informed, caring about public affairs, voting and in other ways *doing* something about public affairs, paying taxes, having opinions, expressing opinions (preferably orthodox ones), being concerned, being favorable and constructive in making remarks, obeying laws and hence not burdening the city with police and court costs, paying taxes, participating in military service, and being true to the country.

Apparently the ideas of production and of work (except as it relates to being a good provider) and of economic function are not assimilated into the idea of citizen in the minds of our men.

The mere listing of the various ideas embodied in the image fails to give a true picture of the variety, not only because it clusters the common notions together under somewhat procrustean categories, but also because it fails to reveal the general lack of syndromes, or groups of attitudes which tend to go together. Such a situation has a meaning which only recently has been explored and about which there is still relatively little literature. The meaning is summarized in the term "role-ambiguity," which refers to situations in which a person feels there is some expected way of behaving but doesn't know what it is. As anyone can imagine, and as research tells us, this kind of a situation creates anxiety, possibly of a critical nature if the role is important; but in our cases it produces rather a kind of diffuse and hardly conscious feeling of worry over unfulfilled duties.

It must be evident, however, that if the vagueness of the contours of this citizen role were sharpened, there might be revealed not ambiguity, but out-and-out conflict. It is this conflict which, as suggested above, Roelofs considers pivotal in the concept of citizenship—a conflict between adequate private life and public duty; a conflict between loyalty and the right to define, at least to some degree, the conditions of service; and, finally, a conflict between pride and identification on the one hand, and the right to criticize and reserve judgment on one's own terms on the other. In point of fact, only the first of these emerges clearly in our interview material—the conflict between private life and public duty; but, in some measure, perhaps, the problem of criticism is adumbrated. Both role conflict and role ambiguity, however, come to much the same thing in the minds of the men of Eastport; and what they come to, for about a third (and certainly not more than half) of the men, is a sense of malaise and guilt. Thus, McNamara, a quiet gentle bookkeeper who believes that most people are pretty close to his definition of the ideal citizen, says, "I probably fall a little short of it. . . . It's a matter of being a little too lazy about reading and following the questions of the day." Ferrera, a salesman, interested in himself and in his moods over time, reveals a certain strength and a certain pathos when, after criticizing others for their civic failures, he describes his weaknesses:

> I was probably speaking about myself—and I have endeavored. I was more or less a (pause) sort of an introvert at least in the past two or three years. I have been trying to get over that introvert-extrovert line. I just mind my own business, and just let the other guy take care of everything, and try to participate as meagerly as possible—as I've been able to in these functions. And I've seen a lot of other people who probably had less than I had—probably had more problems—yet participate in the manner I have been describing.

Ruggiero, a building custodian, too, is not at all satisfied with himself. He sees the demands of citizenship as omniverous. What would an ideal citizen be like to him? "Well, my definition for that would be a person that would take part in his community; uh, just not in this community, of course, in his schooling, and all—everything, *I mean everything in general.*" It is exhausting just to think of it this way. But, continues Ruggiero, people fall down in their duties because, "like myself, we're all interested in money." No wonder, then, he thinks that he does not even come close to being an ideal citizen: "I consider myself one of the ones that are lax in helping my community—for that reason." He is wrong—he is a most active and rather generous man—but he is experiencing this tension of citizenship: a strongly felt demand for an undefined degree of greater participation.

Asked about his own citizenship, Dempsey, a drill operator, says he is not a very good citizen because "I have my differences of opinion towards my fellow men." Sullivan, a truck driver, says he is not a very good citizen because "I'd just as soon let the other guys do it (work with civic groups) now." Sokolsky, a factory operative, says, "I don't know if I'm doing any good to help my country out, but I tried." All but about three of the men are doubtful about their own citizen roles—*but for different reasons.*

The very vagueness of the citizen concept not only encourages doubts about one's performance but also, like any vaguely structured set of demands, encourages a projective style of thought wherein each person reflects some salient feature of his own life problems. Although there is always the possibility that *post hoc* analysis of this sort may lead an observer to "discover" the appropriate life problem in each case, certainly some of the coincidences here are not contrived in this manner:

Ferrera (most obviously) worries about his moodiness, his failure to meet people with the ease and friendliness he feels he should (even though he has many friends), experiences guilt about his failure to participate in civic functions. He is struggling with problems of interpersonal relations.

McNamara, a somewhat passive bookkeeper, whose occupation constantly focuses upon the problem of accuracy and error, feels guilty about not being sufficiently informed on "the questions of the day." He is struggling with cognitive and orientation problems.

Ruggiero, the one member of the sample whose energy and drive is concentrated on making money to the extent that, without finishing high school but with the help of two almost full-time jobs, he has become the highest earner in the sample, feels guilty about spending so much time in selfish pursuits and not doing other unspecified citizenly things. He is struggling with problems of motivation: self- vs. others-motivation.

Dempsey, who lives a retiring life except for his church activity, responded to the first question on politics with the statement, "That I wouldn't like to discuss because I don't care to discuss politics too much. I never argued on that. . . ." But he feels that he has partially failed as a citizen because he holds views which conflict with those of his neighbors. He is struggling with problems of interpersonal conflict and passivity.

Sokolsky, one of two Jews in the sample, is also the only one who mentions national loyalty, "being true to your country," as a feature of citizenship. He feels doubt, at least, about whether he has been "doing any good to help my country." In a period closely following the espionage trials of the Rosenbergs and the establishment of Israel as an independent state, his problem is to prove that he is a good patriotic American (which, from observation, is quite clear).

Sullivan, still burning over frustrations arising from his effort to have the school parking lot converted to an ice-skating rink in the winter, has withdrawn from these civic activities in an angry and bitter mood. He expresses, with more anger than guilt, his current failures as a citizen in terms of "letting the other guy do it *now.*" He is struggling with problems of frustrated leadership (authority), a rejection of his initiative, and especially a wounded vanity.

The essential point here is that the vague and unstructured area of duty implied in the concept of citizenship invites a variety of guilty feelings, each reflecting some more basic problem faced in other areas of life by the "guilty party."

RELIEF OF TENSION

There are a number of ways of resolving this tension over citizenship demands, or, if not resolving, at least repressing it; or, if not even that, of relieving the guilt which may be associated with it in greater or lesser degree. I hardly know whether the devices which the men of Eastport employ are successful in these respects; but they seem to be, because the intensity of feeling of the malaise or guilt in this area of life is, for a number of people, only moderate. This analysis contains much that is in common with other analyses of the methods by which people cope with mental conflict, cross-pressures, or difficult choices.

RESTRICTING THE DEFINITION OF CITIZENSHIP

As a standard by which to study the concept of "restriction," we will first cite the very opposite concept—"engulfment." Ruggiero, reflecting this engulfment style of life, spoke of the need to participate in "everything in general," and he suffers accordingly. Kuchinsky, a roofer, on the other hand, with a narrower frame of reference, sees a good citizen, to the extent that he sees him at all, as simply a person who is "for" the people and "a fellow that would help his neighbors, quite a bit." In one of the longest and certainly least relevant discussions of citizenship, Kuchinsky is finally brought to the point of estimating his own citizenly qualities. He has made it easy for himself with his definition: "I would say this for myself—I'm not going to brag—I mean I would help. . . . I treat everybody right if it's possible"—but only, as he says, "if they're not trying to take advantage" of him. With a restricted view of what society demands of you, it is certainly easier to see yourself as a good citizen.

"OTHERS ARE NO BETTER THAN I AM"

It is, of course, easier to admit some personal deficiency if one conceives this fault to be widespread. About half of the Eastport men saw it this way. So Johnson, a mechanic, says, "The majority of them (people) doesn't seem to be too much interested in it. I mean they'll ride along." How close to an ideal do most people come? Sullivan says "Not too close at all. There's too much letting the other guy do everything." And to the same question Dempsey says, "I, I wouldn't say so. I think that a lot of them have a long way to get up to that," and for Dempsey "that" means voting and "upholding the government." Ferrera, more specific, says that about nine tenths of the people fail to live up to the ideals of citizenship. And Ruggiero says that "there's very few" people who could be described as "good citizens." Of course, the meaning of these remarks varies with the standards set for citizenship, with whether or not the role was idealized. But however the standards were set, whether they thought in ideal or in more practical terms, the tone of response was one of modest disillusionment, understanding, forgiveness—and, in the same breath, self-forgiveness. Only Ferrera, struggling with his problems of introversion, compared himself unfavorably to others. For the most part, the faults of others were useful in avoiding censure of the self.

THE CONFLICTING DEMANDS OF OTHER ASPECTS OF LIFE

As Florence Kluckhohn,[7] Bernard Barber,[8] and others have noted, the American culture, unlike that of Ancient Greece, evaluates occupational success and family life as more important than citizen duty. One might expect some men, therefore, to excuse themselves from their citizenly dereliction by the competing demands of job and home. But this is rare. It is rare partly because some of the men see being a good family man as part of being a good citizen and partly, as we have seen in Ruggiero's case, because occupational life is seen as money-making and therefore selfish. Nevertheless, DeAngelo, a skilled machine operator, avails himself of this argument:

I guess I'm a fairly good citizen . . . get in no trouble. I pay my taxes like anybody else. Of course as far as taking part in any kind of activity that is going on with the kids (Little League, soft-ball coach, etc.) I'd like to. I know even this year they need a fellow to coach the kids' teams. (But) I work around the clock. I work the summer. I just can't do it. I don't have the time. I'd like to do it, you know.

But it is this same DeAngelo who says he has has turned down opportunities to work overtime because he didn't see any sense in working himself to death.

I feel, too, that Farrel, from the eminence of his professional status, is avoiding guilt largely on the grounds that he has an occupation which he, and society, interpret as a special contribution to the social good. Pressed as to the nature of his feelings about the shortcomings he says he has in the area of citizenship, he responds:

Taking my own amount of available time and trying to apportion it to the different needs of life the best I can—while I give some to this concern and probably should give more, I don't feel a particular guilt that I'm not as active in politics or as well read as I should be.

I think, as a matter of fact, that it is an open question whether or not he feels more guilt than he indicates; but at least he is clear in attributing his deficiency to "different needs of life."

A third example of this reliance on other roles to "excuse" this deficiency and alleviate any possible guilt feelings in this area is illustrated most plausibly by our part-time policeman and railroad guard, who says:

As far as my civic duty, what time allows me, I do it. I would say that as far as in the political line—no. For one reason, my job won't allow it. (If) my job would allow it and I could—whether I would do it or not, is another question.

How many civil servants are grateful for their immunity, happy that the Hatch Act and its state companion laws have forbidden them to engage in politics, is a matter of conjecture. The number is probably sizeable.

VOTING: THE PURGING OF GUILT

In a discussion of the effect of the press on civic participation, Lazarsfeld and Merton suggest that instead of stimulating people to engage in greater activity, reading and listening and viewing political material serve as a substitute for such activity. This negative effect on participation is termed the "narcotizing dysfunction" of the media, but there is the further suggestion in their analysis that people satisfy their civic consciences by an evening bout with the paper and a quick tour of the world news by radio.[9]

In my *Political Life*, I took issue with this view and indeed, I find it cast into shadow by the discussions of the Eastport men.[10] None of them, in discussing how close they came to their own images of good citizenship, referred to their keeping up with the news—indeed, this seemed to be the area of greatest sense of deficiency. It seems improbable, therefore, that they are in any substantial way relieving their guilty sense of lack of participation through passive absorption of the media's daily offerings. At least this is true of the working class and lower middle class men of Eastport, whatever may be the situation with the middle classes.

Voting is a different matter. About half of the men featured voting in their descriptions of good citizenship, and many of these relied upon their own record of frequent and regular voting to bolster their somewhat shaky images of themselves as good citizens. It is in this vein that Rapuano, in his enthusiastic voice, almost cracking with excitement, responds to the question about his own citizenship: "Oh gee, I think I'm a perfect citizen. Oh, sure, I mean, naturally, I try to—I vote as many times as I can." (He means, I trust, only once in each election.) Sokolsky, somewhat more modest, puts his voting record in second place, as evidence of his citizenship: "Oh I think I come pretty close to it (the ideal). I mean I don't steal or anything like that. I vote any time I want to. I try to help other people out." This phrase, "any time I want to," is certainly an odd one, but I think Sokolsky means that, as in his definition of a good citizen, he "votes regularly." O'Hara, a factory maintenance man, still boyish and buoyant in spite of his four children, when asked how close he comes to his ideal, says "Well, I vote. I mean—look, I've voted ever since I've been made a voter. I mean I look forward to it, because I figure that I want to vote for the one I figure is going to do the most good for me in there."

Perhaps "the purging of guilt" is too strong a phrase to characterize this sense of relief that, however else one is deficient as a citizen, at least one votes. But, in a general area of slightly bad consciences, this is, for some, a way of relieving self-doubts.

CITIZENSHIP AS A FRAME OF MIND

It was David Riesman who first drew attention to the emphasis the mass audiences put upon the "sincerity" of their entertainers.[11] Similarly, one of the valued qualities for citizens is "being interested in" or "caring about" the public affairs of community and nation. What most irritates O'Hara about the sample of the public that he is familiar with, is that, while he is working with the Little League, others "just sit there. I mean they don't care; they don't seem to care." Flynn, who finds most people are good citizens, suggests that one important criterion is that the citizen "make it his business to consider the condition of the country." Kuchinsky, whose version of citizenship is confused, still manages to convey the idea that being "*for* the people" is pretty important. And Ferrera, in his tortured way, argues that an ideal citizen takes care of his children, votes, goes to church, and is "interested in his country, naturally, and in his state and more immediately in his city."

I do not mean to imply that these men are willing to accept the thought for the deed, the sense of solicitude for the solicitous act. But because of the vagueness in their minds regarding which deeds are called for, they tend to emphasize a generalized "goodness," a tendency, as Farrel says, "not to advance his own interests at the expense of others," or to emphasize qualities of unspecified civic morality. Such a focus, moreover, has the advantage that it permits them to see themselves in a somewhat better light: they can easily experience the requisite "concern"; they know themselves to be "honest" and "well-intentioned." Nor can others deny this; their psychic states are thus not subject to ready confrontation by the evidence of their lives, either as they know themselves or as others know them. This transmutation of good citizenship *from doing to caring*, even more than the use of "faith" as a substitute for "works" in religion, is an easy adjustment and compatible with the demands made upon their lives by modern American society.

THE DEPOLITICIZATION OF CITIZENSHIP

In spite of the long list of qualities which Merriam found to be more or less universally associated with citizenship and civic training—the list given at the introduction of this paper—the political scientist at least, and perhaps any middle class observer, is likely to think of voting and participation in the democratic process as central to the citizen concept. I observed that about half of the men mentioned voting in their definition of citizenship, and a few others included an attention to public issues in one form or another. For these people, it was possible, then, to achieve the status of good citizen by discharge of their electoral obligations.

But for others, the idea of a substantial political element in the idea of citizenship came as an afterthought or not at all. We may illustrate this with Costa's (factory operative) remarks on the qualities of a good citizen:

I would say that a man that works at his factory bench or goes to his law office or goes to his medical practice every day and lives a good life, and contributes time or money to activities in the city, belongs to the Board of Education or belongs to any kind of volunteer group—has a well-rounded life. He's a family man. He has a couple of children, three children—he lives a life, a real well-rounded life with business activity, social work and so on. I would say that makes the best kind of citizen.

There are about four others like Costa in this respect, and many of the others de-emphasize politics. Only Farrel, for example, mentions any kind of association with a political party. Not even the lower middle class members mentioned letter writing or petitioning, though a few mentioned expression of political opinion as desirable; none even dreamed of *running* for office (though *serving* on boards which might happen to be elective is another matter). The truth of the matter is that the public mind still holds partisanship and citizenship to be somewhat antithetical qualities. This is most clearly seen in the remarks of the conscientious bookkeeper, McNamara: "I'd say he (an ideal citizen) sticks pretty much to the middle of the road on most questions." In the American culture it seems that the image of the citizen is at war with the image of the political man in an arena where conflict is the order of the day. This depoliticization leads, thus, into a related interpretation of citizenship as not so much uncritical as anti-critical.

CRITICISM AND CITIZENSHIP

There is a prevalent theme which runs through much of the discussion of citizenship, almost like an undercurrent, affecting the drift of the argument at many points: "be positive," "don't criticize," and "boost, don't knock." This is a theme congruent with many facets of the American culture, not only in the community "booster clubs" and in the refrains, "Accentuate the positive" and "Look on the Bright Side," and in the "silver lining" departments of the Church and the media, but, more basically, in the idea of progress and in a golden, but now dimming, idea of manifest destiny. In a kind of synthetic coda, one might summarize these ideas in the citizenship discussion as:

> Express supportive views of the home community.
> See the merits in every point of view.
> Be loyal to country and community.
> Do not criticize other people or other groups.
> Support community projects.

These views are illustrated in a few of the comments, describing a good citizen as one who "tries to make the city go over the top in anything they are trying" (Ruggiero); "tries to uphold the government" (Dempsey);

is interested in "bettering his community" (Sullivan); "is a man that's true to his country" (Sokolsky); "would try to weigh the merits of everything" (McNamara); would try to "make a better town . . . and would be there willing to pitch in and voice his opinion to help out" (Woodside).

It is too much to expect, no doubt, that there would be much inclination to see the citizen as critic or to give a positive appraisal of the analytic function in this context. People just don't think of the citizen role in this way. And it is the role, at least in part, which accounts for this emphasis on the positive; in another context, when these men were asked about their views on the function of a critic in discussion, there was an overwhelmingly positive reaction. The men did not feel such a person was just a "crab who keeps things from getting decided," but rather felt that the critical function was useful in the discussion of public affairs. Put too simply, but with some evidence to support it, one might say: criticism is not necessarily bad; but the good *citizen* is not a critic.

The question of criticism includes the question of orthodoxy; at least heterodox beliefs usually imply some criticism of the going customs, conventions, and values. Thus, the good citizen is a conventional man, a middle-of-the-roader, as McNamara said. The moralization of citizenship is a moralization of the status quo, conventionality, and the avoidance of trouble. This "staying out of trouble," mentioned by four men, has a broad reference; in the first instance it means avoiding criminality—as when Rapuano says of the good citizen: "I suppose he'd have to stay out of trouble, naturally. After all . . . I wouldn't call him a good citizen if he's costing the city money as far as courts are concerned. Staying out of trouble means something." But it has a secondary meaning closer to Flynn's statement that "he never gets into any kind of trouble of his own making." He doesn't stir up trouble, cause disagreements, or ruffle the surface of a placid community. In this sense for the sensitive and timid, any kind of disagreement is dangerous. Thus Dempsey, asked if he is a good citizen, says: "I'll be honest with you—not very. I have my differences of opinion towards my fellow men, as well as anyone else." In this sentence, aversion to the critical, fear of conflict, and desire for conventionality—as well as concern over his own heart condition—all converge.

It would hardly be possible here to penetrate all phases of the culture which make this combined emphasis upon (a) being a "booster," (b) avoiding unconventionality, and (c) eschewing conflict; but there is one aspect of this sample which may serve to reinforce these more general American themes. It is the Jew, Sokolsky, who emphasizes "being true to your country"; an Irish American, McNamara, who says that his mother was somewhat prejudiced against other national groups and stresses being in the middle of the road; and an Italian American, Rapuano, who twice speaks of citizenship as staying out of trouble. The ethnicity of this sample may well tend to bring to the surface a fear of difference, an overreaction against disloyalty, an avoidance of mutual criticism. The boosters had their greatest spokesman in the indigenous Mr. Babbitt, but exogenous sons of immigrants may come to this position by these other routes.

STATUS AND CITIZENSHIP

The days are long since past when social status, income, or education had any effect on the legal admittance of a man to the rights and duties of citizenship. The fight for equality was fought early and with relatively little difficulty, except on the Negro question, in the United States. As a consequence, it is not surprising to find that almost all of the men were quick to think of the ideal citizen as someone who might easily come from their own status, who could be "a good working man," an "average man," a man who "left the factory bench" to do his duties. Almost all of the men, that is, but not quite. Consider Costa's initial response to the question about the good citizen: "Well, I'm limited because of the fact that I don't know too many different kinds of people—by kinds I mean people in the upper strata." And Sullivan, who feels the union representative should not be a working man, but rather a lawyer, suggests that the ideal citizen is more likely to be a businessman than anything else. Here, and elsewhere, particularly in the related discussion of the concept of civic leader, there is some evidence that at least some members of the working class may be looking to the members of "the upper strata" for citizenship models or, perhaps, relying on them to carry the burdens of civic leadership which they endorse. The line between civics and politics is never sharp; the glance upwards to a higher socio-economic level for civic leadership implies, for these men at least, a wider embrace of upper status leadership in public affairs—including politics.

THE INDIVIDUALIZATION OF THE ROLE

In exploring the sources of the tensions of citizenship, I have suggested the ambiguity of the demands, their moral nature, and the difficulties in satisfying them. But there is one other source of tension worth mentioning: the citizen role imposes impossible demands for "independence" and autonomy.

Curiously, and perversely, the decisions of social man are believed to be arrived at in some mysterious way, without reliance on others. This came out especially in questioning these Eastportians on where they would go for information or guidance if they were badly informed on a local election. Elsewhere I refer to their sense that they get it on their own, without help from any particular source as the "parthenogenesis of knowledge," and treat it as specifically "American."[12] But I have recently run across some evidence that shows that this concept of individualized *political* decisions is not just American, in fact is more British and Italian than American, as may be seen in Table 14-1. In these popular versions, even in the close embrace of the family, voting decisions are not to be made "together," nor is the husband to make the decisions while the wife turns to some other sphere of competence (except in Mexico). In this "idealized" version, husband and wife is each to make his own decision. No wonder citizenship is fraught with tension.

Table 14-1. The Individualization of Citizen Voting Decisions: Percent of Married Population Saying that "General" Decisions in the Family Are Made Individually Compared to the Percent Saying Voting Decisions Are Made Individually, by Nation

	General Decisions		Voting Decisions	
	%	N	%	N
United States	2	(17)	49	(420)
United Kingdom	4	(25)	69	(515)
Germany	1	(8)	38	(294)
Italy	4	(22)	60	(367)
Mexico	2	(19)	23	(256)

Source: Survey data for Almond and Verba study of citizen attitudes in five nations, made available through the Inter-University Consortium for Political Research.

II. The Casual Patriot

> For the modern man patriotism has become one of the first duties and one of the noblest sentiments. It is what he owes to the state for what the state does for him, and the state is, for the modern man, a cluster of civic institutions from which he draws security and conditions of welfare. The masses are always patriotic.
>
> William Graham Sumner,
> *Folkways*, p. 15.

Since William Graham Sumner wrote the above lines, the world has experienced two world wars enlisting the patriotic sentiments of the nationals of the many participant nations. During this time, too, there has been an extensive discussion of patrotism both in scholarly essays and in the more popular media. More recently there have been more analytical studies of the nature of this "noblest sentiment" and some empirical work. As an ideal, patriotism has suffered erosion; efforts to reconcile it with internationalist attitudes have weakened it; as a motive it has, at least in the literary discussion of the time, been down-graded. Sumner's phrases, even more than is true of other aspects of this substantial work on folkways, sounds archaic. And this is made graphic by the testimony and discussion of the men of Eastport.

Patriotism is "love of country; devotion to the welfare of one's country; the virtue and actions of a patriot" (Webster's *New International Dictionary*, 2nd edition). In one of the early post-World War I discussions of patriotism, in the case of a British internationalist, J. L. Stocks, it is defined as follows:

> The disposition which is commonly called patriotism appears to contain three distinct, but closely related, elements—the love of country, the desire for its good, and the willingness to serve.[13]

In a similar vein, Merle Curti defines patriotism as "love of country, pride in it, and readiness to make sacrifices for what is considered its best interest." [14]

Guetzkow, taking off from an earlier definition of patriotism as "love of. or zealous devotion to, one's own country," notes that attachment to fatherland recently has contained an economic and/or ideological component, He distinguishes analytically, moreover, between "allegiance," with its early connotations of attachment to a liege lord; "loyalty," with its implications of "adherence to the sovereign or lawful government"; and "patriotism," with its focus upon identification to a nation or fatherland. In practice, however, he suggests that the three are so intertwined that they may be dealt with "as fundamentally the same attitudinal process."[15]

The distinctions in meaning which scholars make are sometimes reflected in vague, half-conscious discriminations made by the general public. This is hardly the case with the men of Eastport. Indeed, the most significant feature of their discussion of patriotism and the ideal patriot is the confusion and ambiguity of the concept in their minds. Asked about their idea of an ideal patriot, about half of the men responded with such phrases as "Well, you've got me a little buffaloed on that" (Woodside) or "Well, you've got me over a barrel" (Costa). They knew the word, of course, but had not thought much about it—in contrast to the evident thinking they had done about citizenship.

Yet it would be absurd to infer that they did not have ideas and feelings about the area of meaning designated by the literature on "patriot" and "patriotism." What are they? But first, what are they not? What is left out? (a) None of the men mentioned "Americanism" or the "American Way." (b) The concept is not counterposed to ideas of subversion or Communism. Only Sokolsky spoke in these terms: "if he (the patriot) sees anything wrong, he should report it—like any sabotage or Communists or anything like that . . . even though he might start trouble for himself." (c) There was little historical reference. Aside from five men who mentioned exemplars of American patriotism (Thomas Jefferson, Nathan Hale, Patrick Henry, Henry Clay, and Billy Mitchell), patriotism did not seem to be tied in with concepts of history, partly, no doubt, because, as I said in *Political Ideology*, these men are "historyless." And this is true in spite of the suggestion here and there in the discussion that patriotism is an "old-fashioned" virtue, not obsolete, but of another era.

The basic themes are two-fold. On the one hand, patriotism is primarily a quality of men in wartime, when it is revealed by sacrifice and service, particularly if courage and bravery are called forth. Men fighting for their freedom are often cited as exemplifying patriotism, perhaps a reflection of the common use of the term to describe American behavior during the

Revolution. In this sense the quality is a latent one, waiting to be summoned forth. Would Americans respond to the call? Sokolsky says "people talk this or that, but when it really comes to the time, they'll really show their stuff." Ruggiero, estimating whether most people are patriots or not, is, in this context, precise:

> Most of 'em, yes. By most of 'em I say a good 70 per cent are that way. Because if it ever came to the point where the Russians were out on the beach here somewhere, well, then you can see us all be 100 per cent. But we still have the security that we're separated by water, but, uh, those days are gone. It's getting to the point where every man's gonna be thinking about getting into it if it happens again.

All of the men who defined patriotism in this way agreed that the average man was likely to be a pretty good patriot. (How different from the distribution of good citizenship?)

The other main theme is the attachment to country, love of country in peacetime. This is not latent in the same way, but is assumed to be the case without evidence to the contrary. To show that one is not a good patriot, in this sense, one would have to make some negative statements, express disloyalty, prefer another country to this one. And such a state of mind is, to these men, almost unthinkable. They do not know anyone like that. The net result is that they wear their patriotism lightly. Everyone is a good patriot (except for the few who defined it in exotic terms, "blowing up bridges when the country is occupied") and, like the man who really does love his wife, it is not necessary to go around protesting one's love. With one exception, the problem of volunteering for service to be discussed below, patriotism is not a source of tension.

CASUAL PATRIOTISM EXPLAINED

One might have expected it to be otherwise. Napoleon was a Corsican, Hitler was an Austrian, Stalin was a Georgian. Marginal status, such as is conferred by recency of immigration, could well express itself in an intense patriotism and nationalist fervor for one's country. A common and plausible explanation for some of the attitudes associated with the name of the late Joseph McCarthy dealt with the problems of loyalty of the more recent immigrant groups. Even the one Yankee in the group came from a small rural village—the source of the most nationalistic sentiments.[16] Why, then, is their patriotism so casual, their concern about patriotism so minimal, their sense of guilt (with one exception) so unpunishing?

THE MINIMAL ROLE DEMANDS

In the first place, it seems to me, the nature of the demands made upon them as patriots, in the sense in which they view the concept, are minimal. It is certainly not hard to be loyal, when loyalty is compatible with going one's daily round and the pursuit of self-interest. In peacetime there are few demands for acts which must be done at the sacrifice of private and personal goals. And in wartime the government moves into the situation with a massive complement of rules and restrictions which do not provide wide areas of choice. Such choices as are available for civilians, such as engaging in war work, are made much easier by the pay scales, the overtime allowances, and the "excitement" of the sense of urgency. There are, moreover, almost no temptations to engage in patently disloyal or unpatriotic acts—except, perhaps, the temptation to hoard.

The argument that it is easy to be casual about fulfilling a role which either makes few demands, or supports its demands with legal arrangements which strip the role of difficult choices, is supported by the one great exception to this situation—the question of volunteering in the service or of waiting to be drafted. Here, where the individual became involved in a heavily moralized choice central to his conception of the patriot role, there was substantial evidence of guilt and hence of tension. Ruggiero, candid and self-critical, reveals this problem most clearly. Asked about his own patriotism, he says:

> In the sense, uh,—I buy war bonds—I would consider myself not. . . . I consider myself, uh, almost. I mean I didn't volunteer. I waited for them to come get me. But that was before the war. See, now it would be a different thing.

Johnson, asked the same question, hesitates, looks at his shoes, and says, "I feel that, well, in the last war, I waited to be drafted. But I mean, at the time I went, I just—as far as I know—I done everything that was expected of me." Costa first sees the patriot as a person who's "got some military background, even if he was in the army for (only) a year," but goes on to add ruefully, with an embarrassed smile, "which I was not." He cannot stand this situation, for he is a conventional man—and, more than any of the others, was concerned about what I thought of him. He goes on, therefore, to extend the definition of the patriot to someone who "will be interested most of all in the welfare of his country, and the state he lives in, and the community he lives in." And in this sense he qualifies.

At this point, let us pause for a moment to consider a theory of modern patriotism which, I think, runs counter to the prevailing doctrine. In those nations with somewhat repressive laws, or in any group where criticism and discussion of national policy is suppressed "in the national interest," it has often appeared that the repression is a product of the patriotism—the ethnocentric national loyalty of a people—and that the support for these restraints follows from a hyper-patriotic attitude. I would suggest that on many occasions the causal sequence flows the other way; intense patriotism is a *consequence* of the repressive measures and the internal and repressed resentments these measures engender. This is the case because it is under such repressive circumstances that the genuine attachment, the sure loyalty, the secure allegiance do not follow naturally from the situation and hence *must* be inflated into a patriotic fervor in order to keep down the critical impulses. It is the old story: one hates most those forbidden acts of others which one is least sure about not doing oneself. One requires the help of moral indignation (patriotism) to repress acts only tenuously under control.

This line of argument is close to Lewin's belief that in order to bring about group loyalty, a group should require a spirit of self-sacrifice and should be more demanding of its members, not less.[17] For the reasons mentioned above, this is probably true. Greater expressions of patriotism emerge when the nation requires more of its members; and, as Lewin suggests, the patriotism follows the demands, at least as much as it stimulates them. Lacking these demands upon themselves, therefore, the Eastport men are not obliged to develop patriotic fervor to support their sense of duty.

In the preceding paragraphs we have made several points leading to the conclusion that the nature of the role-demands are such as to produce casual detachment. The first is that the patriot role is seen most clearly as a war-time role; hence, in times of peace it may be regarded as latent, a situation easy to fulfill. Second, in wartime the government tends to structure choices so that the degree of freedom is restricted, a situation which does not impose a heavy burden on the conscience. Third, where it does impose such a burden on the conscience—in the instance of volunteering or being drafted (or, even worse, not serving in the armed forces at all), there is evidence of guilt and tension and moral condemnation among draft-dodgers, those who fail to go willingly, etc. And fourth, the lack of repressive measures on the citizen, together with the few demands made upon his time and conscience in peacetime, permits a genuine love of country—so genuine that it does not need "patriotism" to sustain it.

A LEARNED DETACHMENT

There are at least two arguments on the place of patriotic loyalty among other group loyalties. Grodzins argues plausibly enough that patriotism and national loyalty flow naturally from loyalty to a variety of smaller groups— the family, neighborhood, trade union, or school—since these are ingredients in the national life.[18] Guetzkow argues, and finds data to support, the view that international loyalties and a sense of support for the world community or the institutions of the United Nations are not only compatible with national loyalties but, in fact, only arise in people who have learned to have the quality of loyalty by "practising" it with regard to the nation and national institutions. In this sense, only the patriotic can be internationalists (though this argument cannot be reversed).[19] Guetzkow's findings, then, support Grodzins' point and could well be applied to the subnational level—

only those who love their community or their families, perhaps, are capable of genuine (ego-syntonic) patriotism.

Contrapuntal to these arguments, I would say that the sense of detachment which the men of Eastport experienced in their relations with their party, their ethnic groups, their unions, contributes to the casual quality of their patriotism, and that this, in turn, is part of a secure feeling about the country. Nor is this sense of associational detachment an isolated element in the political mind of the Eastport American. His appreciation of the "independence" of certain political leaders, his disapproval of the party partisan spirit, his "official" doctrine of ethnic and religious tolerance, his blurring of class lines and homogenization of many unwanted "differences"—all tend to train him in the qualities of loyalty which make for casualness, detachment, and modest investment of affect. If he does not say of his party or his union or even his family, "my group may she ever be right, but my group right or wrong," why should he say this of his nation? Loyalty is learned; that is true. But the kind of loyalty learned at home, school, and neighborhood or village produces different kinds of national loyalties and patriotic sentiments.[20] Not alienation but detachment is the secret of the Eastport style of loyalty.

NATIONAL PRIDE AND CASUAL PATRIOTISM

In Eastport, it is understood that a good patriot loves his country and especially serves it in time of war, but the matter of national pride is a little different. Eastportians are proud of their country, partly because they compare it to "the old country" which they regard, physically and symbolically, as having been "left behind." But the pride is not the kind that shuts out criticism, or prevents an appreciation of the good in other countries, (except, of course, in Communist countries). Although they are particularly proud of "our form of government," they can criticize with relish the way it works or fails to work—and the same is true of our economic system, and American standards of behavior. In this sense they are typical of their countrymen everywhere who, more than others, single out "governmental and political institutions" as the things they are most proud of,[21] but who, compared to citizens in six other Western countries, are most dissatisfied with "the honesty and standards of behavior" of their countrymen.[22] In Eastport, and apparently elsewhere in America, this country is seen as the best place to live with the best form of government—but it has no monopoly on "the good" and it is far from perfect.

The casual detached style of patriotism comes from lack of abrasive contact where things American are questioned, but also from an assurance about America that must be recent, probably post-World War II. When this assurance is challenged, some of the qualities for which Americans have been known abroad become evident, their braggadocio, and sensitivity, and, in fact, "national pride"—like underdeveloped countries everywhere. I can illustrate this with the amusing and revealing response Rapuano made to Khrushchev's proud statements following Russian sputnik success:

> What made me get mad, really, is the way Khrushchev popped off about what his rockets will do to us, and that he's going to bury us, and so on and so forth. That was—that's what made me mad, and then I became really frustrated, because then I couldn't do anything about it, except sit down and write a card. And I did write a card to Khrushchev . . . I had to let my frustrations go somewhere so I let it go on a card. That really burned me up. I mean I love my country—I really do, and there's nothing that really burns me up as when somebody knocks the hell out of us and threatens—threatens our country. I mean it really made me mad.
> (Lane: What did you say on your card to Khrushchev?)
> Well, I say, "Dear Egghead," I called him an egghead because he's bald, of course, and I told him to keep his big fat mouth shut—whatever he has, that we could—we have better. And I can't remember the rest of it, but anyway on the bottom of it I put down, "A World War II Vet and a working capitalist," I felt better when I put it in the mail box and let it go.

Later, Rapuano says that the fact that the Russians have atomic weapons "hasn't frightened me in the least." It was not fear of the Russians that prompted him to write the note, it was wounded pride. He explains this in words which give an account of "the little man" with an injured ego:

> I'm a peaceful man, we'll say, and I try to mind my own business. And all I do is read the paper and lay down and watch television—don't go anywhere—but those things bother me. I mean, I can't see anybody shooting his mouth off like that. I hate that.

The response is extreme, but the sentiments are typical; when these men's national pride is wounded, something beyond a casual patriotism becomes evident.

The more usual casual kind of patriotism has advantages which may well be admired. As I have mentioned, it does not exclude the good in other nations and accentuate the bad, at least not the malevolent—these others are viewed more in sorrow than in anger. Variations in expressions of "love of country" seem unrelated to authoritarianism.[23] Although Rapuano uses "anti-Communism" as a medium for working through personal difficulties, Ferrera his moralism, and Kuchinsky his anti-Semitism, no one employed nationalism or patriotism for this purpose. Of course, many Americans do try to solve their personal problems through patriotic commitment, but they are, so to speak, working against a cultural friction created by this casual detached style. Not feeling guilty about their love of country and its institutions is one important source of casualness.

CITIZEN AND PATRIOT

How, then, do the interpretations of these two concepts or roles, citizen and patriot, compare? Both are moralized; failure in either respect is a blemish on one's character. But, while most fail to be really good citizens, almost all Americans are good patriots, or at least they would be if called upon. Patriotism, however, is mostly apparent in terms of sacrifice or risk in time of war or other danger; it is a contingent role, while citizenship is a vague, but chronically demanding one. In peacetime patriotism demands, if anything, loyalty—an easy thing to fulfill, while citizenship seems to require something more, some time-consuming or skill-requiring acts, and only defensively can it be interpreted as confined to "right-thinking." This demandingness of the citizen role leads to other defenses: perhaps, one believes, the demands can be satisfied by a ritual act, voting—which is still more than the mere "loyalty" required of the patriot. Or, defensively, it can be said that other worthwhile aspects of life impair one's capacity to carry out the citizenly duties. But one needs no such excuse for peacetime patriotism. (Let war come along, and the matter is infinitely different, with chronic guilt for non-volunteering and other non-performance.) Citizenship can be thought of as a matter for people of higher status, because of the skills and leisure involved. But, in peacetime, there is no need to think in this way of patriotism, hence it is for everyone without question. Althougugh in war-time it is different, peaceful patriotism is generally *ascribed*, but citizenship must somehow be *achieved*.

Notes

1. Mark Roelofs, *The Tension of Citizenship* (New York: Rinehart, 1957), pp. 1–30.
2. Charles E. Merriam, *The Making of Citizens* (Chicago: University of Chicago Press, 1931), pp. 1–26.
3. Gabriel Almond and Sydney Verba, *The Civic Culture* (Princeton: Princeton University Press, 1963), p. 164.
4. New York: Free Press, 1962.
5. They were all men, white, married, fathers, urban, Eastern seaboard. The incomes of all but one range from $2400 (supplemented by wife's wages) to $6300. (The one man whose income was higher was just moving from the development partly because his income in 1957 had been $10,000.)

Ten have working class (blue collar) occupations such as roofer, plumber, mechanic, truck driver, machine operator.

Five have white collar occupations such as salesman, bookkeeper, supply clerk. Their ages range from twenty-five to fifty-four; most are in their thirties. Eleven are Catholic (including one former Protestant); two are Protestant (including one whose father was Catholic); two are Jewish. All are native-born; their nationality backgrounds are: six Italian (two with non-Italian mothers); five Irish (one with non-Irish mother); one Polish; one Danish (with Yankee mother); one Russian, one Yankee. Those with foreign nationality backgrounds are divided about equally between those whose parents were immigrants and those whose grandparents were immigrants. All were employed at the time of the interviews, but many were on short time, in one case permitting supplementary payment by unemployment insurance. Their education distribution was: three had only grammar-school education; eight had some high school; two finished high school; one had some (mediocre) college experience; one had completed graduate training (an apprentice social worker). On Hollingshead's class scale, the group ranked as follows: one II, five III's and nine IV's. See August B. Hollingshead, *Elmtown's Youth* (New York: Wiley, 1949), pp. 27–45.

6. Both role diffusion and partisan role interpretation should be differentiated from the role conflicts which Sutton and associates say produce an "ideology." Cf. Francis X. Sutton and others, *The American Business Creed* (Cambridge, Mass.: Harvard University Press, 1956).

7. Florence Kluckhohn, "The American Family and the Feminine Role," in Hugh Cabot and Joseph A. Kahl (eds.), *Human Relations: Concepts* (Cambridge, Mass.: Harvard University Press, 1953), pp. 247–254.

8. Bernard Barber, "Participation and Mass Apathy in Associations," in Alvin W. Gouldner (ed.), *Studies in Leadership* (New York: Harper, 1950), pp. 477–504.

9. Paul F. Lazarsfeld and Robert K. Merton, "Mass Communication, Popular Taste, and Organized Action," in Lyman Bryson (ed.), *The Communication of Ideas* (New York: Harper, 1948), pp. 105–106.

10. *Political Life: Why People Get Involved in Politics* (New York: Free Press, 1959), p. 283.

11. David Riesman, *The Lonely Crowd* (New Haven: Yale University Press, 1950), pp. 221–223.

12. Robert E. Lane, *Political Ideology*, pp. 373–377.

13. J. L. Stocks, *Patriotism and the Super-State* (London: Swarthmore Press, 1920), p. 14.

14. Merle Curti, *The Roots of American Loyalty* (New York: Columbia University Press, 1946), p. viii.

15. Harold Guetzkow, *Multiple Loyalties: Theoretical Approaches to a Problem in International Organization* (Princeton: Woodrow Wilson School, 1955).

16. See A. Whitney Griswold, *Farming and Democracy* (New Haven: Yale University Press, 1952).

17. Kurt Lewin, *Resolving Social Conflicts: Selected Papers on Group Dynamics* (New York: Harper, 1949), pp. 199–200.

18. Morton Grodzins, *The Loyal and the Disloyal* (Chicago: University of Chicago Press, 1956), pp. 39–50.

19. H. Guetzkow, *Multiple Loyalties*.

20. See David Easton and Robert E. Hess, "The Child's Political World," *Midwest Journal of Political Science*, 6 (1962), pp. 244–245.

21. Gabriel Almond and Sydney Verba, *The Civic Culture*, p. 102.

22. Gallup Affiliates, reported in *Polls*, I (Spring, 1965), p. 64. The seven countries with the percent dissatisfied are: Norway 20%, Switzerland 31%, France 39%, Denmark 43%, Britain 47%, West Germany 51%, U.S.A. 58%.

23. At least as measured by a ten-item, half-reversed version of the F-scale, borrowed from the Survey Research Center. On this scale, Rapuano, quoted above, measures about middle. The man who scores highest, DeAngelo, has this to say about his picture of a patriot: "someone who has fought for his country . . . or any man who has a dangerous job, you know, like a cop or a fireman, protecting the people's lives, you know."

Note: I wish to acknowledge with thanks the help which Robert Evans has given me in preparing this manuscript for publication.

Chapter 15
Good Citizenship:
The Pursuit of Self-Interest

The good citizen is the person who, among other things, pursues his long-term self-interest in the political world with intelligence and understanding. He may also have a number of other qualities; he may be a moral man with a reputation for fair dealing, a responsible man who supports his family and his widowed mother, a self-sacrificing man who can be counted upon to put the interests of others above his own, a patriot who is at his country's service in time of war. But the theme of this essay is that he serves society by serving himself, as though political man in the polity were like his cousin, economic man, in his sphere, the economy.

The relationship of the good citizen to the good society is complex and intricate, but our common coyness about the relationship of good citizenship to the pursuit of self-interest is surely a mistake. In the first place, nothing but trouble comes from a person's misinterpretation of his own long-term interest. Discovering his mistakes at a later point he cannot fail to feel foolish, or cheated, or misled; one harvests embitterment this way. In the second place, misinterpretation is likely to be quite uneven in society, with some well-advised persons pursuing their interests with great cleverness and zeal, while others, in their confusion, fail to reap the rewards of similar intelligence and energy. As everyone can see, the rich and well-educated will be rewarded and the poor and inadequately educated will suffer. Third, the premises of democratic theory embrace the concept of a modified pursuit of self-interest in the polity (as capitalism implies the pursuit of self-interest in the economy); it is a muted theme, as we have indicated, because of the moral

Memorandum for the Research and Theory Committee of the Civic Education Project, Lincoln Filene Center for Citizenship and Public Affairs, Tufts University, Medford, Mass., 1965.

Notes to this chapter will be found on pages 316–317

nature of the discussion, revealed in the very term "*citizen duty*," but the institutions of democracy are intended to present men with opportunities to express their interests; the concepts of "the right of petition" are exactly framed for this purpose, and the concepts of representation rest on the foundation of "self-interest." So, in calling the pursuer of his own long-term self-interest a "good citizen," we accept the implications (but only part of them) of this great body of moral and political thought. Finally, in this day when the themes of alienation and anomie and loss of identity are so glibly on the tongue, I feel obliged to point out that *one* of the links between man and society lies in the identification of satisfying goals and their pursuit through social and political institutions. This is not the high road, perhaps, not the *gemeinschaft* highway, but the low road leads to its destination with equal speed.

So the good citizen is someone who (again, among other things) pursues his long term self-interest with intelligence and understanding. But, observe that it is long-term self-interest. The point is important because much of the ensuing discussion has to do with the differentiation between immediate and long-term, or integrated, or summary self-interest—and this is by no means easy to detect. Observe, too, that I do not use the more usual phrase "enlightened" self-interest. That is because the term "enlightened" is usually the tip of a crowbar employed primarily to open the discussion for extended consideration of preferred social norms. They come into the discussion anyway, but they can be more easily limited by the concept "long-term."

In limiting the concept of "good citizen" to the intelligent pursuit of long-term self-interest, we may be able to exclude some of the considerations of "the good society" and so avoid discussion on the merits of the welfare state or political decentralization, but are we also able to avoid the discussion of what a man's interests *ought* to be? Can we take each man as he is and define good citizenship for him as serving his interests as he conceives them? If we could, then our task would be much simpler, it would be simply the elaboration of means to serve the individual's stated ends. Under these circumstances, "good" would mean "instrumental" and nothing more. The obverse of this is to develop some preferred model of man as suggested in the opening paragraph (he is moral, responsible, self-sacrificing) and then to suggest ways in which such a model man can pursue his self-interest. We choose a middle course, leaning to the first, the man's own interpretation of his interests whatever they may be, but extending it to mean his own interests after reflection. As a psychoanalyst may attempt to discover the main trends or needs of a personality before suggesting the best means for him to satisfy these needs, so, at least in theory, the political analyst may conceive of the long-term, reflected-upon interests of an individual as those which, when successfully pursued in his citizen role, will be most satisfying to him. We need not say what these interests are or should be; we need not specify that men should pursue wealth or power or popularity except as these promise long-term gratifications to the enlarged and consolidated self. Thus, our definition of the "good citizen" is not necessarily the "good man" but rather the integrated or whole man.

This leads us to the matter of the intelligence and understanding brought to bear upon this long-term self-interest. As I conceive it, the basic skill involved here is the capacity to interpret experience, both one's own and others' (even distant others', as reported in the news), with accuracy, empathy, a capacity to foresee consequences, a sense of relevance, in short, in such a way as to reconstruct a situation and use the reconstruction for one's own interests. It has, in our double focus, a double meaning: It means both an understanding of the situation and an understanding of the self. The intelligent pursuit of self-interest lies at the intersection of the two.

But "interpretation" itself has no standardized reference. One of Webster's meanings is useful: "to understand or appreciate in the light of individual belief, judgment or interest; construe as to *interpret* actions, intentions, con·tracts." It is both an understanding, in the cognitive sense, and an evaluation, or judgment. It is not a decision, as we shall see, but decisions flow from an interpretation of the situation. Similarly, it does not imply some action, but no action is possible without an interpretation. It is not a belief system, but it is, so to speak, a product of or a sampling of, a belief system. In short, it is the thinking which takes place when a person must decide on how to pursue his long-term interests in an ambiguous situation. Part of our discussion in the following pages will be devoted to just this problem: What is the nature of political interpretation?

The emphasis upon the process of social interpretation in the pursuit of long-term self-interest has an analogy with the concept of a good consti- tution, as contrasted to the concept of the good society. While the good society must include a specification of the policies of government, the good constitution, while not irrelevant to the policies of government, specifies how governmental policy, whatever it may be, is to be decided upon. Consti- tutional arguments can be stated in terms quite different from those necessary to persuade people on policy matters, and agreements on constitutional matters can be achieved among those who prefer quite different policies. Just as the constitution refers to the process of problem solving on the social level, so our concept of the processes of social interpretation refers to the process of problem solving on the individual level.

If the good citizen, in this limited sense, is someone who has a well- developed capacity for interpreting experience so as to pursue his long-term interests with intelligence, we must have norms for such interpretation. Psychiatric experience is as useful, in analyzing this *process*, as it is in analyz- ing the concept of long-term self-interest. The authors of *Mental Health in the Metropolis*[1] offer a glimpse of the way they sought to define health and "impairment of mental functioning." They define mental health in terms of twelve categories, such as "ease of social interaction," "capacity for pursuit of realistic goals," "feeling of adequacy in social roles," "identification with ethical and moral values," "healthy acceptance of the self," and so forth.[2] Bearing this in mind, they then focus on the impairment of these functions: "Mental health might . . . be defined as the freedom from psychiatric symptomology and the optimal functioning of the individual in his social setting. It could hardly be otherwise assessed."[3] They can do this without specifying which "ethical and moral values" a person should identify with or which social roles a man should "feel adequate" in. In the same way we can outline a set of criteria for social interpretation that does not specify the level of involvement in political life a person should aim for, or the particular policies he should pursue.

At the same time, it is quite clear that unimpaired social interpretation and unimpaired mental health stand on somewhat different footings. Being more specific to some social processes, the concept of the healthy citizen, more than the concept of the healthy man, is likely to imply specific concepts of the proper functioning of society. It requires a closer fit between social norms and individual norms. Citizenship is a role and must fit into a pattern of other roles, whereas being a man (or woman) is not a role but a condition of human life for which virtually everything is or can be relevant. We cannot avoid it. We must say something about the social role for which our concept of the good citizen is appropriate.

The Citizen Role

Although a role is commonly thought to be a set of *reciprocal* obligations, the citizen role is a little different because it is modified by the concept of "rights," that is, more or less unconditional guarantees of certain things the state owes to an individual because he was born or naturalized in a nation state. He does not have to be patriotic to be protected by society; he does not have to vote to get relief payments; he does not have to adopt the going belief system in order to be protected by the courts. At the fringes there are, of course, legal conditions: if he is convicted of a felony he may have his freedom of movement taken away; if he is thought to be disloyal in the specific sense of being an agent of a foreign power, certain limits are put on his behavior; but he cannot have his citizenship taken away, for that is legally considered a "cruel and unusual" punishment. There are many more informal or social sanctions; he may lose his job, his reputation, his friends. But, in one sense, it is true that citizenship is a remnant of the older non-contractual society, where merely being a member of a community was sufficient to partake of its benefits; the contractual approach has not, in this realm, taken over. In this sense, then, the social contract is still only a metaphor and with certain exceptions not legally enforceable.

If the reciprocal expectations of the citizenship role are limited by the rights of man and if, as we must, we insist upon this limitation, it is nevertheless true that this role is still marked by a substantial number of reciprocal expectations, as is any social role. That is, the citizen is expected to behave in a certain way and, indeed, to have certain specified beliefs and values, while he, in return, expects certain treatment from others and from the government. The one is not usually thought to be specifically conditional on the other; yet the situation could be so conceived; and when we consider good citizenship as, in part, the intelligent pursuit of long-term self-interest in the polity, it is useful to view it in this way. It is useful, that is, because it points out to the loyal and obedient citizen the benefits for which he gives up areas of autonomy and self-indulgence.

What, then, are the claims made upon a person when he becomes an adult citizen; and what are the reciprocal benefits which he, in turn, can appropriately claim? As we observed in Chapter 16, C. E. Merriam, in his examination of the requirements of citizenship in nine countries, suggests nine duties placed upon the citizen.[4] To these I will add the reciprocal claim of the citizen against the society, that is, against other citizens or the authorities, either as politicians or as civil servants.

Duties	*Claims*
Patiotism and loyalty	Protection against revolution or invasion
Obedience to the laws of the society	
Respect for officials and government	Enforcement of just laws by fair means on all persons
Recognition of the obligations of political life (voting, keeping informed, etc.)	Respect from officials and government
Some minimum degree of self-control; consideration of others, public decency	Attention to popular (citizen) wishes as indicated in elections and petitions
Response to community needs in times of stress (war, disaster)	Consideration of the citizen's needs by others; self-control by others
Ordinary honesty in social relations	Help from others and authorities in times of personal distress
Knowledge of and agreement with the ideology forming the rationale for the prevailing form of government and the maintenance of limits on criticism of this rationale	Honest dealing by others
	The acknowledgment of one's right of criticism (within these limits); continuing rational exploration and examination of the prevailing ideology; free speech and free association
And, often, belief in the special qualities of one's own people compared to others	A continuing examination of the best qualities of others which might be added to the "special qualities" of one's own people

In some such fashion as this the duties of citizenship serve as a base for reciprocal claims and hence for the pursuit of intelligent long-term self-interest in the polity. But it should be remembered that these "terms" are not contractual; and any effort to make them so, that is, to make the claim conditional on the performance of the duty would not be in the citizen's long-term self-interest. The claims should be properly regarded as conditions of a universal status, citizenship or, perhaps, humanity, rather than a condition of performance.

There is, however, another reason why the pursuit of self-interest in society cannot be made contractual, or conditional on specified performance. Unlike many economic roles, the citizen role is one whose benefits are governed by the principle of joint cost and indivisibility. The principle is recognized in economic theory, of course, where various devices for allocation of factor cost and cost accounting have been created and where pricing follows more closely what the traffic will bear and what the competition will allow (or agree upon), than the more classic principles based on the intersection of marginal cost and marginal demand curves. The pursuit of self-interest in the polity must make allowances for these generalized and indivisible benefits, the main allowance being the generalized support given to the political order by the good and intelligent citizen. There is no point in making a market situation out of the polity where, in fact, the essential characteristics are often missing.

This raises the question of the nature of the qualities which a citizen should have in order to give this generalized support, as well as to fulfill the more specific obligations of citizenship. Almond and Verba,[5] with modern techniques of survey analysis, provide at the same time an explicit portrait of citizen attitudes in five countries and an implicit set of norms for sustaining a healthy "civic culture," including:

A sense of civic competence (a feeling that one can change things through political action)

A sense of subject competence (a feeling that if one should be unfairly treated by administrative authorities, he can bring about redress)

A pride in the national and local political way of doing things

Some emotional investment in politics and elections (caring)

Lack of alienation (a sense of allegiance to the society)

A sense of the obligation to participate in citizen activities

A sense of "open political partisanship" (identification with a political party accompanied by a recognition of the legitimacy of other parties)

Interest in and capacity for free political communication

A relatively high level of political information

A sense of "safety and responsiveness" (general trust in other citizens and in the solicitude of governmental authorities)

A political sense of how to get things done, including how to organize others in *ad hoc* groups, petition authorities, etc.

Integration in society through voluntary organizations

Again, these norms are conceived by the authors of this study as conditions for the good society, which they term "the civic culture," but they might equally well be considered from the point of view of the participants as qualities they develop in return for the generalized benefits of a society in which their self-interests are more adequately cared for. This assumes, of course, that they conceive their interests to lie in a society marked by hetero-geneity, a diffuse rather than a specific cultural or national mission, and in Lipset's term a "democratic class conflict."[6]

So far we have developed the idea of citizenly pursuit of self-interest through the generalized benefits of government following the acceptance of certain norms of behavior and belief. But these norms are not easy to follow and, indeed, they often make conflicting claims on a citizen. Roelofs, as we have observed, examines this problem in his work on *The Tensions of Citizen-ship*,[7] wherein he treats three kinds of conflict: (a) the need for a citizen to be loyal and proud of his country and government versus his need to be critical of it; (b) the need for a citizen to support the authorities and govern-ment versus his need to defy these authorities if they go beyond the prescribed boundaries of their offices or of the constitution; and (c) the citizen's need to participate in the common life and, if necessary, to sacrifice himself for the common good versus the need to protect himself from exploitation and to nurture his private life. These are genuine problems; they confound the pursuit of self-interest in politics and greatly complicate the problem of making those interpretations and evaluations on which such a pursuit must rest.

While Roelofs observes one kind of tension, ambivalence, there is another, the tension associated with the troublesome ambiguity of the citizen role. In the set of interviews with working and lower-middle class citizens in Eastport analyzed in the previous chapter, I found that responses to images of "the good citizen" varied to such an extent that the men hardly knew what was expected of them. Some saw the good citizen as primarily a moral man, others as a good father and husband and breadwinner, others in terms of his community participation (helping the unfortunate, going to church, not being snobbish, and so forth), and still others in terms of political functions and ideas, including a constructive, non-critical frame of mind as well as the more obvious voting-and-keeping-informed criteria. It was clear from further investigation that not knowing what was expected of them at the same time that they felt morally obliged to be good citizens created a special form of tension that involved them in a series of rationalizations and evasive maneuvers.

Finally, while Roelofs stressed the ambivalence and I found the ambiguity of the role to be important, Berelson[8] has stressed the division of labor as a kind of solution both to individual tension and, more especially, to the problem of social theory. He starts with the premise that classical theory has demanded that each citizen have all the qualities desirable in the well-functioning democratic system, whereas he believes that the system require-ments are met by dividing up these qualities so that each person or group can contribute something. Thus if some citizens are intensely involved in politics, it is useful for others to be more or less indifferent to provide "room for maneuvering" by creating a group that might be persuaded by one of the intensely contesting parties. Second, it is desirable for some persons to cling to the traditions of the older values to provide continuity, while others must, in an adaptive system, be more flexibly receptive to the demands for change, indeed, must insist upon change. Third, there is need for some people to retain their loyalties to their class, ethnic, or regional political traditions in order for these groups to be represented in the political struggle, but it is also desirable for some others to break away, to be, for each group tradition, "deviant cases." The usefulness of these hostages in the political camp of the other group (say, white-collar people in a predominantly working-class party) lies in the pressure they put upon the leaders of this "other" party to accommodate some of the interests of their group, that is, in the pressure to compromise. Finally, it is desirable to have some kind of division of labor in the collecting and passing on of political information; some must inform themselves and make up their own minds, but not everyone need be or can be so interested or industrious in this regard. Let the principle of division of labor take over here, says Berelson, and we can have opinion leaders and opinion followers, producers and consumers of political talk and informa-tion.

The Berelson division-of-labor scheme is, of course, descriptive of the way of the real world; but it purports also to be normative, that is, Berelson suggests that this is the way it ought to be. But, as with the economy, it is important to note who does what, because that helps to determine who gets what. There are no clues in Berelson's analysis of the division of the citizen role into a series of sub-roles or at least sub-functions as to how this division of labor should be brought about and, as Walter Berns has commented,[9] how one decides whether or not it is appropriate for him to attempt to be primarily a producer or a consumer of political information, whether he should reinforce tradition or add his weight to the partisans of change, whether to side with his own group or become a useful hostage in the camp of the others. Although the analysis may relieve the guilty consciences of some few who were attempting to do all these things at once (and they could not be many), it does not really solve their problem of how to frame a set of judgments to serve their own long-run interests or to benefit society in some useful way. It is not (nor is it intended to be) a guide to the process of social interpre-tation or of the pursuit of self-interest in politics.

In contrast to traditional society in which the individual is taught to accept the going order as inevitable or, possibly, to petition but not to demand or organize in his own behalf, and in contrast to totalitarian society in which the citizen's self-interest is conceived to be merged with the general interest so as to be indistinguishable from it, democratic pluralist society gives to the individual in his capacity as citizen a license to pursue his interests in political life. The nature of this license varies from country to country, but it commonly includes the following rights:

> The right to vote in accordance with his estimate of how he will be better off
> The right to organize others to support his preferred candidates and policies
> The right to seek office himself
> The right to petition, to lobby, and to propagandize in the pursuit of his interests
> The right to hear all sides of each issue discussed so that he can perceive his interests more clearly
> The right to a free press and minimal censorship on radio and television
> The right to criticize the government and the authorities of church and state without sanctions from them
> The right to privacy and abstention from political life whenever this suits him (with the exception that in some places he may be fined for non-voting and everywhere he can be forced to bear arms for his country and to pay taxes to support it)
> The right to due process and fair trial
> The right to respectful treatment by the authorities
> The right to equal treatment before the law, and equal share in the general benefits

With these instruments and this license he can go about his business of pursuing his interests, not only through the general benefits of government, but more particularly through the special benefits of policy and position and symbolic gain that serve his special needs. How shall he do this?

Social Interpretation—A Simple Paradigm

A citizen can pursue his long-term self-interest with intelligence and judgment only if he has the capacity for unimpaired social interpretations, that is, interpretations of his own long-term needs as these relate to the changing political situation. The main instrument for the pursuit of citizenly self-interest, then, is the social interpretation. So it is to this problem that we devote most of our attention. What is a social interpretation? How is it made? What are its ingredients, processes, and requirements?

I touched on this before, saying that an interpretation was not a decision but a prerequisite of decision making. For this reason decision-making models with their canvas of alternatives, search for information, and commitment to means to serve some determined end will not do. A social interpretation is not nearly so conscious, so specific in its purpose, so rational or conclusive. Social interpretation is often more expressive and less instrumental; it deals with evaluations which are "consumed" in the process; it emerges from less articulate premises; it offers more scope for rationalization, externalization, projection. Like the ideologies Kardiner discusses, it is a "rational system polarized in the direction of unconscious motivations," it has the structure of a rationalization,[10] that is, a later discovery of plausible reasons accounting for an act decided on other grounds. It can retain its projective quality because it is rarely tested by reality. It may emerge in a decision, as with the vote, but the consequences of the decision rarely reveal whether the interpretation was true or false, whether the values implied were the right or the wrong ones for the interpreter himself as measured by some internal pattern of consistency (the discovery of incompatible values, for example) or by some failure to achieve a predicted gratification. A social interpretation, therefore, is a product of a general belief system or primitive (un-thought-through) ideology applied to a particular situation. A social judgement is the evaluative part of this interpretation—implicit or expressed. It is, as I have said, a sampling of the belief system, stimulated by the demands of some particular occasion. The empirical model, then, should reveal how such a mental product is produced.

Just as it is not a decision, a social interpretation is not an opinion; it is a complex of opinions and evaluations and beliefs with supporting comment and data, a kind of argument. An opinion may be stated in a sentence, or, in answer to a question, it may be stated with a "yes" or a "no." An interpretation takes a paragraph or a dialogue to develop. In this sense it has a structure and implies some internal logic or other sets of relationships; it is a small idea-system. Thus forms of analysis inappropriate for opinions may be brought into play: the sequence of statements, the references to authority, the nature of evidence employed, the choice of terms and implied association, use of fantasy material, the ends-means relationships, and so forth.

It is more fruitful to think of social interpretation as a process rather than a product, a verb rather than a noun. As it is a complex process it is difficult to think of it in linear terms, first one thing, then another; but it will be convenient to present a paradigm of social interpretation in this fashion, provided it is not misunderstood. The following model, which will serve as the foundation for the later discussion, may, then, have a heuristic, or at least mnemonic, value.[11]

A. Some internal (remembered) or external (heard or seen) (1) *message or cue* (involving perception of both source and content)
Engages (2) one or more *motives or needs* (with their implied goals),
Shaped by a person's (3) *modes of conflict resolution* (approach, avoidance, psychic withdrawal, repression, scheduling, etc.) and sets in motion a search and striving process.
B. The person's consequent search and striving process is guided by his biologically given and learned (4) *capacities*, as these are reflected in his characteristic modes of

(5) *cognition*, learning, thinking, and knowing

(6) *affection*, giving, and receiving

(7) *evaluation* (especially moral), and

(8) *conation*, or acting-out behavior (operational codes).

C. The person's previous life experience, interpreted through the habitual use of these processes, has produced in him a set of beliefs, emotions, evaluations, and operational codes regarding the important objects of his universe, of which the following are central:

(9) *himself*, self-image, and identity

(10) *others*, and proper modes of interpersonal relations

(11) *society* (the urban man's "nature"), including economic, religious, family, and political institutions,

D. And hence, a more or less loosely structured (12) *belief system* selectively brought to bear on the objects of his thought as they are put in focus by the indicated requirements of the stimulus-motive situation.

E. All of which emerge on a given occasion as (13) *a social or political interpretation* useful to the citizen in the pursuit of his self-interest.

The model implies a series of choice points, although the order presented in the model may have nothing to do with the order of the actual interpretation process. Nor does it adequately reveal a world of interrelationships with enormous importance for the outcome, such as the relationship between identity, including self-esteem, and concepts of interpersonal relationships, or the way the intricate resolution of these two problems structures a larger view of social institutions. Nor, indeed, does it show the differences between a dogmatic belief system and a tentative one, or the differences between one that is learned by rote and one that is interspersed with the precipitates of experience. It is, in short, simply a beginning.

For the good citizen, one who can pursue his self-interest intelligently, the paradigm represents a set of more or less harmonious relationships, the elements of which can be brought together without warring with one another, that is, without violating a person's sense of logic or consistency (whatever that may be) without subjecting him to emotional strains which lead him to withdraw from the field or suffer somatic symptoms (headaches) or moods of depression and crippling doubts about himself and his purposes. The point is that, although a person is never in a state of complete harmonious equilibrium, the conflicts and tensions that are the inevitable consequence of striving (motivated behavior) are, for the good citizen as for the healthy man, tolerable, perhaps even the agents of further maturation. Continuing synthesis, rather than harmony, may be the key term. It is, then, the individual's own purposes and needs, as conceived over the long term, perhaps even a lifetime, and including *his* conscience, that guide the concepts of good citizenship and good social interpretation. Individual needs, not the needs of society as some analyst may conceive them, are the criteria we here employ; but, as we have said, the concept of a good society must rest *in part* on the correct interpretation of his own self-interest in each situation by each citizen of that society.

Intake and Message Reception

Something must trip off the process of social interpretation; it is likely to be a news story, but it might be a comment by a friend, or a changed personal situation, like a notice that a neighbor has asked for a variance in zoning or a letter from the President ordering a man to military duty. The citizen then is confronted with the problem of response: What does he think about it? How shall he behave? The notices come to him; he does not have to search for them. Where he has to search the environment for information and guidance relevant to his citizenly pursuit of self-interest, he must develop a strategy that maximizes a number of values and minimizes cost. What kind of strategy?

THE STRATEGY OF NEWS INTAKE

The relationships of cost to reward in "following the news" are multiple; they should not be lumped together.

1. Some news for some people is "intrinsically" interesting, in the sense that little or no further action or thought is necessary to provide rewards. Following such news is rewarding "in itself," that is, it gratifies one's prurient interests, vanity, moralism, or avocational curiosity. The cost, in these cases, is the opportunity cost—what one gives up by spending time and effort following this segment of news. Here the calculations are relatively simple.

2. Some news is rewarding because it is instrumental in immediate practical terms; it tells of bargains, tax deadlines, public events, each with immediate significance for something one wants to do. The cost in effort is to be weighed against the "practical value" of the information.

3. But some news deals with distant events with problematic relationships to self-interest. The effect on self-interest, that is, one's self, one's values, one's enterprises, and one's friends, is problematic for several reasons. For one thing, how any particular event will affect one's interest, if it does mature in a particular way, may be quite uncertain. This is clearly the case with most foreign affairs, such as events in Berlin and Viet Nam. In the second place, it is uncertain how the course of history will proceed; few people can predict with much assurance, and the assured are often wrong. Then, even if one could make reliable estimates about these matters, there are costs involved, which are threefold. First, there is the cost of acquiring the information about, particularly the understanding of, the situation necessary to make these estimates. Second, there is the cost of modifying one's own situation to adjust to the impact of the events as they mature. And third, there is the cost of

attempting to change the course of events, if this seems possible. These costs vary substantially from person to person.

A concert pianist, remote from the fields of thought most germane to foreign policy, is confronted with news from Viet Nam. How much effort should he put into "following the situation?" For him, especially, the cost is high. Yet the importance of the train of events of which this is or may be a part is also high; and this could be true even if the probability of a general conflagration, as it is called, is low. Moreover, for him the possibilities of action to modify the course of history are low, as are the possibilities of changing his own course of events so as to accommodate with least injury to such a conflagration. He simply would not know what to do.

A Washington lawyer in the same situation finds both the cost of information and the cost of influence much lower, while the possibilities of being effective are higher. Moreover, as he lives in Washington, the costs to him of a general war may be high and his knowledge of the risks involved may be very good.

Suppose the issue is one of civil rights; suppose it has to do with apportionment, judicial reform, or Medicare. Before one judges the correct posture of a man in following the news on these issues, one must judge his situation, his interests, his capacities, as well as the probability that the newsworthy event will, so to speak, mature in such a way as to affect his life or values. Exposure and following the news cannot be said to be good in themselves. The good citizen has a right to choose his strategy without jeopardizing his citizenly status; indeed he has an obligation to himself and to others who may be affected by his actions to consider costs and probabilities and effects in this way.

Perhaps a simple formula will make this clearer. We will state it as a ratio of cost to gain (for the individual, incorporating his concern for other people and abstract values).

$$
\begin{array}{c}
\text{Ratio of cost to} \\
\text{gain in following} \\
\text{the news on a} \\
\text{chain of events}
\end{array}
=
\dfrac{
\begin{array}{c}
\text{Cost of following} \\
\text{and understanding} \\
\text{the news}
\end{array}
+
\begin{array}{c}
\text{Cost of modifying} \\
\text{one's own situation} \\
\text{according to an} \\
\text{estimate of the} \\
\text{impact of an} \\
\text{event on the self}
\end{array}
+
\begin{array}{c}
\text{Cost of any indi-} \\
\text{cated effort to} \\
\text{alter the course} \\
\text{of history}
\end{array}
}{
\begin{array}{c}
\text{Probable gain or loss} \\
\text{implied by an event} \\
\text{in the news}
\end{array}
\times
\begin{array}{c}
\text{Probability that the event will} \\
\text{mature so that the indicated gain} \\
\text{or loss will take place}
\end{array}
}
$$

The calculations are complex. To every probability figure one must attach a degree of certainty, that is, a weight indicating the confidence one attaches to the figure. The ambiguity of distant events may involve calculations of risk not unlike those involved in appraising statistical findings: Is it better to take action when one might be wrong, or not to take action when one might be right? There are many kinds and levels of action possible and every higher level of action implies a greater level of understanding as well as a greater level of "caring" about the outcome. Not only does much so called "apathy" have its roots in these uncertainties, but so do "stereotypes" and blunted perceptions and judgements of every kind.

"Following the news" is not merely a process of exposure, as it so often seems in survey reports. "Following" means understanding, and understanding means a conceptual framework into which items can be placed to give them "meaning," that is, a relationship to other information and evaluative schemes such as "free enterprise," "imperialism," "class warfare," "due process of law," and so forth. Furthermore, as "meaning," like power, is agglutinative, in the sense that one bit of information gathers meaning from other related bits of information, a *history* of following the news has an exponential value, and the cost of "keeping informed" at any one time must fall into place in such a personal history. An interruption is something like the interruption of a statistical time series; it affects the utility of the later elements of the series.

Moreover, information and concepts and interpretations rarely mature into informed judgments without testing them out in conversation. A man who is following the news should talk about his interpretations for them to be properly ventilated, tested, sharpened, and consolidated. Solipsistic news gathering runs the risk, as we noted with one of the Eastport respondents, of curdling, of irrationality and unrealism.[12] Thus the cost figure is likely to run high.

The perceptions of two elements of the formula are likely to be greatly modified by one's psychic disposition. One of these is perception of the personal impact of distant events. For many people, distant events are kept under the threshold of perception because of a preoccupation with themselves, their immediate needs, the demands of others, or a narrow and limited view of life. Impending war is much less important to many people than impending promotions, sick children, or the malicious gossip of the lady next door. Education is a horizon-lifter; the lack of it closes down the world to the dooryard and the factory gate. The other element in the formula which is heavily affected by psychological dispositions is, of course, perception of one's capacity to move and shape events. In Eastport, most of the working class men I interviewed believed that on any general policy issue there was little that they could do to change things. Although a few had attempted to modify the course of events affecting their immediate lives, as when a man petitioned his Congressman to keep open a government arsenal where he worked and another sought to have postal workers' pay increased (he was a part-time postal worker), none had attempted to change the course of American foreign policy. It seemed just too great an effort with too small a chance for success in too ambiguous and distant a situation.

INDEX SCANNING

Nevertheless, men read the news and miss the newspaper when it isn't there, they listen to newscasts on radio and television, and they are, in this sense, "exposed." But, of course, their exposure is selective. As someone has said, we can scan the media as we use an index, searching for the interesting and useful and entertaining, that is, for elements that give us direct or instrumental rewards. The news is no exception. The question, then, is what kind of a "public affairs index" do people use, and how skillful are they in using it? It is convenient to think of five kinds of indexes that people use to guide them in perceiving the relevance of the news to their various interests.

1. *Dogmatism index.* This is employed in order to find items, and within the items particular events and statements, that confirm a certain point of view: to prove that the Democrats are corrupt, or that Wall Street runs the world, or that modern youth is bad, or that only Negroes commit crimes. The dogmatism index is employed by those who use information to give strength to a fragile self, one whose commitment to a position serves, as a repression, to keep down threatening incursions. They use information this way rather than as a tool for further learning or the reexamination of a position held. The dogmatism index is a means of avoiding careful and realistic qualifications, for that which is not white is black, and all black is the same color and implies error and evil to the same degree. The criteria of relevance to self-interest in such a scanning process is this: Whatever shows my view to be right is relevant, whatever shows my enemies to be bad (wrong) and my friends to be good is relevant, and whatever is useful as "filler" material for my "line" is relevant.

2. *Calculus-of-advantage index.* The indexing system of the man on the make creates out of the media one great want-ad. What good is it to me? How can I use it? Local news is better for this, as it tells of friends who have achieved positions of influence, complaints of this and that group of being exploited, functions and social events to which one might want to go, bargains to be had. But there are other versions: the scanning of casualty lists in an airplane crash to see if there are any members of one's own ethnic group on the list and the evaluation of the crash accordingly; the appraisal of business news on the basis of whether or not it is good for the Irish, the Jews, the Italians; the measure of the horror of war by the number of Americans (and only Americans) killed; medical science interpreted as a public effort primarily designed to discover remedies for one's own ailments; the interest in society news (for those who read it at all) limited to me and mine. Our general criterion of relevance was the long-run advantage to the self; but this calculus of advantage is short-run, and the self is parochial. There is no involvement in the world beyond.

3. *Social lubricators' index.* Information can be useful as gambits in con-

versation, not necessarily to get ahead in the usual sense but to amuse, engage, shock, even inform others in the normal course of familiar dialogue. "Did you see the item about ..." is a good opener anywhere. In helping an individual to "make conversation," the news can help him to make friends.

4. *Opinion-leaders index.* There are those to whom others look for guidance; they are the retailers in the opinion business, the ones about whom accounts of "the two-step flow" and "personal influence" are written.[13] They must be guided by the demands of their clientele, of course, and hence they may specialize in labor news, foreign news, business news, or whatever. They scan with a purpose, and a useful one; they need to know so that they can summarize, interpret, and, perhaps, editorialize on the way.

5. *Aficionado's index.* The hobbyist, the cultist, the man who pursues some topic in the news because, as he says, "it's interesting" and nothing more, scans with a special eye. What lies behind that "interest" is also interesting, but beyond our view; suffice it to say that sports, when it is not the lubricating device mentioned above, has, for many people, this aficionado function.

But we are in danger of multiplying the index into as many types until there are as many as there are sources of gratification. There are, for example, those who use the paper as an orienting device and, when the paper is not available, feel vaguely disoriented, if not positively threatened. There are those who use it chiefly as a guide to the films, the sales, the weather. Some read the obituaries with a special kind of interest: They have triumphed over those who are listed here, if only for a little while. Some of this reading behavior is escape, although often from what into what is not so clear. Most often, perhaps, it is escape from themselves into something that either demands thought about something else or prevents it entirely, according to their tastes. In all of these cases, the relevance to the self in the news lies in some immediate gratification (vindication of a point of view, escape, triumph, security, the absorption of the aficionado) or in the instrumental use to be made of it (immediate advantage, social lubrication, opinion leadership).

The impairment of a citizen's scanning capacity lies in his use of only one index, or, of course, his use of the wrong index at the wrong time (search for short-term advantage in a long-term cold war). More than that, one may say that to be an aficionado of the foreign or domestic news, to find it interesting in itself, is a further credit for the citizen scanner, for he finds immediate gratification in something that may provide him with information of great long-term utility. On the face of it, however, it seems that the employment of a dogmatism is never in the citizen's interest. It is worth considering.

DISSONANCE AND PREJUDICE

The dogmatism index, it is true, involves us in a special problem: Is it ever in a person's interest to perceive and believe only what fits his preferences? Selective perception and learning of this kind is an old story in social psychology, well documented by a variety of studies, and it is usually treated as an impairment of a process which should be veridical and true, like the scholar's own perceptions, or so we like to believe. But the citizen is not a scholar (neither is the scholar so scholarly in his "off hours"), and one might do well to consider the costs and limits of the strain to reduce this tendency to confirm one's preferences in political or other affairs. We may list three such costs.

1. Increasingly, the problem of reducing stimulation and strain is regarded as an important social goal. Among my Eastport sample it was not uncommon for the men to complain about the "many tiny messages" they received during the day and evening, or the fact that "everything was all hopped up." Perception is, in any event, selective; but the need for relaxation is in competition with the need for accurate perception and the continuously active pursuit of knowledge.

2. Under certain circumstances, the "secondary gain" involved in immediate reinforcement of a point of view or in the gratification of social support may be worth more, even in long-run terms, than the effort at accurate and "unbiased" perception. The insecure, frightened, weary, and disheartened (as every parent knows) may need the ego rewards contained in confirmation and also need to avoid the stress of uncertainty and ambivalence.

3. In teaching a capacity to tolerate dissonance, to sort out source attributes from message content and to guard against one's own wishes, we may destroy the spontaneity and expressiveness of a person. The man who can never indulge in hyperbole, uncritical enthusiasm, and incautious generalization has lost something; he has been overtaught.

These and other considerations lead to a kind of dual code for news intake and message reception prior to framing a social interpretation:

The impairment of message reception lies in:

1. A chronic state of tension so great that a relaxed confirmatory selection and interpretation of the news is usually necessary AND a chronic inability to relax standards in moments of fatigue.

2. An ego so fragile, a self-esteem so poorly founded, that a person usually needs the rewards of confirmatory selection and interpretation of the news AND an inability ever to reward the anxious self with relaxed standards. And in reverse:

3. A disposition so rigid, or compulsive that a person is chronically and anxiously on guard lest his preferences distort his reading of the news AND an inability to impose rigid standards of accuracy and objectivity on the self when much is at stake.

The key concept is one of flexible capacities; abilities to use veridical standards when much depends upon accurate perception and interpretation and to relax these standards when accuracy is less important. We might train a "cognitively compulsive" nation of news readers, but it would be an unlivable community.

The consequence of these considerations is that we must cease to think of modest levels of interest and blunted perceptions as an impairment of citizenly functions; we must cease to be "shocked" that most people do not know much about current events—it did very little good to take this posture anyway. What we need is a realistic strategy for helping a man with these elaborate calculations so that, in a realistic fashion, he can perceive where his various interests lie and how he may intelligently serve them.

One such strategy is to stop teaching that everyone's destinies are inter-locked and that whenever the bell tolls "it tolls for thee." The counterpart would be to show exactly how and to what degree the welfare of one man depends upon that of another—and where it does not, to say so.

Another would be to state explicitly that the probability of any one individual's vote modifying the outcome of an election is very small indeed and to put the option of voting back on another footing: Men set examples for each other; defections by groups are noticed by elected officials; and *groups* who don't vote tend, in municipal affairs, at least, to suffer loss of benefits; the act of voting has symbolic significance and symbolism is important in specifiable ways to society and to the individual; and so forth.

A third strategy might be to suggest a specialization in following the news, a selective perception of another kind. In this way a person might become an aficionado of that news which lies closest to his interest: labor news, Latin American news, academic news. Surely the building up of broad attentive publics with a capacity to follow events and to make the elaborate calcula-tions necessary to interpret them properly would be a gain. One might take special care to insure that these attentive publics did not become special interests; some might be special watch-dogs.

However it is done, candor in the field of citizenship would go a long way towards defining more realistically the duties of a good citizen.

Notes

1. Leo Srole, Thomas S. Langner, Stanley T. Michael, Marvin K. Opter, and Thomas A. C. Rennie, *Mental Health in the Metropolis* (New York: McGraw-Hill, 1962).

2. *Ibid.*, p. 62.

3. *Ibid.*, p. 61.

4. Charles Edward Merriam, *The Making of Citizens* (Chicago: University of Chicago Press, 1931), pp. 1–26.

5. Gabriel A. Almond and Sidney Verba, *The Civic Culture* (Princeton: Princeton University Press, 1963), *passim.*

6. Seymour Martin Lipset, *Political Man* (Garden City: Doubleday, 1960).

7. H. Mark Roelofs, *The Tension of Citizenship* (New York: Rinehart, 1957).

8. Bernard B. Berelson, Paul F. Lazarsfeld, and William N. McPhee, *Voting* (Chicago: University of Chicago Press, 1954).

9. Walter Berns, "Voting Studies," in *Essays on the Scientific Study of Politics*, H. J. Storing (ed.) (New York: Holt, Rinehart and Winston, 1962).

10. Abram Kardiner, *The Psychological Frontiers of Society* (New York: Columbia University Press, 1945), pp. 41, 46.

11. I have employed a very similar "model of a political 'idea machine' " in *Political Thinking and Consciousness* (Chicago: Markham, 1969), pp. 48–49.

12. See my *Political Ideology* (New York: Free Press, 1962), pp. 99–104.

13. Elihu Katz and Paul F. Lazarsfeld, *Personal Influence* (New York: The Free Press of Glencoe, 1955).

Index